DISCOVERY TO DISCOURSE

DISCOVERY TO DISCOURSE

BECKY WENDLING KIRSCHNER *Michigan State University*

JOANNE MUELLER YATES *Michigan State University*

Macmillan Publishing Co., Inc.
New York

Collier Macmillan Publishers
London

COPYRIGHT © 1983, MACMILLAN PUBLISHING CO., INC.

Printed in the United States of America

Macmillan Publishing Co., Inc.
866 Third Avenue, New York, New York 10022

Collier Macmillan Canada, Inc.

Library of Congress Cataloging in Publication Data

Kirschner, Becky Wendling.
    Discovery to discourse.

    Includes index.
    1. Rhetoric. I. Yates, Joanne Mueller.
II. Title.
PN193.K57   808'042   82-7730
ISBN 0-02-364480-X   AACR2

Printing: 1 2 3 4 5 6 7 8   Year: 2 3 4 5 6 7 8 9 0

ISBN   0-02-364480-X

For Paul and Don, with love.

PREFACE

Discovery to Discourse is a process-centered text designed to introduce you to the composing process experienced writers use. Unlike most writing texts, which focus on the needs of the reader and on the final product, this text makes you conscious of each stage of the composing process and of the needs of the writer as well as those of the reader. By using the process each time you write papers, you will learn to modify and adapt the approaches presented in this book to help you formulate your own approach to writing.

HOW TO USE THIS BOOK

As the discussion above suggests, this book will not be used in the usual manner. Instead of beginning on the first page and working through to the last, Chapter 1 and the first two selections of Chapter 2 will be used once to acquaint you with attitudes about writing and reading.

The assignments in the final part of Chapter 2 and Chapters 3, 4, 5, 6, 7, and 8 will be used each time you write a paper. Each assignment begins by asking you to read several essays from Chapter 9 to stimulate your thinking about the topic to be discussed in the paper. Then you will move to the getting-started approaches in Chapter 3 for discovering an appropriate subject for the writer and the reader. Chapter 4 provides approaches to use to discover a reader, purpose, and form for presenting the ideas, as well as suggestions for writing the first draft and for getting unstuck if you stop writing. Chapter 5 provides forms that a reader can use to react to your first draft. Chapter 6 includes methods for revising and rewriting your paper after obtaining a reader's reaction. Chapter 7 provides editing forms an editor can use to evaluate how well you have met the needs of a reader, and Chapter 8 offers approaches you can use to copyedit the final draft.

As we point out in the discussion of the composing process, you will not move through these stages in the step-by-step way we have just described. You will return to some, combine others, and learn to adapt them to your personal needs and to the writing assignment.

We have written the book in a conversational manner to make you feel at ease. Whenever we use *he* or *she* in discussing a writer or reader, we are referring to both men and women. Most of the student work has been left unedited to help you develop a sense of what writing looks like in the early stages of the process.

ACKNOWLEDGMENTS

Discovery to Discourse has undergone a long gestation, and many people have helped to bring it to birth. We want to take this opportunity to acknowledge our debt and gratitude to all of them.

Over the years, we have worked with hundreds of students. By allowing us to share in their composing process, they have given us insights into the way writers get their ideas on paper. Their contributions are evident in the many approaches and examples found in the following pages. We are especially grateful to those students who gave us permission to use their writing to serve as examples for other beginning writers.

Several of our colleagues at Michigan State University have also played a part in preparing us to write this text. Jane Featherstone nurtured us as composition teachers with her supportive suggestions and enthusiastic interest in our discoveries. Early in our careers, she gave us an opportunity to work together to develop and teach an experimental writing course. In preparing the course, we read (among other works) Mina Shaughnessy's *Errors in Expectations*, which changed our perceptions about teaching writing. The research and experimentation we engaged in while teaching our course is at the heart of this text. Henry Silverman, our department chairman and a participant in the 1979 session of the Iowa Institute on Writing, furthered our academic growth by involving us in the development and implementation of a writing program based on the process model and by introducing us to the work of Richard Lloyd-Jones, Carl Klaus, James Kinneavy, and others. Clinton S. Burhans, Jr., and Michael Steinberg helped us clarify our theories and approaches to teaching writing in a seminar they conducted for ten members of the Department of American Thought and Language in 1978-79. Our discussions of the works of Frank Smith, Ulric Neisser, Jean Aitchison, Peter Farb, Peter Elbow, James Moffet, James Britton, Janet Emig, and many others helped us formulate theories to explain what was happening in our classrooms and inspired many of the approaches presented in this text. Our special debt to Peter Elbow's work can be seen in our chapter on the reader's reaction.

We are also grateful to the people who have helped us revise and prepare the text for publication. Our readers, Stephen Judy, Frank Hubbard, and James Switzer, were generous with their thoughtful criticism and support. At Macmillan, our editor, D. Anthony English, believed in our project from the beginning and has patiently and gently guided us through our writing process. His editorial assistant, Judith Newman, has managed all of the pieces with an expert hand and has freed us from many tedious tasks. Eileen Schlesinger, our production editor, has guided the transformation from manuscript to text with an eye to making the material accessible to students.

We also want to thank our families, who shared in our excitement: our parents, Martha and Russell Wendling, and Greta and Bill Mueller; our children, Charles and Josh, Brian, Juliet, Laurie, Matthew, Robin, and John. Most of all, we are grateful to our good friends and husbands, Paul and Don, who encouraged us, gave us time to write, and knew all along that we could do it.

Finally, we are forever indebted to each other and to the collaborative spirit that imbued our work. Together, we have made discoveries about the teaching of writing that we could never have made alone. In every sense, *Discovery to Discourse* is a product of the interaction of our minds.

B. W. Kirschner
J. M. Yates

CONTENTS

DISCOVERY TO DISCOURSE

CHAPTER 1

Thinking About Writing:
Looking at Attitudes

Attitudes play an important role in everything we do, and writing is no exception. After sharing her writing with classmates for a few weeks, one of our students discovered how her attitude toward her subject affected the reader's reaction to it. "My attitude has a lot to do with the results of my paper. If I think the topic is dull, my finished paper is dull. If I find my topic interesting, most likely the reader will be interested." Other students have found that their definition of a writer, their past writing experiences, and their ideas about the role writing will play in their lives all contribute to their general attitude toward learning to be a better writer.

WRITING INVENTORY

To give you an opportunity to uncover and explore your attitudes about writing, we have developed the writing inventory below. Answer the questions as completely and honestly as possible.

1. What is your definition of a writer? Discuss why you do or do not consider yourself a writer.
2. What kinds of writing experiences have you had? Describe the kinds of things you have written. Describe the one successful or unsuccessful writing experience you remember most vividly.
3. Do you think writing will play an important or useful part in your life? Describe what role you think writing will play in your personal and professional lives.
4. Reread your responses to the previous questions. What do your responses show you about your attitudes toward writing? Describe how you feel about learning to become a better writer.

EXPLORING COMMON ATTITUDES ABOUT WRITING

Assuming that you responded to the Writing Inventory as our students have in the past, you have probably discovered that your attitude about learning to write well is either positive, neutral, or negative. As you read through the responses our students made to Question 4, compare them to your responses and decide if *positive*, *neutral*, or *negative* describes your overall attitude.

Positive: "I am excited about learning to write better." "I enjoy writing and want to learn more about making a reader understand what I am trying to express." "I really do want to learn to write clear, persuasive papers."

Neutral: "Even though I think writing is something I can do with-out, I know I need it. So, I feel that the more I learn about it, the better I will do it in the future." "Since I am an engineering major, I am not as interested in writing as I am in calculus or science, but I guess it will be important." "Although I really would like to learn to be a good writer, I have been writing for quite a while and never seem to improve."

Negative: "I am apprehensive about taking another writing class because of my lack of success in this area." "To be honest, I am tired of writing. After a while, topics and examples seem harder to think of." "I am not particu-larly enthusiastic about taking a writing class."

As these student responses (and no doubt your own as well) point out, general attitudes about becoming a better writer grow out of more specific attitudes. These include attitudes toward writers, past experiences with writing, and what role you think writing will play in your future. A closer look at each of these areas will help you determine how each has shaped your current attitude and, if neces-sary, will suggest ways to replace neutral or negative attitudes with more positive ones.

CONSIDERING ATTITUDES ABOUT WRITERS

In Question 1 of the "Writing Inventory," you gave your definition of a writer and considered why you did or did not think of yourself a writer. Probably some of you, like our students, defined a writer as "a person who puts thoughts down on paper" or as "someone who is writing to communicate an idea to others." Those of you who re-sponded in this way may also consider yourselves writers every time you write a letter to a friend or prepare a paper for a class. Your definition of a writer is related to the act of communication, and you realize that when people communicate in writing, they become writers. Such an attitude helps you understand that writing is a craft everyone can learn and even master. No doubt, you have a positive attitude about learning to write.

On the other hand, many of you probably echo the responses of the majority of our students who think that writers are people who have a special talent that makes writing easy for them. If so, you may have defined a writer like this: "A writer is a person who can sit down and write a story or paper without much previous thought." "A writer can produce a story that is interesting and contains no grammatical errors." "I think a writer is someone with a lot of ideas and is talented enough to create an interesting subject for the enjoy-ment of others." "A writer is a person who has a talent for saying things, not just someone who writes on an assigned topic." "A writer is a person who can arrange his ideas on paper, with a flow from one idea to the next. He is creative and well organized, and his skills are nearly perfect."

Such definitions make it difficult, if not impossible, for you to see yourself as a writer. Therefore, the idea that you can become a better writer does not occur to you. "I never think of myself as a writer because I have trouble putting ideas into words." "Although I have done some writing, I do not have the talent needed to consider myself a writer." Clearly, these statements reflect an attitude that will lessen your ability to become a better writer. But what can you do to replace these attitudes with more positive ones?

Try any of the following approaches to redefine your definition of a writer and to make it clear to yourself that you have the ability to become one. After finishing an approach, look at Question 1 of the "Writing Inventory" again. Is your definition beginning to change?

Approach 1: Gain Strength from Other Writers

Babette Blaushild suggests that when you get frustrated with writing, you should "borrow strength from others who have been there, too." She cites the advice of Eugene O'Neill, who said about the writer's task, "I know what you are up against and how you feel. The only thing is, keep up your confidence that sooner or later you'll come through . . . and keep on writing, no matter what." Our students agree with Blaushild. They find that considering the advice of experienced writers helps them to develop a more realistic definition of a writer and to begin to see that they, too, can be considered writers.

One essay that has helped them is William Zinsser's "The Transaction." In this essay, writer/teacher Zinsser presents a dialogue between himself and a surgeon he calls Dr. Brock. The doctor represents the idea that writers are people with special talents for whom writing is easy and fun. When asked what it was like to be a writer, "He said it was tremendous fun. . . . The words just flowed. It was easy." Zinsser, speaking as a professional writer, contradicts this notion by saying that for him, writing was neither easy nor fun. "It was hard and lonely, and the words seldom just flowed."

THE TRANSACTION

Several years ago a school in Connecticut held "a day devoted to the arts," and I was asked if I would come and talk about writing as a vocation. When I arrived I found that a second speaker had been invited — Dr. Brock (as I'll call him), a surgeon who had recently begun to write and had sold some stories to national magazines. He was going to talk about writing as an avocation. That made us a panel, and we sat down to face a crowd of student newspaper editors and reporters, English teachers and parents, all eager to learn the secrets of our glamorous work.

Dr. Brock was dressed in a bright red jacket, looking vaguely Bohemian, as authors are supposed to look, and the first question went to him. What was it like to be a writer?

He said it was tremendous fun. Coming home from an arduous day at the hospital, he would go straight to his yellow pad and write his tensions away. The words just flowed. It was easy.

I then said that writing wasn't easy and it wasn't fun. It was hard and lonely, and the words seldom just flowed.

Next Dr. Brock was asked if it was important to rewrite. Absolutely not, he said. "Let it all hang out," and whatever form the sentences take will reflect the writer at his most natural.

I then said that rewriting is the essence of writing. I pointed out that professional writers rewrite their sentences repeatedly and then rewrite what they have rewritten. I mentioned that E. B. White and James Thurber were known to rewrite their pieces eight or nine times.

"What do you do on days when it isn't going well?" Dr. Brock was asked. He said he just stopped writing and put the work aside for a day when it would go better.

I then said that the professional writer must establish a daily schedule and stick to it. I said that writing is a craft, not an art, and that the man who runs away from his craft because he lacks inspiration is fooling himself. He is also going broke.

"What if you're feeling depressed or unhappy?" a student asked. "Won't that affect your writing?"

Probably it will, Dr. Brock replied. Go fishing. Take a walk.

Probably it won't, I said. If your job is to write every day, you learn to do it like any other job.

A student asked if we found it useful to circulate in the literary world. Dr. Brock said that he was greatly enjoying his new life as a man of letters, and he told several luxurious stories of being taken to lunch by his publisher and his agent at Manhattan restaurants where writers and editors gather. I said that professional writers are solitary drones who seldom see other writers.

"Do you put symbolism in your writing?" a student asked me.

"Not if I can help it," I replied. I have an unbroken record of missing the deeper meaning in any story, play or movie, and as for dance and mime, I have never had even a remote notion of what is being conveyed.

"I *love* symbols!" Dr. Brock exclaimed, and he described with gusto the joys of weaving them through his work.

So the morning went, and it was a revelation to all of us. At the end Dr. Brock told me he was enormously interested in my answers—it had never occurred to him that writing could be hard. I told him I was just as interested in *his* answers—it had never occurred to me that writing could be easy. (Maybe I should take up surgery on the side.)

Which writer's experience sounds most like your own? Does knowing that professional writers find writing hard give you a new perspective on writers and writing? Do Zinsser's comments help you change your definition of a writer? Many of our students find that once they realize that a professional writer has some of the same writing problems they have, they can begin to consider themselves writers, too.

To gain strength from other writers, try one or more of the following activities:

1. Look for and collect essays that authors have written about their writing experiences. We have included some in this book. Ray Bradbury's "The Impulse to Write" is on page 332, and Malcolm Forbes's "How to Write a Business Letter" appears on page 334. Also, look in magazines or at the feature page in newspapers. Many columnists share their writing problems with their readers. When you get frustrated or discouraged, reread the works that provide you with useful advice and give you strength.

2. Look for and collect cartoons that focus on writing. Cartoonists often produce strips that deal with the frustrations and joys of writing. Artist MacNelly uses his character, Perfesser Fishhawk, to correct the misconception that writers spend all of their time pounding typewriter keys.

And in another cartoon, Charles Shultz lets author Snoopy express the joy a writer feels when he has written something he especially likes.

Reprinted by permission of Tribune Company Syndicate, Inc.

© 1980 United Feature Syndicate, Inc.

Looking for and collecting such cartoons will help remind you that all writers share your frustrations—and joys.

Approach 2: Get to Know the Restraining Critic Inside You

Our students have found Gail Godwin's essay "The Watcher at the Gates" useful for overcoming neutral or negative attitudes about writing. In it, Godwin introduces us to our inner critic who keeps us from putting our ideas on paper. As you read the essay, see if your watcher uses any of these tricks and consider how you might get on better terms with the rogue.

THE WATCHER AT THE GATES

I first realized I was not the only writer who had a restraining critic who lived inside me and sapped the juice from green inspirations when I was leafing through Freud's "Interpretation of Dreams" a few years ago. Ironically, it was my "inner critic" who had sent me to Freud. I was writing a novel, and my heroine was in the middle of a dream, and then I lost faith in my own invention and rushed to "an authority" to check whether she could have such a dream. In the chapter on dream interpretation, I came upon the following passage that has helped me free myself, in some measure, from my critic and has led to many pleasant and interesting exchanges with other writers.

Freud quotes Schiller, who is writing a letter to a friend. The friend complains of his lack of creative power. Schiller replies with an allegory. He says it is not good if the intellect examines too closely the ideas pouring in at the gates. "In isolation, an idea may be quite insignificant, and venturesome in the extreme, but it may acquire importance from an idea which follows it. . . . In the case of a creative mind, it seems to me, the intellect has withdrawn its watchers from the gates, and the ideas rush in pell-mell, and only then does it review and inspect the multitude. You are ashamed or afraid of the momentary and passing madness which is found in all real creators, the longer or shorter duration of which distinguishes the thinking artist from the dreamer . . . you reject too soon and discriminate too severely."

So that's what I had: a Watcher at the Gates. I decided to get to know him better. I discussed him with other writers, who told me some of the quirks and habits of their Watchers, each of whom was as individual as his host, and all of whom seemed passionately dedicated to one goal: rejecting too soon and discriminating too severely.

It is amazing the lengths a Watcher will go to keep you from pursuing the flow of your imagination. Watchers are notorious pencil sharpeners, ribbon changers, plant waterers, home repairers and abhorrers of messy rooms or messy pages. They are compulsive looker-uppers. They are superstitious scaredy-cats. They cultivate self-important eccentricities they think are suitable for "writers." And they'd rather die (and kill your inspiration with them) than risk making a fool of themselves.

My Watcher has a wasteful penchant for 20-pound bond paper above and below the carbon of the first draft. "What's the good of writing out a whole page," he whispers begrudgingly, "if you just have to write it over again later? Get it perfect the first time!" My Watcher adores stopping in the middle of a morning's work to drive down to the library to check on the name of a flower or a World War II battle or a line of metaphysical poetry. "You can't possibly go on till you've got this right!" he admonishes. I go and get the car keys.

Other Watchers have informed their writers that:

"Whenever you get a really good sentence you should stop in the middle of it and go on tomorrow. Otherwise you might run dry."

"Don't try and continue with your book till your dental appointment is over. When you're worried about your teeth, you can't think about art."

Another Watcher makes his owner pin his finished pages to a clothesline and read them through binoculars "to see how they look from a distance." Countless other Watchers demand "bribes" for taking the day off: lethal doses of caffeine, alcoholic doses of Scotch or vodka or wine.

There are various ways to outsmart, pacify or coexist with your Watcher. Here are some I have tried, or my writer friends have tried, with success:

Look for situations when he's likely to be off-guard. Write too fast for him in an unexpected place, at an unexpected time. (Virginia Woolf captured the "diamonds in the dustheap" by writing at a "rapid haphazard gallop" in her diary.) Write when very tired. Write in purple ink on the back of a Master Charge statement. Write whatever comes into your mind while the kettle is boiling and make the steam whistle your deadline. (Deadlines are a great way to outdistance the Watcher.)

Disguise what you are writing. If your Watcher refuses to let you get on with your story or novel, write a "letter" instead, telling your "correspondent" what you are going to write in your story or next chapter. Dash off a "review" of your own unfinished opus. It will stand up like a bully to your Watcher the next time he throws obstacles in your path. If you write yourself a good one.

Get to know your Watcher. He's yours. Do a drawing of him (or her). Pin it to the wall of your study and turn it gently to the wall when necessary. Let your Watcher feel needed. Watchers are excellent critics after inspiration has been captured; they are dependable, sharp-eyed readers of things already set down. Keep your Watcher in shape and he'll have less time to keep you from shaping. If he's really ruining your whole working day sit down, as Jung did with his personal demons, and write him a letter. On a very bad day I once wrote my Watcher a letter. "Dear Watcher," I wrote, "What is it you're so afraid I'll do?" Then I held his pen for him, and he replied instantly with a candor that has kept me from truly despising him.

"Fail," he wrote back.

Did you find out what sends you to watering plants, cleaning rooms, or wasting paper every time you write? To get to know your watcher, try one of the following methods:

1. Write your watcher a letter. Donna Marsten tried this technique and found that it helped her increase her confidence and see herself as a writer. The following is her unedited letter.

Dear Watcher,

I don't want to be rude to you I just want you to know that I'm sick and tired of you interfering at the wrong time. Constantly you cause me to worry about my laundry, writing a letter, washing my hair, reading a book or a newspaper, and so many other little things. You always seem to side track me for some reason or another. Not only do you bother me when I'm writing, but when I'm reading, doing homework, or just trying to concentrate.

Little do you know, but I'm getting the best of you. I'm learning to let my mind go and just concentrate on the line going from my mind to the pencil in my hand. Sure you get the best of me sometimes, but not as much as you used to. I'm really upset with you right now. I know you don't want to read this so you don't want me to write this, but I'm getting the best of you by continually writing without much hesitation.

Someday I would like to come face to face with you. I'm longing to ask you in person why you do this to me. I can hardly wait to see your face. You really aren't such a bad person. I only wish that sometime we could get something worked out so we aren't always fighting.

I'm sure I'll see you shortly so please take care of yourself and stay out of my hair.

Sincerely yours,

Donna

2. Draw a picture of your watcher. Other students decided to use this method in order to know their watchers better and find out why they had been so reluctant to consider themselves writers.

Does our student's watcher look or sound like anyone you know?

CONSIDERING ATTITUDES ABOUT PAST EXPERIENCES

In Question 2 of the "Writing Inventory," you looked back at your past writing experiences, describing the writing you did and your most vivid memory associated with writing. Like our students, some of you found that you have done a great deal of writing. You might have said, "I have many pen pals to whom I write often." Or "I wrote a short story on my own in sixth grade and discovered that I could really write." Or possibly, "I am experienced in writing for publications. I worked on our high school yearbook for four years and was copyeditor for one year and editor-in-chief for another."

These kinds of experiences probably evoked memories of making a friend by writing letters, getting recognition for your writing, or seeing an article with your name on it in print. For the rest of you, responding to the question may have made you realize that you have done very little writing and that most of it has been done for school. Most of our students made this discovery and said, "Outside of school, I have done very little writing" or "Most of my writing experiences were related to class assignments." Such experiences are related to writing a 24-page term paper, or to getting an "A" or a "D" on an essay, or maybe to memories of that long, dark night when you wrote a paper that was assigned three weeks before.

Whether writing experiences are extensive or limited, positive, neutral, or negative, they influence how you view learning to write. Past experiences make many students hesitant to take the risks necessary for learning. Those of you who have written often and who have been rewarded for your efforts may think it is no longer necessary to try new approaches or to work to become an even better writer. Because your old approach worked in the past, you assume it will continue to work. Those of you with limited or unpleasant past writing experiences may be fearful of trying new approaches because you have had so few rewards. Regardless of the cause, however, you will find that if you do not take risks, you will not become a better writer.

In his essay "The Human Use of Language," Lawrence Langer explores two kinds of experiences that keep us from taking risks. The first experience involves a student who wrote in clear prose but was told to rewrite the paper using jargon. She was learning how to write "safe" papers to receive better grades. The second shows a woman trying to communicate her feelings in writing to an unfeeling reader. Langer suggests that this writer will never risk using "human language" again. Although both experiences took place in a school setting, they could have occurred just as well in an office or at home. A boss may have told you to rewrite your report using more professional language, or a well-intentioned friend or parent may have returned a letter with pencilled-in corrections.

Read Langer's essay and consider whether you have had experiences that have made you retreat from using human language.

THE HUMAN USE OF LANGUAGE

A friend of mine recently turned in a paper to a course on behavior modification. She had tried to express in simple English some of her reservations about this increasingly popular approach to education. She received it back with the comment: "Please rewrite this in behavioral terms."

It is little wonder that human beings have so much trouble saying what they feel, when they are told that there is a specialized vocabulary for saying what they think. The language of simplicity and spontaneity is forced to retreat behind the barricades of an official prose developed by a few experts who believe that jargon is the most precise means of communication. The results would be comic, if they were not so poisonous; unfortunately, there is an attitude toward the use of language that is impervious to human need and drives some people back into silence when they realize the folly of risking human words on insensitive ears.

The comedy is easy to come by. Glancing through my friend's textbook on behavior modification, I happened on a chapter beginning with the following challenging statement: "Many of the problems encountered by teachers in the daily management of their classes could be resolved if. . . ." Although I was a little wary of the phrase "daily management," I was encouraged to plunge ahead, because as an educator I have always been interested in ideas for improving learning. So I plunged. The entire sentence reads: "Many of the problems encountered by teachers in the daily management of their classes could be resolved if the emission of desirable student behaviors was increased."

Emission? At first I thought it was a misprint for "omission," but the omission of desirable student behaviors (note the plural) hardly seemed an appropriate goal for educators. Then I considered the possibility of metaphor, both erotic and automotive, but these didn't seem to fit, either. A footnote clarified the matter: "'Emission' is a technical term used in behavioral analysis. The verb, 'to emit,' is used specifically with a certain category of behavior called 'operant behavior.' Operant behaviors are modified by their consequences. Operant behaviors correspond closely to the behavior colloquially referred to as voluntary." Voluntary? Is jargon then an attack on freedom of the will?

Of course, this kind of abuse of language goes on all the time – within the academic world, one regrets to say, as well as outside it. Why couldn't the author of this text simply say that we need to motivate students to learn willingly? The more I read such non-human prose, and try to avoid writing it myself, the more I am convinced that we must be in touch with ourselves before we can use words to touch others.

Using language meaningfully requires risk; the sentence I have just quoted takes no risks at all. Much of the discourse that poses as communication in our society is really a decoy to divert our audience (and often ourselves) from that shadowy plateau where our real life hovers on the precipice of expression. How many people, for example, have the courage to walk up to someone they like and actually *say* to them: "I'm very fond of you, you know"?

Such honesty reflects the use of language as revelation, and that sort of revelation, brimming with human possibilities, is risky precisely because it invites judgment and rebuff. Perhaps this is one reason why, especially in academe, we are confronted daily with so much neutral prose: Our students are not yet in touch with themselves; not especially encouraged by us, their instructors, to move in that direction; they are encouraged indeed to expect judgment and hence perhaps rebuff, too, in our evaluation of them. Thus they instinctively retreat behind the anonymity of abstract diction and technical jargon to protect themselves against us – but also, as I have suggested, against themselves.

This problem was crystallized for me recently by an encounter only peripherally related to the issue. As part of current research, I have been interviewing children of concentration-camp survivors. One girl I have been meeting with says that her mother does not like to talk about the experience, *except with other survivors.* Risk is diminished when we know in advance that our audience shares with us a sympathy for our theme. The nakedness of pain *and* the nakedness of love require gentle responses. So this survivor is reticent, except with fellow victims.

But one day a situation arose which tempted her to the human use of language although she could not be sure, in advance, of the reception her words would receive. We all recognize it. This particular woman, at the age of 40, decided to return to school to get a college degree. Her first assignment in freshman composition was to write a paper on something that was of great importance to her personally. The challenge was immense; the risk was even greater. For the first time in 20 years, she resolved to confront a silence in her life that she obviously needed to rouse to speech.

She was 14 when the Germans invaded Poland. When the roundup of the Jews began a year later, some Christian friends sent their young daughter to "call for her" one day, so that they might hide her. A half hour later, the friends went themselves to pick up her parents, but during that interval, a truck had arrived, loaded aboard the Jewish mother and father — and the daughter never saw them or heard from them again. Their fate we can imagine. The girl herself was eventually arrested, survived several camps, and after the war came to America. She married, had children of her own, and except for occasional reminiscences with fellow survivors, managed to live adequately without diving into her buried personal past. Until one day her instructor in English composition touched a well-insulated nerve, and it began to throb with a painful impulse to express. I present verbatim the result of that impulse, a paper called "People I Have Forgotten":

Can you forget your own Father and Mother? If so — how or why?

I thought I did. To mention their names for me is a great emotional struggle. The brutal force of this reality shakes my whole body and mind, wrecking me into ugly splinters, each crying to be mended anew. So the silence I maintain about their memory is only physical and valid as such but not true. I could never forget my parents, nor do I want to do it. True, I seldom talk about them with my husband or my children. How they looked, who they were, why they perished during the war. The love and sacrifices they have made for me during their lifetime, never get told.

The cultural heritage to which each generation is entitled to have access to seems to be nonexistant [sic], since I dare not talk about anything relating to my past, my parents.

This awful, awesome power of not remembering, this heart-breaking sensation of the conspiracy of silence is my dilemma.

Often, I have tried to break through my imprisoning wall of irrational silence, but failed: now I hope to be able to do it.

Until now, I was not able to face up to the loss of my parents, much less talk about them. The smallest reminder of them would set off a chain reaction of results that I could anticipate but never direct. The destructive force of sadness, horror, fright would then become my master. And it was this subconscious knowledge that kept me paralyzed with silence, not a conscious desire to forget my parents.

My silent wall, my locked shell existed only of real necessity; I needed time.

I needed time to forget the tragic loss of my loved ones, time to heal my emotional wound so that there shall come a time when I can again remember the people I have forgotten.

The essay is not a confrontation, only a prelude, yet it reveals qualities which are necessary for the human use of language: In trying to reach her audience, the author must touch the deepest part of herself. She risks self-exposure — when we see the instructor's comment, we will realize how great was her risk — and she is prepared for judgment and perhaps even rebuff, although I doubt whether she was prepared for the form they took. This kind of prose, for all its hesitant phraseology, throws down a gauntlet to the reader, a challenge asking him to understand that life is pain as well as plenty, chaos as well as form. Its imagery of locked shells and imprisioning walls hints at a silent world of horror and sadness far less enchanting than the more familiar landscape of love where most of us dwell. Language is a two-edged tool, to pierce the wall which hides that world, or build high abstract barriers to protect us from its threats.

The instructor who graded the paper I have just read preferred walls to honest words. At the bottom of the last page she scrawled a large "D-minus," emphatically surrounded by a circle. Her only comment was: "Your theme is not clear — you should have developed your 1st paragraph. You talk around your subject." At this moment, two realms collide; a universe of unarticualted feeling seeking expression (and the courage and encouragement to express) and a nature made so immune to feeling by heaven-knows-what that she hides behind the tired, tired language of the professional theme-corrector.

Suddenly we realize that reading as well as writing requires risks, and that the metaphor of insulation, so central to the efforts of the Polish woman survivor to re-establish contact with her past, is a metaphor governing the response of readers, too. Some writing, like "the emission of desirable student behaviors," thickens the insulation that already separates the reader from the words that throw darts at his armor of indifference. But even when language unashamedly reveals the feeling that is hidden behind the words, it must contend with a different kind of barrier, the one behind which our instructor lies concealed, unwilling or unable to hear a human voice and return a human echo of her own.

Ironically, the victor in this melancholy failure at communication is the villain of the piece, behavior modification. For the Polish survivor wrote her next theme on an innocuous topic, received a satisfactory grade, and never returned to the subject of her parents. The instructor, who had encountered a problem in the daily management of her class in the form of an essay which she could not respond to in a human way, altered the attitude of her student by responding in a non-human way, thus resolving her problem by increasing the emission of desirable student behavior. The student now knows how vital it is to develop her first paragraph, and how futile it is to reveal her first grief.

Even more, she has learned the danger of talking around her subject: She not only refuses to talk *around* it now, she refuses to talk *about* it. Thus the human use of language leads back to silence — where perhaps it should have remained in the first place.

Did the experiences Langer relates evoke any memories that help you understand what might drive you to write "safe" papers? Is it possible that a wish for good grades or a desire to say what the reader expects turns your writing into something that sounds as if it were written by a machine?

If you think that you may have stopped taking risks and retreated from using human language, consider what Carll Tucker says about the danger of never thinking, of never giving yourself time to discover your inner thoughts or the limits of your being. In his essay "Enemies of Thought," Tucker says that the advances made in communications in this century have discouraged people from taking the risk of thinking. He challenges us to consider whether a life of ceaseless activities is more desirable than "a life with time out for reflection, reading, researching, writing letters, formulating one's own thoughts." As you read Tucker's essay, think about the possibility that you have let the advances in communication dictate your life.

ENEMIES OF THOUGHT

Antigua, West Indies I am privileged to be sitting on a balcony overlooking a warm beach and a scarcely populated shore. All the noise I hear is nature's: the tide slapping the reefs, the rustling of the sea grape leaves and palm fronds, some high-pitched chirpers (finches, among others), and the distant, constant hum of the sea. The stillness is conducive to thought, and to one thought in particular: that almost every advance in "communication" in this century has chipped away at our time and incentive to think, and that while our means of communicating have improved fantastically, the quality of our lives has not.

Consider the telephone. Nobody but an eccentric reactionary would dispute the fact that the telephone is one of the grand achievements of man. It shrinks the globe. By facilitating dialogue, it enhances the chances of peace. It frees us to travel. By connecting us with emergency services, it saves lives and alleviates fear. It helps us to maintain relationships, to organize events, to accomplish more in our lifetime. And yet it is also indisputable that telephones discourage thought. They rudely interrupt any conversation or calm. Unlike letters, they do not require us to think out our messages in advance. Pressing us to fill the silence (for time is money), they encourage garrulity rather than concise, thoughtful expression. It is enlightening to browse through an anthology of great letters and ask oneself whether the writers would have written them had telephones been handy. Friendly letters, except as acknowledgments, have become almost quaint archaisms, like teatime and chaperones.

Television is another enemy of thought. Except on noncommercial networks, TV rarely focuses on one subject for more than 10 consecutive minutes. We are asked to consider cowboys, panty hose, deodorants, detectives, news bulletins, soft drinks, station identifications, and more dectectives—in the space of an hour. News "analysts" are allotted enough time to express opinions, not to analyze. "Never a dull moment" being the inevitable ideal of programmers, thinkers who pause to think are barred from talk shows and round table discussions.

The fact that we tend to think less—or rather, less deeply—nowadays is more obvious than the risks we run by doing so. After all, of what benefit is thinking? Isn't a life of ceaseless activity—TV, radio, traveling, movies, one sports season overlapping into the next, happenings, "events"—as desirable as, or more desirable than, a life with time out for reflection, reading, researching, writing letters, formulating one's own thoughts? Isn't advocacy of a quieter life simply nostalgia, or elitism, disguised?

If the aim of civilization is (as it should be) to improve the psychological as well as the physical well-being of mankind, one may well wonder whether this century's advances in communications have resulted in progress. Anthropologists describe ignorant, hungry, and diseased tribes who are nonetheless pleased with their existence, while wealthy Americans pop pills, dabble in religions and enthusiasms, patronize psychiatrists, and wonder what their lives mean and if—as our worst newspapers never stop declaring—their violent death by foreign missle or neighborhood gunslinger is imminent. W. H. Auden called ours "the age of anxiety." Thanks to the rapidity of communications, we are constantly reminded of what there is to fear and seldom of the reasons to hope. We are force-fed information without perspective, which, like food undigested, does not nourish but creates discomfort.

Sitting on a balcony overlooking a darkening beach (it is evening, the toads are singsonging, and a cold wind is coming off the sea), I am reminded that the world is old, that this generation is a drop in the bucket, and that hysteria is a waste of time and energy. True, there is much to concern ourselves about and with, in this generation as in all others: crimes and injustices to be exposed, experiments to be made and assessed, hues and cries to be raised. But our most urgent need of all is an occasional escape from communications—time and stillness to think, and the consolation that comes from thinking.

To make themselves comfortable, some dogs will curl up in impossibly cramped spaces, under bureaus or chairs—literally stuff themselves in boxes so that they may feel their boundaries and know where they are. Human beings feel comfortable in figurative boxes, knowing where we are in relation to the rest of men and in the scheme of things. "Communications" conspire to erode our boxes, which take time and stillness to build.

Could Tucker be right? Do you rely on your old ideas rather than explore new ones? Do you prefer talking on the phone to writing letters? The beat of your radio or stereo to stillness? If so, consider the risk you are taking by never giving yourself time for quiet contemplation.

As you can see, past experiences and the world around you play a part in shaping your attitudes about writing. To increase your willingness to take risks, try the following approach, which has helped our students.

Approach 3: Increasing Your Ability to Take Risks and to Find Time for Thinking

Keeping personal and reading journals can help you feel freer about expressing your ideas on paper. They can also encourage you to take risks with writing and thinking that you would not take in a more public medium. Our students have found that journal writing helps them find their personal writing style, meaning in what they read, and significance in what they experience.

PERSONAL JOURNAL

Consider the personal journal your private place for writing to yourself about subjects you want to explore. There is no need to worry about spelling, punctuation, or penmanship. Although your teachers may ask you to share your journal with them, they will not look at it as they do final drafts of papers.

Use your journal for writing about personal experiences and problems. Many students who start out by thinking of the journal as an assignment are surprised to find how helpful it can become. One student said that he started writing in his journal just to fulfill the course requirement and came to consider it as a friend he could talk to about anything. Others start with the belief that they have nothing to say and find themselves going on for pages about an idea that occurs to them as they write. Still other writers, such as Henry David Thoreau, use their journals to record what they see and then examine the significance of the events or sights.

Our student Steve, who liked to type his journal entries, used the journal to discuss his writing problems. The following is the unedited entry he made while trying to write a paper.

```
I don't know why I am having such a hard time writing this paper,
it should be one of the easier ones for me. I am just not able to put
any thing on paper that I like. I wonder if other writers get to a point
```

where they just can't control the paper like they want to. If you think about it George Orwell had a simailar problem that he told us about in his short story "Shooting an Elephant". In the story he had to do something that he really didn't want to do. This paper is to me as Orwell's story is to him, it is something that I don't want to do but it has to be done.

I have always had a problem with writing papers, because it never fails that when the time comes for the paper to be handed in, mine was finished the night before. I think that most of my problem comes from the fact that I dislike to sit down and write. If there were some other way to express myself besides on paper I would do it. I admit that I am a little lazy in the field of english and I take the blame for that. The real block between me and the paper was school. All throughout my years in high school I think that I turned in four papers total. These were the kind of papers that you write just for the grade and not for the meaning. In school it seemed as there was always an alternative class to take, so that I would not have to take a writing class. I didn't have a writing class until my senior year in high school.

Instead of writing this paper on how I dealt with my fathers drinking or something serious. I decided to give myself a break and just start writing about something relaxing. Maybe I would write about something stupid or something funny, but as I tried to do both I kept pulling blanks from my imagination. I guess that there was a watcher standing behind the door that all my ideas come out of, and he would snatch words and phrases that he did not like. I can see him now sitting in a rocking chair up in my head while words march past him in single file. He takes only the words that sound good to him and makes the others go back to the end of the line.

Writing has become easy for me now as words are going to fast for my watcher to catch them all.

I have finally figured out the solution to writing good papers. I can blame my lack of writing skills on my high school but I can blame my lack of imagination only on myself. I should have finished the other papers before I gave up on them, because maybe the people who made fun of them did not like them, but I didn't give the rest of the class a chance to judge the papers. I really don't think that I need to have an outline for my type of writing. It is more important that I just get something down on paper then how I get it down. I need to do more prewriting in the writing of my papers but it seems that I write the best when I am pressured into writing. Never have I done a paper that was not just finished before the time that it was due.

I really enjoy telling others about experiences that I have had. I enjoy telling about myself because I want others to know and understand what ordeals I have been through and how I dealt them. In high school you were not able to write about sensitive subjects because everyone there knew everyone else. Here a collage I can enjoy what I am writing because I don't give a damn what anyone thinks about what I write. The reason that I feel this way is because personally I don't know the student who sits to the right of me or anyone else who may read my stories. This sort of gives me an anonymous feeling, so that I can write freely and express my feelings without worring who will read the paper.

I consider myself a fairly good "thought expresser"; even in high school I could write a paper with a lot of content but it would be lacking in mechanical skills so then the grade would reflect from the black markings on the paper instead of what was in the paper. I became frustrated by this because I felt that what good is a paper if you do not tell somebody something. All through school I was told that a paper was to be written in a certain order and it had to have an outline, theme, main body, conclusion. Well I would get every thing except what the teacher was looking for, because my papers would never have an outline, and I didn't know what a theme was until my senior year in high school. All through high school the only paper that I enjoyed writing was a descriptive essay that I went all out on. The rest could go to the dogs.

When this entry is finished I will keep it to read and to look back on. It says alot to me that others would not pick up. Like that for the next paper I am to try and have it done at least three days early. I wonder if others have my same problem.

Writing in his journal about his writing problem helped Steve overcome his writer's block. His next paper, "My Place," appears in Chapter 9 and illustrates just how successful journal writing was for him.

GUIDELINES FOR USING THE PERSONAL JOURNAL. To make the personal journal work for you, use the following guidelines.

1. *Keep your journal writing separate from all other writing.* Unless your teacher assigns a specific type of notebook for your journal, choose one in which you feel comfortable writing. Some students prefer writing on paper different from the kind they use for other school work. If this technique may help, select a notebook with paper of a different color or size from the one you are required to

use for class. You might opt for a yellow, legal-sized pad or unlined paper and might even write with red, green, purple, or black ink. Or, if you feel most comfortable writing in the journal when you are propped up in bed or are leaning against a tree, a small notebook that can be carried with you might be a good choice.

2. *Write in your journal every day.* Some days you will write more than others. Just be sure that you write for at least 10 minutes every day. Although you will be responding to questions that we raise, as well as to certain topics assigned by your teacher, the journal will be most beneficial if you also write about your own ideas and concerns every day.

Most students find that setting aside a special time each day for writing in their journals works best. Some prefer the morning before leaving for class. Others like to write in the evening, either after dinner or before going to bed. Make journal writing part of your daily schedule, and you will get the maximum results from it.

3. *Be honest.* Remember, you are keeping a journal for yourself. You can fill in the pages but still hide from your own real feelings and ideas by discussing topics that are superficial and require no risks to express. If you want journal writing to be more than an exercise, respond thoughtfully to the questions we raise or to the topics your teacher assigns. And best of all, talk about subjects or events that really matter to you.

If you cannot think of anything to write about, get started in journal writing by trying one of the following topics. Come back to this list later if you need inspiration.

JOURNAL TOPICS. The following are suggestions for topics you might use for the first journal entry or to refer back to whenever you cannot think of something to write about. They are merely *suggestions;* you are always free to choose your own subjects.

1. Write a letter to your journal telling it what you expect it to do for you.
2. Write a letter to your journal telling it how you feel about writing in it.
3. Describe an event in your life, current or past, using as much detail as possible. Try to re-create it in words.
4. Recall and describe an incident, this time making it end as you would have liked rather than as it did.
5. Write a letter to someone who has made you happy, angry, or sad. There is no need to think of mailing it, but use it to express your feelings on paper. (Abraham Lincoln often used this technique to see how he felt.)
6. Make up a questionnaire for a person, a character, or yourself

to find out what you want to know and what you think about certain subjects by answering the questions.

7. Imagine that you are being interviewed or are interviewing someone you want to know more about. Make up a set of questions that will elicit the answers you want to get or to give.

8. Use your imagination to describe yourself as a specific kind of tree, ice-cream cone, or animal, or to write a dialogue between your right and left hands, your heart and head, or your eyes and ears.

9. Record the sounds you hear as you sit in a certain place. Or record what you feel as you touch different trees or materials. Record smells or tastes.

10. Take a common object and observe all the details or describe all the feelings it evokes for you.

11. Discuss yourself with your journal. Describe your personality or your physical self and write about what you like or would like to change.

12. Describe a dream you have had.

13. Write descriptions of scenes you carry around in your mind, or of fantasies, stories, or daydreams.

READING JOURNAL

Consider the reading journal as a place for responding to what you read. Again, concentrate on your ideas rather than on grammar, punctuation, or penmanship. You can summarize what you read, discuss your reaction to the work, or relate the author's ideas to your own experiences.

Our students tell us that keeping a reading journal improves their reading and even makes it more interesting because it forces them to become active rather than passive readers. By this they mean that they no longer read just the words; instead, they read for meaning and react to what the author says, as if they were involved in a dialogue with him.

GUIDELINES FOR USING THE READING JOURNAL. Use the following guidelines to make the reading journal useful to you.

1. *Become an active reader.* To make the reading journal useful to you, be an active reader. As you read, stop periodically to think about what you are reading. Visualize the scene the author has created, think about a statement the author has made, or imagine what will come next. Make notations in the margin to record your reactions or to summarize the author's idea. Remember, underlining and highlighting are passive activities and do not help you

understand the author's ideas. Instead, when you do find a passage you respond to, discuss it in the reading journal.

2. *Write in your reading journal daily.* Describe your reactions to what you read in papers, magazines, or your assigned readings. In fact, broaden your reading with a visit to the bookstore or library in your area. Look at magazines, current best-sellers, and classics.

3. *Relate what you read to yourself.* Consider how you can use these ideas in your own life. Let the author's ideas evoke memories of past experiences or of people and places you have known. Compare your experience with the author's.

4. *Take risks and say what you think.* Although your teachers may ask to see your journal, they will not look at them as they do final drafts. So, this is your chance to express how you feel about what you read. If it is boring, say so and discuss the reason. If it makes you angry, vent your anger in the journal and try to understand why you reacted as you did.

JOURNAL TOPICS. If you are concerned about finding something to say in the reading journal try one of the following approaches that our students have used.

1. Summarize the author's ideas. This exercise gives you a chance to put the writer's concepts in your own words.
2. Write a letter to the author telling him how you feel about his ideas or how her experience reminds you of your own.
3. Write a dialogue between two characters from different pieces of writing. Ann Byrne did this and had fun writing while coming to understand people and their perspectives on life.

Dee Brown recognized Calamity Jane and what she'd done--so he introduced himself and made sure Calamity knew he was a Sioux Indian.

Calamity wanted to know how an Indian got to heaven--"What are you doing here?"

Dee wanted to know why Indians were not welcome and Calamity said that they weren't civilized--

Dee answered, "We don't need things to prove we're civilized like the white man--our definition is carried in us."

"I suppose killing is part of being civilized," Calamity answered back.

Then...

If you would like to read the entire essay, based on this unedited journal entry, turn to Chapter 9 and read "Gates of Heaven."

4. Imagine a confrontation between an author and one of his characters. Linda White created one to understand what William Styron tried to do in his novel. The following unedited journal entry helped her focus on Nat Turner's perspective.

> It was a typical day in the life of a writer. William Styron sat at his typewriter just staring at it. He just couldn't seem to finish the last page of the chapter. The scene around him showed his present writer's block. The floor was covered with crumpled up paper that contained his great attempts at writing. Suddenly Styron wasn't alone anymore. He felt a presence which he couldn't see or explain. Then a light outline of a person came into view. After a few minutes the vision was clear. This person was black, in ragged, blood-splattered clothing and bound in chains from head to foot. Now Styron recognized the figure. It was Nat Turner, the historical character in Styron's own _The Confessions of Nat Turner_. Styron was in shock and Turner just stood there staring at him. Then Turner began to talk in a purely white voice because that was the only voice Styron could imagine him with. Turner said, "I have been following all of the writings of my history since my death. I read your book and I was deeply upset. I don't understand why my historical life has been altered all for the sake of a good story. There is just too much difference between my real life and your story for it to be seen as a great piece of writing."
> Styron . . .

Linda went on to write a research paper in which she cited historical evidence to support Turner's position.

5. Write about a memory that the work evokes for you. Many of the student essays in Chapter 9 started this way. For examples, read "Letter to Ms. Didion," by Julie Kersul, "Gates of Heaven," by Anne Byrne, or "My Place," by Steve Groholski.

6. Make up questions about the work before you read it. Look at the title, introduction, conclusion, and any headings. What do you predict the piece is going to discuss? What questions do you want answered? Read it and then answer your questions in the journal.

CONSIDERING ATTITUDES ABOUT THE ROLE
OF WRITING IN YOUR PROFESSIONAL LIFE

In Question 3 of the "Writing Inventory," you considered how important or useful writing will be in your future. Many of you may have indicated that writing will be important in your professional life. Our students said, "I am a business major, and I know writing will be an extensive part of my job," or "I think writing will be important because the job I hope to have will involve writing reports." Others may see writing playing a role in preparing them for a career but having little place in the profession itself. "Writing will be important while I am moving up in my profession, but once I am established, it won't be especially important." Still others may suspect that writing will play a limited role in the profession they have chosen. "Because I will work in a scientific field, I doubt that writing will be an important part of my job." "I am going to be a doctor, so I won't have to write as much as I would in other professions."

Like our students, you may not have a very clear picture of the importance of writing in your professional life. Such an attitude may make you feel that learning to write is not necessary because you will write very little after leaving school. Therefore, you may have little motivation to write, or to write better.

Because so many of our students felt this way about writing, we decided to do some research on the subject. With the help of Michigan State University's Placement Service, we found that writing is important not only in getting a job but in advancing in it as well. For years, the service has been asking hundreds of prospective employers in business, industry, and government to rank the qualities they considered most important in hiring an employee. The ability to communicate in writing ranked high and has remained among the five most important qualifications for the past two years. To find out what employers meant by "ability to communicate in writing," we asked Director Jack Shingleton and Associate Director Patrick Scheetz to include the following question in their 1978 survey: "How much importance do the following basic writing skills have in determining success on the job for a new college graduate in your organization?" The figures in the table on p. 26 may give you new insights on how employers view writing.

To learn just how important writing was in each field, we did a follow-up study, interviewing nearly 200 employers and professionals to determine how much and what kinds of writing were required in their fields. We found that writing is important in all professions. A chemical engineer told us that he wrote for 2-4 hours a day and that his advancement in the company was directly related to how well he could write. A doctor told us that his ability to write reports determined how well the treatment was carried out by other health professionals. An accountant said that she spent most of her time

BUSINESS, INDUSTRY AND GOVERNMENT WRITING SKILLS

Writing Skills	A Great Deal of Importance	Some Importance	Little or No Importance
Writing style	117	244	42
Spelling	168	199	19
Punctuation or grammar	144	210	22
Vocabulary	181	197	18
Research skills	148	298	54
Ability to organize ideas	362	36	1
Ability to state and defend a position in writing	237	143	17

Source: Michigan State University Placement Services, *Recruiting Trends Report, 1978–79*, by John D. Shingleton and L. Patrick Sheetz, pg. 23.

writing reports, and a computer programmer from a major corporation stated that she had to write reports to acquire funds for projects and to do progress reports and final papers on completed projects.

To determine the role of writing in your professional life, try one of the following approaches.

Approach 4: Interview People in Your Probable Career Field

Interview people who work in the field you plan to enter. Ask them how often they must write, what kind of writing they do, and how important writing is for getting a promotion within the company or for moving to higher levels in the field. Malcolm Forbes, president and editor-in-chief of *Forbes* magazine, says:

> A good business letter can get you a job interview.
> Get you off the hook.
> Or get you money.
> It's totally asinine to blow your chances of getting *whatever* you want with a business letter that turns people off instead of turning them on.

If you would like to read his essay, "How to Write a Business Letter," turn to Chapter 9. Keep his ideas in mind when you talk to people. Do they say the same things or emphasize the same ideas? One of our students talked to her father in order to find out what writing he was required to do—and she was surprised by his responses. Here are her unedited comments about the interview.

I am very interested in psychiatry because my father is a psychiatrist. I talked to him and he said that he does do a lot of writing.

He has to write up an admission report for every patient that he admitts to the hospital and he admitts at least seven patients everyday. He also has to write up a release notification for each patient including the patients' history and medications. Each of these reports are at least five written pages full of jargon.

A psychiatrist also has to write out reports of all his staff workers such as nurses, dentists, guards, pharmacists, and other employees in his particular ward.

A psychiatrist goes to a seminar each year and earns points for what he writes. A psychiatrist needs 50 points each year to get his medical license renewed.

I haven't exactly declared my major yet but I guess I'm really interested in psychiatry.

Myung Lee

Approach 5: Read About Your Probable Career Field

Read about the field you plan to enter to determine how important writing will be. Find out how much and what kind of writing you will do, and what role it will play in getting the job you want and helping you advance in your career.

Consult the career section in your library or find out if your college placement service has such information. Two of our students did this, and one of them, Robert Sanborn, found out the following about the field of fisheries research.

I learned that communicating (writing and speaking) is very important for a person in the fisheries field.

I hope to be in fisheries research where the importance of writing is lessened but there is still a need for it. A person needs writing in fisheries research because you need to able to discuss your findings on paper so others can read about them.

Writing is needed for fisheries management because write on paper what their management plans are for a certain area. Fisheries managers also need to express themselves for public relations.

Writing is most important in Fisheries Educational Writing and Fisheries Administration. Fisheries Administration needs writing for public relations, developing programs, setting policies and regulations. They also need writing to inform people on radio and television and preparing or overseeing preparation of printed materials for public distribution.

In educational writing, writing is needed for the preparation of literature, scripts and technical reports about advancements in the fisheries field.

I want to learn more about writing so I can express myself to other people. I hope to learn more about writing so I will be able to get a job.

Robert Sanborn

Another student, Bryan Merrill, found out the following about engineering.

To research my career in engineering, I found several related books in the library which pointed out to me the extreme importance of not only good writing ability, but all forms of communication.

In my reading I learned that a good use of vocabulary and grammar was not as important as the ability to express ideas clearly. It was shown that writing increases the ability to think, use logic, and organize ideas for good written and spoken communication.

Writing was described as a display of creativity which, in turn, increases the ability to bring out new ideas. It is very important in engineering to be able to derive new ideas and be able to communicate them effectively.

In college most engineering students don't realize that a surprisingly large amount of an engineer's time is devoted to communicating--particularly writing and speaking. This information startled me and convinced me that it is essential that I learn more about writing for my career.

These unedited comments show how much Robert and Bryan learned from their readings.

CONSIDERING WRITING IN YOUR PERSONAL LIFE

Although some of you may consider writing a part of your professional life, you may not see it figuring in your personal life. Authors Joan Didion and Babette Blaushild talk about what writing means to them in their essays "Why I Write" and "Confessions of an Unpublished Writer." Didion says that she writes to find out what she thinks. "Had I been blessed with even limited access to my own mind there would have been no reason to write. I write entirely to find out what I'm thinking, what I'm looking at, what I see and what it means." She also says that writing gives her power to control others.

In many ways writing is the act of saying *I*, of imposing oneself upon other people, of saying *listen to me, see it my way, change your mind.* It's an aggressive, even a hostile act. You can disguise its aggressiveness all you want with veils of subordinate clauses and qualifiers and tentative subjunctives, with ellipses and evasions — with the whole manner of intimating rather than claiming, of alluding rather than stating — but there's no getting around the fact that setting words on paper is the tactic of a secret bully, an invasion, an imposition of the writer's sensibility on the reader's most private space.

Blaushild repeats these feelings and adds that writing allows her to express herself and to make her world more meaningful. As you read the work of this author (which was never published before this essay was accepted), think about what she says and decide if writing could become important to you.

CONFESSIONS OF AN UNPUBLISHED WRITER

Without being too pompous about it, I think I can say I speak for one of the largest unorganized groups in the world — the unpublished authors. We write as though our lives depended on it — yet we have long since adapted ourselves to the icy truth that we will never get into print. Why do we do it? Because it happens to please us. In my own case I enjoy it.

People who know I write for love and not money probably feel there's something wrong with my moorings. They don't quite comprehend that writing can be an end in itself — and a profoundly rewarding one. In fact, it goes into the making of a good life.

A good life, for me at least, means making all sorts of connections with the world around me. It means a heightened awareness of people and their moods, a sensitivity to all sorts of subtle shadings. It means an existence without murkiness. The discipline of writing conditions the mind for this kind of life. It has enabled me to develop the tri-dimensional or stereoscopic habit. People at a dinner party, who used to fade one into the other with a flat sameness, now take on sharp forms and colors. Women at a committee meeting, or children and their mothers at the school play, now become defined in their own elements of uniqueness. And, as I try to understand them, I find myself liking them better. Take the committee chairman. Why should she be officious and small-minded? After the meeting I talked to her over coffee. Something about her reminded me of my mother's friend when I was small. Doors began to open in my mind; I could go exploring through rooms filled with old memories and feelings. Next: A man seated next to me at dinner. He has always been a bore. But now I look at him through different eyes. He fascinates me; he is literary fodder. True, he is a stereotype: the golf-playing, cigar-smoking, back-slapping businessman who inevitably sits next to you at dinner. But now I talk to him, draw him out, and he lets me have a glimpse now and then of the part of him that is not a cliche. Before I started to write, this kind of evening would numb me; now it excites my imagination.

I remember my first visit to a symphony concert after I took to writing as an important part of my life. I left the hall moved, though not really under-standing why. What was I feeling? My ears had become newly alive. Thereafter I was struck with the difference between live and recorded music. It was as if I had been color blind all my life, seeing everything in grays and blacks, and then suddenly found I could see vivid hues. But there was more. I had a feeling of peace, and of wonder, too: If man is capable of creating this beauty and truth, I thought, here is our supreme elevation, and here is our hope.

As I find myself getting closer to human beings through my writing, I find myself becoming more patient and compassionate, never finding "answers," but perhaps stumbling on small truths. Not for me the novelist who ties up and polishes off the human problem he has posed, who says in effect: that's that. I feel that the novel can only be a search for human truths; and that along the way, some self-discovery is inevitable. In this view, it is not important that my writing be successful. I would of course like to be successful, but even if I do not create best-sellers or "successes of esteem," other rewards are open to me.

But if writing has its pleasures it also has its pain, as when I see my own handwriting on the self-addressed, manuscript envelope the mailman tosses casually on the doorstep. Inside, the melancholy printed rejection slip is clipped to the top page: "Thank you for submitting your work which has been read with interest, but. . . . Sometimes there is a little note of cheer: a "sorry" written across the bottom. Better yet, you may find enclosed a note scribbled on a memo pad by an editor.

Sometimes the manuscript is kept a tantalizingly long time. You then wonder, is this a good omen? Are they passing it up the hierarchy of editors at the magazine, actually liking it? Or is it lying on the desk of an editor who is home sick with the flu? Or is it home with him, not read because his kids are making too much noise? *What is taking so long?* Finally, the mailman brings the story back and there is a crazy kind of relief; you are temporarily liberated from your daily mailbox-vigil. But, full of hope and paper clips, you send another story out, and it starts all over again.

We humans are a mixed lot: scared and lonely and foolish, inhuman and humane, graceful and graceless, full of hope and hopeless. Out of the conflict between reality and our fantasies, art can bring understanding and illuminate truth. To me, this is the supreme function of writing. It is no easy calling, but its rewards go so far beyond the mundane that I expect to practice it for as many years as I have left on earth.

Is it possible that writing can bring you the insights it brings Blaushild? Do you understand how writing might make you feel in control of your world?

Approach 6: Reassessing Your Attitudes

As we said at the beginning of this chapter, the attitudes a writer brings to his craft can determine whether or not he will be successful. Now that you have had the opportunity to consider your own attitudes, take time to reconsider the questions in the "Writing Inventory." Have your answers changed?

Before going on to Chapter 2, answer the following questions:

1. What is your personal reason for wanting to become a better writer?
2. Which approaches will you continue to use to develop a positive attitude toward writing?

Whenever you need to bolster your confidence or find strength in the experiences of other writers, return to this chapter.

CHAPTER 2

Becoming a Writer

Having explored your attitudes about writing and having considered what other writers say about their attitudes and experiences in Chapter 1, you are better prepared to become a writer. To help you further, we have divided this chapter into three sections. In the first section, we help you examine what being a reader has taught you about writing; in the second, we introduce you to the composing process experienced writers use and give you an opportunity to practice it with a warm-up assignment; and in the last section, we provide assignments that lead you from personal to research writing.

THE READER BECOMES A WRITER

Being a reader cannot automatically make you a writer, but the experience you have gained as a reader has helped you to form certain expectations about writing. As you read or were read to, you developed a sense of what makes certain kinds of writing successful and others unsuccessful. So, whether or not you realize it, you possess an understanding of the conventions of successful writing. Completing the "Reading Survey," the "Reading Responses," and "Writing Responses" that follow will make you conscious of what you instinctively know about writing and will help you make the transition from reader to writer.

In order to focus freely on your ideas rather than worry about spelling, punctuation, or grammar, record your responses in your personal or reading journal. Keep in mind that you bring unique experiences to the readings and may respond to them differently from the way we or others do. But your responses are no less valid. Share them and add to the understanding of others.

Reading Survey

Like the "Writing Survey" in Chapter 1, this inventory should help you think about your past reading experiences and help you identify what you expect from successful writing.

Past Experiences
1. What kinds of material do you read most often? Magazines, paperbacks, assigned readings, factual pieces, sports articles, others?
2. What kinds of reading do you most enjoy? Adventures, romances, mysteries, biographies, newspaper or magazine articles, others? Why?
3. Who are your favorite writers? Why?
4. What is the role of reading in your life?

To help you consider what your expectations are as a reader and to answer the next three questions, read any three essays in Chapter

9. If you start an essay but lose interest in it, find another that you prefer. When you have read three essays, jot down their titles and page numbers so that you can refer to them later in this chapter.

Reading Expectations
5. What characteristics do you expect to find in an enjoyable book, article, essay, story, or other piece of writing?
6. What helps you remember what you read?
7. What makes you want to finish a piece once you have started? What makes you stop reading something?

Readers' Expectations

Over the last few years, our students have consistently talked about certain characteristics that they expect to find in writing. They express their ideas in various ways, but essentially they come up with the same list.

1. Writers must care about their subject.
2. Writers need to make the reader care about the subject.
3. Writers must use specifics to convey their ideas to the reader.
4. Writers must make their ideas easy to follow for the reader.

Probably you wrote down the same kinds of ideas because they are important to you, too. If you read mysteries, you want the author to make you care about the innocent, struggling young man accused of murdering his wealthy employer. If you read newspapers or magazines, you want to find out quickly who won the big baseball game or how to lose those 10 pounds without dieting. And if you are reading a chemistry book, you expect all of the specifics on isotopes or valences to be organized in a clear and understandable manner. In other words, you have definite expectations as a reader; when those expectations are met, you read on. When they are not, you stop because reading is a waste of time for you.

By now, you can see that writers have many responsibilities. They must please not only themselves but also the reader. And they must consider this expectation every time they write. By analyzing four of our favorite essays and the readings you choose from Chapter 9, you can see what writers do to fulfill their own needs as well as their readers'.

WRITERS MUST CARE ABOUT THE SUBJECTS

From your own experiences as a writer and after reading Langer's essay in Chapter 1, you realize that writing about topics you care about may be risky business. But if writers ever hope to get beyond comfortable generalizations that are dull and tedious, they must find subjects they can and want to write about. But how do they *show* this concern? As a reader, you know when the writer has succeeded. But because you get involved with ideas, or with plots and characters, you may not be conscious of the writer's involvement with the subject.

One essay we have enjoyed over the years was written by William Allen White, a writer and newspaper editor. Take a few minutes to read it.

MARY WHITE

The Associated Press reports carrying the news of Mary White's death declared that it came as the result of a fall from a horse. How she would have hooted at that! She never fell from a horse in her life. Horses have fallen on her and with her — "I'm always trying to hold 'em in my lap," she used to say. But she was proud of few things, and one was that she could ride anything that had four legs and hair. Her death resulted not from a fall, but from a blow on the head which fractured her skull, and the blow came from the limb of an overhanging tree on the parking.

The last hour of her life was typical of its happiness. She came home from a day's work at school, topped off by a hard grind with the copy on the High School Annual, and felt that a ride would refresh her. She climbed into her khakis, chattering to her mother about the work she was doing, and hurried to get her horse and be out on the dirt roads for the country air and radiant green fields of the spring. As she rode through the town on an easy gallop she kept waving at passers-by. She knew everyone in town. For a decade the little figure with the long pig-tail and the red hair ribbon has been familiar on the streets of Emporia, and she got in the way of speaking to those who nodded at her. She passed the Kerrs, walking the horse, in front of the Normal Library, and waved at them; passed another friend a few hundred feet further on, and waved at her. The horse was walking and, as she turned into North Merchant Street she took off her cowboy hat, and the horse swung into a lope. She passed the Tripletts and waved her cowboy hat at them, still moving gaily north on Merchant Street. A Gazette carrier passed — a High School boy friend — and she waved at him, but with her bridle hand; the horse veered quickly; plunged into the parking where the low-hanging limb faced her, and, while she still looked back waving, the blow came. But she did not fall from the horse; she slipped off, dazed a bit, staggered and fell in a faint. She never quite recovered consciousness.

But she did not fall from the horse, neither was she riding fast. A year or so ago she used to go like the wind. But that habit was broken, and she used the horse to get into the open to get fresh, hard exercise, and to work off a certain

William Allen White, "Mary White," *Emporia Gazette*, May 17, 1921. Reprinted by permission of Mrs. William L. White.

surplus energy that welled up in her and needed a physical outlet. That need has been in her heart for years. It was back of the impulse that kept the dauntless, little brown-clad figure on the streets and country roads of this community and built into a strong, muscular body what had been a frail and sickly frame during the first years of her life. But the riding gave her more than a body. It released a gay and hardy soul. She was the happiest thing in the world. And she was happy because she was enlarging her horizon. She came to know all sorts and conditions of men; Charley O'Brien, the traffic cop, was one of her best friends. W. L. Holtz, the Latin teacher, was another. Tom O'Connor, farmer-politician, and Rev. J. H. J. Rice, preacher and police judge, and Frank Beach, music master, were her special friends, and all the girls, black and white, above the track and below the track, in Pepville and Stringtown, were among her acquaintances. And she brought home riotous stories of her adventures. She loved to rollick; persiflage was her natural expression at home. Her humor was a continual bubble of joy. She seemed to think in hyperbole and metaphor. She was mischievous without malice, as full of faults as an old shoe. No angel was Mary White, but an easy girl to live with, for she never nursed a grouch five minutes in her life..

With all her eagerness for the out-of-doors she loved books. On her table when she left her room were a book by Conrad, one by Galsworthy, *Creative Chemistry* by E. E. Slosson, and a Kipling book. She read Mark Twain, Dickens and Kipling before she was ten—all of their writings. Wells and Arnold Bennett particularly amused and diverted her. She was entered as a student in Wellesley in 1922; was assistant editor of the High School Annual this year, and in line for election to the editorship of the Annual next year. She was a member of the executive committee of the High School YWCA.

Within the last two years she had begun to be moved by an ambition to draw. She began as most children do by scribbling in her school books, funny pictures. She bought cartoon magazines and took a course—rather casually, naturally, for she was, after all, a child with no strong purposes—and this year she tasted the first fruits of success by having her pictures accepted by the High School Annual. But the thrill of delight she got when Mr. Ecord, of the Normal Annual, asked her to do the cartooning for that book this spring, was too beautiful for words. She fell to her work with all her enthusiastic heart. Her drawings were accepted, and her pride—always repressed by a lively sense of the ridiculousness of the figure she was cutting—was a really gorgeous thing to see. No successful artist ever drank a deeper draught of satisfaction than she took from the little fame her work was getting among her school-fellows. In her glory, she almost forgot her horse—but never her car.

For she used the car as a jitney bus. It was her social life. She never had a "party" in all her nearly seventeen years—wouldn't have one; but she never drove a block in the car in her life that she didn't begin to fill the car with pick-ups! Everybody rode with Mary White—white and black, old and young, rich and poor, men and women. She liked nothing better than to fill the car full of long-legged High School boys and an occasional girl, and parade the town. She never had a "date," nor went to a dance, except once with her brother, Bill, and the "boy proposition" didn't interest her—yet. But young people—great spring-breaking, varnish-cracking, fender-bending, door-sagging carloads of "kids" gave her great pleasure. Her zests were keen. But the most fun she ever had in her life was acting as chairman of the committee that got up the big turkey dinner for the poor folks at the county home; scores of pies, gallons of slaw; jam, cakes, preserves, oranges and a wilderness of turkey were loaded in the car and taken to the county home. And, being of a practical turn of mind, she risked her own Christmas dinner by staying to see that the poor folks actually got it all. Not that she was a cynic; she just disliked to tempt folks. While there she found a blind colored uncle, very old, who could do nothing but make rag rugs, and she rustled up from her school friends rags enough to keep him busy for a season. The last engagement she tried to make was to take the guests at the county home out for a car ride. And the last endeavor of her life was to try to get a rest room for colored girls in the High School. She found one girl reading in the toilet, because there was no better place for a colored girl to loaf, and it inflamed her sense of injustice and she became a nagging harpy to those who, she thought, could remedy the evil. The poor she had always with her, and was glad of it. She hungered and thirsted for righteousness; and was the most impious creature in the world. She joined the Congregational Church without consulting her parents; not particularly for her soul's good. She never had a thrill of piety in her life, and would have hooted at a "testimony." But even as a little child she felt the church was an agency for helping people to more of life's abundance, and she wanted to help. She never wanted help for herself. Clothes meant little to her. It was a fight to get a new rig on her; but eventually a harder fight to get it off. She never wore a jewel and had no ring but her High School class ring, and never asked for anything but a wrist watch. She refused to have her hair up, though she was nearly seventeen. "Mother," she protested, "you don't know how much I get by with, in my braided pigtails, that I could not with my hair up." Above every other passion of her life was her passion not to grow up, to be a child. The tom-boy in her, which was big, seemed to loathe to be put away forever in skirts. She was a Peter Pan, who refused to grow up.

Her funeral yesterday at the Congregational Church was as she would have wished it; no singing, no flowers save the big bunch of red roses from her brother Bill's Harvard classmen—Heavens, how proud that would have made her! And the red roses from the Gazette force—in vases at her head and feet. A short prayer, Paul's beautiful essay on "Love" from the Thirteenth Chapter of First Corinthians, some remarks about her democratic spirit by her friend, John H. J. Rice, pastor and police judge, which she would have deprecated if she could, a prayer sent down for her by her friend, Carl Nau, and opening the service the slow, poignant movement from Beethoven's Moonlight Sonata, which she loved, and closing the service a cutting from the joyously melancholy first movement of Tschaikowski's Pathetic Symphony, which she liked to hear in certain moods on the phonograph; then the Lord's Prayer by her friends in the High School. That was all.

For her pall-bearers only her friends were chosen: her Latin teacher, W. L. Holtz; her High School principal, Rice Brown; her doctor, Frank Foncannon; her friend, W. W. Finney; her pal at the Gazette office, Walter Hughes; and her brother, Bill. It would have made her smile to know that her friend, Charley

O'Brien, the traffic cop, had been transferred from Sixth and Commercial to the corner near the church to direct her friends who came to bid her good-by.

A rift in the clouds in a gray day threw a shaft of sunlight upon her coffin as her nervous, energetic little body sank to its last sleep. But the soul of her, the glowing, gorgeous, fervent soul of her, surely was flaming in eager joy upon some other dawn.

Reading Response

Try describing this essay to a friend or classmate. What would you want to say about it? How do you think White showed his involvement?

Perhaps you were impressed that White could even write about his daughter, undoubtedly a painful task, and you described that feeling to your friend or classmate. Maybe you talked about how you would have liked to meet Mary White. She was kind and joyful, and a bit mischievous, too. Or you could have chosen to explain the kinds of things she did: riding her horse, managing Christmas dinners, or loading her car full of people. Or perhaps you had a mental picture of Mary White—smiling, chatty, wearing a cowboy hat, slim and energetic—and that image may have been the center of your description.

By carefully describing the images and memories in his mind, White tried to capture the spirit of his daughter on paper. And in that way, he showed his readers how much he cared for that person who was part of his life for almost 17 years.

Other writers can show involvement in their topics by presenting their ideas humorously, as did William Zinsser. His differences with his fellow writer, Dr. Brock, may not have been as exaggerated as his portrayal of their encounter suggests. But writing about it gave Zinsser the chance to talk about notions concerning writing that genuinely irked him and he displays these feelings in his essay. Other writers may refer to poignant experiences that have affected them deeply in order to convey their ideas. Lawrence Langer in his essay, "The Human Use of Language," did this when he described a Jewish woman's experience in her writing class to show his concern for his topic.

Think back on the three essays you chose from Chapter 9. How did those authors show that they cared about their subjects? In the following box keep a list of what you discover. Later, you can refer to it as a writer to gauge how well you have communicated your concerns, or, as a reader, to suggest how others can show their interest in the subjects of their essays.

Writers show that they care about their subjects by

- *carefully describing their memories and feelings*
- *using humor/exaggeration*
- *relating past experiences to the subject*

Writing Response

As we said earlier, being a reader will not ensure your success as a writer, but it can give you some new insights about writing. In your notebook or journal, try out some of these ideas by first making a list of topics you care about. Include favorite people, passions, books, experiences, childhood memories, pets, places or travels.

Then focus on one subject and write about it for 10 or 15 minutes.

Once you finish, read over your work and think about why this topic is important to you. What is one way you can show this attitude in your writing? Jot down your ideas under what you wrote previously.

WRITERS NEED TO MAKE THE READER CARE ABOUT THE SUBJECT

Writers must do more than find subjects they can and want to write about. They must also consider how to make their topics interesting for their readers. First of all, the writer considers who his readers are and what they are likely to care about. This process entails making decisions: Would it be best to entertain readers? To persuade them to act or to convince them of an idea by giving them a great deal of information? What examples or details would work best? How should the writing begin? Such decisions are necessary if writers hope to communicate their ideas and find ways to involve their readers.

To see how one writer has solved these problems, consider this speech by Martin Luther King, Jr.

I HAVE A DREAM

I am happy to join with you today in what will go down in history as the greatest demonstration for freedom in the history of our nation.

Five score years ago, a great American, in whose symbolic shadow we stand today, signed the Emancipation Proclamation. This momentous decree came as a great beacon light of hope to millions of Negro slaves who had been seared in the flames of withering injustice. It came as a joyous daybreak to end the long night of their captivity. But one hundred years later, the Negro still is not free. One hundred years later, the life of the Negro is still sadly crippled by the manacles of segregation and the chains of discrimination. One hundred years later, the Negro lives on a lonely island of poverty in the midst of a vast ocean of material prosperity. One hundred years later, the Negro is still anguished in the corners of American society and finds himself in exile in his own land. And so we have come here today to dramatize a shameful condition.

In a sense we have come to our nation's capital to cash a check. When the architects of our republic wrote the magnificent words of the Constitution and the Declaration of Independence, they were signing a promissory note to which every American was to fall heir. This note was the promise that all men—yes, Black men as well as white men—would be guaranteed the inalienable rights of life, liberty, and the pursuit of happiness.

It is obvious today that America has defaulted on this promissory note insofar as her citizens of color are concerned. Instead of honoring this sacred obligation, America has given the Negro people a bad check, a check which has come back marked "insufficient funds." But we refuse to believe that the bank of justice is bankrupt. We refuse to believe that there are insufficient funds in the great vaults of opportunity of this nation; and so we have come to cash this check, a check that will give us upon demand the riches of freedom and the security of justice.

We have also come to this hallowed spot to remind America of the fierce urgency of *now*. This is no time to engage in the luxury of cooling off or to take the tranquilizing drug of gradualism. *Now* is the time to make real the promises of democracy. *Now* is the time to rise from the dark and desolate valley of segregation to the sunlit path of racial justice. *Now* is the time to lift our nation from the quicksands of racial injustice to the solid rock of brotherhood. *Now* is the time to make justice a reality for all of God's children.

It would be fatal for the nation to overlook the urgency of the moment.

This sweltering summer of the Negro's legitimate discontent will not pass until there is an invigorating autumn of freedom and equality. Nineteen sixty-three is not an end, but a beginning. And those who hope that the Negro needed to blow off steam and will now be content will have a rude awakening if the nation returns to business as usual. There will be neither rest nor tranquility in America until the Negro is granted his citizenship rights. The whirlwinds of revolt will continue to shake the foundations of our nation until the bright day of justice emerges.

But there is something that I must say to my people who stand on the warm threshhold which leads into the palace of justice. In the process of gaining our rightful place, we must not be guilty of wrongful deeds. Let us not seek to satisfy our thirst for freedom by drinking from the cup of bitterness and hatred. We must forever conduct our struggle on the high plane of dignity and discipline. We must not allow our creative protest to degenerate into physical violence. Again and again we must rise to the majestic heights of meeting physical force with soul force. And the marvelous new militancy which has engulfed the Negro community must not lead us to a distrust of all white people; for many of our white brothers, as evidenced by their presence here today, have come to realize that their destiny is tied up with our destiny, and they have come to realize that their freedom is inextricably bound to our freedom.

We cannot walk alone. And as we walk we must make the pledge that we shall always march ahead. We cannot turn back. There are those who are asking the devotees of civil rights, "When will you be satisfied?" We can never be satisfied as long as the Negro is the victim of the unspeakable horrors of police brutality. We can never be satisfied as long as our bodies, heavy with the fatigue of travel, cannot gain lodging in the motels of the highways and the hotels of the cities. We cannot be satisfied as long as the Negro's basic mobility is from a smaller ghetto to a larger one. We can never be satisfied as long as our children are stripped of their selfhood and robbed of their dignity by signs stating "For Whites Only." We cannot be satisfied as long as the Negro in Mississippi cannot vote and a Negro in New York believes he has nothing for which to vote. No, no, we are not satisfied, and we will not be satisfied until justice rolls down like waters and righteousness like a mighty stream.

I am not unmindful that some of you have come here out of great trials and tribulations. Some of you have come fresh from narrow jail cells. Some of you have come from areas where your quest for freedom left you battered by the storms of persecution and staggered by the winds of police brutality. You have been the veterans of creative suffering. Continue to work with the faith that unearned suffering is redemptive.

Go back to Mississippi, and go back to Alabama. Go back to South Carolina. Go back to Georgia. Go back to Louisiana. Go back to the slums and ghettos of our Northern cities, knowing that somehow this situation can and will be changed. Let us not wallow in the valley of despair.

I say to you today, my friends, even though we face the difficulties of today and tomorrow, I still have a dream. It is a dream deeply rooted in the American dream. I have a dream that one day this nation will rise up and live out the true meaning of its creed: "We hold these truths to be self-evident, that all men are created equal." I have a dream that one day, on the red hills of Georgia, sons of former slaves and the sons of former slave owners will be able to sit down together at the table of brotherhood. I have a dream that one day even the state of Mississippi, a state sweltering with the heat of injustice, sweltering with the heat of oppression, will be transformed into an oasis of freedom and justice. I have a dream that my four little children will one day live in a nation where they will not be judged by the color of their skin, but by the content of their character.

I have a dream today. I have a dream that one day down in Alabama — with its vicious racists, with its governor's lips dripping with the words of interposition and nullification — one day right there in Alabama, little Black boys and Black girls will be able to join hands with little white boys and white girls as sisters and brothers.

I have a dream today. I have a dream that one day every valley shall be exalted and every hill and mountain shall be made low, the rough places will be made plain and the crooked places will be made straight, and the glory of the Lord shall be revealed, and all flesh shall see it together.

This is our hope. This is the faith that I go back to the South with. And with this faith we will be able to hew out of the mountain of despair a stone of hope. With this faith we will be able to transform the jangling discords of our nation into a beautiful symphony of brotherhood. With this faith we will be able to work together, to play together, to struggle together, to go to jail together, to stand up for freedom together, knowing that we will be free one day.

And this will be the day — this will be the day when all of God's children will be able to sing with new meaning:

> My country, 'tis of thee,
> Sweet land of liberty,
>   Of thee I sing;
> Land where my fathers died,
> Land of the Pilgrims' pride,
> From every mountainside
>   Let freedom ring.

And if America is to be a great nation, this must become true.

And so let freedom ring from the prodigious hilltops of New Hampshire. Let freedom ring from the mighty mountains of New York. Let freedom ring from the heightening Alleghenies of Pennsylvania. Let freedom ring from the snow-capped Rockies of Colorado. Let freedom ring from the curvaceous slopes of California.

But not only that. Let freedom ring from Stone Mountain of Georgia. Let freedom ring from Lookout Mountain of Tennessee. Let freedom ring from every hill and molehill of Mississippi. "From every mountainside let freedom ring."

And when this happens — when we allow freedom to ring, when we let it ring from every village and every hamlet, from every state and every city — we will be able to speed up that day when all of God's children, Black men and white men, Jews and Gentiles, Protestants and Catholics, will be able to join hands and sing in the words of the old Negro spiritual: "Free at last! Free at last! Thank God Almighty. We are free at last!"

Reading Response

Jot down how you feel after reading King's speech. Are you sympathetic? Angry? Saddened? What do you remember most after reading his work?

King's task was indeed difficult. Certainly he cared deeply about his ideas, but how could he make his audience believe that his dream, something very personal and intangible, could become a reality? His listeners were well aware of the injustices and social prejudices that existed, but could King convince them that change *was* possible or that there were reasons to hope for a better future? And as for the rest of the nation, how could he capture their attention long enough to persuade them to take some action that would make his dream a reality?

When King begins his speech, he says, "*I* am happy to join with you today" but quickly turns to "*we* have come to our nation's capital." By using personal address with his audience, King is including them in his dream, in his vision of justice and equality. In a similar manner, he draws in a larger, absent audience by saying, "We cannot walk alone." To the nation, King is saying that all men and women, black and white, Jew and Gentile, Protestant and Catholic, must struggle together in order to make the dream come true.

Furthermore, King involves his audience by showing them his dream. Powerful images and descriptions help his listeners see the kind of freedom he sees. King asks his audience to go back once more to Alabama, to Mississippi, to the ghettos in the northern cities, not in despair, but with the knowledge that someday "on the red hills of Georgia, sons of former slaves and the sons of former slave owners will be able to sit down together at the table of brotherhood." Someday freedom will "ring from the snow-capped Rockies of Colorado," and someday "all of God's children. . . . will be able to join hands and sing. . . . 'Free at last! Free at last! Thank God Almighty. We are free at last!' "

Like King, other authors rely on such images and descriptions to involve their readers. William Allen White begins his essay with a brief description of his daughter that reveals her spunk and healthy confidence. "She never fell from a horse in her life. Horses have fallen on her and with her—'I'm always trying to hold 'em in my lap,' she used to say. But she was proud of few things, and one was that she could ride anything that had four legs and hair." Before reading a half dozen sentences, the reader starts to know Mary White and is involved in what her father has to say about her. Gail Godwin is also careful to describe the subject of her essay, the "watcher," to her readers. "They are notorious pencil sharpeners, ribbon changers, plant waterers, home repairers, and abhorrers of messy rooms or messy pages." For a while, White, Godwin, and other authors try to put themselves in the reader's place in order to make him "see" what they are saying. Writers need to reproduce the pictures in their minds, the conversations they hear, or the feelings and moods they remember in order to involve their readers.

The writers of the essays in Chapter 9 had to find ways to capture your attention, too. Take some time to think about how they engaged you and made you feel part of their essays. What techniques did they use? Fill in the following box with your ideas.

Writers involve their readers in the subject by

- *using personal address*
- *describing common experiences*

Writing Response

Look at the topic you focused on in the first "Writing Response." Who would be a suitable audience for your ideas? What can you do to make your subject interesting and your audience responsive to your work? Jot down your ideas in your journal with the material from your first writing response.

WRITERS MUST USE SPECIFICS TO CONVEY THEIR IDEAS TO THE READER

After reading "Mary White" and "I Have a Dream," you can see how specifics are used to involve the reader. But writers also depend on specifics to convey their ideas clearly. Without them, William Allen White could not help readers understand *why* Mary White would "hoot" at the idea that she fell from a horse, nor could Martin Luther King, Jr. make readers understand the abstract concepts he discussed or picture the injustices he mentioned.

Looking at an essay by Ivan Turgenev, consider how he used details to help you understand what he wanted to say.

THE SPARROW

I returned home from the chase, and wandered through an alley in my garden. My dog bounded before me.

Suddenly he checked himself, and moved forward cautiously, as if he scented game.

I glanced down the alley, and perceived a young sparrow with a yellow beak, and down upon its head. He had fallen out of the nest (the wind was shaking the beeches in the alley violently), and lay motionless and helpless on the ground, with his little, unfledged wings extended.

The dog approached it softly, when suddenly an old sparrow, with a black breast, quitted a neighboring tree, dropped like a stone right before the dog's nose, and, with ruffled plumage, and chirping desperately and pitifully, sprang twice at the open, grinning mouth.

He had come to protect his little one at the cost of his own life. His little body trembled all over, his voice was hoarse, he was in an agony – he offered himself.

The dog must have seemed a gigantic monster to him. But, in spite of that, he had not remained safe on his lofty bough. A Power stronger than his own will had forced him down.

Treasure stood still and turned away....It seemed as if he also felt this Power.

I hastened to call the discomfited dog back, and went away with a feeling of respect.

Yes, smile not! I felt a respect for this heroic little bird, and for the depth of his paternal love.

Love, I reflected, is stronger than death and the fear of death; it is love alone that supports and animates all.

Reading Response

Write down what Turgenev told you. What do you think was the main idea he wanted to communicate? Consider how he showed you this idea. What details or images do you remember most vividly?

Turgenev was greatly impressed by this experience. It made him realize that "Love. . .is stronger than death and the fear of death; it is love alone that supports and animates all." This is a fine idea to write about, but alone, it is abstract and has little impact. Few readers would remember it or associate it with their own experiences. Turgenev knew that if he wanted his readers to understand and remember his idea, then he would have to *show* them what he meant. It is the picture of the helpless sparrow, with its "yellow beak. . .down upon its head" and "little, unfledged wings extended," and the dog poised for attack that first involves the reader. Turgenev goes on to to describe the older sparrow that "dropped like a stone right before the dog's nose, and, with ruffled plumage and chirping desperately and pitifully, sprang twice at the open, grinning mouth." These are the sentences readers are more likely to remember because they convey Turgenev's ideas clearly and powerfully.

Details, examples, images, statistics, illustrations, and facts are devices all writers rely on to *show* their ideas to their audience. For a novelist, details develop a character, enrich a dialogue, or create a mood. For scientists, illustrations and facts provide the proof and validation for their theories. For engineers, statistics and descriptions are vital in designing cars, writing environmental impact statements, or getting projects approved.

Thinking about the three essays you read in Chapter 9, which one do you remember most clearly? Why? What idea did the author want to communicate to you, and how did he or she do it? Once you have considered how the author used specifics to dramatize the idea, write down your conclusions in the following box.

Writers convey their ideas by

- *using figurative language*
- *creating pictures in the reader's mind*
- *incorporating facts*

Writing Response

> Reread the writing you have been doing in you journal. Think about the specifics you might use to *show* your reader this idea. Write nonstop for 10 minutes, trying to get down all the details, examples, memories, facts, or illustrations you can recall, sense, or envision. Where and how can these specifics be used to convey your ideas clearly to your reader? Jot down your ideas.

WRITERS MUST MAKE THEIR IDEAS EASY TO FOLLOW FOR THE READER

After finding a subject he can and wants to explore, the writer's next concern is how to make it interesting for the reader by using specifics. But even a fascinating topic, such as the great white shark, or a harrowing childhood experience, such as getting lost in New York City, will not hold the reader's attention for long if the ideas are difficult to follow. Readers expect writers to present their ideas in clear sentences, to organize these sentences in paragraphs, and to order the paragraphs in a pattern that is logical and easy to follow.

The last essay in this chapter was written by Benjamin Franklin and offers some of his observations about people. Notice how he has organized his ideas for his readers.

THE WHISTLE

When I was a child, at seven years old, my friends on a holiday filled my pockets with coppers. I went directly to a shop where they sold toys for children; and, being charmed with the sound of a whistle, that I met by the way in the hands of another boy, I voluntarily offered him all my money for one. I then came home, and went whistling all over the house, much pleased with my whistle, but disturbing all the family. My brothers and sisters and cousins, understanding the bargain I had made, told me I had given four times as much for it as it was worth. This put me in mind what good things I might have bought with the rest of the money; and they laughed at me so much for my folly that I cried with vexation; and the reflection gave me more chagrin than the whistle gave me pleasure.

This, however, was afterwards of use to me, the impression continuing on my mind, so that often, when I was tempted to buy some unnecessary thing, I said to myself, "Don't give too much for the whistle"; and so I saved my money.

As I grew up, came into the world, and observed the actions of men, I thought I met with many, very many, who gave too much for the whistle.

When I saw any one too ambitious of court favor, sacrificing his time in attendance on levees, his repose, his liberty, his virtue, and perhaps his friends, to attain it, I have said to myself, "This man gave too much for his whistle."

If I knew a miser, who gave up every kind of comfortable living, all the pleasure of doing good to others, all the esteem of his fellow-citizens, and the joys of benevolent friendship, for the sake of accumulating wealth; "Poor man," says I, "you do indeed pay too much for your whistle."

When I meet a man of pleasure, sacrificing every laudable improvement of the mind, or of his fortune, to mere corporeal sensations; "Mistaken man," says I, "you are providing pain for yourself instead of pleasure; you give too much for your whistle."

If I see one fond of fine clothes, fine furniture, fine equipages, all above his fortune, for which he contracts debts, and ends his career in prison; "Alas," says I, "he has paid, dear, very dear, for his whistle."

When I see a beautiful, sweet-tempered girl, married to an ill-natured brute of a husband; "What a pity it is," says I, "that she has paid so much for a whistle."

In short, I conceived that great part of the miseries of mankind were brought upon them by the false estimates they had made of the value of things, and by their giving too much for their whistles.

Reading Response

Write down what you think Franklin wanted to tell his readers. Then describe how he organized his ideas to help you follow his work.

One observation you may have made is that Franklin is careful to write about only one subject, making sure that all of his examples relate to it. Instead of trying to explain numerous lessons he learned while growing up, Franklin describes how people overestimate the value of temporary pleasures and, in doing so, create their own miseries. Keeping this idea firmly in mind, Franklin recalls his experiences and shows what happens when a budding politician, a miser, a well-to-do gentleman, and a young woman decide to "give too much for their whistles."

Another organizational aspect you might have described is the order in which Franklin presents his ideas. Because he wants to use the image of a whistle, Franklin must explain what it means to him. So, he begins with his own boyhood experience. Then, to show the readers that his experience is universal, he places specific examples of others who made similar mistakes in the middle of his essay. Finally, to make sure that the reader understands the point of his work, Franklin summarizes: "In short, I conceived that great part of the miseries of mankind were brought upon them by the false estimates they had made of the value of things, and by their giving too much for their whistles."

Still another aspect of the essay you might have described is how Franklin leads the reader from one idea to the next by using certain words and phrases. "When I grew up" helps the reader to understand the time sequence involved. "In short" signals that Franklin is coming to a conclusion. And by repeating certain words or phrases, such as "give too much for their whistle," Franklin reminds the reader of his purpose and shows how the examples support it.

Franklin's piece represents only one of many ways to organize ideas in writing. King decided that his ideas would unfold best if he started by describing past history and then moving on to the present and future. White felt that he could best write about his daughter by starting with the newspaper's perspective and then contrasting it to the real Mary White. Think about the three essays you read in Chapter 9. Can you see how the writers organized their ideas? What did they do to make it easy for you to follow their thoughts? Use the following box to record your conclusions.

Writers make their ideas easy to follow by

- *finding a pattern*
- *using repetition*
- *limiting their subjects*

Writing Response

Look once more at the writing you have been doing in your journal. This time, consider how you might organize your ideas and details. Would it be best to start with a specific experience? Or do you want to tell a story by starting at the end and then recounting what happened before? Would you prefer to describe something by comparing or contrasting it to something else?

Once you have discovered the pattern, use it to organize the material you have writen so far. Write a first draft of your ideas, applying to your writing what you have learned from your perspective as a reader.

Conclusion

As we stated at the beginning of this section, being a reader will not automatically make you a better writer. But now that you understand what you expect as a reader and what writers do to interest you in their ideas, you should have new insight into readers' expectations. Later on, when you work through your assignments or are asked to comment on other students' papers, use the information in this section and from the lists to evaluate you own writing from a reader's perspective and to give suggestions to others.

THE COMPOSING PROCESS

Although being a reader can teach you about the conventions of successful writing and make you aware of the needs of a reader, it cannot explain the process writers use to get from an idea in their heads to the work on the printed page. Because we never see the idea forming in the writer's mind, or the pages of notes he prepares before he tries a first draft, or the false starts crumpled into balls around the wastebasket, or the editor's marginal notes and suggestions, or the scratched-out words, arrows, and circles on the revision, we have no sense of what happens in the composing process that writers use. But by interviewing experienced writers, by observing them while they work, and even by having them talk aloud about the process while they write, researchers have given us a clearer understanding of what happens in those invisible stages.

To introduce you to the composing process, we have broken it into six stages. The following diagram will help you visualize them.

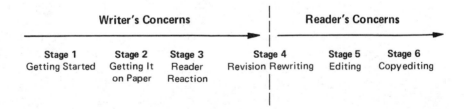

In the early stages of the process, stages 1, 2, and 3, the writer is primarily concerned with his own need to discover a subject, an audience, a purpose, a form for presenting the ideas, a way to express the ideas in a first draft, and a reader's reaction to his first draft. Chapter 3 "Getting Started," corresponds to stage 1, and it suggests several ways to find a subject that you want to and can discuss. Chapter 4, "Getting It on Paper for a Reader," deals with the concerns of stage 2 and includes methods you can use for discovering your audience, purpose, form for writing the first draft, and for getting unstuck if you stop writing. Chapter 5, "Reader Reaction: Discovering How Well You Have Communicated Your Ideas," corresponds to stage 3 and provides forms that can be used for getting a reader to tell you how well you have communicated in the first draft.

The fourth stage of the process is a transitional one in which the writer becomes involved with the reader's needs as well as his own. It is treated in Chapter 6, "Revising and Rewriting: Seeing Your Work Anew to Meet the Reader's Needs," and it focuses on methods for revising the work to make it fulfill the writer's concerns and on rewriting methods to make it meet the reader's expectations about written discourse.

Stages 5 and 6 consider the needs of the reader by focusing on how well the work meets the reader's expectations about focus and purpose, organization, development, spelling, usage, punctuation, and style. Chapter 7, "Editing: Having a Reader Evaluate Your Work," includes editing forms an editor can use to evaluate the writer's work. Chapter 8, "Copyediting: Completing the Writing Process," suggests how a writer can check his work for correctness.

Although this process sounds orderly, it is not. In practice, the process is seldom, if ever, used in this step-by-step fashion. Instead, it is recursive. Most writers move back and forth between the stages, repeating some, combining others, or passing through some quickly depending on what they are writing and how experienced they are. Each writer adapts and modifies the process to fit his needs, and with experience, you will learn to do this also.

To give you a chance to practice the process without using Chapters 3 through 8, we have provided you with a warm-up assignment. First, you will read two essays to stimulate your thinking about the subject; then you will record your reactions to them in your reading journal; and, finally, you will move through the composing process. Instead of asking you to use Chapters 3 through 8, for this assignment we have suggested approaches you can use to gather ideas, write, revise, edit, and prepare your final draft. Like the first three assignments in "The World Inside You" (an upcoming section), this assignment gives you the opportunity to find your own voice by writing about a familiar, autobiographical subject.

Warm-Up Essay

Right now, you may be sitting with some 20 or 30 classmates in your writing class, or perhaps you are in the dorm with a few hundred others. You have signed up for classes, bought your books, and have an ID card with your name and student number that gives you official status. And you may think that you are pretty much like everyone else, or that you see the world in much the same way.

However, such is not the case. Some of you may be the oldest or youngest child in the family, others have gone to parochial or private schools, and some have dedicated years to a particular sport or musical instrument. Many of you have grown up in cities, whereas fellow classmates come from farms or rural communities. All of these differences give you a particular perspective on the world, and if you want to communicate your ideas successfully to a reader, it is important to know that you do see things differently and to discover why.

In this assignment, you will consider what makes you unique. To begin thinking about the topic, read the next two essays by newspaper columnists. The first, by Nickie McWhirter, considers personal reasons for knowing who you are; the second, by Sylvia Porter, discusses how knowing who you are will affect your career choices. Then, complete the "Reading Response," read the assignment, and follow the steps of the composing process.

IT IS IMPORTANT TO FIND THE REALLY UNIQUE YOU

I know a man whose kids have grown up and gone off to live under their own roofs, leaving him with a male version of the empty nest disease.

He's nervous and edgy. He hates to go home from his office at night because he says he hasn't got anything to do at home. Besides, it's too quiet there. He dreads weekends because he can't always plan six projects to fill all the hours. He's talking about taking a course in something, anything, and planning a series of vacations. Maybe he'll remodel his garage or basement recreation room.

He won't do any of those things. He'll just twitch, and argue with his wife.

I don't understand this guy. When the kids were under foot, he never spent great gobs of time with them. He used to complain about their noise and the messes and confusion they caused. When circumstance demanded, he could put in an appearance at a church or school event, but this was hardly his idea of a gala evening. Now that he doesn't have to do any of these things, or make excuses for not doing them, he's convinced himself that he's suffering.

This must be drivel. His home, job, wife, friends, and personal interests are the same as they have been for decades. He's just aware that a significant change has taken place and that his status is affected. Maybe he's beginning to think of himself as "old." Maybe he always defined himself as "father," and now, with no kids around, he can't function as "father" on a daily basis and he is worried that he will disappear altogether. Zip! Gone.

DEAR DEPARTED MOSTLY MALES

Maybe we define ourselves too much according to human relationships, which fluctuate, and we fail to define ourselves in some personal, internal

Reprinted with the permission of the Detroit Free Press.

manner which is lasting. Human relationships are much easier. Obituaries prove that.

For most of my leafing-out years I suspected that women didn't die, except every once in a while, probably if they weren't careful on escalators. (I considered escalators death traps.) That's because I read everything in sight, including the obituary columns of newpapers. I noted that almost all the dear departed were males.

I read about people named Homer Q. Higgins and Percival Pennypacker. They were always retired founders or post chairmen of companies. Sometimes they were former police chiefs or politicians. They were always defined according to their business or work relationships, memberships in clubs and fraternal organizations, military service, philanthropy and above all, genealogy. "Dear husband of Mildred, revered father of Sarah (Mrs. Arthur M. Caldwell) Herkimer and Henry; beloved brother of John, Jacob and Henrietta (Mrs. Marcus P. Quigley) . . ." Stuff like that.

"Yeah," I said to me, "but did he like kids? Did he like Milky Way candy bars? Could he sing? What did he do for fun?" The obituary columns were always a big disappointment to me.

ENTER THE OTHER DEFINITIONS

Later I became aware of other definitions based on relationships. I became a wife and a mother. My mother became a mother-in-law and grandmother. Ed became an executive, whatever that is, and together we became a suburban couple until — whoops! — we became divorced persons.

I didn't mind any of the labels, but I was usually amused when other people accepted them as total definitions of human beings. I began to understand the obituary view of worth: A person who has not accumulated titles and labels is a non-person. That was why women never died. They never lived if all you could say about them was that they married and had kids and worked for their churches.

When I started working for a newspaper I secretly hoped to draw obituary-writing duty so that I could write about some woman and say she baked the best devils food cake anybody at the church supper ever tasted, raised beautiful roses and taught all the little kids how to play hopscotch because none of their mothers remembered. When I drew obituary-writing duty, my boss wouldn't let me write that stuff, so I became a columnist.

The danger of mindlessly accepting labels such as "father" or "mother" or even "columnist" is that you limit your own dimensions and squeeze yourself into a stereotype. One day, when you least expect it, the General Choas strips away the title and challenges you to look at yourself with the name tag. Who and what are you? Do you like Milky Ways? Can you sing? What do you do for fun? What is unique and essential about you that will go on and on even when or if all the human relationships change or vanish? There is something. There is much. It is important to find it before the nest is emptied. Never mind the obituary. You won't care.

JOB HUNTERS: KNOW RISKS by Sylvia Porter

You're a young man or woman, you've had your post-graduation fling and now you're entering the job market for the first time. Or you're more seasoned — your employer has gone on a head-cutting binge and among the heads severed from the payroll is yours. Both of you are facing a key decision which may vitally affect your entire working career and lifestyle.

Yet, it seems a secondary factor which you may not even consider seriously rather than a critical choice that demands in-depth examination. In brief: Should you go to work for a big or small company?

Don't shrug. This digs into the most subtle aspects of your self-identity. It can (and will) be vital in determining where and how you and your spouse live, the atmosphere in which you rear your children, your social and cultural activities — and much, much more. And it's all there in a few words most of you ignore: big or small company?

To help you reach a decision — and no one else should make it for you — here are important guidelines in the form of revealing questions you can answer for yourself when you're under no outside pressure.

1. How significant to you is risk vs. relative security? A large company with, say, annual sales of $20 million-plus that has been a stable force in its industry for 50 or more years obviously will offer you more security than an innovative newcomer. "You're putting your career at risk with the latter if things don't work out," say Dr. Barry Nathanson, president of Richards Consultants Ltd., an executive recruiting firm with offices in New York City, Boston and Westport, Conn. "But if they do, you'll probably move up faster and have a chance at obtaining equity in the company rather than getting just secure pension rights."

2. How deeply do you want to become involved in overall corporate goals and directions? In a smaller company, you'll get greater exposure to senior management and more opportunities to establish corporate goals. In a bigger company, you'll probably be responsible for one part of the business and you'll concentrate on division goals. (Or you might ask yourself: Does deep involvement scare or challenge you?)

3. How vital to you is the chance to express your creativity and reach for self-fulfillment? You'll find the opportunities inherent in this extremely personal (and revealing) question much greater in a small company than in a big company which will have a rigid structure of many layers of management. But you also will be under pressure to produce quickly in a small company and your failures will become more readily apparent. (Frightened or challenged?)

4. Would you prefer to work for a large company first and then find out if you're ready for the greater freedom and risk of the smaller, more innovative concern? This is a compromise decision, of course, but it well might be advisable

for you to go to work for a big company first. In this environment, you'll get better, more standardized training and be taught how to look at situations from many perspectives. You'll also get greater support than you will in a small company where you'll be expected to do more things for yourself. In a large company, too, says Nathanson, you'll have contact with leading experts in your field. Ask yourself honestly whether you should try the big firm for a period of two or three years before striking out for greater freedom.

5. To whom will you be reporting? In a big company, you'll be responsible to many supervisors, while in a small company, you might report directly to the top man or woman. But in each case, will your efforts be recognized and will you be groomed to move up based on those efforts? Or will you simply be an anonymous functionary?

6. How do you see yourself in terms of lifetime goals? Are you willing to pursue a steady upward course in a big company in search of the top? Or does your personality yearn for higher visibility at an earlier date? And are you willing to risk a more precarious life with possibly bigger (but unpredictable) rewards?

What I'm really asking you is: Who are you? Try to answer that and the right job in the right-size company will start to emerge.

Reading Response

In your reading journal, write down what you think McWhirter is saying about the importance of understanding your uniqueness. How did she make you react? Next look at Porter's article. Why does she say you should know yourself? How do you react to her ideas? Which of the two essays do you respond to more strongly? Why? Make a list of the qualities, characteristics, and experiences that make you unique.

Assignment

Write an essay in which you explore what makes you unique. You may write it as a personal essay for your classmates or as a formal essay that would accompany a resumé and serve to introduce you to an employer.

GETTING STARTED

Before starting to write, think about your high school yearbook, with the activities listed by your name or the comments your friends wrote on its pages.

Sailing Club
Debate Team
Senior class,
secretary

Kim Troy

Joel, Don't forget our good times in algebra. Hope to see you at State. Katie

Kim, Always keep your sweet smile. Dave

Wrestling
Photography Club
Student Council

Joel Casey

If classmates or an employer read only those remarks or the activities noted, would they know what you are really like? Or would they know only your "labels" and never realize that you grew orchids, did volunteer work in hospitals, or coached the Little League in the summer?

Referring to your reading responses for McWhirter's and Porter's essays, try either of the following getting-started techniques to find out what you would like to write about and why.

1. Choose one memory or experience that reveals your true character and that could be turned into a selection from your autobiography. Would you write about a terrifying experience? A romance? An adventure? A trip? Write for 10–15 minutes nonstop or until you feel that all of your ideas have been expressed.

2. If you were interviewed by Johnny Carson on his "Tonight" show, what special talents would you reveal? Write down everything that comes to mind as quickly as you can for 10–15 minutes. Or talk into a tape recorder about the things you would discuss on camera.

After you have stated all your ideas, take a few minutes to read what you have written or to listen to the tape. What ideas or words are repeated? Circle or list them. What do the characteristics, experiences, or examples you have included *show* about you? Try writing a sentence or two that sums up why or how you are unique. Why did you choose to focus on this subject? How will this subject reveal the "real" you to a reader?

GETTING IT ON PAPER

After considering your main idea, think about presenting it to readers. Who will the readers be? Do you want to entertain, inform, or persuade them? What parts of your getting-started work are most appropriate for your audience, purpose, and main idea?

Next, do a brief sketch of your ideas. Put your main idea at the top of a sheet of paper and below it list the supporting/developing details, examples, or characteristics. Double-check your list by considering how each item relates to the central idea. Feel free to rearrange your list to find a natural or logical order.

You are now ready to write the first draft. Use your sketch as a reference and start developing a picture of yourself or your talents.

READER RESPONSE

Now that you have a first draft, you can share your ideas with a reader. Find a classmate or roommate who can answer the following questions:

Reader:
1. After reading this essay, what do you know about the writer?
2. What parts of the essay give you the strongest impressions of this person or his or her talents? Underline the sections that support or develop your impressions.
3. Do all the parts of this essay support or develop your impressions? Put brackets around any section that does not.
4. Finally, is there anything you would like to know more about? Put asterisks where you think the writer might develop the ideas more fully.

REVISION

Writer:
Having tried out your ideas on a reader, compare the reader's concept of you or your talents with the impressions you wanted to make. If your ideas do not match, or if the reader did not find the unique you, what parts of the essay could be changed? What could be added? Look at the following revision guide for suggestions.

The beginning—Is your opening interesting, or could you use another method to engage the reader? A quotation? An anecdote? A question? A list of characteristics? A work experience? Are your main idea and purpose clear? Should the main idea be presented more specifically in your introduction? Or should you show the reader why you want to write this piece by developing a scene, an experience, or a mood.

The middle—Does the middle section of the paper fit your main idea? Or should the main idea stated at the beginning be changed to better match what you have written? Should your ideas be rearranged? Should details or experiences be added? Do you need to take out anything that does not fit your main idea?

The ending—Do you tie the ideas together at the end? Does the paper come to a logical conclusion?

Revise the first draft, taking into consideration your reader's comments and the previous questions. Also, use the lists from the first part of this chapter to review what other writers do to meet reader's expectations.

EDITING

Now find a reader who can tell you how well the revisions work by answering the following questions:

Editor:
1. Are you interested in what the writer has to say?
2. Do you have a clear sense of what makes the writer unique?
3. Are there enough specifics to *show* you the writer or his or her talents?
4. Are the ideas easy to follow throughout the essay?

Writer:
Keeping in mind the reader's comments, make any final revisions you think are necessary. Consider titling your work, emphasizing the main idea and purpose with specific words, details, or examples, and making sure that the ideas fall into paragraphs that are easy to follow and are presented in a logical order.

COPYEDITING

Although you may want to do further revision, you have reached the deadline and must hand in the paper. In this last stage, you must concentrate on the more technical needs and expectations of your reader. There are a number of areas you could consider, but for now, focus on spelling, punctuation, and usage.

> *Spelling*—Double-check any word you are unsure of; use a dictionary or ask a friend, roommate, or classmate. Try going through your paper backward to spot any misspellings. (Start from the last word on the last line and continue on to the first word on the first line.)
>
> *Punctuation*—Have someone read your paper aloud. Does the reader pause and stop in the right places? If not, what punctuation is needed? If the reader pauses or stops too often, you may be overusing commas or periods.
>
> *Usage*—Again, have someone read your paper aloud. Does the reader stumble over any sentences or become confused by certain passages? If so, this material should probably be rewritten more simply or clearly. Try explaining aloud what you want to say to help you rewrite.

After revising and polishing your writing, recopy or type it neatly. And if your teacher has special instructions for preparing the manuscript, make sure to follow them.

ASSIGNMENTS

The following assignments are grouped under three headings and move you from expressive to informational to persuasive writing. In the first group, "The World Inside You," you will write about personal experiences. In the second, "The World Around You," you will use your personal experiences to arrive at generalizations about your world and write about these generalizations. In "Expanding Your World," you will use research to arrive at and support generalizations about the world.

Each time you do an assignment, use Chapter 3 through 8 to guide you through the composing process. At the end of each chapter, answer the questions before moving to the next stage.

Remember that you will use the stages recursively. Do not be surprised to discover more about your subject while thinking about audience or form.

The World Inside You—Using Personal Experiences for Writing Topics

This group of assignments focuses on personal experiences and gives you an opportunity to express yourself on familiar subjects. For that reason, you may feel more comfortable directing your work to an audience you know, such as a relative, people in your community, or a friend or classmate. Possibilities for these assignments include personal essays, narratives, or letters to parents, friends, teachers, classmates, or local officials.

Each assignment has an introduction, readings from Chapter 9, and suggested getting-started techniques. After reviewing the assignment and readings, you will turn to a getting-started method in Chapter 3 in order to find ideas for your paper.

ASSIGNMENT 1

To begin this assignment, read these works by authors who express their feelings about places that are important to them. Robert Frost in "Birches" describes a place he visited as a child and, as an adult, wanted to return to when the world got to be too much for him. In an excerpt from *Walden*, Henry David Thoreau recounts his experience at Walden Pond and what it taught him. And Alfred Kazin describes the block he grew up on and how returning to it made him relive his childhood in the essay "The Block and Beyond."

Turn to the following selections and jot down any ideas, reactions, or memories that come to mind as you read.

"Birches," Robert Frost, p. 246
"The Ponds," Henry David Thoreau, p. 248
"The Block and Beyond," Alfred Kazin, p. 253

Describe a place that is special to you.

For this paper, write about a place that is important to you and choose an audience with whom you can share your ideas. You might describe a place from your childhood that you still think about or would like to revisit. Or a place where you go when things become difficult. Or a place that helps you see the world differently or that has had a great impact on you.

To gather ideas, turn to Chapter 3 and read the introduction on page 76. Then use one of the following getting-started methods to discover a topic you can and want to write about.

Survey B, p. 82
Journal Writing, p. 77
The Movie in Your Mind, p. 87
Letters, p. 85

ASSIGNMENT 2

To start this assignment, read these works by authors who discuss influences that have shaped their lives or affected their thinking. Marilyn Krysl in "Genie Women" recalls the Sunday rituals she experienced as a young girl. Louise Bernikow illustrates how peer pressure affected her thinking and actions in the essay "Confessions of an Ex-Cheerleader." John Holt records in his journal school experiences that made him think differently about education. And in "Mending Wall," Robert Frost explores the power of an idea.

While reading the following selections, jot down any ideas, reactions, or memories that occur to you.

"Genie Women," Marilyn Krysl, p. 255
"Confessions of an Ex-Cheerleader," Louise Bernikow, p. 258
Diary entries from *How Children Fail*, John Holt, p. 263
"Mending Wall," Robert Frost, p. 302

> Discuss a person, experience or idea that has been a major influence in your life.

For this paper, write about a person, an experience, or an idea that has played an important role in your life and choose an audience who will be interested in your ideas. You could re-create a vivid childhood memory that has affected your life. Or describe a person whose advice or actions have influenced you. Or show how a certain place has helped you grow or learn something new about the world.

To find a topic you can and want to write about, turn to Chapter 3 and select one of the following getting-started methods. Read the introduction to the chapter if you have not done so before.

Surveys A or C, p. 81 or p. 83
Timed Writing, p. 79
Journal Writing, p. 77
Letter, p. 85

ASSIGNMENT 3

For this assignment, read these works by three authors who describe difficult decisions that confronted them. Liv Ullmann, in her journal, wrestles with the issue of whether to accept the ways of Hollywood or to be herself. Heather Lamb tells Studs Terkel how she has to be impersonal to keep her job and how she feels about this decision. Joan Didion explains what decisions she had to make in order to survive in New York.

Jot down your own ideas and insights while reading the following pieces.

"When Your Profession Takes You to Hollywood," Liv Ullmann, p. 264

"Heather Lamb," Studs Terkel, p. 266
"Goodbye to All That," "Joan Didion, p. 267

> **Discuss a decision you have had to make and its consequences.**

For this paper, focus on a decision you had to make and its effects. Also, consider whom you would like to read your work. You could describe job conflicts or decisions. Or explore tensions in school, or with family or friends, and how you resolved them. Or explain decisions concerning the direction of your life.

Turn to Chapter 3 and select one of the following getting-started techniques to help you discover a topic. If you have not read the introduction to the chapter before, do so now.

The Movie in Your Mind, p. 87
Analysis/Classification, p. 97
Listening/Talking, p. 89
Journal Writing, p. 77

The World Around You—Using the World Around You for Writing Topics

The first assignments gave you a chance to tell the reader who you are and what has affected you. With the following assignments, you will also start with your personal experiences. However, this time you will use these experiences to make generalizations about the world in which you live.

As you do the assigned reading, use your reading journal to record the conclusions these writers draw about their experiences with life, society, or people; how these ideas help them understand something about the world; and memories of your experiences that the readings evoke. This time, your audience can be more formal— employers, government officials, the student body, or the general reading public—and possibilities for the assignments include formal essays, editorials or newspaper articles, persuasive documents, or an excerpt from a history or social science text you would like to write.

Start each assignment by reading the introduction and the selections from Chapter 9. Then choose one of the getting-started methods suggested to discover a topic you can and want to discuss.

ASSIGNMENT 4

The writers of these selections talk about the pressures put on people by their families, friends, or society. Ralph Ellison shows his readers the roles blacks must play because of social and even family pressures. Columnist Sydney Harris and writer Louise Bernikow ask their audiences to consider the roles young people are forced to play because of parental and peer expectations.

"Battle Royal," Ralph Ellison, p. 274
"Burden of Parental Love," Sydney Harris, p. 284
"Confessions of an Ex-Cheerleader," Louise Bernikow, p. 258

> **Consider a role you must play and discuss how that role affects you and the others who have to play it.**

For this paper, describe a role you play and explain to your reader what consequences it has for you and others. You might illustrate how people are invisible because they belong to a certain group, depending on their occupation or background—such as students, Chicanos, athletes, or the handicapped. Or you might describe how pressures from jobs, schools, religious institutions, or communities keep people from being individuals.

To discover what you have to say about the topic, turn to one of the following getting-started techniques.

Timed Writing, p. 79
Reading, p. 94
Listening/Talking, p. 89
Analysis/Classification, p. 97

ASSIGNMENT 5

The readings for this assignment are by three authors who were awakened to the world around them by a specific object or place. Anne Morrow Lindbergh tells how the shape of a certain shell helped her make generalizations about her own world. William O. Douglas recounts his long walks in the mountains and how the mountains not only restored his strength but made him aware of the great physical beauty of nature. John G. Neihardt realized what the American Indian experienced when he compared the shape of their teepees to that of the reservation homes they had to live in.

"Channelled Whelk," Anne Morrow Lindbergh, p. 285
"Polio," William O. Douglas, p. 290
"Circles and Squares," John G. Neihardt, p. 293

> **Discuss an object or a place that has awakened you to the world you live in and helped you to understand it better.**

For this paper, tell a reader how an object or place has helped you understand more about the world. You could focus on a personal object, such as an old photograph, a gift from a relative, or a childhood toy, or a place, such as your grandmother's attic, the neighborhood hangout, or your own spot in the woods or on the block. Or you might choose a more universal object, such as a national monument, a particular car, or the American flag, or a universal place, such as a city, a national park, or a foreign country.

Use one of the following getting-started techniques to gather ideas for this assignment.

Reading, p. 94
Free Association, p. 92
Thinking, p. 93
Questions, p. 96

ASSIGNMENT 6

Start this assignment by reading the works of these authors, who show how events, language, and ideas can influence people. Joyce Maynard discusses the major events of her generation and their effects. Nickie McWhirter, Robert Frost, and James Thurber show how language and ideas can limit people's thinking. Chief Seathl writes to President Franklin Pierce, explaining how the land has shaped the Indians' thinking.

"An 18-Year-Old Looks Back on Life," Joyce Maynard, p. 294
"After All, Moss Is Kind of Nice Stuff," Nickie McWhirter, p. 300
"Mending Wall," Robert Frost, p. 302
"The Rabbits Who Caused All the Trouble," James Thurber, p. 304
Letter from Chief Seathl to Franklin Pierce, p. 304

> **Discuss the major influences, such as events, language, or ideas that have shaped you and your generation.**

For this assignment, explain to your readers how certain events have given you and your generation a particular outlook, or discuss how certain forms of language or ideas affect people's attitudes. You might discuss what values you and your generation hold because of national or political events, economic climates, or technological advances. You might consider how Newspeak, propaganda, jargon, and clichés affect our communication. Or you might show how nationalism, capitalism, idealism, or socialism affects people's attitudes toward the environment, the country, neighbors, schools, or education.

To discover what you have to say about the topic, try one of the following getting-started methods.

Survey, C, p. 84
Reading, p. 95
Analysis/Classification, p. 97
The Movie in Your Mind, p. 87

ASSIGNMENT 7

The writers of the following selections were faced with decisions that affected not only them but their contemporaries and later generations as well. Jefferson and the drafters of the Declaration of Independence outlined their political beliefs and told how they had been violated. Thoreau wrote to his contemporaries, explaining his stand against the government. Ellison's conflict was between his own individuality and society's stereotyped image of him. And Didion told her readers that, like other people her age, she had to make difficult decisions about her life.

"Declaration of Independence," Thomas Jefferson and Others, p. 306
"Civil Disobedience," Henry David Thoreau, p. 308
"Battle Royal," Ralph Ellison, p. 274
"Goodbye to All That," John Didion, p. 267

> Write about a major decision that your peer group, ethnic group, or generation is faced with.

For this paper, explain to your readers what issues confront your generation or ethnic group and what decisions need to be made. You might present your stand or opinions on political issues in your city, state, or country. Or you might describe the kinds of social conflicts you see around you—on campus or in your hometown, state, or country.

Use one of the following getting-started methods to help you gather ideas for this topic.

Letters, p. 85
Analysis/Classification, p. 97
Listening/Talking, p. 89
Interviews, p. 100

Expanding Your World—Using Research in Your Writing

Now that you have begun to make some generalizations about your own experiences, the following writing assignments suggest ways you can gather and analyze new information about the world. Although you will continue to address the audience of the last assignments and may use similar forms for your papers, you will now use research to lead to and support your generalizations.

Again, start by reading the assignments and the selections from Chapter 9. Develop a method for recording information and discussing your own ideas. While you read, use a reading journal, notecards, or a notebook. Then use one of the suggested getting-started techniques or one that you prefer to find out what you have to say about the topics.

ASSIGNMENT 8

These authors write about the conflicts between personal needs and the demands of a career. Gaylord Freeman and Heather Lamb tell Studs Turkel about the personal compromises they had to make in order to keep and progress in their jobs. Columnist Sylvia Porter explains how important it is to know oneself in order to make decisions concerning a career.

"Gaylord Freeman," Studs Terkel, p. 315
"Heather Lamb," Studs Terkel, p. 266
"Job Hunters: Know Risks," Sylvia Porter, p. 57

> **Discuss the conflicts between personal beliefs and career demands faced by working people.**

For this paper, show your readers what you think is essential when considering a job or while working. You could explore the conflicts between a person and his or her job that grow out of ethical, political, social, or economic considerations. To collect information, you might interview someone working in a field that interests you. Or you could research a particular company or survey people in a variety of jobs to find out how they strike a balance between their personal lives and their careers.

To find a subject you want to and can discuss, choose one of the following getting-started techniques.

Interviews, p. 100
Survey, D. p. 85
Questions, p. 96
Researched Topics, p. 101

ASSIGNMENT 9

In the following selections, the writers are concerned about the physical environment. E. B. White and Dennis Farney tell their readers how ideas can bring about changes in the environment. In contrast, Malvina Reynolds shows in her song how people can be shaped by their surroundings.

"Walden," E. B. White, p. 318
"Trying to Restore a Sea of Grass," Dennis Farney, p. 322
"Little Boxes," Malvina Reynolds, p. 325

> **Discuss the relationships between society and the environment.**

For this paper, explain how society's perceptions of the environment affect the world, or how a specific environment shapes the people who live in it. You might consider society's economic and political attitudes and what effect they have on the environment. Or you might look at an environmental issue from several perspectives, such as that of the Department of the Interior, the Sierra Club, or a specific corporation or community. Or you might examine how living in the city, in rural communities, or in different parts of the country affects people. To gather information, you could interview a number of people living in the same area to see how that environment has shaped their lives and attitudes. Or you could survey a group of people who live in contact with common objects in the environment—such as televisions, radios, or automobiles—to evaluate the effect of these objects. Or you could conduct your own demographic survey to see where people on your campus or in your community, state, or country are moving and discuss the reasons for their move.

To get started on this topic, choose any one of the following methods.

Interviews, p. 100
Timed Writing, p. 79
Letters, p. 85
Researched Topics, p. 101

ASSIGNMENT 10

To begin this assignment, read the work of these authors, who show how certain ideas shape attitudes and ultimately affect people's lives. Bill Veeck talks to Studs Terkel about Americans' obsession with winning and its consequences. Germaine Greer and H. L. Mencken write to their contemporaries about women, but at different times and from different perspectives.

"Bill Veeck," Studs Terkel, p. 326

"The Stereotype," Germaine Greer, p. 327
"The Incomparable Buzz-Saw," H. L. Mencken, p. 332

> **Discuss an idea that has influenced our society and the history of that idea.**

For this paper, discuss an idea, its history, and its impact. You could analyze how that idea has become accepted or been turned into a rigid rule or stereotype, and then look at the consequences. Or you might examine a current issue or idea from a variety of perspectives, and then choose a position and support it. To gather information, you can consult back issues of magazines and newspapers to trace the evolution of an idea. Or you can interview older people about their perceptions on a particular idea or philosophy.

Choose one of the following getting-started techniques to find a topic you are interested in exploring.

Analysis/Classification, p. 97
Interviews, p. 100
Researched Topics, p. 101
Questions, p. 96

ASSIGNMENT 11

By now, you have written on a variety of subjects for different readers. Taking into consideration the issues you have raised in previous papers, discuss a specific decision our society will have to make for the future in order to survive. This time, you will be writing a formal college research paper.

Some of the questions you might consider are: Will we need to preserve nature? Plan better cities? Give up individuality? Use different management techniques in business? Change the family structure? Reevaluate our beliefs and attitudes about success?

To get started on this project, reread any of the selections in Chapter 9, review current magazines and newspapers, or watch news programs and specials on television to identify current concerns. Make sure to use the "Researched Topics" getting-started method in Chapter 3 and combine it with any other technique that has helped you gather ideas.

CHAPTER 3
Getting Started

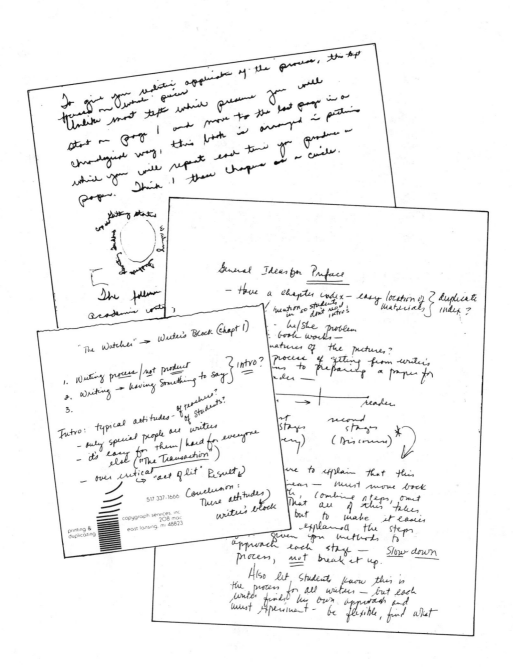

Even for many successful writers, getting started can be the most intimidating part of the writing process. Questions they ask themselves, such as "How can I write 1,000 words on this by Friday?" or "What can I possibly say that will be interesting to all those people?" reflect the real desperation writers feel at times. Naturally, they want to be profound, to be applauded, and to write flawless prose. And these are legitimate concerns that must be considered, but not before writers discover what they want to say. As Kurt Vonnegut says, "your own winning style must begin with the ideas in your head."

To help you get started, we will begin with your need to discover a subject you can and want to write about and your reasons for writing about it. To help you answer these questions, we have compiled a list of getting-started techniques; some come from our students, others from professional writers. When given a writing assignment, look through the suggested techniques that accompany it and find one that suits you best. Feel free to modify any of the methods or to combine them. Remember, there are as many ways to get started writing as there are writers. You will need to find out what works best for you.

Most important for now, write freely and quickly. The object is to get down as many ideas as you can once you start writing. Try not to cross out words or sentences that do not sound right, or to worry about misspellings or what someone will think. Be as open to ideas as you can. You might find yourself wandering from one idea to the next or rambling on about something that seems unimportant. But that meandering is one way you might come upon some interesting ideas or unusual insights you had not considered before. And that discovery is the purpose of this step.

Once you have finished gathering ideas and have written about your subject, make sure to answer the questions included with each getting-started technique. In answering them, you will focus on your main ideas and why you want to express them. This process will prepare you for Chapter 4, where you will define your reader and purpose and discover the form to use in organizing your ideas. However, if you find that the topic you have chosen is not too interesting to you or that your reason for writing about it is unclear, the experience may be too distant or too unfamiliar to explore. If so, try another getting-started method, or see if there is another subject from your writing that is easier for you to approach.

If you are uncomfortable in writing about the topic, it may be too painful or emotional for you to handle right now. If this is true, write more about this topic in your journal and only for yourself. Later, you may be able to share it with a reader. Try another getting-started method, or see if there is something else in your material that you can write about more easily.

JOURNAL WRITING

If you have been using a journal for either personal writing or for recording your ideas about what you read, you have an excellent resource for topics. The first method described for using the journal is aimed at personal writing. The second method will help you use the writing that has come from your reading experiences.

Personal Journal

First, think about your assignment and then read through what you have written, putting a star by any experiences or ideas that might be appropriate. For example, one of our students, whose assignment was to discuss a role she had to play, found the following unedited passage in her journal, written shortly after coming to school.

Journal Entry October 20, 1980

It is a little early in the day to be writing in the journal but I just feel all congested inside. Although, there are some 40,000 students here on campus, 1300 of which live in my dorm, 50 of which I know personally, and 15 of which I consider intimate friends, for some reason I feel alone. I feel very isolated; I am not "one of the gang."

Ever since I was a very little child I have always wanted to be "one of the gang." I felt as if I were an outsider; I needed a place to belong.

When she found this passage, Kim wrote again in her journal, this time pouring out the experiences that made her feel congested.

When I came to Michigan State University, I thought everything would be different. There are very few people here, if any, who know my reputations. My reputation of being a hard-working, friendly individual by teachers; of being friendly and always smiling by my white colleagues; of being nice and a "nectar" by my fellow black colleagues.

The first two reputations are very nice ideas of what a person should be. I like these character descriptions because they transmit a picture of what I consider to be characteristic of me.

The last characteristic of me is not a very good reputation for a black person to have.

This material led her to the idea of writing about the pressures she felt from both white and black society because of the need to act out certain roles in order to be accepted by both groups.

After reading through your journal and finding experiences or ideas that work for your assignment, continue to write in your journal for 2-3 pages, as Kim did. Try to relive the experiences; explore what made you happy, angry, or sad. Then try to explain why you feel or think as you do.

Reread your writing and underline the central ideas or circle the best parts. Then, in a few sentences, describe the subject you want to discuss and how it relates to the assignment. If you have trouble finding a subject, write again in your journal, focusing on the most interesting or important ideas. Once you have identified your subject, answer the following questions:

1. Why is this subject important and interesting to me?
2. Do I feel comfortable writing about this subject?

Answering these questions will prepare you for Chapter 4. Read the introduction to that chapter, page 108, before selecting a method to help you define your reader and purpose and discover the form of your ideas.

Reading Journal

If you have been keeping a reading journal, look through it to find the entries showing that you were excited about or genuinely involved in the reading. Look for passages you may have quoted from the essay, poem, or text or for characters you discussed, letters to authors, ideas you questioned or agreed with, or thoughts that occurred to you while reading.

Rick found the following unedited writing in his journal while looking for ideas for a book review he wanted to write.

Ah, I just got a brainstorm. You know when we talk of a gate watcher, we say he is keeping us from telling or rewriting what we really feel, well I am almost sure that Bilbo and the story of the hobbit is a play on the gate watch. let me explain.

At the very beginning Tolkien brings out that a hobbit is a very conservative person. Except he had this hidden ambition for an adventure. To go against the orthodox — To ask questions and to answer. Oh, he always hid his feelings before but as soon as he is given the chance, as soon as he is pushed to go against his watch, a whole new world opens up. Oh of coarse his watch would stick with him for a while but he (it) doesn't control him for he has beat his watcher!

And what about Tolkien, The first copyright was in 1939, back then do you think that book was orthodox. Hell no. I think the manner in which Bilbo was pushed into a going on adventure was much like the way tolkiens watcher was pushed by his imagination...

When Rick found this insight, he decided to write a rough draft of his ideas in his journal because he felt most comfortable writing there. The final draft appears in Chapter 9 and is an interesting review of J. R. R. Tolkien's *The Hobbit* in which Rick discusses the importance of knowing oneself—despite the interference of watchers.

After finding ideas that work for your assignment, brainstorm in your journal, as Rick did, for a page or so. Once you finish, reread what you have written and underline the main ideas or best passages. At the top of another page in your journal, describe in a few sentences what you want to write about and how it relates to the assignment. Then try writing a rough draft of your ideas for 2-3 pages. If you have trouble with this process, you may have to brainstorm further in order to find what you want to discuss. Make sure that you have a specific subject in mind before answering the following questions:

1. Why is this topic important to me?
2. Can I write about this topic comfortably?

Answering these questions will prepare you for Chapter 4. Read the introduction to that chapter on page 108 before selecting a method that will help you define your reader and purpose and discover the form to use in presenting your ideas.

TIMED WRITING

One way to start getting words on paper is to set a deadline of 10-15 minutes. Make yourself write every second, no matter what you put down. One student thought that the timed writing could not possibly help him, but it eventually led to an idea that he later developed into an excellent essay. His following unedited timed writing illustrates how this approach worked for him.

> Oh ~~jees~~, I've never written for 15 minutes straight. This is dumb – dumb, dumb! What can I say? What can I say? Who cares? Who knows whats important? The sky's blue, the falls finally come. I thought I'd never get to college – but here I am! It was a long summer. So now what do I say? It was a long summer, and hot. We went to Boston. We saw the Red Sox with Uncle Bert and Aunt Gert made loads of great brownies. Had a great time with Bert – what a super guy. I remember once he squirted me with a garden hose. ~~Was I pissed~~ – I wouldn't even talk to him for a day or two – but I sure miss him now. He bought me a new pair of tennis shoes for school when I was eight. Doesn't sound like much, but my dad was out of work – and Bert, he had four kids of his own. It was hot that day, too. But we all piled into his car – an old Chevy station wagon. I had a quarter from mom for some ice cream and we headed down the highway . . .

When Don finished his first timed writing, he had four pages about his trip to Boston, including his impression of the city and how his uncle bought him tennis shoes. The last part described Uncle Bert's taking him to a park to run around and get his shoes dirty and scuffed so that they did not look brand new. Bert did not want his gift to look like charity to our student's parents, so he told them that he found them at a garage sale—for 25 cents! When Don wrote his first draft of this experience, he decided that the main idea was Bert's generosity and kindness, so he developed the last part of his timed writing. Eventually, his idea turned into a fine character sketch of his uncle, who was like a second father to him and who made growing up in difficult times much easier.

To use this method for gathering ideas, simply get out your pen or pencil and the kind of paper you like to use. Go to a comfortable place and think about your assignment for a few minutes. Then start writing *nonstop* for 10-15 minutes. Remember not to censor your ideas or to stop at any point. Timed writing may be difficult to do at first, but if you force yourself to keep the words spilling out and the pen moving across the paper, you will eventually find ideas to write about.

After you finish, read through your writing. Look for any recurring ideas, sentiments, images, or moods, or for the most interesting part of your writing. Try to summarize your central or most important thoughts in a sentence or two and then write once more for another 10–15 minutes. Do not worry if you stray from your original idea; it may lead you to an even clearer understanding of what you want to say.

Finish this getting-started method by looking through your last writing for a central thought, image, or feeling. Underline the sections that reinforce it, and put brackets around anything that does not fit. Then write down in a few sentences what you think is the main idea and answer the following questions:

1. Why is this subject interesting and important to me?
2. Can I write about this subject comfortably?

Once you can answer these questions, turn to Chapter 4 and read the introduction on page 108 if you have not done so. Then use one of the methods that will help you define your reader and purpose and discover the form to use in presenting your ideas.

PERSONAL SURVEYS

Writers' lives provide a reservoir of experiences and events that make fine material for their writing. But less experienced writers often consider their own lives too ordinary—they have no eccentric or wicked aunt, exciting travels in the Brazilian jungles, or double-agent spy stories to tell. And, quite truthfully, most writers do not have those kinds of experiences to write about, either.

To help you discover the kinds of events and experiences in your life that make interesting material for writing, we have included four surveys. Survey A concentrates on the people you know; Survey B looks at the places that are special to you; Survey C considers your experiences; and Survey D treats your interests. If you would like to see how two students used these surveys and turned their experiences into interesting papers, turn to Chapter 9 and read "Joe (Another Love Story)" or "The Last Puff."

To begin, turn to the survey suggested in your writing assignment and focus on the parts or questions that are most interesting to you or that deal most directly with your assignment. Answer the questions briefly and then concentrate on those that trigger the greatest number of memories, ideas, or feelings. After going through this process, turn to the "Conclusion" on page 85 to complete this getting-started technique.

SURVEY A—PEOPLE

After answering the questions you have chosen, go to page 85 to finish this getting-started technique.

Friends: Who was your first friend? Why? Are you still friends? What memories or stories of that friendship do you like to recall or tell? What did that friendship mean to you?

Who is your best friend? Why? How did you meet? What were your first impressions of that person? What story or memory do you recall most vividly about that friendship? How has that friendship affected you?

Do you have different sets of friends? Why? Who are they? How are they alike or how do they differ? What does friendship mean to you?

Relatives: What are some of your first memories of your parents, grandparents, brothers, or sisters? What stories do you like to tell about any of your relatives? What relative has influenced you most? How so?

Who are some of your most memorable relatives? Why? What do you know about your family's history? Have you seen family albums or family trees? Do you recall any stories that your parents, grandparents, aunts, or uncles used to tell about their lives or the lives of other relatives?

People You Work With: What memories do you have of your first teachers? Your best or worst teachers? What teacher has influenced you most? How?

What memories do you have of your first employer? Your best or worst employer? What do you remember about the people on the job with you? Were you influenced by any of them? How?

Do you have any favorite or vivid memories of sports? Marching band? Orchestra? Dance classes? Homecoming? Did you ever hang around in any special gangs or groups? What were the people like in your gang or group, on your team, in the band or chorus? Who were some of the most memorable people you worked or played with? Why?

Real or Fictional People: Who or what is your favorite movie/music/television/cartoon/art/literary figure? Why? How did you become interested in that figure? What do you remember most about him/her/it? What does that character represent to you?

Who or what was the first character to really frighten you? Where? What happened? What did you think? Feel? See? Hear? How did that experience affect you?

Who are the five people you admire most? Why? What are your strongest memories or impressions of them? What do those people represent to you? How did you decide to rank them? Who is number one and why?

Who are the five people you despise most? Why? What are your strongest memories or impressions of them? What do those people represent to you? How did you decide to rank them? Who is number one and why?

SURVEY B-PLACES

After you have found questions to answer, turn to page 85 to finish this getting-started technique.

1. What are your favorite places now? What do you do there? What do they look like? How do they affect you?

2. What were your favorite childhood haunts? What did you do there? What were they like? Why did you go there? What effect did they have on you?

3. Is there a place you consider your own? Why? Is there a place you can go to be alone? What does this place mean to you? How does it affect you? How does it look? Feel? Smell?

4. What place do you spend the most time in? Why? What is it like? How does it affect you?

5. Have you ever visited a favorite childhood spot, an old neighborhood, or a vacation site and seen it change in some way? What do you think has happened – to you and to that place? How do you remember that place? What is it like now?

6. Have you ever hated a place but had to be there? Why? Have you ever left a place you disliked, only to find that you missed it later in life? What do you think happened? What did that place mean to you later on?

7. What traveling have you done? What places have impressed you most? Are there any favorite or vivid travel stories you like to tell? Is there any place you would like to return to? Why? What does it mean to you? What is it like?

8. Do you have a favorite imaginary place? Where is it? What is it like? How did you discover it? Why is it special to you? What has happened there?

SURVEY C–EXPERIENCES

After finding a topic you want to write about, turn to page 85 to finish this getting-started method.

turn to page 85

1. Think about some of the historical events in your lifetime, or in the twentieth century, that you consider most significant. What events would you list as being most important to you? To your generation? Why? Think about how you ranked the events. Which do you consider the most significant? Why? Do the events listed have anything in common?

2. Think about some *firsts* in your life and jot down any memories that occur to you: Your first

date	boss	time in trouble
job	day at work	reward
accomplishment	friend	home
enemy	camping trip	secret
birthday memory	childhood memory	New Year's or other holiday
book	movie	painting or other art form
vacation	day at school	

3. Think about some favorites in your life: Your favorite

food	place	holiday
person	animal	movie/book/poem/play/music
historical period	part of the day	artwork
part of the year	hiding place	experience
entertainer	story	character
job	pastime	home
childhood memory	school memory	vacation
dream	number	color

4. Think about some least favorites: Your least favorite

movie/book/play/music	day in school	day on the job
childhood memory	birthday or holiday	experience
part of the day	part of the year	sport
home	place	dream
color	number	friend/enemy
food/drink	historical period	fear
character	trip	

SURVEY D – INTERESTS

Look at the conclusion below after answering the questions you have chosen.

1. List any hobbies you have. What is your favorite? Why? What affect has it had on you? Which hobby do you know most about? How did you start? What is most interesting about your hobby? Do you think others should be involved in your hobby? Why? Does your hobby play any role in the career you hope to have?

2. List any talents you have, such as playing an instrument, raising animals or plants, drawing, painting, carving, speaking other languages, working on cars, being an athlete, building, cooking, singing, dancing. What special memories or stories do you have about your talents? What do you consider your best talent? Why? Who helped you develop your talent? How would you go about teaching your specialty to another person?

3. List your favorite subjects, such as sports, cooking, fishing/hunting, sharks, a certain historical period, music, science, literature, math, computers, farming, electronics, geography, art, or cartography. Which subject do you know most about? What is the best book or article you have read on this subject? Why is this subject so interesting to you? What do you like to tell others about this subject?

Conclusion

Reread your answers and notes to the questions and go back through your memories once more. Are there any other details—sights, smells, colors, people, facts, impressions, or feelings—that you can recall? Try to visualize the scenes in your memories, hear the sounds, smell the scents, feel the sensations, or recall conversations and write them down.

Next, look through what you have written and focus on one idea, mood, memory, or experience. Write this subject at the top of another sheet of paper and write 2-3 pages on it. Then answer the following questions:

1. Why is the main idea, memory, mood, or feeling important to me?
2. Is this subject easy for me to discuss?

After considering the answers to these questions, turn to Chapter 4, page 108, and read the introduction before using a method for defining your reader and purpose and discovering the form of your ideas.

LETTERS

Letter writing can be a great way to free your mind and let your ideas flow. You can talk to another writer, a character in a story or essay, a politician, the college president, or a teacher or classmate. You can say what you want, raise questions, get angry, or write eloquent prose—and in the end, really write to yourself.

One of our students tried this after reading the account of a man who had visited America 200 years ago and produced the following unedited letter.

Dear Mr. Crevecoeur,

Your paper on America was quite interesting. I suppose I'll never see it as you have. It sounded so friendly and troublefree then. Everyone being so kind to each other and trusting total strangers.

I'd really like to read a paper of yours, on how you would view America today. It would be so very different. You see, people are not so free anymore. They are, in that they can come and go, but we are so tramped by our cruel, unfair, prejudice and violent society. It seems to me that people are doing more arguing and fighting about this and that then I've ever seen before. Some people don't even care that they are Americans, they put her down in everyway that they can. Certain groups like the Ku Klux Klan and Nazi Party try to decide who should live here and who is the best race. It gets a little ridiculous when we all can't just stick together and say, "Hey, I'm an American."

I'm not saying that it is all bad, because it isn't. I wouldn't live anywhere else but here. I just can't understand why so many people hate each other and won't let them live peacefully.

Thanks for letting me see another America,

Laura

Writing this letter helped Laura understand what she thought after reading Jean de Crevecoeur's descriptions of America and the people he met. By writing to him and explaining the changes that had occurred over 200 years, she realized that she saw society as becoming prejudiced and violent, and this is the subject she chose for her paper.

If you would like to use this technique, think about your principal reactions to the assignment or the readings. Are you excited, angry, pleased, amused, saddened, confused, or enthusiastic? Are there questions you have or opinions you want to express? To whom do you want to direct your questions or feelings? Why?

Start writing and do not hold back. Let your emotions, reactions, and ideas take charge. Once you are satisfied that you have said what is important to you, find the central idea of your letter. Underline or circle the parts that express your sentiments best. Rewrite the central idea at the top of another sheet of paper and write 2–3 pages or until you have exhausted your ideas on this subject. Then answer the following questions before moving on to Chapter 4:

1. Why is this idea interesting and important to me?
2. Will I be comfortable writing about it?

Read the introduction to Chapter 4 if you have not done so before. Then turn to the methods that will help you define your reader and purpose and discover the form of your ideas.

THE MOVIE IN YOUR MIND

When you think of grapes, do you recall the taste of your mother's homemade jam or a special bottle of Beaujolais? Do you remember feeling skinned grapes in a Halloween funhouse and being told they were eyeballs? Or do you envision the Napa Valley vineyards, with heavy clusters of dark purple grapes hanging from lush green vines? For many people, their strongest impressions are visual, and for some writers, their ideas are like a series of pictures strung together on 35-mm film. Sound strange? See what Nickie McWhirter has to say about this idea.

THERE'S NO ADMISSION FEE TO THE MOVIE IN YOUR MIND

There are times when I want to write and not read. There are times when I want to read and not write. There are times when I cannot tolerate either. I am sick of words strung together to any purpose whatsoever.

When this happens I ignore all typewriters and written materials and switch over to the thinking mode. That's because I think in pictures, never words.

I was talking about this with another person who makes his living with language. I told him about thinking in pictures. It's a kind of grind movie house in my head where the reality of sight, sound and occurrence mixes with a surrealistic collage of remembrances and fantasies. It's very pleasant and refreshing, not to mention colorful.

The friend to whom I confided this said I was nuts. "Nobody thinks in pictures," he said.

He's nuts. They are fast-moving, living, three-dimensional, Technicolor, wide-screen pictures. What is more fascinating, there are many of these pictures

Reprinted with the permission of the Detroit Free Press.

being shown at the same time and being "seen" all at once, with no trouble at all. It's easy.

If I look at a perfect geranium in my garden, for example, and wonder if I should pick it or leave it alone, I don't think: "Should I pick that geranium? Or, should I just let it look pretty right there? What do you want to do, Nik?"

Nobody thinks like that, in words. What happens is a lot of visual images in no particular order spring up in my head and are processed simultaneously.

I look and see the flower, and that moving image of reality is captured and held in my mind. At the same time, I see the geranium in a vase in the house, by itself as well as with other flowers. It is on the dining table or the coffee table or the night stand. All of them, all at once. It is fresh cut and growing limp and dying, both and at the same time. I see it continuing to bloom and contribute to the garden, then growing limp and dying there. And I see the cutter I will need to cut it, in the basement on its shelf. I see myself going down the stairs to get it. I see the various vases I might choose. I see myself adding water to one of them and sticking the flower in the water.

SCREENING THE CHOICES

I see all of this and much more in a fraction of an instant—whatever an instant is. Sometime during the micro-process one of the pictures is so appealing or troublesome that the decision to cut or not cut the flower is made. No real conscious effort is expended making that decision. It just emerges and feels right.

You do the same thing when you are thinking. You do not form a single word in your mind. Not one. You screen 100 pictures in a wink and make a dozen choices in one flap of a fly's wing.

Thinking is a miraculous, awesome process which hardly anybody considers or properly enjoys. Nobody can explain it or diagram its process either. It is very difficult for me, right now, to translate what happens into this clumsy code of written language in order to try—pathetically, inefficiently, incompletely—to communicate its sense to you. But, you will know, if you think about it. In thinking you will experience the process, which you may have never even considered in yourself and others.

We live surrounded by miracles, peeking out at them from within our body cases, which are, themselves, miraculous. And we complain about being bored. Or we see the hardware around us—the town, the house, the factory, the office—and say we like it or do not like it here. We look at the body cases, our own and others, and say we like this one but not that one. We are happy or unhappy because of these language-definable semi-realities of our existence. We sit around and talk about them, using slow, dull words, for hours and days or lifetimes.

HOME IS INSIDE THE MIND

Actually, we live in our minds, and our minds are full of pictures, not words. So we live in the reality of a personal, surrealistic picture show. It is an enigma inside a paradox.

Not one person on this earth can accurately define in language those things which make him or her happy or sad. The best we can do is to say that a certain place, a certain company, a certain situation makes us "happy." When we think about it and try to grab hold of it, there are only pictures, dozens of them all at once. The words come haltingly, in an attempt to code the pictures and pass them along to another person, or in some effort to label them for ourselves as the essence of what we need or do not need for our happiness.

I thought about this while doing some fairly routine chores around chez moi. I was enjoying the work. I remembered hating the same work in a previous life. The picture show ground away in my thought box. There was no logical reason to be joyful at this work now if I was unhappy in it then. Flash. Flash. Click. Change. The work and its location was obviously irrelevant. Flash. Flash. Click. Change. The difference was in the images, some of which I liked and some of which I did not like. Flash. Flash. Click. Change.

This will be one of those writings of which some readers will say, "What the blazes is she talking about, George?" The answer is our living environment which is not Chicago or Mulberry Street. It is miraculous, very personal, simulcast mind pictures. Lean back and think about it; you'll see.

Taking time to visualize something that you think about can give you new insights, many details, and some interesting perspectives for your writing assignments. Try this method by thinking about your assignment and concentrate on any of the feelings or ideas that come to mind. Where do those feelings or ideas come from? Specific memories or experiences? If you were to make a movie out of your feelings or ideas, what would it be about? What would be the major scenes? The principal characters? Where would it take place? What is the time period? Is the movie in black and white or color? What music would play in the background?

Now concentrate on the major "frames" of the movie and pretend that you are sitting in the audience enjoying the show. Write 2-3 pages describing everything you see and hear for those major scenes.

Does a central idea or feeling emerge from your writing? If not, try writing again until you can express in a few sentences the main idea of your movie. Then answer the following questions:

1. Did I like the movie? Why?
2. Would the ideas or feelings expressed in this movie be easy for me to write about?

LISTENING/TALKING

"Before I can write anything, I have to hear the introduction in my head." Like the student who made this statement, many writers find listening and talking an important part of the writing process because it helps them focus on what they want to say. For some, listening means hearing what others have to say about a topic. For others, such as our student who had to "hear" his introduction, it means rehearsing ideas in the mind until they form a pattern or plan that makes sense. We know of many students who need to listen to music in order to relax enough to turn on their creative juices. Other writers need to read their work out loud or talk to others in order to discover what subject they want to discuss. So, it is not surprising when a writer says that he must use a tape recorder or talk to a friend in order to write.

If you would like to use this method for getting started, there are a number of approaches. Read through them, use one, and then answer the questions before turning to Chapter 4.

1. Listen to what other people say about the assignment, reading, or topic. If your assignment is related to current events or issues, watch television programs, listen to radio broadcasts or music lyrics, or go to movies that might give you insights into the topic. While listening, jot down key words, phrases, or ideas that stimulate your thinking.

Next, focus on one specific idea that interests you and write 2–3 pages about it. If that is difficult to do, try another topic until you find one that gives you enough ideas for 2–3 pages of writing. Then answer the following questions:

1. Why is this topic interesting and important to me?
2. Can I write about it easily?

2. Find a comfortable place where you can listen to a favorite record or kind of music. Concentrate on your assignment and listen for any recurring ideas or themes. Do any conversations in class come to mind? Conversations with friends or teachers? Can you hear what the characters or authors of your readings have to say? Write down the ideas and details that are most interesting and then think about why you respond to them.

Look over your notes and circle the ideas or details that interest you most. Then on another sheet of paper, jot down those circled notes and try to write 2–3 pages based on the ideas they evoke. Does a single subject, feeling, or idea emerge? If not, continue to write or choose other details that give you more ideas. Once you find a subject, answer the following questions:

1. Why is this topic interesting and important to me?
2. Will it be easy for me to discuss?

3. Find someone you like to talk with—a classmate, friend, roommate, or teacher. If that person is not familiar with the assignment or the readings, describe what you are doing and your reactions

to the readings. What did you like most? Least? Propose ideas you might like to write about and consider your listener's reactions. What subjects did you talk about longest? Jot down any notes that will remind you of ideas and your conversation.

If the person is familiar with the assignment and readings, compare your reactions and ideas with his. Do you both look at the assignment and readings in the same way? Why? Do either of you disagree with the readings or with reactions of others in class? Why? Write down the ideas you talk about most or the words that will remind you of your conversation.

Focus on the notes and subjects that you were most involved with in your discussion. Choose an idea that you think will be interesting to explore and try writing on it for 2-3 pages, explaining your views and developing your ideas. If you have difficulty thinking of things to say, recall your conversations or choose another subject. Write again until you can identify a central subject; then answer the following questions:

1. Why is this topic interesting to me?
2. Can I write about it comfortably?

4. Try rehearsing your ideas out loud or in your mind until you reach some conclusions, until you hear the beginning or ending of a speech you might make on the subject, or until you can establish a goal for your writing. What do you want your audience to remember? Why?

Once your ideas become clear, write them down and try to summarize what you want to say in a sentence or two. Then write on that topic for 2-3 pages to develop and explain your ideas. If you get stuck, look at your notes or change topics. When you find a subject you can write about, answer the following questions:

1. Why is this subject interesting and important to me?
2. Do I feel comfortable about presenting these ideas to a reader?

5. Try using a tape recorder. Think about your assignment and then record your thoughts. Do any experiences come to mind that have influenced your opinions or attitudes? Any central ideas or feelings about the readings? Try describing the assignment, the readings, or your reactions, and talk about anything that comes to mind.

When you finish, listen to the tape and be ready to take down notes. Listen for the ideas you talk about most emphatically. Which ideas are you really involved with? What do you talk about for the longest time? This analysis will help you find the central ideas or feelings that will make suitable topics for your paper.

Look over your notes and single out the main idea. Then try writing for 2-3 pages on this subject. Are there experiences or ideas on the tape that can be used to develop your thoughts? Should the tape recorder be used again to record more ideas? Once you can write about a subject for a few pages, answer the following questions:

1. Why is this topic interesting and important to me?
2. Is it easy for me to discuss?

FREE ASSOCIATION

We all make associations with the things around us. An old, scruffy teddy bear or a rusty wagon might bring back childhood memories; a photo might remind you of your prom, or a special place or person. Associating your thoughts with a specific object, symbol, image, or feeling is a way to put your experiences and memories on paper in order to discover what you think or how you perceive the world. Debbie Kaspari captured a flood of memories triggered by a dried crimson rose.

```
A LONG AGO ROSE

Christmas
Roses and perfume
You used to send me roses and poetry...
Even in the school newspaper
Driving in the country
        in the snowstorms
Skipping school to eat donuts
        and more driving in the snowstorms
I cried a lot
Still you sent more roses

Valentine's Day
Just a single rose--no poetry
But not from you
I loved it
Fragile and pink
Weak from the cold
Filled with memories
Of proms and homecomings
Laughter and tears
Gentleness
That's all it took
A single rose
From someone I loved
Long ago
```

```
Graduation--our class flower
And you sent me a dozen roses
I remember you
But I love
My single rose
```

For her essay, Debbie finally wrote about a decision she had made in high school to date a popular, good-looking fellow who was editor of the newspaper, had a car, and was great fun. Not until she received the single rose from her former boyfriend did she realize how much she missed the simple, uncluttered relationship she had shared with him. By making the associations with the old dried rose, Debbie found an experience she could write about, explaining how it helped her realize what she valued.

To use this technique, start by focusing on a specific word or idea from the assignment or by concentrating on an image, symbol, or feeling that comes to mind after reading the assignment or the readings. Once you have the idea or image in mind, jot down any word or phrase that occurs to you and keep writing until you have finished.

Next, select the most important or interesting parts of your writing and expand the words and phrases into whole sentences, descriptions, or memories. Once you finish, think about these impressions and focus on the strongest one. Write down that idea on another page and try writing about it for 2–3 pages. If you get stuck, look over your free association material for more ideas, or find another impression about which you have more to say.

Complete this getting-started method by answering the following questions:

1. Why am I interested in this topic?
2. Will it be easy for me to discuss?

THINKING

A friend of ours who is a well-known detective fiction writer used to tell us how difficult it was to convince his wife that he was really working when he lay on his bed for several hours in the morning. "It used to exasperate her to see me lying on my back looking at the ceiling instead of typing away at my desk. She would dust around me or run the sweeper or decide to move furniture until I finally had to get up. She just couldn't understand that I *was* working when I was lying there—I was *thinking*."

You, too, may need periods of time to mull over your ideas or to let your mind wander until you have discovered an idea or roughed out a plan for your writing assignment. Some writers have to jog or go for walks or drives; others need to listen to music and sit in a special chair or go to their favorite coffee house or doughnut shop; and still others have to turn out the lights and think in the dark.

If this process sounds compatible with your needs, then find a place where you are comfortable and where you can concentrate undisturbed. But be sure to write down your insights before moving on to a formal draft.

After thinking for a while, do you see a general direction for your paper, or have a number of details been generated from your experiences that relate to your assignment? Jot down notes to use later. Or, if you prefer to talk out your ideas, use a tape recorder. Then listen for a central idea, experience, or feeling and write it down on a sheet of paper. Try writing 2–3 pages on this topic. What details or ideas from your thinking can you use? Check your notes if you get stuck, or look for another topic and start writing again.

When you finish, answer the following questions:

1. Why is this topic interesting and important to me?
2. Do I feel comfortable writing about it?

Once you can answer these questions, move on to Chapter 4 to define your reader and purpose and discover the form of your ideas.

READING

Writers frequently find their subjects in what they read. Many use reading to evoke memories and create subjects. Others focus on the author's main idea and support or refute it with their own ideas. "I agree (disagree) with Dennis Farney's observation that there is a growing appreciation of the landscape in the United States because . . ."

Or they react to an author's minor point and discuss it. "Sidney Harris touches on the subject of students who do not try to do well in school. This is a serious issue because . . ."

Others choose to focus on a single sentence or phrase. "Chief Seathl's statement, 'All things are connected. Whatever befalls the earth befalls the sons of the earth,' should make us realize how important conservation is to all of us."

Still other writers formulate their own topic but use the author's work to support and develop their position. "As Martin Luther King, Jr., points out, there were still many vestiges of discrimination 100 years after Lincoln freed the slaves. He cites the example that . . ."

Once the writer is familiar with and clearly understands the material he has read, he can use one of two methods for finding a subject. One involves reading actively and letting the piece evoke personal memories and ideas. The other involves analyzing the author's ideas in order to use them as the center of the writing project.

Using Reading to Evoke Memories and Create Subjects for Writing

If you have been keeping a reading journal and have been using the suggestions we made on page 22 for becoming an active reader, you have discovered how reading helps you find writing topics. Steve Groholski used this approach to find the subject for "My Place" in Chapter 9. Reading Thoreau's description of Walden Pond triggered memories of a place that had been important to him. Authors' discussions of their experiences have probably reminded you, too, of joyful, painful, or meaningful experiences you have had.

Before rereading the selection you want to discuss or use, go back to "Guidelines for Using the Reader Journal," page 22, for suggestions on reading actively and try using one. For example, write a letter to the author explaining how your experience is similar or different. Or try writing to one of the characters. Or make marginal notes.

Once you have used one of the techniques, look through what you have written to see if there is a central idea or feeling. Underline it and then try to express that idea or feeling in a sentence or two at the top of another sheet of paper. If you can write for 2–3 pages on that subject, you are ready to answer the following questions. If not, look for another idea or try another method from "Guidelines for Using the Reading Journal."

1. Why is this topic important and interesting to me?
2. Can I discuss it comfortably?

When you can answer these two questions, you are ready to move on to Chapter 4.

Using the Author's Ideas for Your Subject

To use another person's idea as the subject for your writing, you must first understand that idea well enough to treat it as if it were your own. Unless the idea becomes part of your knowledge, you run the risk of trying to communicate something you do not understand. The result is garbled, noncommunicative writing.

Try either of the following approaches to make sure that you understand the author's ideas well enough to use them in your writing. After you answer the accompanying questions, turn to Chapter 4 to define your reader and purpose and to discover the form to use in presenting your ideas.

1. Read the piece actively, taking notes and stopping frequently to write summaries of major points. Then go back and outline the piece, focusing on the main idea and supporting examples. Read the

outline and focus on a major or minor point or an example that you would like to discuss in your writing. Write 2–3 pages on that idea to determine whether or not you understand it and have enough information to support it. If you have trouble, look for another idea that will be easier to discuss. Then answer the following questions before moving on to Chapter 4:

1. Why is this subject interesting and important to me?
2. Can I discuss it easily?

2. Read the piece and imagine that you are going to teach it to someone. Take notes and write summaries. When you have finished reading, devise a test you could give after teaching the piece. Then take your own test. Go back to the reading whenever you have a problem, answering the questions fully. Once you are familiar with the ideas in the reading, focus on the most important information and try presenting it to a friend or classmate. When you find a subject you can discuss at length, answer the following questions before turning to Chapter 4:

1. Why is this subject interesting and important to me?
2. Can I write about this subject easily?

QUESTIONS

"I find that writers write to answer questions. They may not answer them in a direct way. They arrange words in sentences and paragraphs to describe a picture, and this picture tells the reader what is happening. It is like the writer thinking, only he expresses himself or herself in words. Everyone has questions to be answered; therefore, everyone can be a writer."

To gather ideas for her writing assignments Margaret asked questions, either of herself or of other students. When she worked in a small group of students, her questions were general:

What do you think about the assignment? The readings?
What are we supposed to do? What do you plan to do?

Looking at a specific reading, she might ask:

What do you think the author meant? What was his purpose in writing this?
Why did this happen in the essay?
What did you think of that character? Why?
Do you agree with the author's ideas? With the character's actions? Why? What might you have done?

Once Margaret and her group asked such questions and shared their reactions, ideas, and experiences, they took a few minutes to consider what ideas were most interesting and what they could talk about for the longest period of time. Then each member of the group worked alone, focusing on the subject or question he or she wanted to discuss and writing for 10–15 minutes.

When Margaret worked alone, she often analyzed the assignment and focused on individual words or phrases. For example, one assignment was to discuss the importance of individuality in American life. She broke it down into this series of questions:

> Is individuality important? Why? Do I agree with Heather Lamb?
> What is individuality to me? How did I come to these conclusions?
> What do I consider "American life?" Does Lamb see it the same way?
> Am I an individual? How so? Is Lamb an individual? Why?

These questions helped Margaret to recall experiences, feelings, and ideas that gave her insights into her attitudes and beliefs and direction in discovering what she cared about.

If you would like to try this technique, work with classmates or alone and break down the assignment and readings into questions. Then answer the questions carefully. Focus on the ones that bring back the greatest number of memories, feelings, or experiences. Is there one question you are most interested in answering? If so, try responding with 2–3 pages of ideas and experiences. If not, keep asking yourself or your classmates questions until you find one that stimulates your thinking. Then answer the following questions:

1. Why is this subject important to me?
2. Is it easy to talk about?

Once you find a subject and discover why it is important to you to discuss it, turn to Chapter 4 to continue the writing process.

ANALYSIS/CLASSIFICATION

If you have been given a topic to write about and are not sure what to say about it, one way to put your ideas on paper is to analyze and classify the subject. One of our students used this method for an assignment based on Joan Didion's essay, "Goodbye to All That," in order to consider her own ideas and discover what topic was most important to her. Like Didion, Julie went to New York and found it to be both exciting and disillusioning. But how could she compress three months of experience into a three- or four-page essay?

One way Julie looked at her experiences was to break it down and describe it:

> *Plane flight was exciting—June 1977*
> *Airport in NYC was so crowded—everyone hurrying to get somewhere.*

Taxi ride was terrifying—so many cars, horns.
Subways rumbled, everything seemed to move.

Then she analyzed it by considering what function or purpose her experiences in the city served:

Had to find my own life.
Independence from my family.
It was an escape from a planned, ordered life.
Had to fulfill my dreams. Be somebody.

Once she clarified some of the details and how she felt about her experience, Julie argued for and against her decision to live there:

1. *Chance for a real life—do exciting things.*
   Be alone and independent—find out who I am.
2. *Have to leave friends and family—give up security.*
   Very competitive—no guarantees.
   Will I make it?

After she had broken down and analyzed her experiences, she began to classify those three months by comparing them to the nine years Didion lived there:

Didion: *"too long at the fair"*
         aggrevated
         disappointed
Me: *excitement turned to disillusion*
     became very lonely
     people seemed superficial—I was living a dream

And finally, she tried to place her experiences in a broader perspective by describing her impressions:

New York reminded me of an ice palace—cold and un-
friendly. People seemed dead underneath their busy life. Life
was like a merry-go-round, spinning constantly with no time
for thought . . .

Julie sifted through her getting-started work, looked for the most important ideas, revised, and rewrote. Eventually, she finished a thoughtful paper on following her dreams to New York and the consequences of going there. If you want to read her essay, turn to Chapter 9 and read "Letter to Ms. Didion."

If this method will help you understand what you want to say about an assigned topic, try at least three of the following approaches. Jot down ideas, make lists, or write whole pages until ideas begin to emerge. Then go to the bottom of this page to finish.

Analysis Approaches

1. Describing the subject. Write your subject at the top of the page and break it down by listing its individual characteristics. What parts are most important? Which ones do you know most about? How would you describe those parts? Then explain how those characteristics relate to the whole subject.

2. Finding the subject's purpose. Put your subject on a separate sheet of paper and describe what purpose it serves or how it functions. What are its most common functions? What people use it most often? Why? What effects does it have? Do you see its purpose as primarily positive or negative? Why?

3. Looking at the pros and cons of the subject. Looking at your subject and anything you have written, consider how you would argue for or against this subject. What reasons do you have for supporting or not supporting it? Explain by using your own experiences and knowledge.

Classification Approaches

1. Comparing and contrasting the subject. Put your subject on a sheet of paper and compare it to ideas or experiences that are familiar to you. Jot down any similarities, details, or experiences that help you describe your subject. Then consider how this subject is different from other experiences or ideas and jot down your reasons. What generalizations can you make about this subject based on the similarities and differences you see?

2. Associating the subject with other ideas. Write your subject on a separate sheet of paper and think about the memories it evokes. List your own experiences or those of others, readings, movies, images, or feelings that come to mind. Then explain why you make make about this subject based on the list? Can you develop metaphors, similes, or analogies that symbolize your generalizations?

After trying three or more approaches, look over your work and underline the central or most important ideas. Express those ideas in a few sentences and write 2–3 pages on them. Refer to your lists and notes if you get stuck; or look for another idea, do more detailed writing for one of the approaches, or try the rest of the approaches to find a perspective on the subject you want to discuss.

Before turning to Chapter 4, answer the following questions:

1. Why is this idea important and interesting to me?
2. Is it easy to write about?

INTERVIEWS

One way to gather information, as well as to find out what you think, is to interview people about their beliefs, attitudes, concerns, or experiences. You could interview an older family member, a peer, someone with a specific culture or heritage, or someone who works in a field that interests you. Interviewing is an excellent method for stimulating your own thinking and for developing insights on your own life by comparing what you know with the knowledge and experiences of others.

If you are interested in seeing the possibilities or results of an interview, read "Heather Lamb," "Gaylord Freeman," or "Bill Veeck" in Chapter 9. Those interviews were done with Studs Turkel, the master of the interview, and reflect many hours of work. Make sure that you set aside enough time to make appointments, write questions, and listen to a tape of the interview if you decide to use a recorder.

Preparing for the Interview

To prepare for the interview, write down subjects that interest you, why they are important to you, and what you already know about them. What are your own experiences with these subjects? What concerns and questions do you have? Also, consider doing some background reading to flesh out your ideas.

After doing some warm-up writing and thinking, look for the areas you are most interested in and want to focus on. Then write the main ideas you want to discuss and your goals for the interview on a separate sheet of paper. Below them, list questions that will help you get the information you want. Then make an appointment for the interview, explaining what you want to find out and why it is important to you. This statement will help your subject answer the questions more accurately and fully.

During the Interview

During the interview, take whatever notes seem especially informative. If you take along a tape recorder, make sure that your subject has no objections. It can be a useful backup source that makes it easier for you to listen and be sensitive to the topics the person wants to discuss. Just remember that it must be played back later, and you must allow time for that.

After the Inverview

After you finish the interview, jot down your ideas, reactions, and conclusions as soon as you can. Record this information before your ideas fade away and you lose the opportunity to discover interesting writing topics. Write about what you learned from this experience, how it affected your ideas and attitudes, and what was most interesting.

To find a subject that can be used for your assignment, go through your notes and reactions and listen to the tape recording. Look for any special insights you might have missed or for relationships among the ideas. What generalizations can you make about your experience or new knowledge? What material is most useful? Earmark the notes or write down those parts of the conversation that you will want to use.

Focus on a central or repeated idea and write it at the top of a sheet of paper. Then write 2–3 pages on this idea and integrate the earmarked material and conversation into your discusssion.

Once you find a subject you can write about at length, answer the following questions:

1. Why is this topic interesting and important to me?
2. Can I write about it comfortably?

Move on to Chapter 4 and use a method for defining your reader and purpose and for discovering the form to use in presenting your ideas.

RESEARCHED TOPICS

There are a number of ways to gather information and find out what you want to discuss in longer, more formal writing. Read through all of the suggestions before starting your research. And once you have collected information, read the conclusion of this getting-started technique before turning to Chapter 4.

1. *Focusing on your interests.* If you are allowed to research almost any topic, a good place to start is with what you are interested in and already know. Look at Survey D in this chapter and jot down brief answers to the questions. Is there a topic related to one of your hobbies, talents, or interests that you would like to

know more about? Why? Browse through any material you already have regarding this subject to see if any other ideas occur to you, or check the subject catalogue at your school or local library to see what information is available.

2. *Reading.* If you are given a general subject, such as the American Civil War or alternative energy sources, and need to find a specific topic for your project, look at the reading materials you have on hand (textbooks or handouts from class). Also, go to the subject catalogue in the library to find books on the subject, or check your textbook for bibliographies related to the topics discussed in the text.

Once you find some books, go through the indexes or tables of contents to see if any specific topics look interesting. Read any pages listed for those subjects and write down what you want to know more about. Also, try reading the introductory and concluding chapters of these books to see if the authors suggest what areas related to these subjects require further investigation.

Other sources of information are newspaper indexes and the *Reader's Guide to Periodical Literature* for shorter articles on the topic. For a number of differing views on contemporary and often controversial issues, ask for the *Alternative Press Index.* The librarian will help you use these resources and find the material you want.

3. *Compiling notes.* While doing research, you must take notes and write down your observations. Therefore, you need to develop a system to record the ideas and facts you gather as well as the sources of information. Be careful to write down the exact titles of books and articles, authors' and editors' names, dates and places of publication, publishing companies, editions of books, and critical page numbers. Also, make sure that you indicate when you are quoting directly from an article or a book and when you are paraphrasing the ideas. When using this information later, you will have to document the sources accurately in footnotes and bibliographies. For more details, you may want to refer to the research paper section of a handbook or to a book on writing a research paper.

The system you choose should fit your research and writing habits. Some people use index cards of different sizes to distinguish between the notes they take and the sources of these notes. Others prefer separate notebooks, pads of paper, or notecards on spiral holders. Still others photocopy what they need, underline important passages, or write down the necessary information on the backs of the copies.

After gathering information the first time, look for any repeated or interesting ideas you want to continue researching. These ideas will give you some direction the next time you go to the library and before you go on to Chapter 4. Some of our students like to keep a list of questions that occur to them while reading. The questions they find most interesting to answer and write about later become the topics for their research papers.

4. *Talking/Listening.* When starting your research, do not overlook talking to people who work in related areas. You will find that most people are pleased to share their ideas and experiences about the topic you are investigating. And quite often, they can lead you to other kinds of valuable research materials not easily available through your library. Read *"Interviews"* on page 100 if you decide to try this method.

Also, consider using previously taped interviews with people involved in your subject. Many of the larger university and college libraries have a selection of documentaries or tapes of authors, scientists, educators, politicians, and others who have had some impact on the world.

5. *Using the visual media.* Another way of gathering ideas is through the visual media. News broadcasts, special reports or documentaries, movies, and even cartoons and art can lead you to issues that are often overlooked. One of our students was intrigued by the photographic coverage given to certain contemporary issues and how it sometimes slanted the information reported. This idea led her to investigate the ownership of certain prominent magazines, their publication priorities, editorial policies, and social and political philosophies. Another student followed a nationally syndicated cartoon strip and showed how it gauged the current concerns and problems of Americans.

If you tend to respond to visual forms, you may want to use visual sources to stimulate your thinking and to find topics for your project. While viewing a movie, going through magazines and newspapers, or watching the news, have a pad ready to write down ideas, insights, or questions. When you have made a list of possible subjects, go through them to single out the ones you care about most. Then think about why these topics are interesting and important to you. Go to the library, do some background reading, take notes, and narrow down your list until you find a subject you want to discuss in a research paper.

Conclusion

If, after gathering information, you have not found a specific subject but have identified several general areas of interest, go through your notes, questions, or copied material and look for recurring ideas or specific subjects. In what areas did you take most notes? What books or articles did you most enjoy reading? Why? Use these questions as a guide to finding a specific subject on which you can and want to do further research.

Once you have found a specific subject that interests you and have written some notes on it, take 30-40 minutes to answer the following questions:

1. What do I already know about this subject?
2. Why do I want to know more about it?
3. What do I hope to prove or discuss in a research paper on this subject?
4. What seem to be the best resources so far?
5. Will I be able to research this subject fairly easily?

Answering these questions will prepare you for Chapter 4 and writing a first draft of your paper.

CHAPTER 4

Getting It on Paper for a Reader

Rough Draft--Chapter Six (PartXⅩⅩⅩⅩⅩ I--Revision)

How can I check for organization?

As you discovered in Chapters 2 and 4, there are many organizatinal
patterns available to you. They are predicted by the idea and pur-
ⅩⅩⅩⅩⅩ pose of your paper. It is time now to check how well you
carried out ⅩⅩⅩⅩⅩⅩⅩⅩⅩⅩⅩⅩⅩⅩⅩⅩⅩⅩⅩⅩⅩⅩⅩ this pattern.
First you will need to determine if your ppaer is organized so
your ideas are clear and easy to follow for a reader. Use any one
of the methods below to check this"

Make a MAP of your paper.

What was your destination or goal for the paper? If you used
notes
ⅩⅩⅩⅩⅩⅩⅩⅩⅩ or wrôte your paper using an index card, try mapping
your work now. Using   ide
where you started (ma
within your paragrap
Once you do this, dec
arranged in a logical
understand. ⅩⅩⅩⅩⅩⅩⅩⅩ

Rewriting techniqu
working on the organi

1. Rearrange the
   ⅩⅩⅩⅩⅩⅩ side-
   any ideas that   ⅩⅩⅩ
   A to point c.
2. Write out the

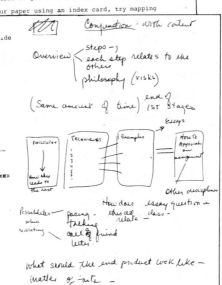

As a paper takes shape, three elements contribute to its form: the subject, the audience, and the purpose. Although the writer's first concern is finding an idea to communicate, he must also consider who his reader will be and why he wants to express this idea to him. Addressing these concerns before writing the first draft helps the writer further limit the subject and find a way to present his ideas in an interesting and understandable way.

Just as there is no one way to find a subject you can and want to write about, there is no one way to define your reader and your purpose for writing. Again, we have suggested several ways you can deal with these concerns. In the first section, "Discovering the Reader and Purpose," you will focus on the questions "Who is my reader?" and "What is my purpose?" Then, in "Discovering the Plan of the Paper," you will consider the question "How can I present my ideas in an interesting and understandable way for my reader?" In each section you can select a method, modify it, or combine it with another method in order to answer these questions. Answering these three questions will prepare you for the third section, "Writing the First Draft."

Sometimes, despite answering these questions, writers still have problems with the first draft. Should you find that you are going nowhere once you start writing, turn to the final section of this chapter, "Getting Unstuck," for suggestions on how to beat writer's block.

DISCOVERING THE READER AND PURPOSE

As a reader, you expect the writer to make you interested in what he or she has to say. And to do this as a writer, you must know for whom you will be writing and what you hope to accomplish by writing to this particular audience. That is why it is important to have a clear sense of your reader and an understanding of his interests.

Even the most talented professional writers encounter problems when they do not fully and accurately assess the interests of their readers. F. Scott Fitzgerald's novel *The Great Gatsby* was set in the Roaring Twenties and focused on the illusions and problems of America's wealthy upper middle class. It immediately captured the interest and imagination of his 1925 audience, who were fascinated by this class of seemingly carefree people. They, too, hoped to share in the glittering success of that era by joining the rich someday. But before Fitzgerald published his next novel, the world had drastically changed. Although *Tender Is the Night* was about the same people who had interested his earlier readers, it was a failure in Fitzgerald's lifetime. His audience of the 1930s, caught up in the Great Depression, no longer cared about the wealthy, whose problems seemed trivial next to their concerns of feeding their families, holding on to their homes, and finding work. It was not until some twenty years later that a new audience appreciated Fitzgerald's ideas and considered his work a success.

From Fitzgerald's experiences, you can understand just how vital it is for the writer to know his audience. Without considering the interests and experiences of readers, the writer cannot be certain that people will want to read what he has written. So, in this section, you will be looking at your reader from three perspectives:

1. Who is the reader?
2. What does the reader know about the subject?
3. Why would the reader be interested in this subject?

Who Is My Reader?

Use any of the following methods to answer these questions. Make sure that you read about all the techniques to find one that is congenial to you. If you still cannot answer the questions after using the method you have chosen, select a different one or combine it with another technique.

BRAINSTORMING THE READER

If you think you know a great deal about your reader, you can discover just how well you do know him or her by using this method.

Find a place where you will not be disturbed for at least ten minutes. Writing nonstop, put down all the ideas you have about the reader. You can write these ideas in sentences, phrases, or lists. Write as fast as you can and do not worry about spelling, penmanship, or grammar. Simply record as many details as possible and focus on the reader's interests, his knowledge of your subject, and his likes and dislikes.

After you have filled a page or more, look over what you have written. Do you have a clear sense of who the reader is? What interests him or her? How the reader feels about this subject? If so, write a paragraph that makes a clear statement and that answers the following questions:

1. Who is my reader?
2. What does my reader know about this subject?
3. Why would my reader be interested in this subject?

Once you finish, turn to page 112 to define your purpose for writing on this topic.

TALKING ABOUT THE READER

Some of you have found that you generate the most ideas by talking to others about your subject. If this works for you, try discussing the reader with someone to get a clearer sense of who he is, how he will react to this subject, and what interests this person.

First, consider your reader's personal characteristics, such as age, background social class, and gender, and how these might influence his or her attitude toward your subject. Then consider what the reader may already know about the subject or what prejudgments he may have made about it. While exploring these subjects, jot down any notes or insights you have about the kinds of things that will interest the reader and whether or not your subject or your perspective on it is likely to appeal to him.

After you have discussed these ideas, read over your notes. Has a clear image of the reader emerged? If so, prepare a sketch of the person for whom you will be writing. Include all the material that will help you understand the following:

1. Who is my reader?
2. What does my reader know about this subject?
3. Why would my reader be interested in this subject?

Once you finish, turn to page 112 to define your purpose for writing on this topic.

PICTURING THE READER

In "Why I Write," Joan Didion says that ideas come to her as images that "shimmer around the edges." If ideas come to you in the same way, take some time to think about how you picture the reader. Sit back; let the images float to the surface of your mind. When the images start to develop into clear pictures, start writing to find out what you are thinking.

Read over what you have written. If the images are not clear, think about your reader once more. Is your reader male or female? How does your reader dress? Does the reader's clothing give you clues about his or her peer group, educational background, or occupation? Do you associate your reader with an age group? Why? What do you imagine this reader does on weekends or after work?

Now try writing a paragraph about your reader, describing his or her interests, social or political views, and what this person knows about your subject. When you finish, read your paragraph and answer the following questions:

1. Who is my reader?

2. What does my reader know about this subject?
3. Why would my reader be interested in this subject?

Once you finish, turn to page 112 to define your purpose for writing on this topic.

SURVEYING THE READER

If you are not well acquainted with your reader, using this survey can give you insights on who the reader is and how to present your ideas to him. Take a few minutes to ask your reader these questions and to jot down the answers.

1. Age
   Occupation
   Educational background
   Interests

2. What strong political, social, or religious views do you have? Why?

3. What do you know about _____ ?
   (your subject)

4. What are your views or opinions on _____ ?
   (your subject)

5. Are you interested in learning more about _____?
   (your subject)
   Why?

After you finish the survey, read over the responses and write a 10-minute timed summary about the reader that explores his or her interests, views, and knowledge. Then answer the following questions:

1. Who is my reader?
2. What does my reader know about this subject?
3. Why would my reader be interested in this subject?

Once you finish, turn to page 112 to define your purpose for writing on this topic.

RESEARCHING THE READER

When writing more formally for an audience you cannot easily survey or meet, you can do some brief research that will be helpful in predicting your audience's interests, knowledge of, and reactions to your ideas. For example, if you intend to write an editorial or article for a particular publication, find a recent issue of that newspaper, magazine, or periodical and consider the following questions:

1. Does the principal readership of this publication seem most like yourself? Your parents? Grandparents? Younger or older siblings? Your teachers? Or employers?
2. In what section of the publication would your work most likely appear? What kinds of ideas do you find there, and what do they tell you about the audience's interests or political and social views? Educational background? Sex? Are they likely to be interested in your ideas?
3. What do the advertisements in this publication tell you about the interests of its readers?
4. What did other writers use to capture their reader's attention? Principally facts, statistics, illustrations, personal experiences, or opinions? What can you do to gain the interest of your readers?

Review your answers to these questions and describe your audience in a paragraph. Then answer the following questions:

1. Who is my audience?
2. What are they likely to know about this subject?
3. Why would they be interested in this subject?

Once you finish, turn to the next section to define your purpose.

What Is My Purpose?

Once you have a clear picture of your reader and why he is interested in your subject, you are ready to consider your purpose for writing. To answer this question, you will have to define (a) why you want to write about this subject and (b) what you hope to accomplish by presenting your subject to the reader you have in mind.

As you learned in Chapter 1, writers have many reasons for writing. Some, such as Blaushild and Didion, write to express their ideas and to discover what they think. This kind of writing, *expressive writing*, is primarily writer-oriented. Sometimes the writing is very personal, such as that in diaries or journals. At other times, the writer wants to involve a reader and may express his feelings to a close friend, a public official, or a newspaper editor. Besides expressing himself, a writer may have a public purpose, such as informing or persuading his audience. For example, William Allen White no doubt started to write his editorial about his daughter to express his own feelings about her. But he also wanted to make some impact on his readers. His central purpose became showing his audience just who Mary White was, so that they might see her as he did.

Some writers write mainly to give information or transact business. *Informational writing* is used to record and pass on information. It, too, can be very personal. It is the grocery list you wrote out this morning or the class notes you took down yesterday afternoon. Or informational writing can be public, such as a test or an essay for class, a report for interdepartmental use, a letter written to a customer, or a major research project for a teacher or boss. In these cases, the author writes in order to share information with the reader. Sometimes this is done by presenting the ideas in an amusing way. Art Buchwald informs his readers about current issues by using satire and other forms of humor. Political columnist Jack Anderson prefers to present facts or statistics to inform his readers about similar events.

Finally, some writers write principally to persuade others to see the subject as they do. As Joan Didion put it, *persuasive writing* is the act of saying, "See it my way." The writer wants to persuade the reader to understand and perceive the subject as he sees it, to change the reader's mind, or to make the reader react in a certain way. Although part of the writer's goal may be to give information, his ultimate purpose is to make the reader *act*. Martin Luther King, Jr., was writing to express his feelings, to inform his audience about injustice, but his most important goal was to incite his audience to act.

If you hope to interest your reader in what you have to say about your subject, you must be certain that you have a real reason for writing and know how you want him to react to your ideas. And, most of all, you must be certain that your reason for writing relates to your subject and not to some secondary purpose. For example, you may discover that you have settled on a subject, not because you have strong feelings or opinions about it but because you think it will impress the reader. Or you may find that your only reason for writing is to complete the assignment or to get a good grade. These are all legitimate motivations, but first of all, you must care about your subject in order to interest your reader. He will be impressed only if *you* show that the subject is important. Remember, meeting a deadline may help you to finish your paper or report, but writing only to meet the deadline will not make your writing interesting or understandable.

To be certain that you have a clear purpose for writing about your subject and know how you want to affect your reader, we have suggested the following methods to help you answer the question, "Why am I writing about this subject for this reader?" Make sure to consider them all. Then choose one or a combination of methods that will help you complete these statements.

1. My purpose in writing about this subject is
   to _____ .
2. I want my reader to _____ .

After completing these statements, turn to "Discovering the Plan of the Paper, p. 116.

BRAINSTORMING YOUR PURPOSE

If you think you have a clear purpose in mind, put your subject at the top of a sheet of paper and write down your reasons for writing about it, as well as how you want your reader to react.

After you have written a page or more, read over your ideas. Does a clear purpose emerge? Do you have a sense of how you want your reader to respond? If so, complete the following sentences:

1. My purpose in writing about this subject is
   to _____ .
2. I want my reader to _____ .

FINDING THE PURPOSE IN YOUR
GETTING-STARTED WORK

Look over the material you generated in the getting-started stage. Did you use any words that reveal how you feel about your subject? Are there words or phrases that suggest how you might want the reader to respond to your writing? Underline the words, phrases, and sentences that reflect your purpose. Martin Luther King, Jr., might have discovered words and phrases such as *injustice, I have a dream, all God's children, shameful, defaulted,* and *now* in the material he wrote or used to gather ideas. By considering these expressions, he could have realized that he wanted to reveal his deep feelings about this subject, to inform his audience, and most of all, to convince them that his dream was possible.

Look over the material you underlined. Does it give you a clear sense of your purpose? Does it help you see how you want to affect your reader? If so, write a paragraph telling yourself why you want to write this paper and how you want it to affect your reader.

Then read over what you have written and complete the following sentences:

1. My purpose in writing about this subject is
   to _____ .
2. I want my reader to _____ .

TALKING ABOUT THE PURPOSE

Discuss your subject with someone. Be conscious of the way you talk about it. Are you talking merely to express your ideas and feelings? If so, you probably do not expect much response from the listener, aside from his being interested in or entertained by your ideas. Or are you trying to explain something to the listener? Are you watching his face and listening for reactions that tell you whether you are communicating clearly or not? If so, you are trying to give your reader information. Or are you trying to get the listener to agree with you? Are you trying to change his mind or spur on your listener to action? Then, no doubt, you are hoping to persuade your listener in some way.

After finishing your discussion, write yourself a brief letter describing it. Were you merely expressing your ideas in an interesting way for your audience? Or were you trying to inform or persuade your audience?

After reviewing your letter, complete the following sentences:

1. My purpose in writing about this subject is
   to ——————————.
2. I want my reader to ——————————.

USING LISTS TO FIND THE PURPOSE

List every reason you have for writing about this subject. Do not stop thinking and writing until you have at least five to ten reasons. If William Allen White had done so, his list might have looked like this:

1. Want to tell everyone that Mary did not *fall* off her horse.
2. Writing about her will bring her back for a while.
3. Want people to know the person she was.
4. Want to capture her indomitable spirit on paper.
5. Writing makes me feel better.
6. Want to show people how full of life she was.
7. Want to think of her as she was.
8. Want to show what she thought about the people she knew.
9. Want to write a tribute to her.
10. Want to put my feelings for her on paper.

After writing your list, look over your reasons. Are some of them similar, so that they can be grouped in some way? What seems to be the most common or important reason or group of reasons? What effect do you want to have on your readers? Why?

Now complete the following sentences:

1. My purpose for writing about this subject is
   to _____.
2. I want my reader to _____.

USING MEDIA FORMS TO FIND THE PURPOSE

Imagine that instead of turning your ideas into a paper, you were writing for a specific medium. Would the ideas you want to express be most suited to a television drama or a movie? Would they be appropriate for a newspaper article or a professional journal? Would you write about them in a letter to the editor? Think about how the audience would react to the subject. Would the television or movie audience be entertained or informed by your ideas? Would the newspaper or journal readers be informed or persuaded by your article?

Once you have a clear idea about the form your presentation would take, write a one-paragraph review of your show, movie, article, or editorial. Read it and then complete the following sentences:

1. My purpose for writing about this subject is
   to _____.
2. I want my reader to _____.

DISCOVERING THE PLAN OF THE PAPER

Now that you have a subject, an audience, and a purpose in mind, you are ready to consider how you can present your ideas in an interesting and understandable way. Finding a plan for the paper is important for two reasons. One, the plan will guide you through the writing of the first draft. Two, it will help you decide how you can present the ideas to make them easy to follow and interesting to your reader. Before you consider how to present the ideas, look back at the lists you started in Chapter 2. Do your observations of what other writers do to make their ideas interesting and understandable suggest techniques you could use? If so, keep these techniques in mind as you begin this part of the process.

As with other stages of the discovery process, you are still focusing on what you want to say, but now you must see how those ideas can be organized. Writers approach this stage in different ways. Some like to use an organic approach that lets them discover how one idea grows out of another. Others like to make an open-ended plan that gives them a general direction for the paper but does not focus on specific details. Still other writers like to plan the paper in a careful, step-by-step manner, deciding what ideas will be presented and how they will be discussed. Indeed, in attempting to find a form for a paper, some writers have to use more than one approach.

Whichever approach you use, keep in mind that the form is important only because it helps you communicate your ideas. *Each subject will dictate its own form.* In order for you to discover that form, use any one of the methods suggested. If you think an organic approach suits you, look at the methods on pages 117–120. For open-ended techniques, choose one from pages 120–126. And if you prefer a more formal technique, try one of the methods on pages 126–138.

Organic Approaches

Organic writing is just that: One idea grows out of another. If you have used timed writing, brainstorming, or even lists to discover your subject or define your reader and purpose, you have been doing organic writing.

Once he has discovered his subject and defined his audience and purpose, author Frank O'Connor uses a form of organic writing to find the design of what he is writing:

> "Get black on white" used to be Maupassant's advice – that's what I always do. I don't give a hoot what the writing is like, I write any sort of rubbish which will cover the main outlines of the story, then I can begin to see it.

If this way of finding the form of your paper appeals to you, try one of the following organic approaches to discover how to organize your ideas in an understandable and interesting way.

ZERO DRAFT

Unlike the subsequent drafts of your paper, which will be written for a specific reader, the zero draft is written only for you. Like the timed writing or brainstorming you have done before, the zero draft gives you a chance to see where your ideas are headed.

Find a quiet place where you will be undisturbed for an hour or so. Read the material you have generated in the getting-started stage and in defining your reader and purpose. Write the subject you want to discuss at the top of a sheet of paper and think about what you want to accomplish. Then start pouring out your ideas.

After completing the zero draft, use either Option A or Option B to discover the form of your paper.

OPTION A. Read what you have written. Draw a line through any ideas that do not relate to the subject at the top of the page.

Reread what remains and look for a beginning, a middle, and an end. Bracket that material and label it in the margin.

Next, focus on the middle part. Are the ideas arranged in a natural and logical way? Rearrange them if necessary by using numbers to indicate the order in which they should appear. Then check to see if you included enough specifics to show what you mean. Look through your getting-started materials for details and add them to the paper.

Then focus on the ending. Have you pulled together all the ideas presented in the middle? If not, add material or repeat words and phrases that help tie together your ideas. Also, decide if the ideas you left out indicate that the material in the middle section may not belong in the paper. Then think about how you want to affect the reader and decide if the conclusion reinforces that purpose. Will the reader understand your feelings or ideas? Will he realize that he has gained new information? Or will he feel compelled to act or think differently?

Finally, focus on the beginning. Does it reach out and capture your attention? Will it capture your reader's attention? If you think not, consider raising a question, giving background information, or entertaining your reader in some way. Then think about how you prepared the reader for what will come in the middle section. If there is not enough background information to introduce the subject, look through your getting-started materials for details. Or if you find that the main idea is not clear enough, restate it more specifically or omit any information that sidetracks you from the main idea.

Use the work you have done to answer the following questions before turning to page 139, "Writing the First Draft":

1. What will I do to make the ideas easy to follow?
2. What will I do to make the reader interested in my ideas?

OPTION B. Read what you have written. Then write an outline of the zero draft, using complete sentences to show the ideas discussed in the beginning, middle, and end. This does not need to be a formal outline, but it should show in the order in which ideas are presented and how you will make them interesting.

Next, read over the outline. Are the ideas organized in a logical and understandable way? Draw lines through ideas that do not relate to the subject you want to discuss. Then, using numbers, indicate the order in which the ideas should be presented.

Now focus on the beginning. Do you want to continue reading after finishing the beginning? Will your reader? Do the ideas lead into the middle of the paper? Think about the changes you should make to interest your reader and to prepare him for the ideas presented in the middle section.

Consider how you have used specifics in the middle section. Have you shown the reader what you want to say? Look through your getting-started work if it is necessary to add information that will make your ideas easier to understand or more interesting.

Finally, focus on the ending. Does it tie together the ideas in the middle section? Does it leave the reader with the impression or effect you wanted? Cross out parts that do not fit and think about how you can make the reader react as you want him to.

Use the work you have done to answer the following questions. Then turn to "Writing the First Draft," p. 139.

1. What will I do to make the ideas easy to follow?
2. What will I do to make the reader interested in the ideas?

THE PARTS

Our student Lynn must see the parts of her paper before deciding how to organize them. She concentrates on what she wants to say about each part of the subject and how to make those ideas interesting. Then she decides how to arrange the ideas before writing the first draft. If certain parts or images come to you before you see how they all fit together, you might like to try Lynn's approach.

Look over the ideas you generated in the getting-started stage. What points or ideas have you decided to present that are part of the larger subject of your paper? Use as many sheets of paper as you have ideas and write one idea at the top of each sheet. Focusing on a single point or idea at a time, write what you want to say about it. After you have written on each point, go back and read your work. Think about how those sheets of paper can be arranged. Is there a natural or logical order? Can one point serve as the beginning or ending of your paper? Do any parts seem irrelevant?

After you decide how to organize the parts, look at each one to see if it is interesting and clear. Are there enough details to show the reader what you mean? Are there some details that interfere with your ideas?

Finally, consider what you want your introduction and conclusion to do. How will you introduce your reader to your ideas and then interest him? How can you prepare him for the points you will raise later? And for the conclusion, consider how you will tie together the ideas and what impression you want to make.

Looking at your answers to the above, consider the following questions:

1. What will I do to make the ideas easy to follow?
2. What will I do to make the reader interested in my ideas?

Answering these questions will prepare you for "Writing the First Draft," page 139.

TALKING OUT THE IDEAS

Several of our students have found that talking their ideas into a tape recorder helps them discover a form for the paper. If you find talking about your subject easier than writing about it, you should try this method.

Find a place where you will not be disturbed and where you can talk into a tape recorder. Reread what you wrote about your subject, audience, and purpose. With these ideas in mind, begin talking about your subject and discuss everything you want to say.

When you are finished, listen to the tape. Try to determine where you began to focus on your subject, where you began using specifics, and where you ended the discussion. Then write down a list of topics you addressed in the middle section. Look at them to see if a pattern emerges. Do all the ideas fit together? If not, what should be left out? For the remaining ideas, can you add more details to make them clearer or more interesting? Look through your getting-started work for this material.

Next, listen to the ending again. Write down the points you made. Did you just stop talking, or did you try to pull the ideas together? Do you think another listener would care about the ideas, react in some way, or understand the information given after listening to your conclusion? If not, think about the effect you want to make and how you can have a greater impact on your audience.

Listen to the beginning once more and write down a description of what you said and how you presented your ideas. Were you interested in the beginning? If not, what specifics and background can you add? Does the introduction lead into the ideas presented in the middle part of the discussion? If not, how can you emphasize the main idea? Write down any ideas that will make your introduction more interesting and understandable for the reader.

Use your notes and tape to answer the following questions:

1. What will I do to make the ideas easy to follow?
2. What will I do to make the reader interested in my ideas?

Once you can answer these questions, turn to page 139, "Writing the First Draft."

The Big Picture

Some writers like to have a general goal in mind for their work but prefer to discover the details of their ideas as they write. One short-story writer and essayist, Jorge Luis Borges, says that he always knows how his stories will begin and end before he starts, but that he has to write in order to find out what happens in the middle. This kind of writer has a "big picture" in mind, but he also needs the freedom to change or modify that picture as the ideas become clearer.

If this is the way you like to work, get a general view of your paper by using one of the following methods.

ROUGH PLAN

Many writers like to write down phrases or sentences that evoke ideas, memories, or emotions. These statements serve as a reminder of what the writer wants to accomplish, but they also provide the opportunity to experiment with different ideas or to follow creative impulses while writing.

If you want to try this approach, start by going through your getting-started materials and your statements about your reader and purpose. Underline the words, phrases, or sentences that sound especially good or that make you respond in some way. On a separate sheet of paper, copy them down in list fashion. Which ones are most interesting and help bring to mind a number of ideas, details, or images? Jot down some of these ideas as a reminder for later on. These specifics will help make your ideas interesting to the reader.

Next, consider what relationships exist among the ideas you have listed. Do they follow a time sequence? Do some of the ideas naturally follow or grow out of others? Or can you group some of the phrases and sentences into two or three larger categories? Number your list of words, phrases, and sentences to show the order that makes sense to you. Now, try writing a few sentences that identify your subject and how you plan to present it.

Finally, think about how you want to begin and end your draft. Do any of the phrases give you an idea about how you might catch your reader's attention? Do others give you an idea on how you can make your reader react at the end of your draft? Write down any insights you have and, if you want, rearrange your ideas and omit or add others so that you have a general plan for a beginning, a middle, and an end.

Once you have done this, use your plan to answer the following questions:

1. What will I do to make my ideas easy to follow?
2. What will I do to make my ideas interesting to the reader?

After answering these questions, move on to page 139, "Writing the First Draft."

SKETCH

Before carefully filling in the details, illustrators like to rough out their drawings by arranging the images they envision on paper or by sketching in the outlines of the figures that will appear in their work. Like these artists, some of our students need to see where their ideas fit in relationship to others before they consider the details. They sketch their ideas by using arrows, lines, bubbles, dots, and boxes that only they understand.

Other students use index cards. Carrie wrote about the first time she really got into trouble, not just because she disobeyed her mother but because she almost died. She knew she wanted to write about falling into the pond during the winter, and so she wrote down the main ideas on index cards so that she could move them around until the ideas followed a logical order.

Once she saw the order, Carrie decided that the most important part of the story was falling through the ice. She felt that leading up to that event would make her paper more dramatic and interesting,

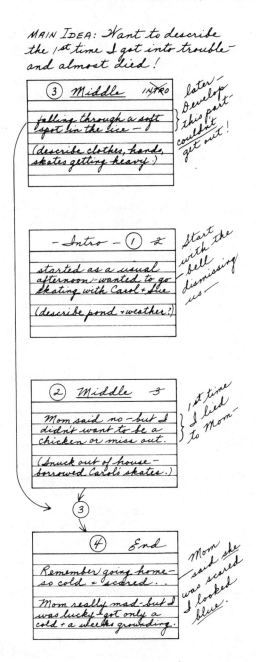

MAIN IDEA: Want to describe the 1st time I got into trouble — and almost died!

Middle ③ INTRO — later — Develop this part — couldn't get out!
falling through a soft spot in the ice —
(describe clothes, hands, skates getting heavy.)

Intro — ① 2 — Start with the bell dismissing us.
started as a usual afternoon — wanted to go skating with Carol + Sue
(describe pond + weather?)

Middle ② 3 — 1st time I lied to Mom —
Mom said no — but I didn't want to be a chicken or miss out.
(Snuck out of house — borrowed Carol's skates.)

③

End ④ — Mom said she was scared — I looked blue.
Remember going home — so cold + scared . .
Mom really mad — but I was lucky — got only a cold + a week's grounding.

so she changed the numbers of the cards and drew arrows to show the flow of ideas. When she felt she had a sequence that worked, she began filling in some of the details from her getting-started material that would help the reader feel what she went through that afternoon.

If you want to sketch your paper, start by writing your main idea and purpose at the top of a sheet of paper. Then find and summarize the major points of your main idea. To do these two steps, look through the getting-started material and the work on your purpose and audience. Put your major points on index cards or write them in boxes, bubbles, or groups under your main idea. Then start looking for the relationships among your ideas and use arrows, lines, or words to show the pattern you see. Remember, this process usually takes a few tries. Keep rearranging and modifying until you see how the pieces all fit together—or until you decide which pieces or ideas do belong in your big picture.

Once you think you have a workable sketch of your paper, start filling in with words or phrases that remind you of how you can develop your ideas. Look at your getting-started materials for the specifics you need to interest your reader and to make your ideas clear.

Looking at your sketch, consider the following questions:

1. What will I do to make my ideas easy to follow?
2. What will I do to make the reader interested in my ideas?

Answering these will prepare you for "Writing the First Draft," page 139.

JOURNALISTIC APPROACH

Journalists use the headings *who, what, where, when* and *why* to categorize their material. Then, depending on the point they want to emphasize in the piece, they stress one or more of the *w's*. For example, a journalist covering a plane crash might give the *what, when,* and *where* in the lead or first paragraph. The *who*—the people involved, the number of survivors—and the *why*—what caused the crash, how the investigation is proceeding—will be the focus of the rest of the article.

To use this approach, spread out your getting-started materials and the work on your purpose and audience. Then arrange the ideas according to the five headings. Make marginal notations or separate notes on another sheet of paper. If you find that you do not have material for each heading, decide whether you need it for this paper. If you do, generate more information by brainstorming or thinking through your ideas once more. If the information seems unnecessary, decide which category you will emphasize in your work.

Determine what information or material can be used for the introduction, the center of your paper, and the conclusion. Finally, consider what specifics you need to make your ideas interesting and clear to your reader.

Use your notes and ideas to answer the following questions:

1. What will I do to make my ideas easy to follow?
2. What will I do to make the reader interested in my ideas?

Then turn to "Writing the First Draft," page 139.

INTRODUCTION

As a reader, you know how an introduction can engage your interest in a subject. As a writer, doing an introduction for yourself can help clarify what you want to say and can give you direction in presenting your ideas.

If this technique sounds useful, imagine that instead of writing a paper, you are going to present your ideas in a speech. You are sitting behind the podium, waiting to be announced, and the master of ceremonies begins his introduction. Would he say, "Ladies and gentlemen, our guest speaker tonight will *tell us of his travels on the Amazon,*" suggesting a story or narrative? Or would he begin with, "Tonight, our speaker is going to explain *how you, too, can be a fine Italian cook,*" implying that you will give your audience the steps for preparing pastas, white sauces, and rum cake desserts? Or would your host say, "Our speaker tonight, ladies and gentlemen, will *show you that unlike other sports, mountain climbing is more exciting than . . .,*" suggesting that you will contrast the thrill of hanging by a rope in the Himalayas to that of sinking a putt or shooting a basket?

Think about what you want to say and how you might be announced at an after-dinner gathering, departmental meeting, or school rally. Will you be telling a story? Raising several points? Contrasting or comparing things? Or showing a process? What plan will you use to present your ideas? What ideas do you want to talk about first? Second? Third? Or fourth? What final impact do you want to have on your audience?

Once you have considered these issues, begin thinking about how you will make your ideas interesting to your audience. How will you catch their interest at the beginning and help them see your ideas later on? Jot down any ideas you get by looking at your getting-started work and what you wrote about your reader and purpose.

Use your answers and notes to consider the following questions:

1. What will I do to make my ideas easy to follow?
2. What will I do to make the reader interested in my ideas?

Once you can answer these questions, move on to "Writing the First Draft," p. 139.

CONCLUSION

One day in class, a student said, "I guess this will sound crazy, but I always start with my conclusion first. Once I do that, I can write what leads up to it." Not crazy at all—knowing where you want to end can often help you plan the best route for getting there. If you work better with a goal in mind, you might want to try this approach.

Read your getting-started material and the statements you made about your purpose and audience. Pretend that you have just written your paper, and all that is left is the conclusion. Go ahead and write it.

Once you have finished, read it over to see what point you made and what impression you left. What points or ideas in your getting-started work will lead up to the main idea or conclusion you have drawn? Did you want to give information in your paper? Persuade or convince your audience? Entertain the reader? What material in your getting-started work will emphasize this purpose?

Write down the ideas that lead to your conclusion and look at them to find some order. What relationships do you see? Which idea should come first? Second? Third? Fourth? Which one might serve to introduce your paper?

Finally, consider how you will interest your reader and make your ideas understandable. Will you use experiences, facts, or descriptions? Use your getting-started materials and jot down any ideas.

Once you have finished, use your answer and notes to consider the following questions:

1. What will I do to make my ideas easy to follow?
2. What will I do to make my ideas interesting to my reader?

Answering these questions will prepare you for "Writing the First Draft," page 139.

The Formal Plan

Some writers are comfortable and secure in writing their first draft only when they have a detailed plan. To achieve greater control over their work, they might use a thesis statement that directs their ideas, an outline that organizes all the details, a diagram that tells them what to say and when, or a rhetorical form that groups and orders their ideas. If you are this kind of person, these approaches will appeal to you. In most cases, you will find that they work best after using an organic or big-picture approach.

TENTATIVE THESIS

In its final form, a thesis tells the reader what the writer will say. It prepares him for the ideas by focusing on a single subject, making an assertion about it, and predicting the pattern of the paper. In this form, the final thesis is designed to help the reader. The tentative thesis does exactly what the final thesis does, but, instead of being designed for the the reader, it serves to help the writer identify the subject, decide what he wants to say about it, and determine how he will present his ideas. And because it is a tentative guide, it is often revised once the writer sees his ideas on paper or has a new perspective on his subject.

If this approach sounds helpful, then first focus on your subject. Read the statements you made about it at the end of your getting-started work. In a sentence or two, write down what you want to discuss. Then focus on the person, place, thing, or idea. Have you limited this statement as much as possible? For instance, have you used a word such as *people* when you really mean *college students my age?* Or have you used an abstract term such as *privacy* when you want to say *the right to have one's own room?* Look at your subject carefully to see if you can state it more precisely.

Next, look at what you have said about your subject. Have you stated it in a general way? For example, if you were making an assertion about our national forests, did you simply say "They should be preserved" when you wanted to say "They should be preserved to ensure the balance of oxygen and carbon dioxide in our atmosphere?" Think again about what you want to prove and state it as directly as you can.

Now look over your statements about the subject, reader, and purpose. How are you going to arrange your ideas to make them easy to follow and interesting for the reader? Does any organizational pattern emerge? For example, if you were to use the thesis "Our national forests should be preserved to ensure the balance of oxygen and carbon dioxide in our atmosphere," would you want to write a narrative piece depicting life in 2001 without an abundance of oxygen on our planet? Or would you prefer to interest the reader and arrange your ideas by comparing the effect of city air on people today with its effect on people 100 years ago? Or would you explain the major contributions our forests make to that nation's ecology?

There are different ways to state these relationships and to indicate what pattern you want to use for your draft. Notice how the following tentative thesis statements predict the form of the paper.

From the moment we left in her jeep, I knew my back-packing trip in the Grand Canyon with my seventy-three-year-old grandmother would be an experience to remember.

Here, the italicized words signal a story that will probably be told in chronological order.

> *Because my seventy-three-year-old grandmother does not consider herself old, she still does unusual things*, such as backpacking in Grand Canyon National Park.

This tentative thesis indicates a cause-and-effect relationship between the grandmother's attitudes and her actions.

> *Unlike most seventy-three-year-olds*, my grandmother is still active. *Instead of staying home and watching television*, she went backpacking last spring in the Grand Canyon.

The italicized sections in these sentences suggest a contrast that will be developed by describing her trip.

> My grandmother is still young at seventy-three *because* she does not consider herself old. She keeps doing new things each year, and she spends as much time as possible with younger people to keep up with the changes in society.

Here, the italicized word shows why the writer's grandmother is still young by leading to the reasons (or causes) for her youthfulness.

Try writing a tentative thesis to guide you through the first draft by limiting the subject, by making a specific assertion about the subject, and by suggesting an organizational pattern.

Then test your tentative statement by answering the following questions:

1. What will I do to make the ideas easy to follow?
2. What will I do to make the reader interested in the ideas?

Go through your getting-started materials for ideas and specifics that will help you answer these questions. Then turn to page 139, "Writing the First Draft."

TENTATIVE OUTLINE

Are you a person who plans your life carefully and fully? For example, if you will be taking a trip, do you trace your route on a map, plan just how far you will drive each day, and call ahead for motel reservations? If so, you will find that one of the following outlining techniques will give you more control when writing.

MAKING A TENTATIVE OUTLINE*. Some writers like to know what they will do in the beginning, middle, and end of their work, as well as what they will say in each part. Therefore, they make a tentative outline of their ideas to discover the pattern of their paper. These outlines are not like the formal ones discussed in handbooks, but tentative maps of where the writer will go, what points he will develop, how he will organize them, and what specifics he will use to develop those points. Because writing the first draft is still part of the discovery process, the writer remains flexible enough with the tentative outline to change ideas or the direction of the paper if new insights occur to him. And even though the writer uses the guide for his first draft, the final draft may be different from the initial plan.

To use this method, first look over your getting-started material. Write the subject of the paper at the top of another page and then read the work on your reader and purpose. Now you must make a decision about the form your paper will take. Keeping in mind your reader and effect you want to have on him, decide whether:

A. You want to state the conclusion about your subject first and then prove or show why it is correct or valid in the middle section.
B. You want the reader to be a detective who must pick up the clues in the beginning and middle sections that lead him to the conclusion you present at the end.

OPTION A: DEDUCTIVE PATTERN. If you decide to present your conclusions about the subject at the beginning of your paper and then add specifics, you have chosen to use the deductive method. That is, you will present the generalization first, and then proceed to support and develop it. For example, if you have realized that "The Niagara River has been polluted by the chemical companies adjacent to it," you would state this idea at the end of the introduction and use the body of the paper to support it. Then you might restate the idea in the conclusion to wrap up your work.

A tentative outline for this subject and assertion might look like this:

Beginning: Background info—in 1955 fishermen began to notice that . . .

End with: People in the Niagara Falls area realize that the river is being polluted by the chemical companies there.

---

*If you are doing a research paper, see the Final Note on this technique, page 132.

Middle:	Now mention facts:
	1. Plant life is deteriorating because . . .
	Plants affected are . . .
	When this happens, the water becomes . . .
	The cause for this deterioration is . . . and the company producing this chemical is . . .
	2. Fish populations are dying—mention perch, trout, and walleye.
	This is happening because . . .
	This shows that the water cannot . . .
	Tests and company documents show that . . .
	The long-range effects of this will be . . .
Ending:	Restate what is happening.
	But also mention that something must be done.
	People must . . .
	Government must . . .

The writer using this outline might change a point or two, re-arrange the order of the specifics, or leave out certain points once he starts writing and ideas become clearer. However, this outline does give him a firm grasp on his subject, purpose, and specifics as well as control his writing.

OPTION B: INDUCTIVE PATTERN. On the other hand, if you decide to make the reader a detective who comes to the same conclusion you have reached, you will be presenting your ideas in an inductive manner. That is, you will present specifics first, and then state the generalization in the conclusion. For example, using the same subject as before, you would start by suggesting that the Niagara has undergone many changes in the last twenty-five years, some of them troubling. This is a hypothesis that you would investigate and prove by citing evidence of the changes caused by pollution. By piling fact upon fact in the middle section of your paper, you (and your reader) would conclude that the Niagara River has been polluted by the chemical companies in the surrounding areas.

An outline for this paper is quite similar to the preceding one, but the emphasis is different:

Beginning:	Describe the changes—fewer fishermen, less boating, swimming areas closed in the falls and river areas.
	At the same time, many chemical companies have plants built there because . . .
Middle:	Why there are fewer fisherman—
	Fewer fish, contaminated fish (mention perch, walleye, trout)

Source of contamination is . . .

Company that produces this is . . .

They came to the area in 1955 just before the changes.

Second reason for fewer fish is loss of plant life . . .

Caused by . . .

Manufactured by . . . who moved to the area in 1957.

Ending: People in the Niagara Falls area realize that the river is being polluted by the chemical companies.

This means that people cannot use the facilities— only look at them. Few tourists realize the seriousness of this.

People should write . . .

That way, the waters can be made safe again.

Again, this outline orders the material for the writer and gives him control over the ideas. There is still room for changes or additions, but the goal and direction of the paper are clear.

If you want to choose one of these outlining methods, spread out your getting-started material and your work on the reader and purpose. In a sentence or two, state the subject and how you want to affect your reader. Then decide if it is best to give your main idea at the beginning or to lead up to it in the conclusion. Once you have done that, you can plan your outline.

Beginning: Decide what information you want there, and how it will affect your reader and prepare him for the middle section.

State this decision in complete sentences.

Middle: Think about the evidence or points you want to present.

Write each point as an assertion, and jot down the specifics that make that assertion clear and interesting for the reader.

Ending: Finally, plan what you want your conclusion to do for you and your reader. Consider your purpose for this paper, and write down the information and ideas that will reinforce it.

When you finish your outline, make sure you can answer the following questions before turning to page 139, "Writing the First Draft."

1. What will I do to make the ideas easy to follow?
2. What will I do to make my reader interested in these ideas?

Final note. This approach often works well when you are writing longer or more formal papers, such as research projects. If you decide to use an outline for a term paper or longer report, you can modify it by using index cards along with a rough outline.

After you have decided on the general direction of your paper by using a rough outline, write down the specific points you want to make on index cards—one point to a card. Then fill in the cards with notes or references that will support that point. This will make it easier if you want to rearrange, add, or leave out any ideas.

Once you have established an order for your ideas, number or mark the cards so that you know how they correspond to your outline. The outline will help you keep in mind the overall goal and direction of your paper.

TRADITIONAL RHETORICAL FORMS

Subjects for papers sometimes suggest the preestablished patterns of one of the traditional rhetorical forms. These organizational forms include narration, spatial description, comparison/contrast, cause and effect, process analysis and argumentation. To determine whether you can use one of these patterns, look over your getting-started materials to see if you can present your subject by:

a. Telling a story ("Narration," p. 132).
b. Showing spatial movement, going from left to right, inward to outward, top to bottom, inside to outside ("Spatial Description," p. 133).
c. Comparing or contrasting two or more subjects ("Comparison/Contrast," p. 134).
d. Showing a cause-and-effect relationship (("Cause and Effect," p. 136).
e. Presenting a step-by-step description of a process ("Process Analysis," p. 136).
f. Presenting a position and defending it ("Argumentation," p. 137).

If your getting-started material indicates that your subject may be organized by one of these traditional rhetorical forms, read the explanation of the appropriate form noted above. Then move to the "Conclusion," page 138, to complete this method.

NARRATION. Narratives or stories rely on time order for their organization. Generally, they fall into one of the following patterns.

Starts at the beginning. Some works start at the beginning of an event and progress forward. Marilyn Krysl's essay, "Genie Women," on page 255, follows this pattern. She opens with the sentence "Sundays were different . . ." and recounts the events of a typical Sunday for her. The work starts with an account of the women family members dressing for the day. Next, she moves to the scenes during and then after the church service, and on to the preparation and eating of Sunday dinner. Then she concludes with the afternoon nap. The following diagram illustrates the movement of the work.

1. Bedroom Scene *Beginning* → 2. Church Service → 3. Sunday Dinner → 4. Nap *End*

Starts in the middle. Some works follow a modified version of the pattern just described. They start in the middle of the action, go back to events preceding that point, and then move forward in time. The following diagram shows how Krysl's piece would look if it had followed such a pattern.

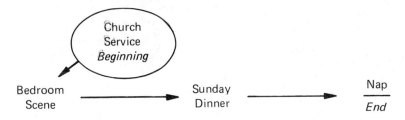

Following this order, Krysl would have started with the events in church, flashed back to the account of the women dressing, and then moved forward to the scenes following the church service.

Starts at the end. Works that open after the action has occurred employ a third pattern. The story begins with the final scene and then traces the earlier events that led up to it. Had Krysl used this approach, she would have started with the nap scene and then would have shown the events leading to it.

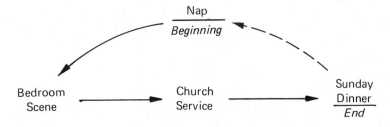

SPATIAL DESCRIPTION. Spacial descriptions rarely provide the form for whole works; more often, they order a paragraph or section of the paper. This form organizes movement from left to right, front to back, top to bottom, inward to outward, and outward to inward. Henry David Thoreau used the inward-to-outward movement in the first paragraph of "The Ponds," page 248, to describe the pond, then the trees, and then the hills surrounding the pond. Beginning with the lake, he says, "A lake is the landscape's most beautiful and expressive feature. It is earth's eye; looking into which the beholder measures the depth of his own nature." Then he moves outward to describe the trees: "The fluviatile trees next the shore are slender eyelashes which fringe it." And, moving outward to the hills, Thoreau writes, "and the wooded hills and cliffs around are overhanging brows."

The following diagram illustrates the movement of Thoreau's first paragraph.

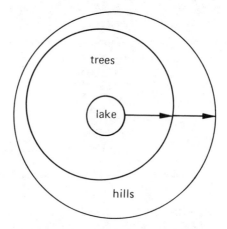

Other works might describe movement from inside a room to the out-of-doors or from one place to another. Alfred Kazin in "The Block and Beyond," page 253, describes his movement away from his home, down the street to Blake Avenue, and beyond Blake Avenue to the park and the fields.

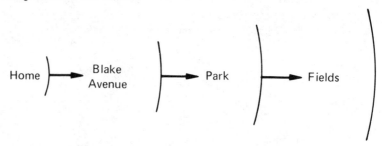

COMPARISON/CONTRAST. Comparison shows how two or more topics are similar, and contrast shows how topics are different. Works following these forms can be organized in two ways.

Subject by subject. Works using the subject-by-subject pattern give all the information about one subject and then all the information about the other. For example, if the writer wants to show a contrast between two vacation spots, he would discuss all the pros and cons of one place and then all the pros and cons of the other.

Germaine Greer uses a subject-by-subject pattern in her essay "The Stereotype," page 327. In the first part of the essay, she develops society's view of women. By focusing on elements of women's physical appearance, she shows what traits make up the feminine stereotype. In the second part of the essay, Greer presents her objection to equating femininity with physical appearance. In this way, she shows the contrast between her beliefs and those of society. The following diagram shows the subject-by-subject pattern she uses.

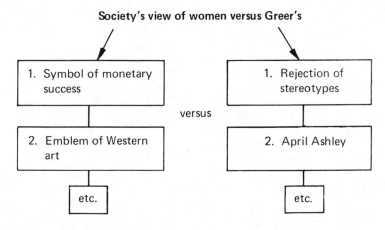

Point by point. In works using the point-by-point form, the writer deals with each point of the comparison or contrast, showing how the subjects are similar or different on each point. For example, if a writer used this method to compare and contrast two vacation spots, he might first consider the climate of both places, then the entertainment facilities, and finally the costs.

E. B. White uses the point-by-point pattern in his essay "Walden," p. 318, to compare his experiences in the Concord and Walden Pond areas with Thoreau's. First, he focuses on his experiences in Concord and shows how they contrast to Thoreau's. Then he focuses on Walden Pond and illustrates how the area has changed since Thoreau lived there. Finally, he shows what his trip cost and how his expenses far exceeded Thoreau's. The following diagram illustrates this pattern.

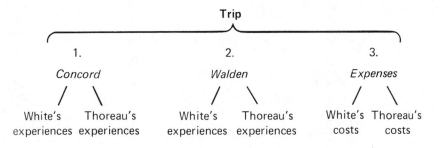

CAUSE AND EFFECT. Cause-and-effect patterns show the relationships between causes and effects. Works using this form can be organized in one of two ways.

Effect to cause. Some writers present an effect that is known and then consider the causes leading up to it. For example, a writer might state that a flood occurred and then explore its possible causes.

An example of this pattern is presented in Sydney Harris's column, "Burden of Parental Love Can Be Too Heavy to Bear," page 284. In the opening, he states the effect: "The boy returned home from college for the Christmas holidays, and he seemed drawn and depressed." In the rest of the piece, Harris explores the possible causes for the boy's state. A diagram of his column shows this relationship.

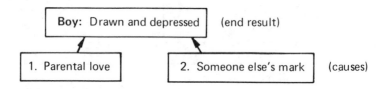

Cause to effect. Some works present a cause that is known and then consider the effects growing out of it. A writer using this pattern to discuss a flood would first state that the dam burst and then explore the consequences of this event.

Dennis Farney uses this pattern to present his subject in "Trying to Restore a Sea of Grass," page 322. In an early paragraph, he says, "Whatever the [cause], there is a growing appreciation for the landscape." In the remainder of the piece, he explains what is happening because of that attitude. The following diagram shows how he used the cause-to-effect pattern.

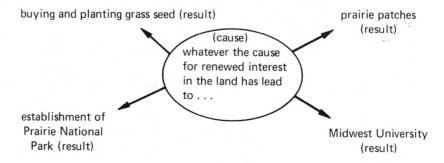

PROCESS ANALYSIS. A process analysis breaks up a process into steps and presents these steps in a sequential pattern. Works following this pattern are arranged like the recipe on the back of a box of brownies or the directions for assemblying a carburetor.

Edward T. Thompson uses a process pattern in "How to Write Clearly," page 337. His subject is broken down into seven steps:

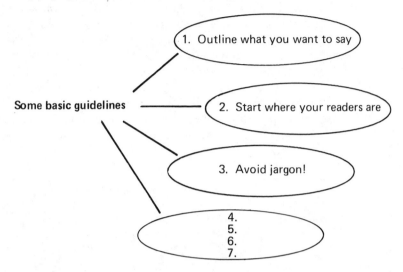

ARGUMENTATION. Argumentative pieces present a proposition or thesis in the opening section and support it in the rest of the essay. A number of patterns are used to persuade the reader to accept the writer's views.

Thesis and support. Some works state a thesis at the end of the introductory paragraph and then offer support in the following paragraphs to persuade the reader to accept this position. The thesis is then restated in the conclusion.

Nickie McWhirter's piece, "After All, Moss Is Kind of Nice Stuff," page 300, uses this pattern. She states her thesis, "We tend to live according to cliches, and for every useful one there are a couple of others that are downright dangerous to the human psyche," in the first sentence of the work.

Her following paragraphs present examples to support this proposition. Then in the conclusion, she restates the thesis: "Cliches and I never got along very well after the fifth grade."

The following diagram shows how she used this form.

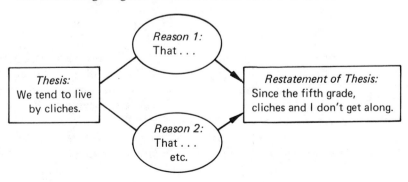

Thesis, opposition, concession or refutation, and support. Writers who use the pattern of thesis, opposition, concession or refutation, and support follow one of two forms. Both forms state the thesis in the introduction. The next part either presents the *opposition's* stand and *concedes* that it has some validity, or it presents the *opposition's* stand and *refutes* it. The final section in both forms presents *support* to convince the reader that the thesis is true.

Henry David Thoreau in "Civil Disobedience," page 308, uses the second form. He states his thesis in the introduction and then presents the opposition's views and refutes them. Then he supports his own position in the rest of the essay. A diagram of the form he used looks like this:

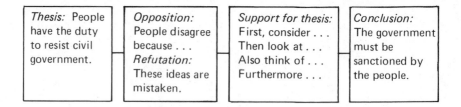

Had Thoreau used the first form, a diagram of his ideas would have looked like this:

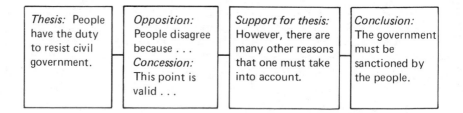

CONCLUSION

If you still think you can use one of these forms after reading the explanation, look through the getting-started material and your work on the reader and purpose. State your subject and purpose in a sentence or two; then diagram your ideas, using the appropriate rhetorical form as a guide. Does the pattern suggest an interesting and understandable way to present your subject? If so, use it and write down the specifics you can use to illustrate your ideas.

If you find that the form is not useful, do not try to force your subject into a pattern it does not innately possess. Perhaps the form you are considering is useful for only part of the paper; you may need to choose another form for the rest of it.

Once you have diagrammed your ideas and filled in your plan with specifics, answer the following questions:

1. What will I do to make my ideas easy to follow?
2. What will I do to make my reader interested in these ideas?

Now turn to the next section, "Writing the First Draft."

WRITING THE FIRST DRAFT

Preparing the First Draft

By now, you have done a great deal of writing and thinking to discover what you want to write about, who your reader will be, how you want him to react to your ideas, and how you can present your ideas in an interesting and understandable way. This work has prepared you for the next stage of the discovery process, writing the first draft. But remember, even though you have considered these writer's concerns carefully, you may continue to gain new insights into your subject and how you will present it to a reader.

Although we have given you several methods for approaching the other stages of the discovery process, we cannot do so for this step. However, we can share with you some advice from other writers and our students. Writer William Zinsser says that too many writers try to "commit an act of literature" in their first draft. Instead of being eloquent and profound in the first draft, Zinsser suggests concentrating on what you want to say. There is plenty of time later on for revising and rewriting.

In "The Impulse to Write," page 332, Ray Bradbury comments on how one should approach writing—especially the first draft:

> If you are writing without zest, without gusto, without love, without fun, you are only half a writer.... For the first thing a writer should be is excited. He should be a thing of fevers and enthusiasms. Without such vigor, he might as well be out picking peaches or digging ditches. God knows it'd be better for his health.

And commenting on the writing process, he says:

> The history of each story, then, should read almost like a weather report: Hot today, cool tomorrow. This afternoon, burn down the house. Tomorrow, pour cold critical water upon the simmering coals. Time enough to think and cut and rewrite tomorrow. But today—explode—fly apart—disintegrate! The other six or seven drafts are going to be pure torture. So why not enjoy the first draft, in the hope that your joy will seek and find others in the world who, reading your story, will catch fire, too?

So if you take Bradbury's advice, enjoy writing the first draft and ignite the reader with your interest as well.

Along with this advice, our students pass on these suggestions:

- Write your subject on a 3 X 5 index card and keep it in front of you as you write.
- Rehearse your paper in your head. Listen to the words before you put them on paper.
- Talk the paper into a tape recorder while looking at your map, diagram, or outline.
- Get excited about the subject. Imagine that you are the only person in the world who can discuss it and that your paper will affect the course of the world!
- Once you are ready to write, don't talk to anyone about your ideas. You might lose your excitement.
- Write until you finish the whole draft. Don't stop, because it's hard to get back on the same track.
- Find a place where you like to be alone. Try the library, student union, or somewhere outside.

Should you get stuck somewhere in this stage and realize that you are writing in circles, turn to the last part of this chapter, pages 143-145, for suggestions on getting unstuck. And if you are doing a longer research work, look at the next section for alternatives to writing complete first drafts. When you have completed the first draft, move on to Chapter 4 to get a reader's reaction to what you have written.

Preparing the First Draft of Research Projects

When writing research papers or business or project reports, it is not always possible to write complete first drafts because of time limits or your need to do further research. And it is not always easy to find a reader who has the time to read through fifteen to twenty pages of handwritten material. However, it is still important to try out your ideas in order to see if they are interesting and easy to follow.

Two alternatives to writing a complete first draft are talking through an outline and filling in the details as you speak, or writing an introduction and conclusion to detailed notecards and giving this material to a reader.

OUTLINE APPROACH

Express your major ideas in complete sentences, and write down the specifics as notes to remind you of your research. Try to reinforce the relationships among your ideas so that you help the listener know what you are doing and where you plan to go. For example:

Beginning

In the beginning, I want to give some background on the American automobile industry.

Henry Ford — Detroit, Mich.
1920's — Ford built . . . .
 People worked . . .
1950's — Industry had grown . . .
 Competition from . . .

This will help the reader for my main idea: There was little change in the industry's philosophy until recent social and economic pressures arose.

Middle

1. The first social pressure came during the 1960s.

— Familys were having fewer children so they needed . . .
— More mothers were working which created a market for . . .

2. The second social pressure came during the 1970s.

People became more interested in the foreign car because . . .

3. Now, explain what effects these pressures had on the industry.

— The change in the family unit created . . .
This resulted in . . .
— Demand for foreign cars produced . . .

4. The first major economic event that pressured . . . etc.

With more people working, the economy blossomed. This ment the car industry . . .

Ending

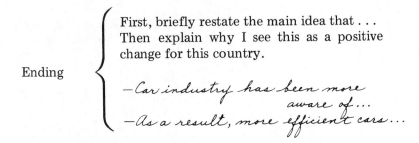

First, briefly restate the main idea that . . .
Then explain why I see this as a positive
change for this country.

—Car industry has been more
             aware of . . .
—As a result, more efficient cars . . .

DETAILED CARD APPROACH

Look over your cards and decide what information can be used for the introduction, middle, and conclusion of your paper. Review the cards for the middle section and summarize the main idea you want to make. Then, using the other cards as a guide, write a first draft of your introduction and conclusion.

Looking once more at the cards for the middle section, arrange them in the order that makes your ideas easy to follow. For each group of cards that deals with a specific point in your paper, write down the point or main idea and how it relates to the whole paper. Do this on separate notecards. The process will help your reader or listener understand what points you are making and how they relate to one another and to the whole paper.

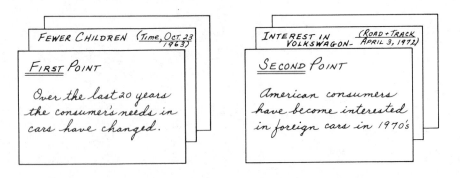

Either approach works well if you want to read and talk through your ideas. The second approach is better if you prefer having someone read your work. Remember, even though this is a more formal writing assignment, let your excitement show in presenting your ideas and in any writing you do. What is most interesting to you and your reader will help you limit your subject when you consider writing out a complete draft. You will find that with most research projects, you will have far more information than you can use; so, it is very important to find a way of limiting your subject.

© 1979 United Feature Syndicate, Inc.

GETTING UNSTUCK

Even with all the writing and planning you did before starting to write the first draft, you still may find that, like Sally, you have not accomplished much. There are many reasons for this problem. To help you get unstuck and begin writing again, we suggest you try to understand why you have developed a writer's block. Look over the following techniques to find out why you are getting nowhere and to see how you can get started again.

When you can write again and have finished the first draft, turn to Chapter 5 to continue the process.

1. *Did you choose a subject you cared about?* You might have thought you wanted to write about this subject, but it is possible that you are not as excited about it as you imagined. Look back over what you wrote about your reason for wanting to discuss this subject. Did you answer the questions honestly? If not, and if you do not feel like writing with gusto, love, or fun, then go back to the getting-started stage and review your writing. Look for a better topic or try another approach that will help you discover a topic you *really* do want to write about.

2. *Did you choose a subject that is too painful or personal to explore?* Remember Lawrence Langer's essay, "Human Use of Language," page 12? Are you trying to write about something you still cannot talk about or share with a reader? If this is the case, focus on another subject or another aspect of that experience that is less difficult to discuss and write about it. Or use another technique from the getting-started stage that will direct you to a topic you can write about.

3. *Are you trying to write about a subject you do not fully understand?* This can happen if you are writing about something you have just learned or read. Before you can write about the subject, you must understand it and feel confident about discussing it. To do this, reread the material and discuss it with a friend or classmate. Or

pretend you are teaching this subject to your class. Focus on what is important by listing the main ideas you discuss. Use this process as your getting-started technique and continue writing for fifteen to twenty minutes on these topics. Once you are more familiar with your subject, start writing the first draft again.

4. *Are you too worried about the reader's reactions?* If you are concerned about the reader's response, remember that you will share this first draft with someone who will simply let you know how well you are communicating your ideas. Try writing this draft for a friend or close relative. Or try writing yourself a letter explaining why you are having trouble with this draft and what you really want to say. Then use these ideas to help you write the first draft.

5. *Are you being too critical, judging too soon, trying to be perfect?* Ah ha! You *do* have a watcher. Perhaps you did not think so when you read Godwin's essay, "Watcher at the Gates," in Chapter 1. Go back and reread it now. Then use one of her suggestions to confront the bully. Draw a picture of him, write him a letter, hold the pen for him. Or trick him by writing on different-colored paper with green ink or on the back of a math test. Then try writing your first draft again.

6. *Are the distractions of the outside world keeping you from thinking?* Get away from the telephone, television, stereo, and conversations with friends or roommates. Go someplace quiet and peaceful where you can think. Listen to your ideas and try writing again.

7. *Are you concentrating on how your paper will be evaluated?* This is an honest concern, given the importance of grades in our educational system. If your ideas are becoming secondary to the mark you might receive, read the passage below. It comes from Ivan Doig's autobiography, *This House of Sky*, and in it he recounts one of his first experiences with grades in college. Doig was from a small town in Minnesota where he had always done well in school. But then came those first traumatic weeks at school, and his first test:

> Small tight penciling at the top of the quiz paper: *Please see me after class.* Above the words, like a cold half-moon hung over a battlefield, the reason: the grade of D, the first of my life. The history class went its hour with fear after fear sawing at the back of my mouth. *Godalmighty, am I going to flunk out of here? . . . must have been a mistake, must . . . what will I tell . . . what could I have . . . how am I going to . . .* After eternity, the bell rang, the instructor walked me to his office. In a dozen steadying ways he said a single thing: that memorized dates and facts would not carry me in college as they had in high school, I must think out essay answers now. When I at last stood to leave, his wide, horn-rimmed glasses caught me like headlights. *Don't let it throw you, Mr. Doig. You'll do better here than*

you've started out. Those first earthquake weeks of Northwestern, his was the one classroom voice to say such words to me. His course was the one I felt my way through to my first college grade of A.

The teacher's comments show that he did understand and did care about how well Doig did. His advice to Doig was sound: Concentrating on minor details will not make anyone a better writer. But thinking about what those details mean and what is important to say will.

If your concern over grades is keeping you from writing, then remember that you will not be graded on this draft. You have many opportunities to rewrite and revise before handing it in for a mark. Try again, and give your creative impulses freer reign.

CHAPTER 5

Reader Reaction: Discovering How Well You Have Communicated Your Ideas

Reviewer's Response

The proposal for <u>Discovery to Discourse</u> demonstrates that the authors are capable of accomplishing the objectives they set for the text. I am particularly impressed by the direct, honest tone used in the sample material. The questions, exercises and examples are, generally, pertinent. Occasionally, however, they need ___ ain them- selves more completely. Points II and III in Chapter 4 ___ t as clearly developed as points I and IV where specif ___ assign- ments amplifies the authors' theme ___

2. Though it is ___ ___ certain text ___ cular pes) chieve

MACMILLAN PUBLISHING CO., INC.
866 Third Avenue, New York, N.Y. 10022

Questions for Referees

Kirschner/Yates: DISCOVERY TO DISCOURSE: THE COMPOSING PROCESS

1. From the material submitted do you feel the authors will accomplish the objectives they set forth in the prospectus?

2. Can the theory outlined in this book be applied to another composition text? Specifically, could you use the format outlined in this text in your classroom without adopting this book?

3. Is the material written in a style that your students would find under- standable? Enjoyable? Is sufficient motivation provided to sustain the student reader's interest?

4. What do you think of the reading selections? Will they be effective pedagogically? Will they hold the student's interest? Are the ques- tions and exercises applied to the reading selections appropriate and motivating?

5. Will the writing assignments ease the student writer into the process of writing?

6. The authors intersperse many questions which, overall, seem rhetorical, but which are, in fact, for use by the student as he or she proceeds from a rough draft to a finished product. Do you think the form in which these questions are posed will confuse students or be ignored by them? In other words, do you see the design of this book as a problem to its adoption? Can this problem be eliminated by the publisher's design of the finished product?

7. What is your opinion of the sample feedback and editing forms? Will they be effective in assisting the student to go from rough draft to final form?

8. Do you like the authors' use of conference-centered techniques? Have you ever used this method to advantage in the classroom? Do you believe the authors' conference-centered techniques outlined in the material would work in the classroom?

9. Using the text outline contained in the prospectus, do you feel that the "apparatus" accomplishes the "objectives"? Are any "objectives" or "apparatus" included that you feel would be ineffective? Can you think of any "objectives" or "apparatus" that would be more effective?

10. Would you advise Macmillan to publish a text derived from this begin- ning?

11. Would you consider assigning this text in your own courses?

This stage of the process gives you the chance to have a reader react to the ideas in your first draft. You will be working in pairs or small groups, reading or listening to each other's work, and describing your reactions to what another writer has said. At this stage of the process, you will become a reader whose job is to tell the writer how a reader will look at his work. Assuming this role will also prepare you for looking at your own writing from a reader's perspective.

Like the other stages of the writing process, responding to writing takes practice and patience. And as Barb Zakowski points out, it requires an open attitude.

Reader Reaction—Does It Help?

I feel that having a paper read by a classmate is extremely important and helpful if the person is honest and willing to write down what he feels can be useful to the author.

Very often I find that people are too lenient and polite when they respond to a paper. They tend to write down all positive points because they feel guilty or foolish cutting down the paper. This does not benefit the author at all. The reason for getting reader reaction to a paper is to receive a second or third opinion. Let's face it, in most cases there is room for improvement in any paper. The job of the reader is to make helpful comments so that the author can go back and write an even better paper.

Fortunately, I had a very good reader. Kim Zilke helped me out in many ways. She did encourage me and said that I could have a very good paper. But she also pointed out to me that my ideas weren't developed clearly. She told me that I needed to have some "backing" for what I said. She also told me that examples would help a lot and would help tie the ideas together, too. And she brought to my attention that my conclusion was weak. Then she gave me what I hope was a good idea for a conclusion.

After Kim finished reading and reacting to my paper, I went back and rewrote the whole paper, trying to develop and link my ideas together. I do feel that there was a definite improvement from my first rough draft to the second. Therefore, I feel having a reader's reaction is very beneficial to the writer and should be used when writing any paper!

As you can see from Barb's comments, sharing a first draft can be crucial to the success of an essay, business report, or editorial. However, readers sometimes feel that they cannot be helpful in this role;

or they may even feel uncomfortable reacting honestly to what they read. If you feel this way, first, remember what Barb, a student and writer, has said. Second, keep in mind that you will be using reader reaction forms that will guide you through the paper. These forms ask you to describe your reactions or to point out what did and did not work for you.

We have included three types of reader reaction forms. Forms A and C ask you to describe your reactions to the paper by focusing on the subject and what the writer did to make his ideas interesting and easy to follow. In Forms B and D, you will point out what the author did to make his subject clear, interesting, and understandable. Form E provides a guide that helps you devise your own reader reaction form. Use form E whenever you want the reader to comment on specific elements in your first draft.

After completing the reader reaction form and returning it to the author, set aside time to review what the reader has said about your draft. Then read your own paper again and answer the following questions on a separate sheet of paper:

1. What particular comments help me see my draft from a reader's perspective?
2. What areas should I revise in the next draft?

Keeping your responses in front of you, go on to Chapter 6. Read the introduction, if you have not done so before, and then begin revising.

READER REACTION FORM A

Writer_____   Reader _____

Writer: Trade your paper with a classmate, or read your paper aloud to someone.
Reader: Fill out this form carefully after reading or listening to the writer's paper. Return it to the writer when you finish.

General Reaction: Describe your general reaction to the paper. What did it make you think or feel?
Example: "The paper made me think of vacation posters – it was exciting."

1. Describe what you learned about the subject and your impression of the ideas.
   Example: "Because my family has never spent any time at a lake cottage, I was surprised to learn that a family can have . . ."

2. Describe how you felt as the paper unfolded. Did you know at all times where the writer was taking you? Did you get lost at any point?
   Example: "At first, I thought you were going to talk about your parents, but then I realized by the end of the introduction that you were going to describe the time you spent . . . But I was surprised at the end when you talked about going back to school because . . ."

3. Describe what you envisioned as the paper unfolded. Which ideas were most vivid? Also, explain what made the paper interesting to you.
   Example: "I could see the cottage in the woods as the paper began, and the more I heard the more I could see the lake with the pine trees around it. Then I saw . . ."
   Or: "I really liked the beginning; it made me see what you did. But my mind wandered a bit when . . ."

Final Reactions: Describe what the writer might do to make his ideas more interesting or easier to follow. Refer to the lists you made in Chapter 2 if you need reminders.

READER REACTION FORM B

Writer_____   Reader_____

Writer: Trade papers with another writer.
Reader: After reading the paper, fill out this form carefully. Return this form to the writer once you are finished.

General Reaction: Write down what you remember most vividly or how you feel after reading the draft.

1. Did the writer make you care about this topic? Put asterisks next to the passages where you were most involved, or jot down the words that were especially vivid to you.

2. Do you understand the main idea the writer wants to express? Write it down in a sentence or two.

3. Where is the main idea sharply in focus? Underline it in the paper.

4. Does a pattern emerge that helps make the ideas easy to follow? To make sure, do a map or diagram of the paper.

Does the pattern revealed by the map or diagram work for you and show that the ideas in the paper are clearly organized? If not, put a question mark next to any section that is difficult to follow.

5. Is there any place where the central idea seems blurred or completely lost? Bracket the material that distracts you or interferes with your reading of the paper.

6. Is there any idea you want to know about? Put a + where you feel that further information is needed.

Final Reactions: When you return this form to the author, make sure to discuss your comments with him and explain the questions or marks you made in the margin.

READER REACTION FORM C

Writer_____   Reader_____

Writer: Trade your paper with another classmate, or read your paper aloud to someone. *Reader:* Make sure to fill out this form carefully after reading or listening to the paper. Return it to the writer once you are finished.

General Reaction: Imagine that this essay is a mural. Describe how you feel after looking at it.
Example: "After reading this and thinking about the images, I felt quiet and thoughtful."

1. What do you think the title of the mural should be? Can you think of one word or phrase that summarizes what you see?
   Example: "Perhaps 'dream' or 'hope' should be part of the title because . . ."

2. Describe how you see the scenes relating to the title of the mural.
   Example: "The first scene fits well because . . . But the second scene seems extra — not part of the whole picture."

3. In what order do you see the scenes? Are the scenes easy to follow? Describe your impressions.
   Example: "I remember the last scene most because . . . The others helped lead up to it and made me realize what you hoped for in the future."
   Or: "I remember the middle scenes most because . . . Maybe you can start with those and . . ."

4. Describe the scenes that are clearest in your mind. Do you need more specifics for any scene?
   Example: "The last scene is the clearest. I see people joining hands. But I don't remember the middle scenes as well."

Final Comments: Describe to the writer what he can do to reorganize, emphasize, or make the ideas more interesting or easier to follow. If you need reminders, look through your lists in Chapter 2.

READER REACTION FORM D

Writer_____   Reader_____

Writer and Reader: Exchange papers and work with this form carefully. You will do most of your commenting on the draft itself. Use this form to guide you in making suggestions to the writer.

To begin this approach, do the following: Read the paper. What is the main idea of the work? Look for a sentence or sentences in the draft that state this idea and underline them. Then copy the main idea at the top of the draft. If you cannot find any sentences that state the central idea, summarize it in your own words and write it at the top of the draft.

Focusing on the paragraphs one at a time, do the following:

1. Read the paragraph carefully to determine the central idea. In the margin beside the paragraph, summarize the main idea. If there is a summarizing sentence in the paragraph, draw an arrow to it. If there is none and you think one is needed, note your suggestion on this form.

2. Next, reread the main idea at the top of the draft and your paragraph summaries to determine what the author has done to make his ideas easy to follow. In doing so, explain in the margin how the ideas in the paragraph relate to the main idea of the paper. Circle the words or phrases in the paragraph that make this connection clear. If no relationship seems to exists, put a question mark in the margin and suggest on this form how the writer could clarify the relationship.

3. Finally, determine what the specifics in each paragraph do to make the main idea interesting and understandable. Underline the examples, details, illustrations, facts, statistics, or experiences in the paragraphs. Reread the main idea and indicate in the margin how the specifics support and develop it. If the paragraphs do not supply information that help you understand the writer's idea more clearly, suggest on this form what could be added.

Comments and Suggestions: Discuss with the author what worked well for you and what might be done to revise the draft.

READER REACTION FORM E

Writer _____ Reader _____

Writer: Ask you reader to describe his or her reactions to your ideas and to the sections of the paper that most concern you. Or have the reader point out what did or did not work well. Devise your own questions that focus on one or more of the following areas.

Reader: React to the paper and answer the writer's questions to explain how you see the work. After you finish, discuss your comments with the writer.

General Reactions and Feelings:

Subject:

Pattern:

Specifics:

Final Comments and Suggestions:

CHAPTER 6

Revising and Rewriting:
Seeing Your Work Anew to Meet the
Reader's Needs

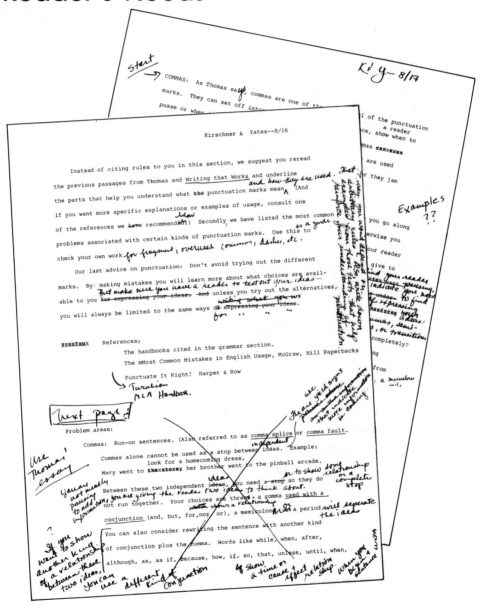

In the revision and rewriting stage of the writing process, the writer alternates between the roles of writer and reader. As a writer, he must look at the first draft and consider what can be done to make the meaning clearer. As a reader, he must take into account how his work will fulfill the conventional expectations of his audience.

Revision is the more chaotic and complex part of the processs. The writer must relinquish control over the work. Sometimes the order of the first draft disappears before his eyes as the paper is pulled apart and reshaped. Or an idea developed in only one paragraph may become the central part of the paper, sending the writer back to the getting-started stage for more information—and the majority of the first draft to the wastebasket. The writer may even see the conclusion as the real introduction to his paper because it gives a sharper focus to the main idea and a clearer organizational pattern to the paper. The reward for giving up control is seeing ideas become distilled, focused, and reordered, and finding a clarity the paper did not have before.

Rewriting is more orderly and usually requires less extensive changes. It may include rewriting the introduction to make it more interesting, expanding a paragraph, or inserting transitional words or phrases to improve the flow of ideas. In this part of the process, the writer takes the paper one step further and gains the joy of producing a piece that is far better than anything he hoped to write.

REVISION AND REWRITING MODEL

To illustrate the process you will go through in this stage, we have included the unedited first draft and reader response form for a student's paper and have described what he did to revise and rewrite it.

What Makes Me Unique?

Being versatile, is one of the aspects of my personality that makes me most unique. I think that being versatile is very important, as to minimize the doldrums of life. It is very easy for people to get themselves into a rut of always doing and liking the same things, but a greater challenge is trying something different. There is a much greater awakening of all the potential you have, when you try new things.

The job I hold, truly puts versatility to the test. I am a tour guide at Henry Ford Museum and Greenfield Village, and am placed in different situations with the public every day. Whether it is acting as an interpreter in one of the historical buildings, or giving a personal tour to the heads of Egypt or even personalities such as John Davidson or Joan Rivers, flexibility is very important.

I am somewhat of an extravagant person who likes to do things big and bright. I like spending my summers in Europe and holidays in New York, and I am a push-over for Broadway plays, formal gatherings such as the symphony or opera, and a bustling city. In a sense, I am a worldly person, but at the same time I still like the simple things in life. There are times when I am perfectly content just being curled up in a quilt by a roaring fire, walking in the woods, or running along the beach.

Acting is another way in which my versatility surfaces. I have been doing drama and musicals for four years, and have portrayed characters from the likes of an undertaker to an English butler. Transforming yourself into another character on stage means that you must have a varied background in different areas of speech, dress, and action. A good actor, is one who can place himself in any position, and carry it off as if he had always been that character. Versatility is one of an actor's most useful tools.

Being versatile allows me to branch out in many different situations that I am face with, and to enjoy the different paths that I sometimes choose to follow. It is very important to me, because it makes me the individual that I am.

READER REACTION FORM A

Writer _Al Sebastian_   Reader _Steve Troy_

Writer: Trade your paper with a classmate or read your paper aloud to someone.
Reader: Make sure to fill out this form carefully after reading or listening to the writer's paper. Return it to the writer when you finish.

General Reaction: Describe your general reaction to the paper. What did it make you think or feel?

> There are some really interesting ideas in your paper. I wish you could tell me more about your job at Greenfield Village. I love the place.

1. Describe what you learned about the subject and your impressions of the ideas.

> Well, I was impressed by the interesting experiences you've had, but I can't say I feel I know the unique you.

2. Describe how you felt as the paper unfolded. Did you know at all times where the writer was taking you? Did you get lost at any point?

> When I read the first paragraph, I felt lost. The ideas seemed so vague. Are you sure "versatile" is the word you want to keep repeating? "Flexible" seems to be a better word to explain you.

3. Describe what you envisioned as the paper unfolded. What ideas were most vivid? Also, explain what made the paper interesting to you.

> Like I said before, I liked the part about Greenfield Village. I've been there often so I could see it, but I don't think a person who hadn't been there would.

Final Reactions: Describe what the writer might do to make his ideas more interesting or easier to follow. Refer to the lists you made in Chapter 2 if you need a reminder.

> Maybe it is just me, but I think the paper would be better and show more about you if you centered on the part about your jobs at Greenfield Village. That does sound unique and it would show how flexible you have to be.

To begin the revision part of the process, Al assembled his first draft, the Reader Reaction Form, his predrafting material from Chapters 3 and 4, his lists from Chapter 2, and plenty of fresh paper.

First, he reread his first draft, the Reader Reaction Form, and his own comments on what helped him see the paper from a reader's perspective. Then he looked at the lists of what writers do to make their readers care and to make the ideas interesting and easy to follow.

Next, he decided to focus on the reader's statement that the part of his paper about Greenfield Village was most interesting. How could that part be developed to show why he was unique? To think out this idea, Al talked to himself on paper:

```
What does my job at Greenfield Village tell the reader about me?
Well, I guess it shows that I have lots of different jobs there and that
I have to relate to different kinds of people. I guess it does show I am
flexible like I say in the last sentence of the paragraph. Hey, that
might be better than saying I'm versatile. Ok. I'll use that for my main
idea and describe my job in the Village to show that I am unique because
I am flexible. But what am I going to do with all the good stuff about
acting and New York. Throw them out--unless I could use it in my intro.
That might show that my interest in travel and dramatics makes me
different from some people--but it's my flexibility that really makes
me unique.
```

At this point, Al went back to his getting-started material to decide what to use in developing his experiences at Greenfield Village. He had to generate a few more ideas before deciding to organize his paper into two parts, one describing his job as an interpreter and the other his job as a tour guide. Both showed his flexibility. He started with his work as an interpreter, noting that he had to wear different costumes and give different speeches for each building he worked in. He pointed out that working in five different buildings in one week really emphasized his flexibility.

Next, he developed the part about being a tour guide, stating that he had to be flexible enough to take Cub Scouts, Egyptian officials, and celebrities on the tours and feel at ease with all of them. And he had to be prepared to answer any group's questions, some of which he used to illustrate how different the groups were.

Then he began to focus on the introduction, integrating the material on his acting and trips to New York to make it interesting. He was not sure what to use for the conclusion, so he wrote down a few ideas and planned to discuss them later with a reader.

Finally, he answered the questions at the end of the revision strategy, "Talk to Yourself," to determine how much he had revised.

1. What is my main idea?
2. What have I done to make it easy to follow?
3. What have I done to show my ideas to the reader?
4. What have I done to make the ideas interesting for the reader?

Before moving on to the rewriting stage, Al asked his first reader to read through his second draft to decide if the ideas were more interesting and better developed. And he discussed the possibilities for a conclusion to see what might work best.

With the reader's comments in mind, Al began the rewriting process by using the checklist on page 178. This helped him focus on the conventions that readers expect. Going through the list, he discovered that he needed to improve the transition between the section of his paper describing his work as an interpreter and the one on his work as a tour guide. After doing this revision and adding another example of an incident that happened on one of the tours, he exchanged papers with an editor.

You may find that you have to do more than Al did to revise and rewrite your first draft—or maybe you will do less. But remember, this is an important part of the process; even experienced writers, such as E. B. White, say that they revise and rewrite everything more than once. So, do not be surprised or discouraged if you must again revise or rewrite after an editor reads your next draft. This process is part of writing. It takes time to do what will work for a reader.

REVISING—MAKING THE MEANING CLEAR

In the revision part of the process, you will focus on making your meaning clear. This entails making your ideas easy to follow, showing what you mean, and making your ideas interesting for the reader. To guide you through revision, we have suggested three steps for you to follow. During step three, you will concentrate on four areas: "Make the Main Idea Clear," "Make the Ideas Easy to Follow," "Show the Reader the Ideas," and "Engage the Reader's Interest." And finally, you will answer four questions to evaluate your revision.

Keep in mind that you must now try to see your writing as a reader sees it. Your experience in Chapter 5 should have prepared you for making the transition from writer to reader and should have suggested a perspective you can use for looking at your paper anew. Also, your reactions to your reader's comments should help you see your paper differently. To further prepare yourself, look back at Chapter 2 to remind yourself of what writers do to show that they care about their subject, to make their readers care, and to make their ideas easy to follow and interesting to read.

Make sure to have these materials on hand when you begin to revise:

Lists from Chapter 2
Predrafting materials from Chapters 3 and 4
First draft
Reader Reaction Form and your comments

1. To begin the revision, reread your first draft and the Reader Reaction Form. Then review your responses to the reader's comments.

2. Consider what parts of your paper the reader reacted to and what kinds of revisions he suggests. Where might you begin? If the reader said, "I'm not quite sure what you are trying to say," he could be telling you that you need to state your main idea more clearly or focus on one point. A comment such as "The idea is good, but your paper is confusing to read" tells you to work on making it easier to follow. And when a reader says, "I think I know what you mean, but I can't really see it," you know that you have to add more details and specifics.

3. Focus on the following areas and try *one or more* of the revision methods suggested to guide you through this part.

Make the Main Idea Clear
Look at the reader's comments about your main idea, p. 165
Talk to yourself, p. 166
Focus on what you like best, p. 167
Discuss the paper with another person, p. 167
Focus on the conclusion, p. 168
Take your paper apart, p. 169
Revise or add a thesis, p. 172

Make the Ideas Easy to Follow
Focus on the conclusion, p. 168
Take your paper apart, p. 169
Ask questions, p. 169
Look at the reader's reaction to find a pattern, p. 170
Make a descriptive outline of your paper, p. 171
Revise or add a thesis, p. 172
Focus on the details, p. 173

Show the Reader the Ideas
Listen to the paper, p. 173
Imagine a reader who disagrees, p. 174
Look at the specifics the reader liked, p. 175
Visualize your paper, p. 176
Look at the reader's questions, p. 177

Engage the Reader's Interest
Discuss the paper with another person, p. 167
Focus on the real introduction, p. 177

When you think you have made enough changes, answer the questions at the end of the revision method used. They will help you to focus on the main idea and to decide whether you made it clear, interesting, and easy to follow. It may take more than one revision to answer these questions; but once you can, you will turn to the section on "Rewriting," page 178.

Look at the Reader's Comments About Your Main Idea

If the reader's comments show you that your main idea is not clear or is not what you intended to discuss, then do the following before revising:

- Reread your paper and summarize the main idea as you see it now.
- Consider what the main idea is, according to the reader, and compare it with the statement you just wrote.

If you find that the idea in your summary statement is different from the reader's, reread your draft, circling the main idea you want to discuss and any supporting sections. Revise by doing *any* of the following:

- Rearrange the introduction so that the main idea falls at the end and leads into the middle section of the paper.
- Write a sentence that specifically states your main idea and put it in the introduction if necessary.
- Develop the sections that reinforce the idea you want to discuss.
- Omit the sections that distract the reader.
- Rewrite your conclusion to reinforce your main idea if you decide not to state it in the introduction.

If you need to gather more ideas, clarify your purpose, redefine your reader, or find a new plan for your ideas, make sure to review any section in Chapters 3 and 4 that is helpful.

Once you write the revision, answer the following four questions and go to the section on "Rewriting," page 178. If you want a reader to react to your draft before going on to "Rewriting," use one of the forms in Chapter 5.

1. What is my main idea?
2. What have I done to make it easy to follow?

3. What have I done to show my ideas to the reader?
4. What have I done to make the ideas interesting to the reader?

Talk to Yourself

Sometimes talking to yourself or writing yourself a letter is the only way to bring your meaning to the surface. Even in writing a first draft, it is very easy to be distracted by introductions, conclusions, paragraphs, and punctuation, leaving what you really want to say buried in your mind.

Here is what one student typed as he began the revision process:

What am I trying to do in this paper anyway. Here I am trying to show the reader that I am a shy person but all I do is just tell him. What should I do? This is so frustrating--hey! Maybe I am being shy right now--maybe I just tell because I am too afraid to really show through the words. Do I really want my reader to understand what being shy is like? When has it really screwed things up for me? I know it ruined a perfectly good evening when I sat home afraid to ask Kelly for a date-- and she sat home wondering why I didn't like her. I remember how mad she was the next day....

This idea was enough to give Steve the idea of writing a how-to essay on overcoming shyness. First, he told the story of his nondate with Kelly and how she ignored him. In the middle of the paper, he developed some ideas on overcoming shyness. Finally, he ended by describing the afternoon he finally asked Kelly to the Christmas dance.

If you want to try this method, do the following:

- Get out your journal and start writing to yourself; or start talking to yourself in order to focus on your real concerns.
- When you find an answer that leads you to memories or experiences, write or talk about them until you see what they mean.
- After you finish, try to summarize what you want to say in a few sentences and list the details or experiences that support this idea.

Use this material to begin your revision. If you need to gather more ideas, clarify your purpose, redefine your reader, or find a new plan for your ideas, make sure to review any section in Chapters 3 and 4 that is useful.

Once your write the revision, answer the following four questions and turn to the section on "Rewriting," page 178. If you want a reader to react to your draft before going on to "Rewriting," use one of the forms in Chapter 5.

1. What is my main idea?
2. What have I done to make it easy to follow?
3. What have I done to show my ideas to the reader?
4. What have I done to make the ideas interesting to the reader?

Focus on What You Like Best

Reread the paper and circle the parts you like best. Why are they most interesting to you? What is the main idea that is communicated

One student decided that she liked the telephone conversation in her essay best. So, she made it the introduction and then used flashbacks to help the reader understand what was going on. Gradually, the story led to the main idea at the end of the piece.

If you think this method might work for you, do the following:

• Focus on the part of the first draft you liked best.
• Decide what idea it communicates or how it interests the reader.
• Think about where you can use that idea and how you can develop it. Review your getting-started materials for ideas.

If you need to gather more ideas, clarify your purpose, redefine your reader, or find a new plan for your ideas, make sure to review any section in Chapters 3 and 4 that is helpful.

Once you write the revision, answer the following four questions and go to the section on "Rewriting," page 178. If you want a reader to react to your draft before going on to "Rewriting," use one of the forms in Chapter 5.

1. What is my main idea?
2. What have I done to make it easy to follow?
3. What have I done to show my ideas to the reader?
4. What have I done to make the ideas interesting to the reader?

Discuss the Paper with Another Person

Find a person who has not read your paper and tell him about it. What do you want to accomplish? How do you want your reader to react? What do you want to say? As you discuss your paper, do the following:

• Listen to the person's questions.
• Listen to what he says and *how* he says it.

- Jot down the subjects you talk longest about or most enjoy discussing.

Your listener's questions and comments are very revealing. They can tell you what is confusing, what is most interesting and most dull, whether you really care about the subject or not, or if you know enough about it to discuss it fully. When you have to backtrack in a story, you know that you did not give the listener enough information. If he starts yawning or shifting in his chair, you know the subject is dull. But when your listener cannot wait to find out what happened, you are beginning to find out what you want to talk about most.

If you need to gather more ideas, clarify your purpose, redefine your reader, or find a new plan for your ideas, make sure to review any section in Chapters 3 and 4 that is helpful.

Once you write the revision, answer the following four questions and go to the section on "Rewriting," page 178. If you want a reader to react to your draft before going on to "Rewriting," use one of the forms in Chapter 5.

1. What is my main idea?
2. What have I done to make it easy to follow?
3. What have I done to show my ideas to the reader?
4. What have I done to make the ideas interesting to the reader?

Focus on the Conclusion

Read the conclusion and summarize its main idea. Then read the rest of the paper. Is your conclusion a summary of what comes before, or does it state the idea you really want to discuss? The latter is not unusual; writing the first draft may have clarified your ideas. By the time you reached the conclusion, you knew what you wanted to say. If this has happened, do the following:

- Write down the idea you want to discuss in your revision at the top of a sheet of paper and list any of the points from the first draft you want to keep.
- Or use the conclusion of the first draft as the introduction for your revision.
- Go through your getting-started material, looking for details or examples you can use to develop the idea you focused on in the conclusion.

If you need to gather more ideas, clarify your purpose, redefine your reader, or find a new plan for your ideas, make sure to review any section in Chapters 3 and 4 that is helpful.

Once you write the revision, answer the following four questions and go to the section on "Rewriting," page 178. Or if you want a reader to react to your draft before going on to "Rewriting," use one of the forms in Chapter 5.

1. What is my main idea?
2. What have I done to make it easy to follow?
3. What have I done to show my ideas to the reader?
4. What have I done to make the ideas interesting to the reader?

Take Your Paper Apart

Take the first draft apart and look at the pieces to see if you have said what you meant. Start by reading the individual paragraphs and summarizing each on a 3 × 5 card. Look at the cards and shuffle them until a clear relationship emerges. If you have trouble finding the relationship, decide if all the ideas fall under the main idea of your draft. Is one idea more important or interesting than the others? If so, start with the paragraph that is most interesting to you and think about how you can develop it.

- Check through your getting-started material for ideas.
- Think about why this idea is interesting to you.
- Focus on the clearest pictures in your mind or the most vivid emotions you have on this subject.

If you need to gather more ideas, clarify your purpose, redefine your reader, or find a new plan for your ideas, make sure to review any section in Chapters 3 and 4 that is helpful.

Once you write the revision, answer the following four questions and go to the section on "Rewriting," page 178. If you want a reader to react to your draft before going on to "Rewriting," use one of the forms in Chapter 5.

1. What is my main idea?
2. What have I done to make it easy to follow?
3. What have I done to show my ideas to the reader?
4. What have I done to make the ideas interesting to the reader?

Ask Questions

One way some writers adopt a reader's role is to set their work aside for a few hours. When they come back to it, they ask themselves questions about it or even write questions in the margin. "What does this mean?" "Why is this so important?" "Why do you believe this?"

"How do you know this is true?" "Where does this fit in?" "Why did you start here?" Questions such as these help writers discover what is most important to them and why they want to discuss that subject.

If you would like to use this method, put your paper away for a few hours. Then read through it, ask any question that occurs to you, and do the following:

- Choose the questions you would like to answer and write about them in your journal.
- After answering the questions, summarize your answers or find the sentences that explain what you want to talk about and why.
- Arrange the answers in some order, or think about the details, facts, or experiences that support your answers and try to organize them.

If you need to gather more ideas, clarify your purpose, redefine your reader, or find a new plan for your ideas, review any section in Chapters 3 and 4 that is helpful.

Once you write the revision, answer the following four questions and go to the section on "Rewriting," page 178. If you want a reader to react to your draft before going on to "Rewriting," use one of the forms in Chapter 5.

1. What is my main idea?
2. What have I done to make it easy to follow?
3. What have I done to show my ideas to the reader?
4. What have I done to make the ideas interesting to the reader?

Look at the Reader's Reaction to Find a Pattern

If your reader told you that your ideas were difficult to follow, use his comments about the paper to help you revise its pattern.

If the reader said that the whole paper was confusing, do the following:

- Reread the paper and note the reader's comments.
- Write down the main ideas in the order in which they occur.
- Determine and mark where the reader got lost.

If the reader got lost in the introduction, reread it to see if it focuses on the main idea and decide whether it prepares the reader for the way you ordered the ideas. If not, rewrite the introduction to match the order of your ideas. Or rearrange and rewrite the ideas to reflect the pattern you established in the introduction.

If the reader became confused in the middle of the paper, try the following:

- Write down the main ideas in this section.
- Underline the words that reinforce the pattern or relationship of the ideas.

If the ideas do not seem clear or logically presented, do the following:

- Eliminate the ideas that do not clearly relate to your main idea.
- Rearrange the order of the sentences of paragraphs in a logical order.
- Think of a different pattern that could explain your ideas more clearly.
- Emphasize relationships by expanding transitional words to phrases or sentences.
- Add transitions if there are few or none.

If you need to gather more ideas, clarify your purpose, redefine your reader, or find a new plan for your ideas, make sure to review any section in Chapters 3 and 4 that is helpful.

Once you write the revision, answer the following four questions and go to the section on "Rewriting," page 178. If you want a reader to react to your draft before going on to "Rewriting," use one of the forms in Chapter 5.

1. What is my main idea?
2. What have I done to make it easy to follow?
3. What have I done to show my ideas to the reader?
4. What have I done to make the ideas interesting to the reader?

Make a Descriptive Outline of Your Paper

To find out what you must revise to give the paper a clearer focus and a better organizational pattern, try writing a descriptive outline.

Start by identifying the main idea of the paper and writing it on a separate sheet of paper. Then read each paragraph to determine what it says and how it functions within the paper.

- Look for the main idea of each paragraph (including the introduction and conclusion) and summarize these ideas on the separate sheet in the order in which they occur.
- Determine what each paragraph does in the paper. Does it introduce, support or develop, or tie together ideas? Indicate the function on the descriptive outline.

If a paragraph does not serve to develop the main idea, do the following:

- Add sentences that clarify the meaning of the paragraph.
- Add sentences or transitional material that clarifies the function of the paragraph.
- Take out the paragraph and, if necessary, substitute relevant material.

If you need to gather more ideas, clarify your purpose, redefine your reader, or find a new plan for your ideas, review any section in Chapters 3 and 4 that is helpful.

Once you write the revision, answer the following four questions and go to the section on "Rewriting," page 178. If you want a reader to react to your draft before going on to "Rewriting," use one of the forms in Chapter 5.

1. What is my main idea?
2. What have I done to make it easy to follow?
3. What have I done to show my ideas to the reader?
4. What have I done to make the ideas interesting to the reader?

Revise or Add a Thesis

A thesis can be useful for making your main idea and organizational pattern clear to the reader. If you used a tentative thesis as a guide in writing the first draft, or if you think the meaning of the paper could be clarified by adding a thesis, try the following:

- Reread the paper.
- Underline the tentative thesis or summarize the main idea of the paper.
- Do a brief outline of the statements that support or develop the main idea.
- Read these statements. Summarize the main idea they develop and compare that idea to the thesis or summary written before.

Make sure that the tentative thesis matches the idea developed in the middle section of the paper. If it does not, revise so that it does. Next, look at the pattern you used to develop the ideas in the middle section. Does your thesis reflect this pattern? If not, either revise the thesis or rearrange the paragraphs.

If you need to gather more ideas, clarify your purpose, redefine your reader, or find a new plan for your ideas, review any section in Chapters 3 and 4 that is helpful.

Once you write the revision, answer the following four questions and go to the section on "Rewriting," page 178. If you want a reader to react to your draft before going on to "Rewriting," use one of the forms in Chapter 5.

1. What is my main idea?
2. What have I done to make it easy to follow?
3. What have I done to show my ideas to the reader?
4. What have I done to make the ideas interesting to the reader?

Focus on the Details

Some writers start with details, facts, or examples but never tie the parts together for the reader. Before you reread the first draft, express the main idea in a sentence or two. Then as you read the paper, look for sentences or phrases that show the main idea or overview. If you find that this material is missing, do any of the following:

- Think about where to add a sentence or two that presents the overview or main idea of your paper.
- Group the details or examples you develop into larger categories and then arrange the categories in a logical order.
- Disregard the details that do not reinforce your main idea or purpose.
- Write an introduction or conclusion that gives your reader the main idea of your paper.

If you need to gather more ideas, clarify your purpose, redefine your reader, or find a new plan for your ideas, make sure to review any section in Chapters 3 and 4 that is helpful.

Once you write the revision, answer the following four questions and go to the section on "Rewriting," page 178. Or if you want a reader to react to your draft before going on to "Rewriting," use one of the forms in Chapter 5.

1. What is my main idea?
2. What have I done to make it easy to follow?
3. What have I done to show my ideas to the reader?
4. What have I done to make the ideas interesting to the reader?

Listen to the Paper

Find a roommate or classmate who will read your paper aloud to you and carefully listen to it. Do the sentences you hear match the ideas, pictures, memories, or feelings in your mind?

Ann, a volunteer nurse during the summer, wrote about some of her experiences for her first paper. But because she could not understand why her writing seemed flat and uninteresting, she did not know how to revise it. When she listened to another classmate read her work, she began to hear the discrepancies between what she was saying and what she meant. For example, she said that she often *talked* to patients while inserting an intravenous line, but she really meant that she had to *comfort* them, make them *smile* or *feel that she listened* to them. Focusing on what she meant to say, she jotted down more exact words, memories, and descriptions that matched her ideas.

If you need to listen to your paper to find out what you mean, do any of the following:

- Note the sections that puzzle you or seem abstract.
- Jot down the memories that come to mind as you listen that did not find their way into the draft.
- List the concrete, definite words that represent what you see, hear, or imagine. Do not forget conversations or dialogue.
- Listen for the real center of your ideas or for the sections that are most interesting. Leave out the sections that get in the way of what you really mean when revising.

If you need to gather more ideas, clarify your purpose, redefine your reader, or find a new plan for your ideas, review any section in Chapters 3 and 4 that is helpful.

Once you write the revision, answer the following four questions and go to the section on "Rewriting," page 178. If you want a reader to react to your draft before going on to "Rewriting," use one of the forms in Chapter 5.

1. What is my main idea?
2. What have I done to make it easy to follow?
3. What have I done to show my ideas to the reader?
4. What have I done to make the ideas interesting to the reader?

Imagine a Reader Who Disagrees

If you want to write an editorial or persuade your reader in some way, try pretending that you are a reader who disagrees with the main idea of the draft. If you want to use this method, do the following:

- Read the paper and write a response to it.
- Or write a dialogue between you, the writer, and you, the reader.

Next, focus on the sections of your response or the dialogue that are most interesting. What do you need to add to the draft? What parts should be developed? How can you get the reader to respond positively to your ideas?

If you need to gather more ideas, clarify your purpose, redefine your reader, or find a new plan for your ideas, review any section in Chapter 3 and 4 that is helpful.

Once you write the revision, answer the following four questions and go to the section on "Rewriting," page 178. If you want a reader to react to your draft before going on to "Rewriting," use one of the forms in Chapter 5.

1. What is my main idea?
2. What have I done to make it easy to follow?
3. What have I done to show my ideas to the reader?
4. What have I done to make the ideas interesting to the reader?

Look at the Specifics the Reader Liked

If the reader told you that some of your ideas *show* while others just *tell*, use the parts the reader liked to help you decide how to develop the parts that *tell*.

- Reread the paper and circle the sentences or parts the reader liked.
- Look at those sections and decide what you did that attracted the reader. Did you give detailed examples, lists, or illustrations? Detailed descriptions or facts?

Now look at the parts that *tell*. Could you apply any of the methods used in parts that *show* to further develop your ideas? If so, revise and do any of the following:

- Add more examples, illustrations, descriptions, facts, or statistics.
- Omit sections that are not crucial to the development of your main idea.
- Do more research or reading to get the information needed to develop your ideas.

If you need to gather more ideas, clarify your purpose, redefine your reader, or find a new plan for your ideas, review any section in Chapters 3 and 4 that is helpful.

Once you write the revision, answer the following four questions and go to the section on "Rewriting," page 178. Or if you want a reader to react to your draft before going on to "Rewriting," use one of the forms in Chapter 5.

1. What is my main idea?
2. What have I done to make it easy to follow?
3. What have I done to show my ideas to the reader?
4. What have I done to make the ideas interesting to the reader?

Visualize Your Paper

If you have used descriptive images to develop your paper and want to be certain that you have created the clearest picture possible, try this method:

- Underline all of the parts that you consider descriptive.
- Focus on one image at a time and visualize the picture you have created.

Do further images come to mind? Do you see more details? Should you put them into the paper to sharpen the picture you want to create or to enhance the mood?

Continue to focus on the central images of your work and revise by doing any of the following:

- Brainstorm to capture feelings, sounds, scents, and sights. Add these details to show your ideas to the reader.
- See your ideas as a movie. Jot down what you see and describe it to your reader.
- Hear the characters talk. If you envision your main characters talking, try to capture what they say and use this dialogue to develop your ideas.

If you need to gather more ideas, clarify your purpose, redefine your reader, or find a new plan for your ideas, review any section in Chapters 3 and 4 that is helpful.

Once you write the revision, answer the following four questions and go to the section on "Rewriting," page 178. Or if you want a reader to react to your draft before going on to "Rewriting," use one of the forms in Chapter 5.

1. What is my main idea?
2. What have I done to make it easy to follow?
3. What have I done to show my ideas to the reader?
4. What have I done to make the ideas interesting to the reader?

Look at the Reader's Questions

Use the questions the reader raised in the Reaction Form or noted on the draft to help you decide what kind of information to add.

- Reread the paper and the reader's comments or marginal notations.
- Bracket the parts where the reader raised questions and consider the kinds of questions raised.

If the reader said, "I don't see what you mean here," you need to explain the idea more fully or use an example to help the reader see the idea.

If the reader says, "Why is this idea here?" or "How does this fit in?" then you need to make the relationships within the paper or paragraphs clearer by adding transitions.

If the reader says, "Such as?" "How so?" or "Why?" you will have to add examples or illustrations to prove that your idea is valid and convince your reader of its merit.

If you need to gather more ideas, clarify your purpose, redefine your reader, or find a new plan for your ideas, review any section in Chapters 3 and 4 that is helpful.

Once you write the revision, answer the following four questions and go to the section on "Rewriting," page 178. If you want a reader to react to your draft before going on to "Rewriting," use one of the forms in Chapter 5.

1. What is my main idea?
2. What have I done to make it easy to follow?
3. What have I done to show my ideas to the reader?
4. What have I done to make the ideas interesting to the reader?

Focus on the Real Introduction

Sometimes it takes two or three paragraphs before the writer starts talking about the ideas that most concern him. This material is the *real* introduction to the paper. If you think you have used this approach, reread your draft.

- As you read it, mark the section where you really become involved in the ideas.
- Write down the main idea of that section.
- List the details, examples, or experiences you focus on after that section or that are part of the section that interests you most.

Consider dropping the first part of your draft and starting with the paragraph that helps you focus on what you mean. Then think about what you can use to develop that idea.

If you need to gather more ideas, clarify your purpose, redefine your reader, or find a new plan for your ideas, review any section in Chapters 3 and 4 that is helpful.

Once you write the revision, answer the following four questions and go to the section on "Rewriting," page 178. If you want a reader to react to your draft before going on to "Rewriting," use one of the forms in Chapter 5.

1. What is my main idea?
2. What have I done to make it easy to follow?
3. What have I done to show my ideas to the reader?
4. What have I done to make the ideas interesting to the reader?

REWRITING—MEETING THE READER'S NEEDS

The final part of the revision/rewriting stage involves reshaping the paper to make it meet the conventions of discourse. At this stage, you must consider your reader's expectations about focus and purpose, organization, and development. Although we discuss these concerns in some detail, offer methods for checking your paper in each of these areas, and provide approaches for rewriting, you may also want to consult the lists you began in Chapter 2 and a handbook on writing while you rewrite. Your lists will be useful because they can direct you to examples of writing approaches that have worked for you as a reader. The handbook will provide a detailed discussion of the writing conventions and can be helpful if you think of the material it presents as an analysis of what a reader expects to find in a final draft.

Use the following checklist to guide you through the rewriting process. As you focus on each convention, turn to the section indicated for an explanation on what the reader expects, the methods for checking your draft, and the approaches for rewriting. Consult your lists from Chapter 2 or a handbook whenever you need more detailed explanations or want to consider other approaches for rewriting. Be certain that you look at all the conventions and answer the questions relating to each, and that you complete all rewriting before you share your paper with an editor in Chapter 7.

Checklist:

Focus and Purpose
(Reader's Expectations About Focus and Purpose, page 179)
1. What methods can I use to check for focus and purpose? (Pages 179–180)

2. Have I given the paper a clear focus?
3. How have I made my purpose clear?
4. What can I do to improve the focus and purpose? (pages 180–181)

Organization
(Reader's Expectations About Organization, page 181)
1. What methods can I use to check the methods used to organize and tie together my ideas? (pages 181–182)
2. How is the whole paper organized?
3. How are the paragraphs organized?
4. How does the introduction prepare the reader for the pattern?
5. How does the conclusion reinforce the pattern?
6. How are the ideas in the paragraphs tied together?
7. What can I do to organize my ideas and tie them together? (Pages 182–183)

Development
(Reader's Expectations About Development, page 183)
1. What methods can I use to check the development? (page 183)
2. How have I developed my ideas?
3. What can I do to improve the development? (page 184)

Reader's Expectations About Focus and Purpose

Readers expect a writer to focus on a single subject, to limit the range of the discussion, to state the subject clearly, and to relate all parts of the paper to that subject. Readers are confused when they have to stop and ask, "What is this writer trying to say? How are all these ideas related?"

The writer must also take into consideration the reader's interest in and knowledge of the subject in order to carry out the purpose. Readers become bored when they are informed of something they already know. They are not entertained by long accounts of personal experiences or anecdotes in business reports or research papers.

If you consult a handbook, *focus* will be treated under the headings of *subject, thesis, unity, central idea,* and *introductions. Purpose* is most often discussed under *introduction, conclusion, mood, tone,* and *purpose.*

METHODS FOR CHECKING FOCUS AND PURPOSE

To check for focus and purpose, do *one or more* of the following:

- Write the main idea of your paper as a headline. Do all the paragraphs and supporting ideas fit under that headline?

- Compress your paper into a telegram message. Remember that your are paying 36 cents per word. State your message clearly. Do all the paragraphs and supporting ideas belong in that telegram?
- Think of your paper as a painting or other work or art. What is its title? What mood does it create? Does everything relate to the title and mood?
- Think of one word that describes your paper. How does everything in the paper relate to that word? What purpose does that word evoke?
- Read the first 20 words of your introduction. Would you read on if you did not have to? Would you know what the writer wants to accomplish?
- Describe how you felt as you wrote this piece. Were you comfortable? Uneasy? Sure of your ideas? Hesitant or apologetic? Angry? Excited? Look for words that reveal these attitudes. What feelings do you want to convey to your reader?
- Read the introduction to be sure that it prepares the reader for the main idea of the paper. Can you predict what is to follow? Is your prediction accurate? Does it indicate your reason for writing?
- Check the title to see if it is interesting and indicates your central idea or purpose. If you saw this title in a magazine or newspaper, would you be tempted to read the article?
- Check the conclusion to make sure it reinforces your purpose. Picture your reader for a moment. How will he react after finishing your piece?

APPROACHES FOR REWRITING FOR FOCUS AND PURPOSE

To achieve a clearer focus or purpose, do *one or more* of the following:

- Use a title that prepares the reader for the subject or indicates your purpose.
- State the main idea or proposition in a thesis sentence(s) that appears at the end of the introductory material.
- Omit material that does not clearly relate to the main idea or reinforce your purpose.
- Repeat key words from the main idea or thesis in other parts of the paper.
- Repeat key words that reinforce the tone or mood of your work; find words that create a consistent mood or reinforce your purpose.
- Take out lengthy material the reader already knows.
- Use specifics or examples appropriate to your purpose.

- Rewrite the introduction or conclusion so that your main idea and purpose are emphasized.

Reader's Expectations About Organization

Readers expect writers to organize their papers in patterns that make ideas easy to follow. They assume a writer will use a common logical pattern such as beginning-middle-end, a general-to-specific order, or a traditional rhetorical form for presenting ideas. Readers also expect paragraphs to be arranged in a logical pattern and to contain general ideas that help explain the specifics and their relationship to the main ideas. Strings of figures, facts, statistics, or details do little to keep the reader's attention if he does not understand what they mean.

In addition, readers expect writers to use transitional markers to show relationships between the ideas in the paper and those in the paragraph. These markers encourage the reader to continue reading because the ideas flow smoothly from one paragraph to another. If you consult a handbook, *organization* will be discussed under *introductions, conclusions, paragraphs, transitional words* and *sentences, rhetorical modes* (*forms*), *topic* and *thesis sentences, coherence, consistent verb tense,* and *point of view.*

METHODS FOR CHECKING ORGANIZATION AND TRANSITIONS

To check for organization, do any of the following:

- Think of your paper as a picture. What are the principal objects in the picture? What do you want your audience to see first? Second? Third or fourth? Does this concept match the organization of your paper?
- Think of your paper as a machine. What is its function? How are the pieces organized? What product does it create? How does this concept match the order of the ideas in your paper?
- Think of your paper as a map. What is your destination? What places on the map must you visit in order to arrive at the destination? In what order must you visit those places? How does your map compare with what you did in the paper?
- Read only the introduction. Write down what you predict will happen in the rest of the paper. Then read the rest of the paper. Are your predictions right?
- Read only the conclusion. Where does the conclusion say you have been? Read the rest of the paper. Does it lead up to the conclusion?
- Summarize the main idea of each paragraph. What is the func-

tion of each paragraph? How does each paragraph fit into the organizational pattern of the paper?

- Look for the main idea of each paragraph. What does that idea predict? Or to what conclusion do the details of each paragraph lead? Are the details and the main idea (or conclusion) compatible?
- Look at the rhetorical forms in Chapter 4 if you have used a traditional pattern. Use these forms as your organization guide.
- Read the last sentence of the first paragraph and the first sentence of the next paragraph. Can you follow the ideas easily? Do you find any abrupt jumps or changes when you read these sentences in the other paragraphs?
- Underline the words that show relationships. How many are there? Do they help to reinforce the organizational pattern of the paper?
- Check the tense you have used throughout the piece. Have you been consistent, or have you mixed up the past, present, and future tenses?
- Consider the audience you address or point of view you take in this paper. To whom do you want to speak? Who is doing the talking in your paper? Do you switch your point of view or address different audiences?

APPROACHES FOR REWRITING TO IMPROVE ORGANIZATION AND TRANSITIONS

To improve your organization, do any of the following:

- Provide a thesis statement at the end of your introductory material to help the reader predict what will follow.
- Rewrite the conclusion to reinforce your main idea and purpose.
- Use topic sentences or words that reinforce the organizational pattern of the paper.
- Use words or phrases to show how the details in your paragraphs relate to the purpose and main idea of the paragraph.
- Rewrite the thesis of your paper (or the introduction) to match what happens in the middle of the paper.
- Rewrite the topic sentences so that they reinforce the organizational pattern of the paper.
- Rewrite the topic sentences so that they *tell* what the details *show*.
- Omit paragraphs or details that do not function within the organizational pattern.

- Follow the conventions mentioned in Chapter 4 if you have used a specific rhetorical form to organize your ideas.
- Use transitions between sentences and paragraphs that reinforce your organizational pattern.
- Repeat key words from your main idea, thesis statement, or introduction that remind the reader of your main idea.
- Organize the ideas in a natural and recognizable order.
- Maintain a consistent verb tense.
- Maintain a consistent point of view.
- Use words that reinforce the mood or feeling of the piece.

Reader's Expectations About Development

Readers expect writers to develop fully the main idea in the paper and to provide examples, illustrations, details, statistics, and facts that help them understand the writer's idea. They do not like to fill in gaps or be left wondering, "What does the reader mean here? What is he trying to show me?" If you are going to talk about the Rocky Mountains, let your reader see the treeless tundra, smell the air, or hear the wind.

If you consult a handbook, *development* will be discussed under headings such as *rhetorical modes (forms)*, *developmental paragraphs*, *concrete* and *abstract nouns*, *general to specific*, *details*, and *emphasis*.

METHODS TO CHECK FOR DEVELOPMENT

To check for development, do any of the following:

- Underline the general statements in your paper and circle the concrete descriptions or specifics. Does underlining outweigh circling? What does that tell you? Is there little underlining? If so, can you understand the purpose or main idea of the specifics that are circled?
- Ask yourself questions. How do you know that your general assertions are true? What experiences have led you to your conclusions? Why do you believe as you do? How can you *show* your reader, not just *tell* him, that your ideas are valid?
- Look for clichés, jargon, or pat expressions. What do you really mean when you use them? Can you find another way to develop your ideas?
- Ask someone to describe your paper to you. What ideas did he miss or forget? Does that mean he did not have enough details to remember or notice these ideas?

APPROACHES FOR REWRITING TO
IMPROVE DEVELOPMENT

To improve development, do any of the following:

- Use dialogue to let the reader hear what the people in your paper say. As Mark Twain once put it, "If you want to say the old lady screamed, drag her out and let her scream." Bring out your characters; a bit of dialogue can add life to even a shadowy character.
- Use facts or statistics to support your statements. This method of development is especially useful if you have researched your subject. Use books such as *Information Please Almanac, New International Year Book, Statistical Abstract of the United States,* or the *CBS News Almanac* to find material to reinforce your ideas.
- Use comparison and contrast to develop an idea. You might show how one idea is different from another or how the two are the same. This method is an excellent way to get your reader involved. Relate your ideas to something he already knows.
- Analyze the subject. Take the idea apart and look at its components.
- Classify ideas. If you are working with several ideas, develop the relationships between them so that the reader sees how they are being grouped.
- Define an idea. If you are working with an idea a reader may not understand, one way to develop it is to define it. This approach is especially useful when writing about abstract subjects such as love, peace, friendship, or prejudice.
- Quote others on the subject. Just be careful not to let the experts take over your paper.
- Consider how other writers make their subjects interesting. If you think your introduction is dull or you cannot find ways to describe your ideas, analyze what other authors do to get you interested.
- Avoid clichés, jargon, and pat expressions that are someone else's thinking and not your own. (See Chapter 8, page 230.)
- Define the abstract terms you use. If you talk about love, *show* us the fireworks, the roses, the comfortable routines, the unexpected pleasures.
- Add more details so that your reader can feel, sense, hear, or smell what you experienced.
- Find another way to present your ideas so that they are more interesting, such as writing a story, editorial, speech, comparative essay, or dialogue.

CHAPTER 7

Editing:
Having a Reader Evaluate Your Work

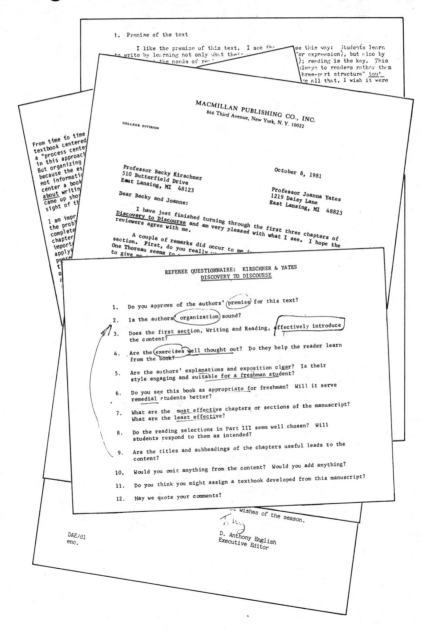

Editing is an essential part of the writing process. It gives you a chance to have an editor look carefully at the work in order to tell you how ready it is for a reader. The editor will comment not only on your ideas and how they interest him but also on how well you have focused on your subject, taken your reader into account, organized the ideas and tied them together, and on how well you developed your ideas. In effect, editing is pointing out areas of the paper that will create problems for a reader and suggesting how the writer can make changes.

In this stage, you will exchange your paper with a classmate and edit his paper while he edits yours. As with reader reaction, your editing skills and those of your editor will improve with practice. You might like to see what experienced writers say about this stage. If so, see "How to Write with Style" by Kurt Vonnegut and "How to Write Clearly" by Edward Thompson in Chapter 9 for ideas on how to edit and revise or rewrite.

As an editor, use the form suggested by your teacher or the one that best suits the writer's work. Answer the questions carefully and thoughtfully, and make helpful suggestions. After editing, return the paper to the author.

When the editor has returned your paper and the editing form for it, decide what you will do to rewrite. Reread your paper, consider the editor's comments, and answer the following questions:

1. Which areas of my paper (focus and purpose, organization, development) will create problems for a reader?
2. What should I do to rewrite the paper to make it meet a reader's expectations?

Rewrite by using the suggestions your editor made and referring to the section on "Rewriting: Meeting the Reader's Needs," in Chapter 6. Before moving on to Chapter 8, ask an editor to review your rewritten draft.

EDITING FORM A

Writer and Editor: Trade papers and use this form to evaluate the work you read. Your written responses and suggestions will help the writer understand how well he or she has met a reader's conventional expectations.

General Comments: Write a short letter to the author describing what was most interesting to you.

Focus and Purpose: Use *one or more* of the following methods to check for focus and purpose.

1. Write down the main idea of paper as you remember it. Then look for sentences that state this idea and underline them. Note any problems the writer's audience might have in finding or understanding the main idea.

2. Circle the words that help you understand the main idea and purpose of the paper. Explain how these words reflect the main idea or reinforce the purpose, or note where such words could be added.

3. Reread the title and introduction. Describe how well they limit the subject and make it interesting for the writer's audience.

4. Reread the conclusion and write down how you feel or what you think. Then predict how the writer's audience will react.

Suggestions: If you were the writer of this paper, what is one thing you would do to make the focus and purpose clearer? Suggest any of the approaches given on page 180 in Chapter 6 under "Approaches for Rewriting for Focus and Purpose."

Organization: Use *one or more* of the following methods to check for organization.

1. Reread the introduction and explain how you expect the paper to unfold. Underline the words that suggest this direction and then describe how well the paper follows your predictions. Note any problems the audience might have with the organization of the paper.

2. Reread the conclusion and describe its purpose. Consider how well it ties together the ideas. Or how well it reinforces the paper's purpose. Or how well it leads the audience to new insights about the subject.

3. Make a descriptive outline of the paper by writing down the main idea and then explaining how each paragraph or section relates to it. Note any section that does not show a clear relationship to the main idea.

4. Look at the individual paragraphs or sections of the paper and summarize the main ideas. Explain what the writer has done to organize these sections, and note any problems the audience might have in following the ideas.

5. Underline or circle the words that help you move smoothly from one idea to the next. Describe any problems you had following the author's ideas.

6. Look at the tenses used and the point of view of the paper. Note in the margin any inconsistencies or places where the audience could become confused.

Suggestions: If you were the writer of this paper, what is one thing you would do to make the ideas easier to follow? Suggest any of the approaches given on page 182 in Chapter 6 for "Approaches for Rewriting to Improve Organization and Transitions."

Development: Use *one or more* of the following methods to check for development.

1. Make a list of the ideas and details you remember most clearly and explain why they stay in your mind.

2. Make a list of questions that you want the writer to answer, or that you think the audience might ask after reading the paper.

3. Underline the general ideas and then describe how they are developed within the paragraphs or sections of the paper. Note in the margin where the writer's audience might need additional information, or where a general idea should be added to pull together the specific information given.

4. Underline or circle any phrase or word that the audience will consider inappropriate or that does not clearly communicate the writer's ideas. Consider jargon, clichés, and trite or pat expressions.

Suggestions: If you were the writer of this paper, what is one thing you would do to develop the ideas more fully? Suggest any of the appraoches given on page 184 in Chapter 6 for "Approaches for Rewriting to Improve Development."

EDITING FORM B

Writer: Trade papers with your editor. After he finishes, the editor will discuss your paper with you or will provide you with a written record of his responses. Take down any notes that will help you revise or rewrite.

Editor: As you read the paper, jot down what you want to discuss with the author or make notes in the margin of the paper. Use this form to guide you in preparing your written or oral responses to the following:

General Comments: Explain to the writer what you liked best about the paper.

Focus and Purpose: Use *one or more* of the following methods to check for focus and purpose.

1. Discuss the kind of audience you see for this paper and what their reactions might be. Consider what they already know about the subject, what will interest them, and whether they will disagree or agree with the ideas.

2. Describe the introduction to the author and discuss how well it limits the subject. Explain what you see as the main idea and point out the words, phrases, or sentences that would make the main idea especially clear and interesting to the audience. Mention any problems the audience might have with the introduction.

3. Think about how you felt or what you thought when you came to the end of the paper.

Discuss with the author how well the conclusion helped to reinforce the purpose of the paper or reflect the main idea.

Suggestions: What do you think the writer could do to make the main idea clearer or more interesting? Suggest any of the approaches given on page 180 in Chapter 6.

Organization: Use *one or more* of the following methods to check for organization.

1. Read the introduction and describe how you expect the paper to be organized. Point out the words that reinforce your expectations and discuss how well the paper follows this pattern. Mention any problems the audience might have with the organization.

2. Read the conclusion and explain what you see as its function within the paper. Consider how well it reflects the main idea of the paper or reinforces its purpose. Or how well it leads the audience to develop new insights about the subject.

3. Make a map of the paper by describing the main idea and identifying the organizational pattern. Discuss where the paper starts, each point it develops, and the paper's final destination. Point out the words and phrases that reinforce the organizational pattern or note where the relationships in the paper need to be clarified.

4. Look at the individual sections or paragraphs within the paper and summarize the main ideas to the author. Explain what the author has done to organize these sections and discuss any problems the audience might have in following the ideas.

Suggestions: What is one thing the writer could do to make the ideas easier to follow? Suggest any of the approaches given on page 182 in Chapter 6.

Development: Use *one or more* of the following methods to check for development.

1. Describe the ideas or pictures that you have in mind after reading this paper. Explain why they are vivid to you. Also, point out any section or idea that might be unclear to the audience.

2. Point out the specifics the writer used and explain how well they supported or developed the general ideas. Also, mention any areas where the audience might need a general statement to understand the specifics used.

3. Ask the writer any questions you have about the ideas discussed. Or think about what kinds of questions the writer should answer for his audience and discuss these with him. him.

Suggestions: What is one thing the writer could do to develop the ideas more fully? Suggest any of the approaches given on page 184 in Chapter 6.

EDITING FORM C

Writer and Editor: Trade papers and use this form as a general guide for evaluating the piece you read. Jot down the conventions you look for in each area, the methods you use to check for these conventions, and any suggestions that will help prepare this draft for the final audience. Refer to Chapter 6 for rewriting approaches when necessary.

General Comments: Write down what you think will be most interesting and enlightening to the writer's audience.

Focus and Purpose:

1. What are you looking for?

2. What methods can you use to check on the focus or purpose?

3. What can the writer do to make the focus sharper or the purpose clearer?

Organization:

1. What are you looking for?

2. What methods can you use to check on the organization?

3. What can the writer do to make the ideas easier to follow for the audience?

Development:

1. What are you looking for?

2. What methods can you use to check on the development.

3. What can the writer do to develop the ideas more fully?

EDITING FORM D

Writer: Tailor this form to your paper by asking your own questions. Keep in mind the specific conventions you want your editor to look for and how he can do so. Make sure to cover the three areas listed on this form.

Editor: Answer the writer's questions as carefully and helpfully as you can. Refer to Chapter 6 when necessary to give suggestions.

General Comments:

Focus and Purpose:

Organization:

Development:

CHAPTER 8

Copyediting: Completing the Writing Process

~~about writing as being a useful means of communication.~~

If you are to improve your writing ability, you will be more successful
if you can recapture the enthusiasm and desire you (first) had when you λlearned
to write your name, and if you can once again see writing as a way to share
your ideas with another person. As with learning to do anything, from walking
to swinging a golf club, your attitude is crucial. If you are be become a

These statistics were compiled through the Michigan State University's Placement
Center, one of the largest college placement services in the country. Each
year, Director Jack Shingleton and Aossciate Director Patrick Sheetz survey
Associate   *sp ??*
hundreds of potential employers to determine which qualities are most important
in potential employees. The ability to communicate in writing has been near
the top of the list for many years, But in 1980, it was cited as the number
one quality. Keep in mind that these employers were looking for recruits in
all areas including business, engineering, journalism, communications, medicine
and liberal arts (among many others)

To learn just how important writing is in each field, we did a follow-up
study in which we surveyed and interviewed nearly two-hundred recruiters on
campus who came looking for qualified, potential employees in all major fields.
From those responses, we learned that writing is a major part of the job for
every college graduate. One engineer suggested we advise engineering students
to take as much English and writing as possible. He said he was surprised to
learn that his progress in the company he worked for had depended heavily on
his ability to communicate in writing. A computer programmer told us that he
spent most of his time writing proposals for future projects while graduates
from technical schools worked on the computer. While the amount of time writing
var ied, most recruiters said the new employee would write letters, memos, proposals, and reports on a weekly if not daily basis.

Writing Response: If you have not felt that writing will be important
to you in your future, why not talk or write to a number of successful people who work in the field you consider entering. Ask them
how much they write, how often, how much their chances for promotion
are tied to their writing ability. ~~This might just be the motiva-~~

Even though a writer might like to revise and rewrite further before handing in the final manuscript, he must take time to fulfill the reader's last expectation: correctness. Because language is a social act, every time a person writes for a reader, he enters into a contract. If he is to communicate and have the reader understand his ideas, then the writer must use the accepted conventions of spelling, usage, punctuation, and style expected by the reader.

Correctness would not be a problem if language were a simple act governed by only a dozen rules. But as you know, it is possible to write almost any sentence in a variety of ways, each with a different meaning. And it is this flexibility and richness of language that create almost limitless possibilities for error. The hundreds of rules in grammar texts attest to this problem.

Unlike standard handbooks, this chapter offers you copyediting methods to check spelling, usage, punctuation, and style. Instead of giving you rules, it identifies the most troublesome areas, such as confusing *their* with *there* or overusing commas, and provides checklists and strategies for finding and correcting problems in your work. We suggest reliable reference books that you can consult when you are concerned about rules. Because you will be writing throughout your college career and at work, your own reference library—a good dictionary, a handbook, and any other writing guide you need—is a worthwhile investment.

Use the General Checklist that follows to find the areas you need to focus on. Review the introductions to each area, complete the checklists, and consult the general strategies and common problems when necessary. If you want a reader to copyedit your paper, ask him to use the Copyediting/Proofreading Form on page 198.

GENERAL CHECKLIST

Use this guide to look for common problems in spelling, usage, punctuation, and style. If any of the conventions are unfamiliar to you, make sure to read the explanations provided in this chapter or refer to a handbook for more detailed examples. And if you need strategies for copyediting, turn to the appropriate pages.

Spelling:

General strategies for checking spelling, p. 204

_____ Apostrophes, p. 205

_____ Homonyms, p. 206

_____ General spelling problems, p. 206

_____ The spoken word vs. the written word, p. 207

_____ Capitalization, p. 207

Usage:

General strategies for checking usage, p. 210

_____ Pronoun references, p. 211

_____ Subject/verb agreement, p. 212

_____ Faulty syntax, p. 212

_____ Parallel structure, p. 212

_____ Missing or faulty relationships, p. 213

Punctuation:

General strategies for checking punctuation, p. 219

_____ Commas, p. 220

_____ Periods, p. 221

_____ Semicolons, p. 221

_____ Colons, p. 222

_____ Dashes, p. 222

_____ Exclamation marks, p. 222

_____ Question marks, p. 222

_____ Quotation marks, p. 222

Style:

General strategies for checking style, p. 228

____ Denotation vs. connotation, p. 229

____ Homonyms and synonyms, p. 229

____ Abstract vs. concrete words, p. 230

____ Clichés, pat expressions, and jargon, p. 230

____ *At this point in time* vs. *now*, p. 231

____ Voice, p. 231

COPYEDITING/PROOFREADING FORM

Writer _____   Editor _____

1. *Spelling:* Use one of the strategies for checking spelling and circle or list any general problems you see. Also, note any of the following areas the writer must double-check.

   ____ Apostrophes (p. 205)

   ____ Homonyms (p. 206)

   ____ Word endings (p. 207)

   ____ Names (p. 207)

   ____ Capitalization (p. 207)

2. *Usage:* If you have to stop and reread a sentence, it may have a usage problem. Put a "?" in the margin where you are confused or have difficulty reading the sentence.

   Do you see any repeated problem? If so, check the areas that you think are interfering with the writer's ideas.

   ____ Pronoun reference (p. 211)

   ____ Subject/verb agreement (p. 212)

   ____ Faulty syntax (p. 212)

   ____ Parallel structure (p. 212)

   ____ Missing or faulty relationships (p. 213)

   ____ Other (explain) _____

   If you do find recurrent problems, what reference book or handbook do you suggest the writer look at? _____

What specific section or pages? _____

What one strategy would you suggest the writer use to state his ideas more clearly? _____

_____

3. *Punctuation:* Any sentence you need to read again may be flawed by incorrect or missing punctuation. Put an asterisk where you think punctuation is needed or is used incorrectly. Double-check by reading the sentence out loud or by writing it alone on a separate sheet of paper.

Do you see any repeated problems with run-on sentences _____ or fragments _____?

Does the paper flow? _____

Are there any choppy sections? _____ If so, point these out.

Are there any sentences that seem too long? _____ If so, point these out.

Is there any handbook or reference book that you think the writer should look at for punctuation? _____ What specific pages? _____

What is one strategy you think will help the writer punctuate his sentences so that they are easy to read and understand? _____

_____

4. *Style:* Has the author helped you see, feel, or understand the ideas in his paper by using definite, concrete words? _____ Point out the sections that are most successful. Also, let the writer know if any section, sentence, or idea is vague.

Is there any area in the style section of this chapter that you think the writer should review? If so, which one? _____

Why? _____

After reading the paper, how do you feel about it? _____

How do you think the vocabulary contributed to your impressions? _____

_____

Is there any one recommendation or compliment you would like to make? _____

_____

_____

SPELLING

English is one of the most active, colorful languages in the world. We enjoy hot *chocolate* and *demitasses* of *expresso;* we have tremendous *orange* groves in the South and Southwest; we have all gone to *kindergarten,* and some of us watched the first *Sputnik* circle our *planet.* The American Indian, the French, Italians, Arabs, Germans, Russians, and Greeks are only a few of the peoples who have enriched the language with their own words and ideas. But this variety has also created problems. Can you imagine someone sitting down at a desk, pen in hand, trying to create logical and all-encompassing spelling rules?

Impossible, you say? The following essay presents one man's solution to part of this problem. He is an imaginary radio sports announcer who has irregularized all our troublesome verbs to make them conform to logical rules of spelling and usage.

WHO FLANG THAT BALL?, by W. F. Miksch

My assignment was to interview Infield Ingersoll, one-time shortstop for the Wescosville Wombats and now a radio sports announcer. Dizzy Dean, Red Barber and other sportscasters had taken back seats since the colorful Ingersoll had gone on the air. The man had practically invented a new language.

"I know just what you're gonna ask," Infield began. "You wanna know how come I use all them ingrammatical expressions like 'He swang at a high one.' You think I'm illitrut."

"No, indeed," I said. Frankly, I *had* intended to ask him what effect he thought his extraordinary use of the King's English might have on future generations of radio listeners.

But a gleam in Infield's eyes when he said "illitrut" changed my mind. "What I'd really like to get," I said, "is the story of how you left baseball and became a sportscaster."

Infield looked pleased. "Well," he said, "it was the day us Wombats plew the Pink Sox . . ."

"Plew the Pink Sox?" I interrupted. "Don't you mean played?"

Infield's look changed to disappointment. "Slay, slew. Play, plew. What's the matter with that?"

NO THINKING THIS WAY

"Slay is an irregular verb," I pointed out.

"So who's to say what's regular or irregular? English teachers! Can an English teacher bat three hundred?"

W. F. Miksch, "Who Flang that Ball," in *This Week Magazine,* 1951. Reprinted by permission of Maxwell Aley Associates.

He paused belligerently, and then went on. "What I'm tryin' to do is easify the languish. I make all regular verbs irregular. Once they're all irregular, then it's just the same like they're all regular. That way I don't gotta stop and think."

He had something there. "Go on with your story," I said.

"Well, it was the top of the fifth, when this Sox batter wang out a high pop fly. I raught for it."

"Raught?"

"Past tense of verb to Reach. Teach, taught. Reach, —"

"Sorry," I said. "Go ahead."

"Anyhow I raught for it, only the sun blound me."

"You mean blinded?"

"Look," Infield said patiently, "you wouldn't say a pitcher winded up, would you? So there I was, blound by the sun, and the ball just nuck the tip of my glove—that's nick, nuck; same congregation as stick, stuck. But luckily I caught it just as it skam the top of my shoe."

"Skam? Could that be the past tense of to skim?"

"Yeah, yeah, same as swim, swam. You want this to be a English lesson or you wanna hear my story?"

"Your story please, Mr. Ingersoll."

"Okay. Well, just then the umpire cell, 'Safe!' Naturally I was surprise. Because I caught that fly, only the ump cell the runner safe."

"Cell is to call as fell is to fall, I suppose?" I inquired.

"Right. Now you're beginning to catch on." Infield regarded me happily as if there was now some hope for me. "So I yold at him, 'Robber! That decision smold!'"

"Yell, yold, Smell, smold," I mumbled. "Same idea as tell, told."

Infield rumbled on, "I never luck that umpire anyway."

"Hold it!" I cried. I finally had tripped this backhand grammarian. "A moment ago, you used nuck as the past for nick, justifying it by the verb to stick. Now you use luck as a verb. Am I to assume by this that luck is the past tense of to lick?"

NOBODY LUCK HIM

"Luck is past for like. To like is a regular irregular verb of which there are several such as strike, struck. Any farther questions or should I go on?"

"Excuse me," I said, "you were saying you never luck that umpire."

"And neither did the crowd. Everyone thrould at my courage. I guess I better explain thrould," Infield said thoughtfully. "Thrould comes from thrill just like would comes from will. Got that? Now to get back to my story: 'Get off the field, you bum, and no back talk!' the umpire whoze."

"Whoze?"

"He had asthma," Infield pointed out patiently.

I saw through it instantly. Wheeze, whoze. Freeze, froze.

"And with those words, that ump invote disaster. I swang at him and smeared him with a hard right that lood square on his jaw."

"Lood? Oh, I see—Stand, stood, Land, lood—it lood on his jaw."

"Sure. He just feld up and went down like a light. As he reclone on the field, he pept at me out of his good eye."

"SO I QUAT"

"Now wait. What's this pept?" I asked.

"After you sleep, you've did what?" Infield inquired.

"Why, slept—oh, he peeped at you, did he?"

"You bet he pept at me. And in that peep I saw it was curtains for me in the league henceforward. So I beat him to it and just up and quat."

"Sit, sat. Quit—well, that gets you out of baseball," I said. "Only you still haven't told me how you got to be on radio and television."

"I guess that'll have to wait," Infield said, "on account I gotta hurry now to do a broadcast."

As he shade my hand good-by, Infield grun and wank at me.

After reading this essay, you can see how inconsistent English usage and spelling are. For example, there are two *f* sounds, the *f* in *fast* and the *f* sound in *enough*. The past tense of the verb *dream* can be spelled either *dreamed* or *dreamt*. With all this inconsistency, you need a reliable guide to help you check spelling because misspellings are not only annoying to many people, they can interfere with the communication of ideas. No doubt you had a difficult time trying to make sense out of the spellings and forms in Miksch's essay, but he used them to prove a point and to prove it humorously. Unless you want to make a similar point and entertain your reader, it is crucial to spell correctly in order to communicate your ideas effectively.

References

Any standard dictionary with contemporary spellings and explanations of usage is fine. Should you want to invest in a specialized text, you might consider any one of these:

The Mis-Speller's Dictionary, Time Books

Look It Up, A Deskbook of American Spelling and Style, Harper & Row

Handbook of American English Spelling, Harcourt Brace Jovanovich

Dictionary of Homonyms: New Word Patterns, Amereon Ltd.

Webster's New World Speller/Divider, Simon & Schuster

Correct Spelling Made Easy, Dell Paperbacks

Words Most Often Misspelled and Mispronounced, Pocket Books

SPELLING CHECKLIST

Use this page to note any spelling problems you have. Make sure that your copyeditor sees this list to spot any misspellings. Also, mark down any of the references and specific page numbers that are especially helpful to you. Most handbooks have excellent sections on spelling that cover areas not mentioned in this chapter. Last, note the strategies that help you most in spotting misspellings.

General Problem   *Reference*   *Strategies*

General Strategies for Checking Spelling

1. *Use a checklist.* Look at papers you have done in the past to see if common spelling problems occur. Do you confuse *des-* and *dis-* or *in-* and *im-* prefixes? Or endings such as *-ence* or *-ance* or *-ible* and *-able?* Do you miss apostrophes, confuse certain homonyms, leave off word endings, or chronically misspell the same word(s)?

Make a list of any spelling problems on the form on page 203. When proofreading, make several passes through the last draft, looking only for those words.

2. *Read your paper backward.* Even though you try to look for misspellings while going through a draft, it is easy to get caught up in ideas instead of looking at individual words. By reading for meaning, you will miss errors. Reading your paper backward means starting with the last word of your conclusion, moving your eye from right to left on each line, and ending with the first word of the introduction. This method will help you spot the words that look wrong—the kinds of words that give you problems.

3. *Find a spelling whiz to check your work.*

4. *Underline or circle words you are unsure of.* In writing the early drafts, you may not remember how to spell certain words or may not be sure of some spellings. Do not bother to look them up then, but do underline or circle those words as a reminder to check them later.

5. *Use an eraser.* Some students prefer to focus on individual words by putting the eraser end of a pencil under each word. That way, they are less inclined to try rewriting or rephrasing sentences. They stop under each word for a second or less, with the eraser forcing their eyes to look at single words instead of whole phrases or sentences.

6. *Type your paper.* Many of our students have found typing papers the biggest help in spotting spelling errors. Not only do they have to concentrate on each letter of every word when typing, but they have a chance to see the words in printed form. (If you use this technique, make sure to proofread your typed draft for typographical errors as well as misspellings.)

7. *Double-check names.* Do yourself a favor and check the proper names that appear in your essay, report, or job application. There is nothing quite so annoying to an employer as seeing his name misspelled. And when the principal subjects of an essay or report are misspelled, the teacher, boss, or other reader begins to wonder how accurate your work really is.

Common Problems

Being aware of what spelling problems are most common will help you copyedit your work more efficiently and hand in better-prepared final drafts.

APOSTROPHES

Apostrophes rank high on the list of most common spelling problems. Remember, they are most often used in one of two ways:

1. To replace missing letters in contractions.
2. To show possession.

Example: Do not = don't   Here the apostrophe replaces the missing *o* in *not.*

The cat's mouse   Here the apostrophe indicates that the mouse belongs to the cat.

If possession is confusing or if you have trouble distinguishing when to use the apostrophe and when not, this concept may help. The letter *s* at the end of the word is used to indicate a number of things: number, single-subject verbs (he builds, she runs), and possession. However, *s* cannot represent more than one function at a time. So, if you have a plural noun, the *s* will tell you that more than one person, place, or thing is involved. And if you have a plural noun that possesses something, say three cats who have a mouse, then you need to indicate both functions. In *cats's mouse*, the first *s* indicates number, the second possession. However, in the last 20 years, a stylistic change has occurred; the second *s* has been dropped. Some handbooks recommend retaining the double *s* (cats's), and others advise dropping it. And that is why you see *cats'* today more often than *cats's.* If you want a more detailed description or specific examples, consult one of the references in the sections on "Usage" and "Punctuation."

Most of our students understand how possession works for people and objects, but they have trouble with abstract nouns. For example, *a society has many rules.* To convey this idea in fewer words, you can either write *rules of society* or *society's rules.* If you have trouble with this concept, ask yourself what idea you want to express or try rewriting the passage.

Example: The nations industries are gradually changing.

> *Question:* Do the industries belong to the nation? Yes. Then you need to put an apostrophe between the *n* and *s*. (And if your answer is that the industries belong to the nations, then the apostrophe must go after the *s* because that *s* signifies number.)
>
> *Rewrite:* The industries *of* the nation(s) are gradually changing. The industries that *belong to* the nation(s) are gradually changing.
>
> Because both of these rewritten sentences indicate possession, an apostrophe is needed if you want to write, "The nation's industries . . ."

Another way you can check for apostrophes is by looking at any word ending in *s* and deciding what that *s* shows. If it represents number or a single-subject verb, no apostrophe is needed. If the *s* stand for possession, then you need the apostrophe.

HOMONYMS

The next common problem is confusing certain words that sound alike but have different meanings. The words most often confused are:

they're	there	their		your	you're
two	too	to		then	than
are	our			affect	effect
it's	its			principle	principal

Everyone knows the meanings of these words, but when you are concentrating on ideas, it is easy to overlook spelling. If homonyms are a problem for you, put these words on the spelling checklist and make a special effort to look for them when copyediting.

GENERAL SPELLING PROBLEMS

Almost everyone has general spelling difficulties. Some writers cannot remember when to use an *-ible* or *-able* ending. Others have difficulty with *-ence* or *-ance* endings. Look over papers you have written for previous classes and see if any common spelling problems appear. Find out what kinds of words give you difficulty, make a note on the spelling checklist, and proofread specifically for such words.

THE SPOKEN WORD VERSUS THE WRITTEN WORD

Another problem area is the discrepancy between how we pronounce certain words and how they are actually written. Although we mean to say *should have, could have, would have,* or *might have,* the words sound more like *should of.* The message here is to use your eyes more than your ears.

At other times, the endings of words, especially *-ed* or *-g,* are not clearly pronounced, but they are required in accurate written work. You may not say the *-ed* in *supposed to* or mash*ed potatoes,* but that ending should be there when you write those words. The same goes for words such as *going* (instead of *gonna* or *goin*) or *feeling* (instead of *feelin*).

CAPITALIZATION

Because more people are publishing and writing on a greater variety of subjects, the spelling conventions have become more inconsistent over the years. Social scientists capitalize terms that literature students might not and advertising writers use conventions that are different from general usage. So, a general rule to follow is to capitalize specific proper nouns.

Persons:	Agatha Christie, President Carter
Places:	Grand Canyon, Hyde Street
Months:	February
Peoples:	Native Americans, Jews, Asians
Nationalities:	Bolivians, New Zealanders
Languages:	Danish, Vietnamese
Religions:	Buddhism, Judaism

Usually, seasons such as fall or summer, racial groups such as blacks and whites, and general directions such as north or west are not capitalized. When in doubt, refer to the University of Chicago *Manual of Style.*

Make sure to find out what spelling conventions exist in your discipline, profession, or area of research. And double-check any word you are unsure of in a current handbook or dictionary.

USAGE

Imagine that your car just landed in a ditch. You call a wrecking service, and when the tow truck comes, you explain to the driver what happened: "I pulled away from the side of the road, glanced at my mother-in-law, and headed over the embankment." Unless your mother-in-law rides a broom and wears a black hat, she probably did not send you heading for the ditch, as your sentence implies.

Or suppose you are an officer taking down a police report, and a driver tells you, "The guy was all over the road. I had to swerve a number of times before I hit him." You would probably want to arrest and handcuff the driver for being a public menace.

As you can see, writing a sentence that says what you mean involves more than putting nouns and verbs in the right place. Sentences have to make good sense to your reader as well. The examples given come from actual insurance claims. They are humorous, and you can probably guess what the people meant to say in both cases. However, in essays, term papers, or application forms, you do not want your audience to guess at your ideas or think that you are trying to be a comedian. For help with usage, look at the references we suggest in the next section and at the common causes of sentences that betray your ideas.

References

Every writer has occasional questions or problems concerning usage. Any one of the following references serves well for explaining particular grammar and usage points.

Elements of Style, Strunk and White, Macmillan
Handbook, Macmillan
Questions you always wanted to ask about English*
    *but were afraid to raise your hand, Pocket Books
The New York Times Manual of Style and Usage, Times Books
Students' Guide for Writing College Papers, University of Chicago
    Press
The Writer's Hotline Handbook, Mentor—New American Library
The Business Writing Handbook, Bantam Books
Writing That Works, St. Martin's Press

USAGE CHECKLIST

List the problems or questions you have with usage. Jot down the reference and specific pages that are most helpful to you; then note what strategies help you find and correct errors.

General Problem   *Reference*   *Strategies*

General Strategies for Checking Usage

Use any one of the following strategies to find grammar problems that interfere with communicating what you mean. At first, you may not be able to focus on all the problems mentioned in this section. Instead of concentrating on too many things, start with the usage problems you want to work on and use one of the handbooks for more detailed explanations.

1. *Make up a checklist and reference guide.* Look through your previous papers to see what kinds of usage problems are most common. Note these problems on the form on page 209, along with the pages from this text or another handbook that help you understand what is needed in revising or rewriting. If you find usage problems not covered in this chapter, consult one of the references cited and list the pages that are most helpful. That way, you will have a quick reference guide for answering the usage questions that occur.

2. *Read the paper out loud.* You have several options. First, read your paper aloud to someone in class or in your dorm. Have the listener stop you whenever an idea is unclear, and try to explain what you mean. Make a note where you need to rewrite. Second, have someone in class or in the dorm read your paper aloud to you. When that person stumbles or needs to reread a sentence, it may mean that your idea should be expressed more clearly and simply. Try to explain what you mean and note that place on your draft. Finally, if it is 3 A.M. when you are proofreading and you cannot find a willing audience, go to a place where you can either read the paper out loud to yourself or into a tape recorder. *Listen* to your ideas. When something does not sound quite right or a sentence does not say what you mean, stop and try to explain your idea again. If stopping does not work, note where you need to rewrite and go back to the draft later.

3. *Think of your ideas as pictures.* Once you have found sentences that need work, try to think of your sentence as a series of pictures that develop in a logical sequence. Keep the order straight in your mind and then find words that make the relationships clear; or rearrange the parts of your sentences until they match the order in your mind; or take out or add what you need to bring the series of pictures in focus for your reader. As Joan Didion says in "Why I Write," "The arrangement of the words matters, and the arrangement you want can be found in the picture in your mind. The picture dictates the arrangement."

4. *Isolate problem sentences.* If you have problems in finding out why a sentence is confusing or seeing how to rewrite it, take it out of the paper and write it on a separate sheet of paper. Think about what you mean and what the sentence actually says. Change what you want or throw the sentence out and write another.

5. *Rewrite the idea, not just the words.* Instead of plugging in different words or rearranging the parts of the sentence, you may have to consider the idea once more, throw the problem sentence out, and write a new sentence. If the idea you want to express is not quite clear to you, take time to think about it and try it out in your journal. Or try rereading the ideas that come before or after the problem sentence. Once you know what you want to say, try writing it in your journal. Do not worry about grammar until you get the idea on paper.

6. *Say it aloud.* If you get stuck on a sentence, pretend you are talking to a friend and express the idea out loud as simply and directly as possible. As soon as you say what you mean, jot down the sentence. If necessary, have a roommate or classmate listen or take down your thoughts.

Common Problems

Confusing sentences are sometimes caused by a word that signals an inaccurate relationship, by the order of the words and phrases within the sentence, or by individual words. Sometimes, it is the whole sentence that fails to communicate. The following are some of the causes of sentences that do not say what the writer means.

PRONOUN REFERENCE

What do the following sentences actually say?

I was taking my canary to the hospital. It got loose in the car and flew out the window. The next thing I saw was his rear end, and there was a crash.

Undoubtedly, it was not the canary's rear end the driver saw, but the tail end of another car. Remember that words such as *his, hers, its, theirs, he, she,* and *it* do not name the subject you have *in mind.* If you use these words, make sure they correspond with the logical or most recently cited subject. If you change subjects or introduce new ones, make sure to let your reader know by announcing who or what that new subject is.

Another area of confusion is using the correct pronoun with words such as *everyone, anyone,* and *someone.* Although these words do not name a specific person and seem to refer to many people, they are considered singular nouns and require the use of singular pronouns—*he, him, she, her.*

Example: Everyone carries *his* umbrella on rainy days.
Someone called today. *She* left her number for you.

Finally, be careful when using *I* and *me*. *I* is always properly the subject of a sentence, and *me* is the object of a sentence or a preposition. People have become so conscious of using *me* incorrectly that they tend to avoid it altogether.

> *Example: I* am leaving tomorrow. Did you bring *me* the ticket.
> Between you and *me*, I am very weary of typing.

SUBJECT/VERB AGREEMENT

Keep a firm grasp on your subject so that the verb you use corresponds to it. Do not let the information between the subject and the verb distract you, so that you write sentences such as these:

> One of you lucky people are going to Hawaii! (*One* of you . . . *is* . . .)
> Some types of music defies understanding. (Some *types* . . . *defy* . . .)

FAULTY SYNTAX

Although a sentence represents one main thought, it is composed of many parts. And the way you put those parts together helps the reader understand what you mean. For example:

> The indirect cause of the accident was a little guy in a sports car with a big mouth.

This sentence literally says that the car has a big mouth, which is not what the writer means. Even in very brief communications, syntax is important:

> Lost: Large, red woman's purse.

The order of the words in this ad may make the reader think that a large, red woman has lost her purse.

To keep from muddling the syntax of your sentences, make sure that you understand the relationships among the words and phrases and put the related words together.

PARALLEL STRUCTURE

The writer must make sure not only that the parts of the sentence work together in a logical order but that the parts are compatible as well. By starting a sentence in a particular way or by selecting a certain pattern, you determine how that sentence will continue and end. For example:

> Running a marathon requires that you eat well, lots of practice, and comfortable shoes.

Although the list of requirements is plain, the sentence begins with one grammatical structure and ends with another. Parallelism means that all the parts of a sentence follow the order predicted:

> Running a marathon requires *that you* eat well, (that you) practice often, and (that you) wear comfortable shoes.

MISSING OR FAULTY RELATIONSHIPS

Often, while putting down a sentence, writers have several thoughts in mind and do not always make the right connections within the sentence. Sometimes this problem occurs at the beginning of the sentence, and the connection is missing altogether:

> Being in a dilapidated condition, I was able to buy the house for only $25,000.

The house is dilapidated, not the buyer, but the sentence says the opposite. In this example, it is obvious what the writer means, but what about the following sentence?

> Running down the street, the dog bit me.

Does the writer mean that a dog was running down the street *and then* attacked him, or that *while* he was out jogging, a dog bit him?

Sometimes the relationship within a sentence is faulty, and the writer needs to choose a different word or way of expressing the idea. For example:

> The pedestrian had no idea which direction to take, so I ran over him.

Here the word *so* makes it sound as though the pedestrian deserved to be hit because he did not know which way to go. The writer most likely means that the pedestrian froze, not knowing which way to go, and *he could not avoid* hitting him. Rewriting the sentence makes the relationship between what the pedestrian did and what the driver did clear and accurate.

At other times, a writer may start a sentence with one idea in mind but end it with a different idea and without the bridge the reader needs to connect the thoughts. Here is one example:

A truck backed through the windshield into my wife's face.

The writer may have had three ideas or events in mind while he wrote this sentence. First, a truck backed into his car. Second, the truck's trailer or flatbed smashed into the windshield. Third, the pieces of glass from the windshield went into his wife's face, not the truck. Although the writer meant one thing, his sentence suggested several meanings.

PUNCTUATION

Learning to use commas, periods, colons, semicolons, dashes, and the other punctuation marks correctly involves far more than avoiding red pencil marks on your papers. Punctuation marks are signals to the reader. They tell him when to pause, when information is being added or listed, when a writer has come to the end of an idea, or when he is delighted with something.

The next essay, by an American physician and writer, shows how expressive punctuation is for the writer and how necessary it is for the reader.

NOTES ON PUNCTUATION, by Lewis Thomas

There are no precise rules about punctuation (Fowler lays out some general advice (as best he can under the complex circumstances of English prose (he points out, for example, that we possess only four stops (the comma, the semi-colon, the colon and the period (the question mark and exclamation point are not, strictly speaking, stops; they are indicators of tone (oddly enough, the Greeks employed the semicolon for their question mark (it produces a strange sensation to read a Greek sentence which is a straightforward question: Why weepest thou; (instead of Why weepest thou? (and, of course, there are parentheses (which are surely a kind of punctuation making this whole matter much more complicated by having to count up the left-handed parentheses in order to be sure of closing with the right number (but if the parentheses were left out, with nothing to work with but the stops, we would have considerably more flexibility in the deploying of layers of meaning than if we tried to separate all the clauses by physical barriers (and in the latter case, while we might have more precision and exactitude for our meaning, we would lose the essential flavor of language, which is its wonderful ambiguity))))))))))).

The commas are the most useful and usable of all the stops. It is highly important to put them in place as you go along. If you try to come back after doing a paragraph and stick them in the various spots that tempt you you will discover that they tend to swarm like minnows into all sorts of crevices whose existence you hadn't realized and before you know it the whole long sentence becomes immobilized and lashed up squirming in commas. Better to use them sparingly, and with affection, precisely when the need for each one arises, nicely, by itself.

I have grown fond of semicolons in recent years. The semicolon tells you that there is still some question about the preceding full sentence; something needs to be added; it reminds you sometimes of the Greek usage. It is almost always a greater pleasure to come across a semicolon than a period. The period tells you that that is that; if you didn't get all the meaning you wanted or expected, anyway you got all the writer intended to parcel out and now you have to move along. But with a semicolon there you get a pleasant little feeling of expectancy; there is more to come; read on; it will get clearer.

Colons are a lot less attractive, for several reasons: firstly, they give you the feeling of being rather ordered around, or at least having your nose pointed in a direction you might not be inclined to take if left to yourself, and secondly, you suspect you're in for one of those sentences that will be labeling the points to be made: firstly, secondly and so forth, with the implication that you haven't sense enough to keep track of a sequence of notions without having them numbered. Also, many writers use this system loosely and incompletely, starting out with number one and number two as though counting off on their fingers but then going on and on without the succession of labels you've been led to expect, leaving you floundering about searching for the ninethly or seventeenthly that ought to be there but isn't.

Exclamation points are the most irritating of all. Look! they say, look at what I just said! Hòw amazing is my thought! It is like being forced to watch someone else's small child jumping up and down crazily in the center of the living room shouting to attract attention. If a sentence really has something of importance to say, something quite remarkable, it doesn't need a mark to point it out. And if it is really, after all, a banal sentence needing more zing, the exclamation point simply emphasizes its banality!

Quotation marks should be used honestly and sparingly, when there is a genuine quotation at hand, and it is necessary to be very rigorous about the words enclosed by the marks. If something is to be quoted, the *exact* words must be used. If part of it must be left out because of space limitations, it is good manners to insert three dots to indicate the omission, but it is unethical to do this if it means connecting two thoughts which the original author did not intend to have tied together. Above all, quotation marks should not be used for ideas that you'd like to disown, things in the air so to speak. Nor should they be put in place around clichés; if you want to use a cliché you must take full responsibility for it yourself and not try to fob it off on anon., or on society.

The most objectionable misuse of quotation marks, but one which illustrates the dangers of misuse in ordinary prose, is seen in advertising, especially in advertisements for small restaurants, for example "just around the corner," or "a good place to eat." No single, identifiable, citable person ever really said, for the record, "just around the corner," much less "a good place to eat," least likely of all for restaurants of the type that use this type of prose.

The dash is a handy device, informal and essentially playful, telling you that you're about to take off on a different tack but still in some way connected with the present course — only you have to remember that the dash is there, and either put a second dash at the end of the notion to let the reader know that he's back on course, or else end the sentence, as here, with a period.

As you can see, Thomas feels strongly about the subject and has given you his views as both a writer and a reader on what the different punctuation marks mean. Others have slightly different perspectives. For example, the authors of *Writing That Works* say of colons and of exclamation marks:

> The colon is a mark of anticipation and introduction that alerts the reader to the close connection between the first statement and the one following.

> The exclamation mark (!) indicates an expression of strong feeling. It can signal surprise, fear, indignation, or excitement but should not be used for trivial emotions or mild surprise. Exclamation marks cannot make an argument more convincing, lend force to a weak statement, or call attention to an intended irony — no matter how many are stacked like fence posts at the end of a sentence.

> The most common use of an exclamation mark is after an interjection, phrase, clause, or sentence to indicate strong emotion.

Although these writers have slightly differing judgments about punctuation, their message is the same: Punctuation is a *meaning system*, not a set of arbitrary rules a writer must master.

So, instead of citing rules in this section, we suggest that you reread the previous passages from Thomas and *Writing That Works* and underline the parts that help you understand what punctuation marks mean. If you want more specific explanations or examples of usage, consult one of the references listed in the "Reference" section. There is a checklist you can use to note specific problems in your work and list of general strategies for checking punctuation. Also, we have listed the most common problems associated with certain kinds of punctuation marks that can serve as a guide for checking your own work.

Our last advice on punctuation: Do not avoid using the different marks. By making mistakes, you will learn more about what choices are available for expressing your ideas. And unless you try out the alternatives, you will always be limited to the same ways of writing.

References

All the following texts give detailed, current explanations of punctuation. The last two are especially useful guides for writing term papers.

Any of the previously mentioned handbooks.
The Most Common Mistakes in English Usage, McGraw-Hill Paperbacks
Punctuate It Right!, Harper & Row
A Manual for Writers, University of Chicago Press
MLA Handbook, Modern Language Association

PUNCTUATION CHECKLIST

Note any particular problems or questions you have regarding punctuation. Jot down the reference and specific pages that are most helpful to you; then note what strategies help you spot and correct errors.

General Problem   *Reference*   *Strategies*

General Strategies for Checking Punctuation

Use any of the following strategies to copyedit for punctuation.

1. *Use a checklist.* If you look over your past papers and see that certain punctuation problems persist, note them on a checklist and refer either to the introductory remarks to this section or to one of the references we have mentioned. Write down the problems and then the rules or ideas from a handbook that help you understand punctuation as a meaning system.

2. *Read your paper out loud.* This can be done in different ways. Have a roommate or classmate read your work aloud. If the reader stumbles over any sentences or needs to reread them, the problem may be faulty punctuation. Take out, add, or change the punctuation marks so that the sentence is easy to read and makes good sense.

You can also try reading your paper into a tape recorder and listening to your voice. When you paused on the tape, did you indicate that pause on the paper? When you stopped or took a breath between ideas, did you use a stop in the draft? Listen carefully to your voice, noting when it falls and rises. That analysis will help you determine when you need to break up your ideas, pause for extra information, show surprise or excitement, or ask a question.

3. *Look for danger words.* If you find that your writing has many fragments, look for the danger words that most often introduce fragments. Make sure that the information introduced by words such as *after, when, while, whenever,* or *since* is not broken off from the main idea of the sentence with a period. If it is, simply replace the period (or semicolon) with a comma.

4. *Isolate problem sentences.* If you read a sentence that seems wrong but the problem is not obvious, write the sentence on a separate sheet of paper without the original punctuation. Read the sentence by itself out loud, think about what you mean, and then put in the marks that help you read the sentence most easily.

5. *Ask yourself questions.* If you feel befuddled by all the punctuation rules, think about your ideas and how you want the reader to respond. Do you want the reader to pause? To stop? To know that something important is coming? To anticipate another idea? To puzzle over an idea? To share your excitement or terror? Asking yourself these kinds of questions can help you find the punctuation that reinforces the purpose of the sentence.

Common Problems

The following is a brief list of the most common problems caused by misusing certain punctuation marks. Consult a handbook about other questions you may have on punctuation.

COMMAS

As Thomas says, the comma is one of the most useful punctuation marks. It can set off introductory material in a sentence, show a reader when to pause or when information is being added, or emphasize certain ideas. But when the comma is used incorrectly, it can stop the reader too often or jam too much information into one sentence.

OVERUSE. Add commas to your work as you write the second or third draft, or when you read your draft aloud. If you try to go back and put them in here and there, you may fracture your sentences (and ideas) into so many pieces that the reader will give up reading.

Example:
The writer, with a love of commas, will, eventually, kill his, poor, reader's interest.

To avoid overusing commas, consider what signal you want to give your reader. Do you want him to pause, to understand that you are adding information or listing material to accompany your main sentence, or to focus more sharply on a particular word or phrase? Answering these questions will help you determine when commas are appropriate.

RUN-ONS. Another comma problem is *run-ons* (also known as *comma splices* or *comma faults*). Commas cannot be used alone to signal a complete break between independent thoughts. When too much information is jammed together in one sentence, the reader may stop reading because he is confused.

Example:
Some writers misuse commas, they put them where a period or semicolon belongs.

Between these two thoughts, the reader needs enough time to register all the information. A comma is a split-second pause and, by itself, does not give the reader enough time. To provide a long enough break, a writer can use a period, a semicolon, or a comma *with* a coordinating conjunction such as *and, or, but, for,* or *nor.* So, you could rewrite the example putting a period or a semicolon between the first and second independent thoughts. Or rewrite by adding a coordinating conjunction after the comma, as follows:

> *Example:*
> Some writers misuse commas, and they put them where a period or semicolon belongs.

PERIODS

Periods let the reader take a breath between one thought and the next. If used too often, they create a machine-gun style or sentence fragments.*

MACHINE-GUN STYLE. This kind of style is tedious. It is boring. It limits ideas. Find words that relate your ideas. Use punctuation to link your ideas.

FRAGMENTS. Most often, fragments are introductory remarks to sentences that have been broken off with a period. When this happens. The writer has made the reader stop when the reader should only pause. If this happens too often. The reader will stop reading altogether.

If you begin sentences with words such as *after, while, when, whenever, although, as, as if, because, how, since, so, that, unless,* and *until,* you are giving the reader introductory information that will help him understand the main idea of your sentence. So, it is important not to separate that information from the rest of your idea.

SEMICOLONS

The semicolon is a compromise between a comma and a period, and, as Thomas says, invites the reader to ponder. It allows the reader more time to pause between ideas than does the comma; but the semicolon is a less complete break than the period. (Perhaps it should have been named the *semi-period* instead.)

Semicolons are used incorrectly when they appear in place of commas. When they are used this way, the parts of the sentence are

---

*Sometimes sentence fragments help to emphasize an idea or a word. They are used especially in advertising, creative writing, and persuasive essays. If you feel that a fragment is the most effective way of communicating an idea, use it. But be careful not to excuse dangling thoughts or strings of phrases punctuated with dots as writing that communicates.

separated and the result is a string of fragments. Remember, if you have ideas that you want to link but a comma cannot handle all the information and a period is too severe a break, then the semicolon is a fine solution.

COLONS

The colon is excellent for emphasizing an idea or a word. But it cannot be used to enumerate a point or to list a series in a sentence. That is the job of the comma.

Example:
(Incorrect) I had to get: toothpaste, orange juice, and soap.
(Correct) You can get almost anything at a drug store: frying pans, grass seed, rakes—anything.

DASHES

The dash is one of the most versatile punctuation marks. However, when writers begin to use it, they often overuse it or incorporate the dash when they cannot think of more appropriate punctuation. Do not fall into the trap of using it—whenever you cannot think of something else—because it can be disruptive—and distracting.

EXCLAMATION MARKS

As you have been warned, the exclamation mark can be used too frequently and can detract from your ideas. But remember, at times it is the only punctuation mark that really suits your meaning. So do not be afraid to use it.

QUESTION MARKS

The only problem is forgetting to use the question mark. If you pose a question, reinforce it with the appropriate signal.

QUOTATION MARKS

For accurate and detailed descriptions on how to use quotation marks, consult a handbook. They are used appropriately only when quoting someone else's ideas or citing the title of a work.* Some writers use them to call attention to colloquial terms, clichés, or jargon, trying to excuse their use of such phrases. If you use these forms, do not apologize. Just make sure that they are the *best* way of stating your ideas or making your point, and do not use quotation marks.

STYLE

Turn on the radio, grab a newspaper, or flick the dial to your favorite news broadcast, and there it is: *nontalk.* Between the ideas is a new language manufactured by people who have to fill up space or air time but have little to say or do not want to speak in simple, clear English. It is exasperating to trudge through *in terms of, the reason why is because, as it were or if you will, in my opinion it seems to me that I think,* and all the other meaningless phrases tacked on to ideas. Perhaps people think that nontalk makes them sound more impressive or knowledgeable, but when that filler creeps into an essay or an oral report, it robs both the author and his audience. Space is taken away from the ideas of the writer or speaker, and time is wasted for the reader or listener, who must muddle through to find out what is being communicated. The end result is something like the following essay.

HOW TO SAY NOTHING IN 500 WORDS, by Paul Roberts

It's Friday afternoon, and you have almost survived another week of classes. You are just looking forward dreamily to the weekend when the English instructor says: "For Monday you will turn in a five-hundred word composition on college football."

Well, that puts a good hole in the weekend. You don't have any strong views on college football one way or the other. You get rather excited during the

*When writing specialized reports, term papers, bibliographies, or footnotes, make certain that you know the different conventions for using punctuation. You will need to know when to underline titles and when to use quotation marks, when to use ellipses, or when to use periods, commas, and colons in footnotes and bibliographic entries. *A Manual for Writers* and the *MLA Handbook* are the two most widely used guides. For business reports or writing, *Writing That Works* and *The Business Writing Handbook* are excellent resources.

season and go to all the home games and find it rather more fun than not. On the other hand, the class has been reading Robert Hutchins in the anthology and perhaps Shaw's "Eighty-Yard Run," and from the class discussion you have got the idea that the instructor thinks college football is for the birds. You are no fool. You can figure out what side to take.

After dinner you get out the portable typewriter that you got for high school graduation. You might as well get it over with and enjoy Saturday and Sunday. Five hundred words is about two double-spaced pages with normal margins. You put in a sheet of paper, think up a title, and you're off:

WHY COLLEGE FOOTBALL SHOULD BE ABOLISHED

College football should be abolished because it's bad for the school and also bad for the players. The players are so busy practicing that they don't have any time for their studies.

This, you feel, is a mighty good start. The only trouble is that it's only thirty-two words. You still have four hundred and sixty-eight to go, and you've pretty well exhausted the subject. It comes to you that you do your best thinking in the morning, so you put away the typewriter and go to the movies. But the next morning you have to do your washing and some math problems, and in the afternoon you go to the game. The English instructor turns up too, and you wonder if you've taken the right side after all. Saturday night you have a date, and Sunday morning you have to go to church. (You can't let English assignments interfere with your religion.) What with one thing and another, it's ten o'clock Sunday night before you get out the typewriter again. You make a pot of coffee and start to fill out your views on college football. Put a little meat on the bones.

WHY COLLEGE FOOTBALL SHOULD BE ABOLISHED

In my opinion, it seems to me that college football should be abolished. The reason why I think this to be true is because I feel that football is bad for the colleges in nearly every respect. As Robert Hutchins says in his article in our anthology in which he discusses college football, it would be better if the colleges had race horses and had races with one another, because then the horses would not have to attend classes. I firmly agree with Mr. Hutchins on this point, and I am sure that many other students would agree too.

One reason why it seems to me that college football is bad is that it has become too commercial. In the olden times when people played football just for the fun of it, maybe college football was all right, but they do not play football just for the fun of it now as they used to in the old days. Nowadays college football is what you might call a big business. Maybe this is not true at all schools, and I don't think it is especially true here at State, but certainly this is the case at most colleges and universities in America nowadays, as Mr. Hutchins points out in his very interesting article. Actually the coaches and alumni go around to the high schools and offer the high school stars large salaries to come to their colleges and play football for them. There was one case where a high school star was offered a convertible if he would play football for a certain college.

Another reason for abolishing college football is that it is bad for the players. They do not have time to get a college education, because they are so busy playing football. A football player has to practice every afternoon from three to six and then he is so tired that he can't concentrate on his studies. He just feels like dropping off to sleep after dinner, and then the next day he goes to his classes without having studied and maybe he fails the test.

(Good ripe stuff so far, but you're still a hundred and fifty-one words from home. One more push.)

Also I think college football is bad for the colleges and the universities because not very many students get to participate in it. Out of a college of ten thousand students only seventy-five or a hundred play football, if that many. Football is what you might call a spectator sport. That means that most people go to watch it but do not play it themselves.

(Four hundred and fifteen. Well, you still have the conclusion, and when you retype it, you can make the margins a little wider.)

These are the reasons why I agree with Mr. Hutchins that college football should be abolished in American colleges and universities.

On Monday you turn it in, moderately hopeful, and on Friday it comes back marked "weak in content" and sporting a big "D."

Granted, it is not easy to get excited about this topic. But a writer can still try to say something thought-provoking instead of something trite. Of course, it is important to start with an idea you care about, but even caring will not guarantee success if the words you choose do not convey your passions or the pictures in your mind.

So, how do you say something in 500 *interesting* words?

References

Any standard dictionary with clear, contemporary definitions is an excellent starting point in choosing the words that will communicate your ideas in an accurate, interesting way. You might consider some of the following specialized references found in most school and local libraries.

Dictionary of Homonyms, New Word Patterns, Amereon
Dictionary of American Slang, Crowell Company
The Jonathon David Dictionary of Popular Slang, Jonathon David
The Oxford American Dictionary, Avon Press

Oxford English Dictionary, Oxford University Press
Room's Dictionary of Confusibles, Routledge & Kegan Paul

We find that any one of these references will serve you better than a thesaurus. The thesaurus can help when a writer cannot think of the exact word he wants to use, but it should not be used to plug in a fancy word to impress the audience.

STYLE CHECKLIST

Note any particular problems or questions you have regarding style. Jot down the reference and specific pages that are most helpful to you; then note what strategies help you examine the language you use more critically.

General Concern   *Reference*   *Strategies*

General Strategies to Check for Style

Use any of the following strategies to express your ideas simply and directly.

1. *Use the word that suits your idea and purpose.* If your idea is big and fancy, then use the words that express it. And if your idea requires simplicity, choose the lean, precise words that best communicate this feeling.

2. *Be honest.* Talk for yourself and believe in what you want to say. If a book is boring, then say so and do not apologize. If you disagree with an idea or a person, let your reader know what you think.

3. *Sound like yourself.* Even though some types of writing are more formal than others, let your audience know that there is a real breathing, feeling, thinking person behind those words on the paper.

4. *Make sure that you understand your subject.* If you find sentences galloping away from you and are not quite sure where they are headed, you may be using terms or words you do not understand fully. You may have to do more reading in order to double-check the terms and feel comfortable using them. Or, if there is not time for checking, say what you mean in the words you can use confidently.

5. *Check homonyms and synonyms.* If you think you are confusing words that sound alike or are not sure of the connotations or usage of certain words, check a contemporary dictionary.

6. *Think of your ideas as pictures.* If a sentence seems to be only a vague notion or feeling, think of your idea as a series of pictures that develop. Describe those pictures until your ideas are clearly in focus and use the words in your sentences that are most accurate.

7. *Question yourself.* Ask yourself questions such as "What does this word mean to me?" "Why did I choose this word?" or "What does this word make me feel or remember?" This process will help you find more precise and concrete words that represent your ideas.

8. *Expand your vocabulary.* If you want to improve your vocabulary—and not by memorizing 20 words each week—then try to read more often. When you come across words you want to know more about, check a dictionary to find out how those words came into being. And do not be afraid to use the words you learn and enjoy. A bigger vocabulary will not help you impress your friends, but it will let you express your ideas more effectively.

Problem Areas

Guarding against the following common problems will help you express your ideas more powerfully and clearly.

DENOTATION VERSUS CONNOTATION

All words have a literal meaning: A *mother* is a woman who has borne a child, and *apple pie* is a baked dessert made of pastry and apples. These are the denotative meanings. However, *mother* and *apple pie* also have strong positive associations to most Americans. (That is why one car company uses these words and images in their advertisements). But not all words carry such favorable connotations. A word such as *politician* is colored by negative associations or images, such as illegal campaign funds and bribes.

It is important to be aware of the connotations of the words you use. The words in your essay should suit your purpose and create the right images in the reader's mind. If you want to stir patriotic fervor, you might use terms such as *apple pie* and *mother*. If you want to write a persuasive editorial endorsing a certain candidate, you might use the word *statesman* instead of *politician*, or describe him as an *honest individual*.

Remember that words have great power because of the associations people make. If you want to sell an idea or a product, use words that have positive images. If you want to stimulate people or move them to action, use words that will make them angry or determined enough to write letters or support your cause.

HOMONYMS AND SYNONYMS

Because many words sound alike, they are often confused. This confusion not only creates spelling problems but also disrupts the meaning of the sentence. Homonyms such as *pair* and *pare*, *beat* and *beet*, *passed* and *past*, or *sun* and *son* have distinct meanings and cannot be used interchangeably. Make sure that you understand your idea well enough to use the words that say what you mean.

Synonyms may not look similar, but they have similar meanings. The problem with synomyns is that most of them are not interchangeable because they carry different connotations or must be used in specific ways. For example, *home* and *house* are similar in a general sense, but a *home* means far more than the four walls and roof of a *house*. In the same way, *convince* and *persuade* or *motivate* and *stimulate* may have similar meanings, but they are used in different ways. And as you know from grammar lessons, *less* and *fewer* or *well* and *good* cannot be used interchangeably either.

Most handbooks have glossary sections listing the homonyms and synonyms that are commonly confused or misused. And if the word you want to double-check is not included, any standard dictionary will tell you whether its meaning is appropriate for the idea you want to communicate.

ABSTRACT VERSUS CONCRETE WORDS

In Chapter 2, many of you may have listed "details," "specifics," or "sentences that grab you" as methods writers use to make you interested in their ideas. They create interest by using words that are precise, definite, and concrete—especially when choosing the nouns and verbs for their ideas. For example, if you write *people* instead of *students at San Fransisco State*, or *sometime in the late sixties* when you mean *1969*, or *disagreed* when you mean *marched against*, then your ideas will be too general and fuzzy to interest most readers.

Choosing your words carefully is especially important when writing about abstract ideas such as freedom, injustice, or love. In order to help your reader see your ideas, to persuade or startle him, you need to find words that will create pictures for him, make him feel or hear what you do in your mind. And if you realize that a specific date or fact is needed to replace a generality, two quick references can help you find what you want:

> *Columbia Viking Desk Encyclopedia*, Columbia University Press
> *Encyclopedia of American Facts and Dates*, Crowell Company

CLICHÉS, PAT EXPRESSIONS, AND JARGON

Should you look before you leap? Or is it true that he who hesitates is lost? What will happen if you hitch your wagon to a star? Will you bite off more than you can chew? Or do you find yourself *maximizing, finalizing, impacting on,* or *interfacing* in your papers? Writers who rely on clichés and jargon are taking shortcuts in thinking and padding their work with fluff (they are also killing off their readers with that stuff).

Clichés and jargon are the easiest kinds of padding to spot, but pat expressions are more difficult because they seem like generalizations that everyone understands. What does *everything will turn out one way or the other* really mean? And what about *the American way of life?* Is your American way of life the same as ours? As you see, the real danger with these expressions is that each reader has his own definition of them. So, the reader is not learning about your ideas, and you are not finding out what you really think.

AT THIS POINT IN TIME VERSUS *NOW*

When writers become concerned with turning out a specific number of words, they often find ways to express their ideas in five or six words when one or two would do. Using a phrase such as *in the event that* instead of *when* adds nothing but excess baggage to your paper. Do not take the chance of obscuring your ideas and boring your reader by explaining too much or adding unnecessary words to your paper.

VOICE

Finally, writers need to keep in mind their audience as well as their own ideas and purpose when choosing words. Imagine describing the wild party you attended last weekend to three different people. What would you say and how would you describe it to a close friend, a teacher, or a parent? Not only would you select certain experiences, but you would use a different *voice* or vocabulary for each as well.

Try to use the vocabulary that suits your audience and is still natural to you. You can sound authoritative and logical without becoming a stuffed shirt. And you do not have to be mushy or feverish when you want to be caring.

One last consideration regarding voice is knowing what is and is not acceptable to your reader. Some audiences prefer that the writer avoid *I* in formal kinds of writing, such as business reports, term papers, and researched writing. Writers do not have to avoid subjects they care about, only to find alternatives to saying *I think* or *I believe.*

If your reader prefers that you not use *I*, you can simply state your convictions directly:

(I think that) Knowing alternative energy sources gives Americans greater freedoms.

Or use a lead-in:

It is important that ⎫
It is imperative that ⎬ Americans develop alternative energy sources
It is time that ⎭

And when you do use *I* in your writing, do not use it to apologize or hedge: "I think this is true, but . . ." Make sure *I* emphasizes your beliefs and ideas: "I applaud John Smith's efforts in Congress to halt nuclear proliferation."

Lastly, make sure that you know your reader's idiosyncrasies—almost everyone has some. Some people cannot stand dashes, whereas others abhor contractions or abbreviations. Make sure that you know the expectations of your final reader in order to prepare your manuscript accordingly.

CHAPTER 9

Readings

STUDENT WORKS

Introduction to "Letter to Ms. Didion"

After reading "Goodbye to All That," Julie Kersul put her own experiences into perspective by writing back to Joan Didion. Julie explained what had happened to her during her three-month stay in New York by describing, analyzing, classifying, comparing, and associating her memories. In doing this, she came to some fundamental conclusions about her life and what she wanted.

LETTER TO MS. DIDION

Dear Ms. Didion:

I had to write and tell you how much "Goodbye to All That" meant to me. After reading about your experiences in New York, a mirror image of myself stood before my eyes. It was hard for me to believe that someone else had shared the same dream that I once had. And the interesting part of your story is that it resulted in exactly the same consequences as did my experiences. I, too, found, "It is distinctly possible to stay too long at the fair." The only difference between our "visits" to New York is that I realized before you that the merry-go-round had stopped.

Ever since I was a little girl, I wanted to visit New York. I think it all stemmed from seeing pictures of it on television. No matter how many times I saw the City, my fascination never lessened. I remember fantasizing about climbing to the top floor of a skyscraper and looking down at all the people below me. I imagined them looking like little ants crawling around the sidewalks in search of something. As much as this excited me, I think that in actuality I was looking for certain promises too. Exactly what kind of promises, I am still not sure. Deep down, I think those promises dealt with doing exciting things and meeting new and interesting people. In essence, I wanted to start a whole new life.

To begin with, I arrived in New York in June of 1977. Then I was 17 years old and full of life. My first thought as I stepped off the airplane was, "I have made it. I am finally here." And when I got to Manhattan itself, I was so thrilled that even the rumbling sounds of the subways sent shivers up my spine. It was even more exciting than what I had seen on television.

For the first few weeks, the city totally enveloped me. I loved everything about it: the people, the places, and even the noise. I actually enjoyed waking to the sounds of screeching tires and screaming horns. I was excited about looking for jobs and walking in the great crowds of people. I just could not get enough of anything New York had to offer.

Well, as the saying goes, "All good things must come to an end." It was not too long before the excitement began to fizzle. The noise began to irritate me, the places were not nearly as enchanting, and it truly seemed that the great masses of people began to blend together. I had to laugh when your friend told you it was impossible to see new faces. He was right; I found out that I had seen each and every face before. It seemed that most of the people were just like me. They all hoped their dreams of adventure and fulfilling their promises would not turn into an everlasting nightmare.

I honestly believe that many people go to cities like New York to escape their already planned out lives. Like me, they go to start life all over again, to make their dreams real and to keep the promises that they have made to themselves. Finding adventure in New York is easy. It is fulfilling the promises that is difficult. The toughest part of all is when the adventures become boring and you suddenly realize that you have not kept a single vow or made a single change. And as you pointed out, that is when you see every past moment lost to an adventure that has not made you into a new person or given you the exciting life you dreamed of. This is when the city becomes unbearable. I remember how French poodles, elevators, and even taxi drivers made me dizzy.

As it was, I stayed in New York for only three months. That was all the time it took for me to discover that the big city was in reality an icy glazed fortress surrounded by gates that only a certain privileged few had keys to. These were the people who let the skyscrapers and mink coats keep their dreams in the dark corners of their minds. There was no time for them to dream anymore; for if they did, they, too, would see all of the promises left unkept.

There are many times when I wish I had never gone to New York City. All of my beautiful visions were obliterated by faceless people. However, my experiences did teach me something: Life is too short to be spent at a fair. If ever again I feel the need to start my life over, I am going to look around and be thankful for the things life has already offered me. In other words, the next time I find myself on another merry-go-round, I will get off before the music begins to play.

I thank you, Ms. Didion, for such an inspiring essay. You made me realize that I am not the only person who has had dreams shattered, and you helped me see that life does have one golden opportunity: Me.

Sincerely,
Julie A. Kersul

P.S. I hope for your sake that the manufacturer discontinues L'Air du Temps.

Introduction to "Gates of Heaven"

For her writing assignment, Anne Byrne wanted to show how specific cultures affect the attitudes of the people living within them. She chose the Indian and white cultures of the late 1800s and early 1900s and used the author Dee Brown and the character Calamity Jane to represent her ideas. Before she started, Anne needed to understand the ideas and beliefs expressed in the excerpts she read from Dee Brown's novel, *Bury My Heart at Wounded Knee*, and Edward L. Wheeler's *Barkin' Up the Wrong Tree*. So, she began by pretending that the two people, Dee Brown and Calamity Jane, met and exchanged views. Eventually, she developed the dialogue into a short story that exposed the kinds of misconceptions one culture had projected on another.

GATES OF HEAVEN, by Anne Byrne

Climbing the stairs to the gates of Heaven, Dee Brown focused on the lone guard standing in the mist outside the gates. When he arrived at the top, he tapped the man on the shoulder and inquired, "What time do the Pearly Gates open?" The guard turned and, to Dee's surprise, it was a woman.

"Oh, excuse me. I thought you were a guard here," he apologized.

With a chuckle, Calamity Jane introduced herself.

Recognizing the name and the history that went with it, Dee Brown introduced himself and proudly stated he was a member of the Sioux tribe.

Calamity Jane looked at him closely and asked, "What's an Injun doing at these Pearly Gates?"

"What makes you think a white man is more worthy of entering these gates than an Indian?" Dee countered.

Calamity Jane answered, "A white man lives a more civilized life and thus deserves the reward."

Dee questioned, "Isn't your definition of civilized materialistic? Would you have us cut our hair for fancy hats, wear pants and fine clothes or live in big houses? Can't you see that an Indian's idea of being civilized is in his heart?"

"But aren't you Indians always fighting among yourselves? Don't you see that your people live primitively and barbarically?" Calamity asked.

"What was so civilized about the American Revolution?" Dee replied. "That was Englishmen fighting Englishmen. And the Civil War was Americans fighting other Americans—even brother against brother. But I guess you weren't around for that one. Tell me if wiping out a whole Indian tribe—including women and children—is barbaric or not." Dee's voice began to rise.

"Now let's not get hostile," Calamity Jane said warily. "You Indians were always hostile toward the white man."

"Tell me how you would feel if some foreign person came to your homeland with deadly sticks that shot fire and killed all your braves. Then what if they burned your villages and drove you to a dry, deserted land where nothing was productive and finally told you to live there?" Dee asked pointedly.

Calamity reasoned, "But we put you there because you didn't want to be part of us. You wouldn't accept our offer to help you progress. Don't the Indians want to learn modern techniques for farming and living?"

Dee chuckled and said, "If I have my history straight, it was the Indians who helped the Pilgrims with planting. We're the ones who taught you about fertilizer."

"But you didn't let us show you our ideas," Calamity countered. "You just stayed in a rut. Can't you see you not only slowed yourselves down, but the white man too?"

Dee paused for a moment as if deep in thought. Then he said softly, "I guess the white man's idea of progress is quite different from the Indian's. You see, we strive for inner maturation and peace. We want our spirits to progress to a state of wisdom and personal happiness. An Indian places little importance on material wealth. We only seek survival in this world until it is our time to greet our ancestors here. That is why I have approached these Pearly Gates."

"But what about all that killing and scalping you did?" asked Calamity. "Do you think God would let you into Heaven after that?"

"Let me tell you a story," Dee said. His eyes softened as he told Calamity about Big Foot and the Hotchkiss Gun Massacre at Wounded Knee. After he finished, Dee asked, "Do you think that the white man was justified for doing that? Do you think God should let you into Heaven after that?"

"But I wasn't involved in Wounded Knee."

"And I never scalped a white man either."

Calamity Jane couldn't look Dee in the eyes when Dee said, "You see, we're all responsible for our own actions. Maybe some of my people killed white men for various reasons: revenge, hate or even self-defense. But tell me something. If you were to see an Indian riding toward you, what would you do? Shoot him?"

"Well it depends on if he were a friendly one or not," Calamity answered.

"And how could you tell if he were friendly?"

Chagrined, Calamity said, "Well I guess it would be hard to tell. But if I didn't shoot him, he would attack me!"

"So you're afraid of Indians. Why?" asked Dee.

"Because they seem like savages. Besides, weren't the Indians afraid of the white man?"

"Indians aren't afraid of anything on earth; not even death," Dee replied softly. "They only fear the evil spirits, and even then we are protected from them by the Almighty one."

Calamity looked at Dee with a growing respect, and thought how mistaken she had been. "Maybe there is hope for us humans yet!" And without warning, the gates of Heaven quitely opened and Calamity Jane and Dee Brown walked through them together — arm in arm.

Introduction to "Review of *The Hobbit*"

After reading J. R. R. Tolkien's *The Hobbit*, Richard Preuss captured his impressions by brainstorming in his journal. In his final paper he used his insights from the entry to focus on a single important idea.

REVIEW OF *THE HOBBIT*, by Richard Preuss

The Hobbit, though written in a fairy tale style, has a theme that directly pertains to real life. By the use of fictional characters in realms only dreams can reach, the author, J. R. R. Tolkien, brings out the importance of knowing one's self. Through the major character, Bilbo Baggins, he shows how to achieve happiness through the development of individual capabilities that lead to discovering one's personal identity.

At the start, Bilbo Baggins is not the individualist he is later, but rather a social conformist. As a hobbit, he is a short, chubby and furry little man-like creature. Most hobbits are what Tolkien calls "respectable" and Bilbo is no exception. Tolkien describes Bilbo's family:

> The Bagginses had lived in the neighborhood of The Hill for time out of mind, and most people considered them very respectable, not only because most of them were rich, but also because they never did anything unexpected: you could tell what a Baggins would say on any question without the bother of asking him.

This passage shows the social conformity of Bilbo's family and how he was expected to act and think.

Yet Bilbo breaks away from the tradition of the hobbits by joining in an adventure with thirteen dwarves. Because of demanding situations during the adventure, Bilbo begins to develop skills that he never knew he had or ever thought would be useful.

> Bilbo saw that the moment had come when he must do something . . . Bilbo was a pretty fair shot with a stone . . . While he was picking up stones, the spider reached Bombur [one of the dwarves] and soon he would have been dead. The stone struck the spider plunk on the head, and it dropped.

Through experiences like these, Bilbo becomes more and more confident; as the author puts it: "He felt a different person, and much fiercer and bolder." Near the end of his adventure, Bilbo's confidence has grown so much that at times he takes it upon himself to guide the expedition. "'No time now!' said the hobbit. 'You must follow me!'" Bilbo becomes a very interesting character because he becomes an individual. He no longer acts as society wants him to, but instead, as his true self responding to the needs of others with his refined and practiced abilities.

When he returns to The Hill, Bilbo finds he is no longer respectable to his family and is rejected by almost everyone. Does that make him a failure? Will he mourn his solitude? Hardly. As Tolkien says, ". . . he did not mind. He was quite content."

Introduction to "Joe (Another Love Story)"

In this essay, Lisa Lezovich focused on a person who was very important to her and described the relationship they once shared. She began gathering ideas by using Survey A—People and continued the process by revising and rewriting until she finished "Joe (Another Love Story)."

JOE (ANOTHER LOVE STORY), by Lisa Lezovich

As the leaves fell around me, I sat waiting for Joe. A few hours before, he had asked me to meet him at the park. Joe said there was something he wanted to tell me and, by the tone of his voice, it sounded important. Since he said he had some things to pick up at the house, I agreed to meet him here at our special place. So I sat in the park waiting for him.

As I sat there, I began looking around. Flashbacks of the summer came back to me: This place had been paradise. Joe and I had spent much of our summer here together and during that time he and I became closer to each other than we ever were before.

Joe and I had known each other most of our lives, but we did not really know one another until this summer. He says he remembers when I was five years old and how we always played together. I even remember those times and how I loved every minute of it.

As I stared off into the distance, I daydreamed about the summer thinking of the talks we had and the walks we had taken. I remembered the time we got caught in a rainstorm, and we laughed all the way home with the rain coming down harder and harder each passing moment. It was our little world, and with each day, we understood and enjoyed each other more and more.

I awakened from my daydreaming when I saw him coming in the distance. I watched him walk toward me, and I noticed how tall and proud he walked, even with his bad leg. He had a tall slender body, but it was solid as cement. His muscles showed through his light-colored shirt making him look strong. He looked as if he could kill a grizzly with his hands, but when he held me, he was as gentle as a pussy cat.

His face almost always had a hard look, as though he had had a tough life. But at times I know his face could be turned into a puppy dog's face that showed gentleness within him. His hair, like usual, was not combed, so he looked like a street dog; but he liked it that way. Of all his face, I liked his eyes the best. They were a deep, dark brown, and when I looked into them, I could see his love for me.

Not too many people liked Joe because they judged him by his appearance and not by what was inside of him. I had found out what he was like underneath all that messed up hair and that was the person I liked. I overlooked his stern expression and uncombed hair and found a bright and intelligent person there. But not too many people could do this; so they left him all by himself.

Joe walked to me, but he did not greet me with a happy face. We said our usual hello's and gave each other a kiss on the cheek. He turned away for a moment; then he turned around and took me by the shoulders.

"I have something to tell you and it will be very hard for you to take. I will not beat around the bush." He took a deep breath. Then he said, "I have cancer of the liver and not very long to live." He looked at me for a moment; then he went on talking. "There is a good hospital in California that specializes in this sort of thing and I'll be leaving to go there soon."

By the time he started that last sentence I had started to cry. Through the tears I asked, "When are you going?"

"In just a few minutes because my plane leaves in a half hour. Don't worry about me—I have some close relatives out there so I won't be alone."

"Have you told my family yet?"

"Yes, I told them about a week ago, but I wanted to tell you at a special time and place."

It was so still we could hear each other breathe. I stared at him and silently asked myself, "Why him and why me?" Then I broke the silence and asked, "What did you pick up at the house?"

"I had to pick up some of my clothes and this." He handed me a tiny box. "I want you to have this."

I looked at him and then opened it. Inside was the most beautiful ring I had ever seen. It was a simple gold band with four small diamonds in the center.

Joe said, "It was my mother's and she said I was to give it so someone special."

I felt numb. I liked it so much, but I could not find the words to tell him. Finally I got out a thank you.

He asked, "Do you like it?"

"Of course I do, and I will cherish it the rest of my life."

He smiled and kissed me; then he left. With the box clenched in my hands and tears running down my face, I saw him walk out of my life. There was nothing I could do to keep him.

Joe died two months later in California. They tell me there was no real suffering because he died in his sleep.

My aunt sent me a picture of his grave site. On the head stone it says, "Here lies Jospeh H. Lezovich, Sr. Let him sleep in peace."

But that did not mean much to me because I never did call him by his name. I just called him Grandpa.

Introduction to "The Last Puff"

Kim Troy used one of the personal surveys in Chapter 3 to find ideas for her assignment. After listing the events she remembered most vividly in her life, she decided to focus on the first time she got into trouble—real trouble—and developed her memories in the following essay.

THE LAST PUFF, by Kim Troy

It was early on a summer morn. The sunlight shown bright and as it broke through my bedroom curtain it made my face feel very warm. The morning's air smelled fresh and full of lilacs as it blew about my room. When I sat up and raised my arms high over my head, I could feel the cool sheets under me and could hear the birds chirping and singing outside my window.

I went into the kitchen and, by myself, made a tall glass of ice tea to cool me from the summer's heat. The tea seemed to slide down my throat like fresh spring water down a mountain. Then I started to think about my birthday, which was getting close, and how grown-up I felt. No one would dare squeeze my cheeks or call me "little Kimmie" again.

Just then the telephone rang. I slowly picked up the receiver and in a very mature voice said, "Heellooo!"

"Madelyn," answered the voice in a hurried tone. "Who have you been talking to? Girl, I've been trying to reach you for hours. Did you hear that . . ." At that very moment I stopped her and told her who I was. Although I was a "big girl," I did not think that I was big enough to hear the latest gossip from Mrs. Jones. I put the receiver on the table as I called mother to the phone.

I must really have sounded grown-up if Mrs. Jones mistook my voice for my mother's. As I walked back to my glass of tea, I began practicing other ways to sound mature. "Heellooo. Troy residence . . . Yes, my name is Kimberly . . ."

As I added another spoon of sugar to my tea, I spotted "it" on the table. There "it" was in plain view. The sunlight hit the plastic cover just right and made the wrapper shine. The reflection was so bright that it hurt my eyes. I had to squint to read the name on the red and white label. In clear, thin white letters it read: PALL MALL CIGARETTES.

I began to think of what it meant to be grown-up. Mother was always telling me how grown-up I was becoming. She was grown-up and she smoked cigarettes. Dad was grown-up and he smoked a pipe. Most of the grown-ups I knew smoked cigarettes. I guess if Mother said I was grown-up then I could do grown-up things too — like smoking.

I turned my back to my mother and took a cigarette out of the pack, carefully placing it into my shirt pocket. Then I tip-toed over to the kitchen cabinet and quietly nabbed a book of matches which I carefully placed in my blue jean pocket.

In a very slow and dignified manner, I reached for my tea and walked casually through the house. As I walked out of the door, I rubbed my jean pocket as if to tell myself, "well done."

Once outdoors I placed the glass of tea on a porch rail and pulled up a lawn chair. I tried to put my legs up on the rail, but I was too far away. I slid the chair toward the rail and again tried to put my legs up. Still too far away. So I rose completely out of the chair and pushed it at least three more inches. Then I sat down and, with tea in hand, succeeded in placing my feet on the rail.

I took a few sips of tea as the wind blew my braids about my head in a frantic dance. Hmmm, not a bad glass of tea. I lowered my glass and placed it between my legs. While looking behind me, I took the cigarette out of my shirt pocket and eased it between my lips. I cupped my hands around the freshly struck match, put it to the cigarette and immediately started puffing. I was so thrilled; I did not cough, not even once. I was so engrossed in the smoke, the puffing and the light-headed feeling that I did not hear my mother walking toward the front door.

All of a sudden there was a loud bang as my mother let the door slam shut. "What the hell do you think you're doing," she exclaimed. I was so frightened that I fell out of the chair; my tea and I went tumbling onto the porch. Totally speechless, I stood up quickly and put my hands behind my back. I tried to clench the cigarette with my fingers as I had seen her do so many times before. Ouch! I burnt my fingertips. Mother then grabbed my hands from behind me. There I was standing with a half lit cigarette in my hand. I looked up at her with sorrowful eyes but swiftly brought them down to my glass of tea, spilled in a hundred little pieces. I had never seen my mother so angry.

Without hesitation she grabbed the cigarette, threw it to the floor and crunched it. "Go get a switch from the lilac bush," she said. My mother was not one to spank her children, but I knew I was in for it when I heard the word, "lilac." The lilac bush was only a few feet from our house. The new, thin young branches made excellent spanking rods since they were young and sturdy and did not break easily.

When I returned from the bush, mother was waiting. She looked down at the large branch I had in my hand and shook her head. Even though it was a large branch, it was much too fat and brittle to be used for spanking. Mother made me go back to the bush and bring another switch. That was a double ouch; I had to go back again.

The bush itself was beautiful in the summer. Its leaves were green and the blossoms were light lavender and filled the air with their scent. But I could not appreciate that as I found myself walking to it to find a switch – a switch for my spanking.

The tears began to flow as I headed back to the house. No matter how hard I tried to keep them inside, they just kept falling down my face. Like a leaky faucet they ran and ran, each tear burning a path down my face.

She gave me a "it's-gonna'-hurt-me-more-than-it-will-hurt-you" look as she took the switch from my one hand and held the other. As I turned my head away from her, I heard the thin branch whistle in the air before it hit my skin. Oh . . . OUCH! The thin branch seemed to tear right through my bluejeans. Each swat seemed to make my buttocks numb. Swat. (Ohhh!) Smack. (Ughh!) With each blow from the switch I screamed louder. But I still could hear my mother saying, "I . . . don't . . . want . . . to ever . . . see you . . . with a . . . cigarette . . . in . . . your mouth . . . again." She angrily continued. "Do . . . you . . . under-. . . stand me?" A quick nod was the only response I could muster from my aching body.

Did I understand? How could I help not understanding. I understood that I was never to smoke again. Believe me, mother, I understood. And to this day I do not smoke, nor do I ever plan to smoke. Do *you* understand?

Introduction to "My Place"

After writing in his journal to get away from doing safe, uninteresting papers, Steve Groholski wrote the following essay. In "My Place," he compared his experiences to those of Henry David Thoreau and described a place that not only helped him to see the world differently but to survive in it as well.

MY PLACE, by Steve Groholski

After I finished reading Thoreau's story about Walden Pond, I began to wonder why he had chosen to write about something as common as a pond. Surely there are other, more exciting stories he could have written. Why did he want us to know about this pond of his? I think that I have the answer to that question, but I will have to tell you about my place first.

The first time that I sought shelter in "my place" was the day I almost shot my father. Four years ago my parents were in the process of a divorce. During that time between filing for divorce and actually getting one, my father would make frequent stops by our house to take anything he wanted. One day when my mother and I returned from a camping trip, we stumbled across my dad trying to take all our livingroom furniture. My mother is not one to take such things calmly. When she realized what was happening, she ran into my room and got my hunting gun. I knew that she did not know how to use it, so I grabbed it from her. I do not know what I was feeling as I aimed the gun at my dad's forehead, but rage controlled me and I really did not care. I ordered him to take everything of ours out of the truck, which he did. All of the time, I watched over him with the gun still pointed at him. As he was leaving, I told him never to come back or I would pull the trigger next time. He shifted the truck into reverse and looked at me with a sly smile. Behind the sweat on his face and the fear in his eyes, he knew that I would never shoot him.

After this incident, I felt as though the whole world closed in around me. I needed some place to go, something to do so that I could take my mind off of what had just happened. Behind our house is a small woods about the size of the Farm Lane Woodlot. Right after this incident the woods seemed to beckon to me. Never before had I been so fascinated by this collection of timber. Before I thought of it only as an obstacle that divided our farm into two equal parts. Now I looked on it as a refuge, a place where I could let all my feelings go and be whatever I wanted.

As I waded through the waist-high weeds and hurdled the fallen trees of years past, I saw the woods for what it really is. It is a haven of beauty and serenity. The beauty lies in the trees; some spiral gracefully towards the sky while others, twisted and torn by nature, take on strange and grotesque shapes. The serenity comes from a calm that prevails over the woods, a calm so peaceful that it makes me feel as though I have left this world for awhile. After that day, I returned to the woods whenever I needed to recapture that peacefulness.

I cannot say that I spent all of my time there, but I did go out when I became depressed—which was quite often that summer. When I would go into the woods with a problem, I could always count on it to lift my worries and leave me refreshed.

As fall and winter came and went, so did my need for the security of the woods. But, with spring, my problems returned and my place called to me again. As I looked around, I could see the woods coming to life. It seemed as though all the trees were in competition with each other to see which one would be the first to burst into full bloom. The weeds, waist high in the summer, had been killed off in the winter frost. But their offspring were beginning to push through the blanket of leaves that protected them during the harsh winter.

During my walks through the woods, I noticed other signs of nature renewing itself. One day I saw that an old maple had joined the ranks of its fallen comrades. To the right of the fallen tree, a sapling was all ready to take its place. Each autumn the fallen maple had lost its green overcoat and had built up the rich soil preparing a home for its replacement. Another day I ran across a squirrel who must have been cleaning house. I watched its every move as old acorns came flying out of an old hollow tree. Seeing the squirrel making room for the new, I realized I had to go on with my life and put the past behind me.

That spring I started going out with a girl with whom I could discuss my problems. So my need for the woods ended almost as suddenly as it began. Time rolled endlessly on and I began to see the woods as an obstacle again. One day when I started out to cut wood for our furnace, I ran across some of the memories that I had left behind: an old fort, my favorite shirt lost long ago, a hollow tree with a squirrels's nest still in it. And I remembered what the woods had meant to me.

Thoreau wrote the story about the pond to show us that we all need to have a place that we can go to renew our spirits. The world is a very big place with a very fast-paced society. No one can be expected to keep up with every change, advancement or every pressure without having a place to rest once in awhile. Like Thoreau, my rest stop had been the woods and nature had shown me how to go on with my life.

My Place

I look all around and laugh.
But the world goes on.
I do all that I can and cry.
But the world goes on.
Do they never stop, I scream.
But the world goes on.
I take a rest and sigh.
The world goes on, but a little slower.

PROFESSIONAL WORKS

BIRCHES, by Robert Frost

When I see birches bend to left and right
Across the lines of straighter darker trees,

I like to think some boy's been swinging
    them.
But swinging doesn't bend them down to
    stay
As ice storms do. Often you must have seen
    them
Loaded with ice a sunny winter morning
After a rain. They click upon themselves
As the breeze rises, and turn many-colored
As the stir cracks and crazes their enamel.
Soon the sun's warmth makes them shed
    crystal shells
Shattering and avalanching on the snow
    crust—
Such heaps of broken glass to sweep away
You'd think the inner dome of heaven had
    fallen.
They are dragged to the withered bracken
    by the load,
And they seem not to break; though once
    they are bowed
So low for long, they never right themselves:
You may see their trunks arching in the
    woods
Years afterwards, trailing their leaves on the
    ground
Like girls on hands and knees that throw
    their hair
Before them over their heads to dry in the
    sun.
But I was going to say when Truth broke in

With all her matter of fact about the ice
    storm,
I should prefer to have some boy bend them
As he went out and in to fetch the cows—
Some boy too far from town to learn base-
    ball,
Whose only play was what he found him-
    self,
Summer or winter, and would play alone.
One by one he subdued his father's trees
By riding them down over and over again
Until he took the stiffness out of them.
And not one but hung limp, not one was
    left
For him to conquer. He learned all there
    was
To learn about not launching out to soon

And so not carrying the tree away
Clear to the ground. He always kept his
   poise
To the top branches, climbing carefully
With the same pains you use to fill a cup
Up to the brim, and even above the brim.
Then he flung outward, feet first, with a
   swish,
Kicking his way down through the air to
   the ground.
So was I once myself a swinger of birches.
And so I dream of going back to be.
It's when I'm weary of considerations,
And life is too much like a pathless wood
Where your face burns and tickles with the
   cobwebs
Broken across it, and one eye is weeping
From a twig's having lashed across it open.
I'd like to get away from earth awhile
And then come back to it and begin over.
May no fate willfully misunderstand me
And half grant what I wish and snatch me
   away
Not to return. Earth's the right place for
   love:
I don't know where it's likely to go better.
I'd like to go by climbing a birch tree,
And climb black branches up a snow-white
   trunk
Toward heaven, till the tree could bear no
   more,
But dipped its top and set me down again.

That would be good both going and coming
   back.
One could do worse than be a swinger of
   birches.

THE PONDS [THE WATERS OF WALDEN], by Henry David Thoreau

A lake is the landscape's most beautiful and expressive feature. It is earth's eye; looking into which the beholder measures the depth of his own nature. The fluviatile trees next the shore are the slender eyelashes which fringe it, and the wooded hills and cliffs around are its overhanging brows.

Standing on the smooth sandy beach at the east end of the pond, in a calm September afternoon, when a slight haze makes the opposite shore line indistinct, I have seen whence came the expression, "the glassy surface of a lake." When you invert your head, it looks like a thread of finest gossamer stretched across the valley, and gleaming against the distant pine woods, separating one stratum of the atmosphere from another. You would think that you could walk dry under it to the opposite hills, and that the swallows which skim over might perch on it. Indeed, they sometimes dive below the line, as it were by mistake, and are undeceived. As you look over the pond westward you are obliged to employ both your hands to defend your eyes against the reflected as well as the true sun, for they are equally bright; and if, between the two, you survey its surface critically, it is literally as smooth as glass, except where the skater insects, at equal intervals scattered over its whole extent, by their motions in the sun produce the finest imaginable sparkle on it, or, perchance, a duck plumes itself, or, as I have said, a swallow skims so low as to touch it. It may be that in the distance a fish describes an arc of three or four feet in the air, and there is one bright flash where it emerges, and another where it strikes the water; sometimes the whole silvery arc is revealed; or here and there, perhaps, is a thistledown floating on its surface, which the fishes dart at and so dimple it again. It is like molten glass cooled but not congealed, and the few motes in it are pure and beautiful like the imperfections in glass. You may often detect a yet smoother and darker water, separated from the rest as if by an invisible cobweb, boom of the water nymphs, resting on it. From a hilltop you can see a fish leap in almost any part; for not a pickerel or shiner picks an insect from this smooth surface but it manifestly disturbs the equilibrium of the whole lake. It is wonderful with what elaborateness this simple fact is advertised – this piscine murder will out, – and from my distant perch I distinguish the circling undulations when they are half a dozen rods in diameter. You can even detect a water-bug (*Gyrinus*) cease-lessly progressing over the smooth surface a quarter of a mile off; for they furrow the water slightly, making a conspicuous ripple bounded by two diverging lines, but the skaters glide over it without rippling it perceptibly. When the surface is considerably agitated there are no skaters nor water-bugs on it, but apparently, in calm days, they leave their havens and adventurously glide forth from the shore by short impulses till they completely cover it. It is a soothing employment, on one of those fine days in the fall when all the warmth of the sun is fully appreciated, to sit on a stump on such a height as this, overlooking the pond, and study the dimpling circles which are incessantly inscribed on its otherwise invisible surface amid the reflected skies and trees. Over this great expanse there is no disturbance but it is thus at once gently smoothed away and assuaged, as, when a vase of water is jarred, the trembling circles seek the shore and all is smooth again. Not a fish can leap or an insect fall on the pond but it is thus reported in circling dimples, in lines of beauty, as it were the constant well-ing up of its fountain, the gentle pulsing of its life, the heaving of its breast. The thrills of joy and thrills of pain are undistinguishable. How peaceful the phe-nomena of the lake. Again the works of man shine as in the spring. Ay, every leaf and twig and stone and cobweb sparkles now at mid-afternoon as when covered with dew in a spring morning. Every motion of an oar or an insect produces a flash of light; and if an oar falls, how sweet the echo!

In such a day, in September or October, Walden is a perfect forest mirror, set round with stones as precious to my eye as if fewer or rarer. Nothing so fair, so pure, and at the same time so large, as a lake, perchance, lies on the surface of the earth. Sky water. It needs no fence. Nations come and go without defiling it. It is a mirror which no stone can crack, whose quicksilver will never wear off, whose gilding Nature continually repairs; no storms, no dust, can dim its surface ever fresh;—a mirror in which all impurity presented to it sinks, swept and dusted by the sun's hazy brush,—this the light dustcloth,—which retains no breath that is breathed on it, but sends its own to float as clouds high above its surface, and be reflected in its bosom still.

A field of water betrays the spirit that is in the air. It is continually receiving new life and motion from above. It is intermediate in its nature between land and sky. On land only the grass and trees wave, but the water itself is rippled by the wind. I see where the breeze dashes across it by the streaks or flakes of light. It is remarkable that we can look down on its surface. We shall, perhaps, look down thus on the surface of air at length, and mark where a still subtler spirit sweeps over it.

The skaters and water-bugs finally disappear in the latter part of October, when the severe frosts have come; and then and in November, usually, in a calm day, there is absolutely nothing to ripple the surface. One November afternoon, in the calm at the end of a rain storm of several days' duration, when the sky was still completely overcast and the air was full of mist, I observed that the pond was remarkably smooth, so that it was difficult to distinguish its surface; though it no longer reflected the bright tints of October, but the sombre November colors of the surrounding hills. Though I passed over it as gently as possible, the slight undulations produced by my boat extended almost as far as I could see, and gave a ribbed appearance to the reflections. But, as I was looking over the surface, I saw here and there at a distance a faint glimmer, as if some skater insects which had escaped the frosts might be collected there, or, perchance, the surface, being so smooth, betrayed where a spring welled up from the bottom. Paddling gently to one of these places, I was surprised to find myself surrounded by myriads of small perch, about five inches long, of a rich bronze color in the green water, sporting there and constantly rising to the surface and dimpling it, sometimes leaving bubbles on it. In such transparent and seemingly bottomless water, reflecting the clouds, I seemed to be floating through the air as in a balloon, and their swimming impressed me as a kind of flight or hovering, as if they were a compact flock of birds passing just beneath my level on the right or left, their fins, like sails, set all around them. There were many such schools in the pond, apparently improving the short season before winter would draw an icy shutter over their broad skylight, sometimes giving to the surface an appearance as if a slight breeze struck it, or a few rain-drops fell there. When I approached carelessly and alarmed them, they made a sudden plash and rippling with their tails, as if one had struck the water with a brushy bough, and instantly took refuge in the depths. At length the wind rose, the mist increased, and the waves began to run, and the perch leaped much higher than before, half out of water, a hundred black points, three inches long, at once above the surface. Even as late as the fifth of December, one year, I saw some dimples on the surface, and thinking it was going to rain hard immediately, the air being full of mist, I made haste to take my place at the oars and row homeward; already the rain seemed rapidly increasing, though I felt none on my cheek, and I anticipated a thorough soaking. But suddenly the dimples ceased, for they were produced by the perch, which the noise of my oars had scared into the depths, and I saw their schools dimly disappearing; so I spent a dry afternoon after all.

An old man who used to frequent this pond nearly sixty years ago, when it was dark with surrounding forests, tells me that in those days he sometimes saw it all alive with ducks and other water fowl, and that there were many eagles about it. He came here a-fishing, and used an old log canoe which he found on the shore. It was made of two white-pine logs dug out and pinned together, and was cut off square at the ends. It was very clumsy, but lasted a great many years before it became water-logged and perhaps sank to the bottom. He did not know whose it was; it belonged to the pond. He used to make a cable for his anchor of strips of hickory bark tied together. An old man, a potter, who lived by the pond before the Revolution, told him once that there was an iron chest at the bottom, and that he had seen it. Sometimes it would come floating up to the shore; but when you went toward it, it would go back into deep water and disappear. I was pleased to hear of the old canoe, which took the place of an Indian one of the same material but more graceful construction, which perchance had first been a tree on the bank, and then, as it were, fell into the water, to float there for a generation, the most proper vessel for the lake. I remember that when I first looked into these depths there were many large trunks to be seen indistinctly lying on the bottom, which had either been blown over formerly, or left on the ice at the last cutting, when wood was cheaper; but now they have mostly disappeared.

When I first paddled a boat on Walden, it was completely surrounded by thick and lofty pine and oak woods, and in some of its coves grape vines had run over the trees next the water and formed bowers under which a boat could pass. The hills which form its shores are so steep, and the woods on them were then so high, that, as you looked down from the west end, it had the appearance of an amphitheatre for some kind of sylvan spectacle. I have spent an hour, when I was younger, floating over its surface as the zephyr willed, having paddled my boat to the middle, and lying on my back across the seats, in a summer forenoon, dreaming awake, until I was aroused by the boat touching the sand, and I arose to see what shore my fates had impelled me to; days when idleness was the most attractive and productive industry. Many a forenoon have I stolen away, preferring to spend thus the most valued part of the day; for I was rich, if not in money, in sunny hours and summer days, and spent them lavishly; nor do I regret that I did not waste more of them in the workshop or the teacher's desk. But since I left those shores the woodchoppers have still further laid them waste, and now for many a year there will be no more rambling through the aisles of the wood, with occasional vistas through which you see the water. My Muse may be excused if she is silent henceforth. How can you expect the birds to sing when their groves are cut down?

Now the trunks of trees on the bottom, and the old log canoe, and the dark surrounding woods, are gone, and the villagers, who scarcely know where it lies, instead of going to the pond to bathe or drink, are thinking to bring its water, which should be as sacred as the Ganges at least, to the village in a pipe, to wash their dishes with—to earn their Walden by the turning of a cock or drawing of a plug! That devilish Iron Horse, whose ear-rending neigh is heard throughout the town, has muddied the Boiling Spring with his foot, and he it is that has browsed off all the woods on Walden shore; that Trojan horse, with a thousand men in his belly, introduced by mercenary Greeks! Where is the country's champion, the Moore of Moore Hall, to meet him at the Deep Cut and thrust an avenging lance between the ribs of the bloated pest?

Nevertheless, of all the characters I have known, perhaps Walden wears best, and best preserves its purity. Many men have been likened to it, but few deserve that honor. Though the woodchoppers have laid bare first this shore and then that, and the Irish have built their sties by it, and the railroad has infringed on its border, and the ice-men have skimmed it once, it is itself unchanged, the same water which my youthful eyes fell on; all the change is in me. It has not acquired one permanent wrinkle after all its ripples. It is perennially young, and I may stand and see a swallow dip apparently to pick an insect from its surface as of yore. It struck me again tonight, as if I had not seen it almost daily for more than twenty years,—Why, here is Walden, the same woodland lake that I discovered so many years ago; where a forest was cut down last winter another is springing up by its shore as lustily as ever; the same thought is welling up to its surface that was then; it is the same liquid joy and happiness to itself and its Maker, ay, and it *may* be to me. It is the work of a brave man surely, in whom there was no guile! He rounded this water with his hand, deepened and clarified it in his thought, and in his will bequeathed it to Concord. I see by its face that it is visited by the same reflection; and I can almost say, Walden, is it you?

> It is no dream of mine,
> To ornament a line;
> I cannot come nearer to God and Heaven
> Than I live to Walden even.
> I am its stony shore,
> And the breeze that passes o'er;
> In the hollow of my hand
> Are its water and its sand,
> And its deepest resort
> Lies high in my thought.

The cars never pause to look at it; yet I fancy that the engineers and firemen and brakemen, and those passengers who have a season ticket and see it often, are better men for the sight. The engineer does not forget at night, or his nature does not, that he has beheld this vision of serenity and purity once at least during the day. Though seen but once, it helps to wash out State-street and engine's soot. One proposes that it be called "God's Drop."

I have said that Walden has no visible inlet nor outlet, but it is on the one hand distantly and indirectly related to Flint's Pond, which is more elevated, by a chain of small ponds coming from that quarter, and on the other directly and manifestly to Concord River, which is lower, by a similar chain of ponds through which in some other geological period it may have flowed, and by a little digging, which God forbid, it can be made to flow thither again. If by living thus reserved and austere, like a hermit in the woods, so long, it has acquired such wonderful purity, who would not regret that the comparatively impure waters of Flint's Pond should be mingled with it, or itself should ever go to waste its sweetness in the ocean wave?

THE BLOCK AND BEYOND, by Alfred Kazin

The block: *my* block. It was on the Chester Street side of our house, between the grocery and the back wall of the old drugstore, that I was hammered into the shape of the streets. Everything beginning at Blake Avenue would always wear for me some delightful strangeness and mildness, simply because it was not of my block, *the* block, where the clang of your head sounded against the pavement when you fell in a fist fight, and the rows of storelights on each side were pitiless, watching you. Anything away from the block was good: even a school you never went to, two blocks away: there were vegetable gardens in the park across the street. Returning from "New York," I would take the longest routes home from the subway, get off a station ahead of our own, only for the unexpectedness of walking through Betsy Head Park and hearing the gravel crunch under my feet as I went beyond the vegetable gardens, smelling the sweaty sweet dampness from the pool in summer and the dust on the leaves as I passed under the ailanthus trees. On the block itself everything rose up only to test me.

We worked every inch of it, from the cellars and the backyards to the sickening space between the roofs. Any wall, any stoop, any curving metal edge on a billboard sign made a place against which to knock a ball; any bottom rung of a fire escape ladder a goal in basketball; any sewer cover a base; any crack in the pavement a "net" for the tense sharp tennis that we played by beating a soft ball back and forth with our hands between the squares. Betsy Head Park two blocks away would always feel slightly foreign, for it belonged to the Amboys and the Bristols and the Hopkinsons as much as it did to us. *Our* life every day was fought out on the pavement and in the gutter, up against the walls of the houses and the glass fronts of the drugstore and the grocery, in and out of the fresh steaming piles of horse manure, the wheels of passing carts and automobiles, along the iron spikes of the stairway to the cellar, the jagged edge of the open garbage cans, the crumbly steps of the old farmhouses still left on one side of the street.

As I go back to the block now, and for a moment fold my body up again in its narrow arena — there, just there, between the black of the asphalt and the old women in their kerchiefs and flowered housedresses sitting on the tawny kitchen chairs—the back wall of the drugstore still rises up to test me. Every day we smashed a small black viciously hard regulation handball against it with fanatical cuts and drives and slams, beating and slashing at it almost in hatred for the blind strength of the wall itself. I was never good enough at handball, was always practicing some trick shot that might earn me esteem, and when I was weary of trying, would often bat a ball down Chester Street just to get myself to Blake Avenue. I have this memory of playing one-o'-cat by myself in the sleepy twilight, at a moment when everyone else had left the block. The sparrows floated down from the telephone wires to peck at every fresh pile of horse manure, and there was a smell of brine from the delicatessen store, of egg crates and of the milk scum left in the great metal cans outside the grocery, of the thick white paste oozing out from behind the fresh Hecker's Flour ad on the metal signboard. I would throw the ball in the air, hit it with my bat, then with perfect satisfaction drop the bat to the ground and run to the next sewer cover. Over and over I did this, from sewer cover to sewer cover, until I had worked my way to Blake Avenue and could see the park.

With each clean triumphant ring of my bat against the gutter leading me on, I did the whole length of our block up and down, and never knew how happy I was just watching the asphalt rise and fall, the curve of the steps up to an old farmhouse. The farmhouses themselves were streaked red on one side, brown on the other, but the steps themselves were always gray. There was a tremor of pleasure at one place; I held my breath in nausea at another. As I ran after my ball with the bat heavy in my hand, the odd successiveness of things in myself almost choked me, the world was so full as I ran—past the cobblestoned yards into the old farmhouses, where stray chickens still waddled along the stones; past the little candy store where we went only if the big one on our side of the block was out of Eskimo Pies; past the three neighboring tenements where the last of the old women sat on their kitchen chairs yawning before they went up to make supper. Then came Mrs. Rosenwasser's house, the place on the block I first identified with what was farthest from home, and strangest, because it was a "private" house; then the fences around the monument works, where black cranes rose up above the yard and you could see the smooth gray slabs that would be cut and carved into tombstones, some of them already engraved with the names and dates and family virtues of the dead.

Beyond Blake Avenue was the pool parlor outside which we waited all through the tense September afternoons of the World's Series to hear the latest scores called off the ticker tape—and where as we waited, banging a ball against the bottom of the wall and drinking water out of empty coke bottles, I breathed the chalk off the cues and listened to the clocks ringing in the fire station across the street. There was an old warehouse next to the pool parlor; the oil on the barrels and the iron staves had the same rusty smell. A block away was the park, thick with the dusty gravel I liked to hear my shoes crunch in as I ran round and round the track; then a great open pavilion, the inside mysteriously dark, chill even in summer; there I would wait in the sweaty coolness before pushing on to the wading ring where they put up a shower on the hottest days.

Beyond the park the "fields" began, all those still unused lots where we could still play hard ball in perfect peace—first shooing away the goats and then tearing up goldenrod before laying our bases. The smell and touch of those "fields," with their wild compost under the billboards of weeds, goldenrod, bricks, goat droppings, rusty cans, empty beer bottles, fresh new lumber, and damp cement, lives in my mind as Brownsville's great open door, the wastes that took us through to the west. I used to go round them in summer with my cousins selling near-beer to the carpenters, but always in a daze, would stare so long at the fibrous stalks of the goldenrod as I felt their harshness in my hand that I would forget to make a sale, and usually go off sick on the beer I drank up myself. Beyond! Beyond! Only to see something new, to get away from each day's narrow battleground between the grocery and the back wall of the drugstore! Even the other end of our block, when you got to Mrs. Rosenwasser's house and the monument works, was dear to me for the contrast. On summer nights, when we played Indian trail, running away from each other on prearranged signals, the greatest moment came when I could plunge into the darkness down the block for myself and hide behind the slabs in the monument works. I remember the air whistling around me as I ran, the panicky thud of my bones in my sneakers, and then the slabs rising in the light from the street lamps as I sped past the little candy store and crept under the fence.

In the darkness you could never see where the crane began. We liked to trap the enemy between the slabs and sometimes jumped them from great mounds of rock just in from the quarry. A boy once fell to his death that way, and they put a watchman there to keep us out. This made the slabs all the more impressive to me, and I always aimed first for that yard whenever we played follow-the-leader. Day after day the monument works became oppressively more mysterious and remote, though it was only just down the block; I stood in front of it every afternoon on my way back from school, filling it with my fears. It was not death I felt there—the slabs were usually faceless. It was the darkness itself, and the wind howling around me whenever I stood poised on the edge of a high slab waiting to jump. Then I would take in, along with the fear, some amazement of joy that I had found my way out that far.

GENIE WOMEN, by Marilyn Krysl

Sundays were different. It was the women who were in power. All my aunts and uncles and cousins were there, and of course we had to go to Sunday school and church, but it was the women, my grandmother, their leader, who insisted on attending church and in fact looked forward to it. Church was a social, not a religious occasion. Church was an excuse for dressing up, for making up your face. Everyone knew this, and that was why the women loved it and the men prayed for the day to pass quickly.

My grandfather and uncles and my father got scant pleasure on this day.

When they could not work, they were out of their element. My grandfather had gotten the idea from Genesis that man was born to wrest a living from the land by the sweat of his brow, and he took this as a mandate. Work was what there was to do, except Sundays, when work was forbidden. Play was also forbidden, but that was because my grandfather didn't know how. The younger men might have preferred whiskey and indolence, but they knew what was expected of them. They shaved dutifully, put on their graceless white shirts and suits, and that was that.

The women conceived the occasion as a celebration. Sunday mornings, my cousin Ruthie and I met with them in grandmother's bedroom. Lingerie was made of satin and had to be ironed, but the shiny smoothness was worth all the trouble. Lolling on the bed in peach colored satin, they looked like movie stars. These goddesses drew us to their shimmering sides, washed us and patted us dry with thick towels, powdered us with sweet talcum. I rose with the cloud of powder floating, nebulous, in a shaft of sunlight. I liked the downiness of my belly afterwards. They rubbed glycerine and rosewater on our cheeks and noses to protect our baby skin from sun and dry wind. I liked this too, the soft slide of the oil and its heavy smell, the luxurious attention to my sweet flesh.

Then they let us help them powder and perfume themselves. *Bring me the lavender.* Ruthie's mother, Hope, might say. And one of us would hurry to Grandma's dressing table to fetch it. We observed carefully as she perfumed the inside of her wrists, the lobes of her ears. She was a small woman, and delicate. The scent of lavender seemed right for her. We wondered if someday we too would grow up to be small and delicate, if lavender would someday be right for us too. But why behind the ears, we wondered. *Because,* she said, the man who stands behind you will smell the perfume and want to see your face.

"Give the powder puff to Grandma." It was my grandmother's habit to poke the powderpuff into the cleavage at the top of her slip and let the powder drift down inside unseen. My mother was brisk and extravagant, filling the bedroom with a pale, dry mist until my grandmother called her name: "Evelyn!" Hope powdered her belly and breasts, then asked one of us to powder her back. Soft shoulder blades fanned from her spine, silk smooth, cream white. I dusted her slowly, lightly, wanting to make the experience last. The powder puff drifted like white cumulus across her skin. I imagined sky, light wind, a long afternoon.

Bathsheba and her women. Demeter and her daughters. Face powder and rouge. The bright red oil sticks of lipstick. Black dye for eyelashes. The tinkle of garters, the putting on of white gloves to prevent runs when pulling on stockings. The adjusting of seams in the stockings. Are my seams straight? No, the left one turns out at the ankle.

Strings of pearls, pearl earrings, flower printed dresses, linen suits. And hats with veils. Round boxes lifted carefully from closet shelves. Boxes of hats of all sizes and descriptions. Cloche hats, straws with wide brims, pill boxes, black straw with cherries, pink linen with net veil, white straw with blue ribbons. And the last touch was a handkerchief, in purse or pocket or carried in the hand.

I felt in the presence of ease, luxury, affection, time without duties. I felt our importance. Here women admired themselves. They praised and approved each other. Hope massages my mother's shoulders and the headache goes away. They comforted each other with the small amenities of the body.

They comforted each other and they put on power. If at other times they were depressed or terrified into silence, here they were not afraid. No one judged, no one condemned. We were at ease, did as we pleased, and we took time, great, lazy amounts of time. There was no one to tell us we were wasting it. Each at leisure studied her own nature. A color or cut that was right for one might be wrong for another. Each worked out her particular series of allurements. Each helped the others perfect their particularities.

I came to understand the power of presence. That one's presence had overtones, undertones, reverberations. That to walk into a room meant the room changed. That even if acknowledgment was unspoken, still presence imposed in space and time, demanded and exacted acknowledgment. I understood presence was enhanced by color, by jewelry and scent, that these things encouraged the manifestation of an essence that was invisible but real.

As the toilet progressed, their power increased. By the time these women left the bedroom, they knew who they were. They were not afraid of themselves or each other and certainly not of the men. The men were, in turn, bewildered, uncomfortable in their starched white shirts and ties, not up to their ladies. And how could they be—there was little stylish or expressive about their clothes, nothing sensuous or daring in their manner. They were solemn, dressed for a solemn occasion.

But what was intended as a solemn occasion became instead a carouse. In church it was the women who sang. The men mumbled or held back, embarrassed. Their toilet had not primed them for this frank, full-bodied expression of emotion. The women sang lustily, with florid vibrato. They leaned into hymns with nasal intensity. They held the tied whole notes bravely to the end. Then, during the sermon, some women wept. Whether they wept at the minister's message or for private griefs, no one could tell, but they were not ashamed. Nor were those brazen women who dozed, sunk in their gorgeousness. The rest, though more circumspect, were just as wicked. They quietly admired each other, letting the minister drone on unheeded, communing by glance and sideways smile.

Afterward, everyone had to shake the minister's hand. Ruthie and I dreaded this custom, but once past him, we were free. We ran wild with the others, played tag, gathered in a bright cluster behind our mothers, wanting to hear what they were saying about the minister's wife, wanting to know what dish each woman planned to bring to the pot luck supper. Their voices buzzed, rose to laughter, modulated down to gossip. They had waited a week for this meeting. They had prepared and saved remarks for this meeting. They were glad to see even their enemies. They were in no hurry to go home.

The men had to stand and smoke and wait. The men were boring. They didn't talk much. Also they seemed to have nothing to do. They stood with hands in their pockets, studied the sky. Ruthie and I hung at the edge of the circle of women. When they hugged us, we could smell their perfume, the powder they used to brush their teeth. Sometimes they would unpin the home-made corsages from their shoulders and give us the flowers.

The women made Sunday dinner, and the men had to sit and wait some more. They had to read the weekly paper and bide their time. Sometimes they tried to stroll in the yard, but they were stiff in their suits, and they still couldn't find anything to do with their hands. They talked about the weather and the price of corn, then lapsed into silence. As a last resort they walked to the barn, looked over the cattle, then came back to the driveway and kicked the tires of my father's car. They looked at the tractor. They looked at their watches. How implacably slow the earth's turning must have seemed to them.

How deliciously slow it seemed to me. Dinner was big, colorful, heavy. Afterward everyone took a nap. My mother and Hope lay on the bed, talking softly. Grandmother did embroidery. Aunt Mildred showed Ruthie and me how to crochet and to tat. Sometimes one of the women would read to us. Sometimes we lay on the bed with them, listening to them talk until we fell asleep.

I tried to stay awake, listening to the sound of my mother's voice. On these Sunday afternoons her voice had an easiness, a softness and grace I heard at no other time. Her words threaded the afternoon lightly, without tension or rancor. The sound of her voice left me with the impression of loosely woven cloth, a texture that would comfort the body.

I felt comforted there, lying next to her, or close by, within hearing. I believed this ease would continue, that we would not be tested. My grandmother's bedspread was printed with peacocks, those regal birds I had read about, but never seen. Their wide tails spread like full skirts seemed exotic beyond believing. I took it for granted all peacocks were female, and their images are imprinted on my memory still, an emblem of that uroboric feeling and that time.

I didn't worry about God and his ten inexorable commandments on those days. My grandfather did of course. He always did what he was supposed to do. The rest of us knew we were supposed to worry, but there in that inner chamber amidst down comforters, crewel pillows, blue glass perfume droppers and ivory combs, God and the fear he was to inspire seemed distant and unreal. What interested us was us. We were real, we were vibrantly alive, and we had let ourselves out of the bottles. We were genie women, and we wove our magic for a day among ourselves.

CONFESSIONS OF AN EX-CHEERLEADER, by Louise Bernikow

The trick is to be up in the air with a big Ipana smile on your face, touching the heels of your saddle shoes to the back of your head, bending your elbows as close as you can get them behind you. This makes your short red dress rise, revealing a quick glimpse of thigh and underpants. It also makes your 16-year-old tits, aided and abetted by stuffings of cotton or the professional padding of Maidenform, stick far out.

I am doing this of my own free will on a spring afternoon in Madison Square Garden. The year is 1957, halfway between my sixteenth and seventeenth birthdays. I have aimed at, plotted and waited for this moment. It is living up to my

From "Confessions of an Ex-Cheerlreader" by Louise Bernikow, in *MS Magazine*, 1973.

expectations. The Garden is crowded. This is the play-off game for the New York City championships: Forest Hills against Boys High.

The old Madison Square Garden smells like a locker room, which is what makes it such a triumph that I find myself the center of attention in it. I am a star at last on male turf. There are 10 of us at halftime in the middle of the wooden floor with all the lights out except for the spotlight shining on us. I turn my face upward into the smell of sweat, into the applause and whistles dropping like confetti from the tiers of spectator seats above me.

Tip of my head to Maidenform padding to saddle-shoed toes, dizzy with ecstasy, I go into the first cheer.

WE GOT THE T-E-A-M

I shake my shoulders and wiggle my ass.

IT'S ON THE B-E-A-M

I do some chorus-girl high-kicking, wiggle and shake a little faster, and smile my smile a little bigger.

COME ON, FOREST HILLS, SKIN 'EM ALIVE!

Up in the air, head back, back arched, trembling all over. I hit the ground squarely on my feet and run off to the sound of thunderous applause. The team emerges for the second half.

I am a cheerleader.

Forest Hills is defeated. I am sitting in the ladies' room, having changed the short red dress for a gray flannel skirt and button-down pinstripe shirt. The Garden is dark and silent. The cheerleaders are dark and silent, too. We are all quietly weeping. When we leave the ladies' room to meet the team in the corridor, each of us embraces each of them. I move from one boy to another, despondently hugging. No funeral has brought more grief.

On the way home, I see the *Daily News* centerfold photograph of the Forest Hills cheerleaders. We are lined up like chorus girls, grinning, shoulders back. I feel as though I am looking at faded glory. When I get home, the telephone is ringing. My mother answers and says it is for me. I can tell from her face that she does not recognize the voice, and she hovers near my shoulder, monitoring me.

"Hello?"

There is no sound on the other end, then there is heavy breathing, then faster huffing and puffing. I am terrified. I hang up.

"Who was that?"

"No one."

And not until 16 years later do I understand the connection: obscene phone calls are the other side of the cheerleader glory.

Glory. I was hell-bent on glory when I started high school. On my awkward first day, I saw that cheerleaders were the queens of the school, and I determined to become one.

Forest Hills was a "rich" neighborhood, but not everyone at the high school was rich. I wasn't. In fact, I didn't live in Forest Hills at all, but in Kew Gardens Hills, on the other side of the tracks. I always felt like an outsider. When I became a cheerleader, every time I put on that red dress and went out there to jump and shout, every time I looked at the gold megaphone on my charm bracelet, and every time I walked through the corridors of the school knowing freshmen and sophomores were whispering and pointing with envy, I thought that I had managed, by hook and by crook, to wiggle my way into the ruling class.

Methodical, ruthless, ambitious, and manipulative, I studied the way "in" and discovered that, since cheerleaders chose their replacements, I had to learn how to charm women. Everything else in my life had depended on charming men and I, the original all-time Daddy's Little Girl, had that one down pat; but women?

Sororities were the key. Although they were officially outlawed, sororities ran things. The school cafeteria had special tables by custom for each sorority. As a sophomore, I would walk by those tables on my way to the nonspecial area where nobodies like me downed egg salad and Oreo cookies. I studied the sorority girls.

At night, I stood before the mirror "doing" my hair as I had seen it on the girls at those tables. I studied *Mademoiselle* and *Glamour*, full of girls who looked like cheerleaders, and there I discovered that fuzzy hair was my problem. Fuzzy Jewish hair. The girls in *Mademoiselle* had sleek blonde hair. Not me. The most popular cheerleaders at Forest Hills had sleek blonde hair. Not me.

I pin-curled as per instructions, every night, half going left and half going right. Still, in the morning, I combed it out to find kinks and fuzz. Somehow, in spite of it, I was "rushed" by sororities and, in blue serge Bermuda shorts and pink knee socks, was accepted.

I discovered how you charm women: you imitate them.

From Nora I picked up the names of painters and "acquired culture"; from Ellen I got my taste in plaid pleated skirts; from Arlene I saw how to bite my lower lip cutely. I was a sorority girl. I felt myself on shaky ground, always, but I hung in there, selling bananas on the streets of Manhattan as a "pledge," making the carfare back to Forest Hills where I joined my "sisters" who had dumped me off without a penny. We had an initiation ceremony; the fraternity boys came over afterward.

Two sorority sisters were cheerleaders. When "tryouts" time came, they taught the cheers to those of us who were going to try. We practiced all the time. I did cheers in my sleep and on the bus and in the shower. My family went nuts from the "Yea, Team" thundering from my bedroom.

"I wanna use the bathroom," my brother pounded at the door.

"Forest Hills—Forest Hills—THAT'S WHO!" I screamed from within, my teeth all freshly Ipana white.

If I made cheerleaders, my mother would stop clicking the hall light off and on when I came home from a date and "lingered" in the hall.

If I made cheerleaders, boys would arrive in rows and rows bearing tennis rackets, basketballs, baseball gloves, and fencing masks to lay in tribute at my feet.

If I made cheerleaders, Jimmy Dean and Marlon Brando would fall in love with me.

If I made cheerleaders, my hair would be straight.

Many tried; few were chosen. A jury of gym teachers and cheerleaders watched as we, with numbers on our backs, went through the cheers. I was

Number Five. Something of the Miss America pageant in all this and something of the dance marathon. Girls were tapped on the shoulder and asked to leave the floor.

What were the criteria? I have gone over the old photographs in vain. They do not say. It was not "looks," for even by fifties standards, the cheerleaders were not the best-looking girls. My own photograph shows an ordinary middle-class Jewish girl. Her hair is short and flipped-up, with bangs. Her large nose has a bump on it. (I resisted the nose-job binge my friends went on. I have no idea where I got the courage.) She is wearing dark-red lipstick and her eyebrows are heavily lined. She looks older in the high school yearbook than she does now.

It wasn't looks that made a cheerleader, but "personality" or a certain kind of energy. Something called aggressiveness. Or bitchiness. Or pep.

Pep is what happened in American history before *vigah*, but it only applied to females. Pep was cheerfulness. It mysteriously resided in the Ipana smile. "Weird" or "eccentric" girls, moody girls or troublemaking girls did not have pep. We who had it became cheerleaders, committing ourselves to a season of steady pep, bouncy activity, and good clean dispositions.

I do.

We played some humid swimming meets in Far Rockaway and Flushing, tottering at the edge of the pool and getting our hair all fuzzy, but basketball was the main attraction. (There was no football. Rumor said a boy had once been killed on the field and the sport discontinued.) Cheerleaders as a group were married to the basketball team as a group. We played wife.

Our job was to support the team. We were the decorative touches in the gyms they played. We had some "prestige" in the city because the team was good that year. They had a little of our prestige rub off on them, too, for Forest Hills was known for the good-looking stuck-up bitches there. We learned to cater to the boys' moods, not to talk to Gary after he had a bad game (he would glower and shake us off), and yet to *be* there when he or Stanley or Steve came out of the locker room all showered and handsome. We were there for them always, peppy and smiling. Boys had acceptable temper tantrums on the court, but cheerleaders never did. We were expected to be consistently "happy," like the Rockettes at Radio City Music Hall.

We were the best athletic supporters that ever lived.

We paired off, cheerleader and basketball player, like a socialite wife and corporation executive, leading lady and leading man. My social life was defined by my "status." I only went out with jocks. "Who's *he*?" or "What a creep!" applied to boys who wore desert boots or girls who were "brains." We knew kids "like us" in other middle-class ghettos in the city, and we stayed away from the Greek and Italian kids in our school, from "rocks" like Howie and Dominic who played cards and drank and "laid girls," and from girls like Carole and Anita whom we called "hitter chicks" and who, we whispered, went all the way.

Cheerleaders had a reputation for chastity. No one ever said it, but we all understood it. On top of the general fifties hangups about sex, cheerleaders had a special role to play. Vestal virgins in the rites of puberty. Jewish madonnas.

Half the time, in real "civilian" life, I had to keep pulling those gray flannel skirts down, making sure "nothing showed," keeping my legs crossed. I would have been incarcerated on the spot by my mother if, one morning, I refused to layer the top of my body with a bra and all its padding followed by a slip followed by a blouse. Even if I were to evade Mother, my peers would have condemned me as a "slut" if I appeared less dressed.

The other half the time, as a cheerleader, I dropped a skimpy red costume over only bra and panties and got out there in the middle of a gym full of screaming spectators to wiggle my hips all over the place.

What does it do to the mind of a 16-year-old girl to be Marilyn Monroe one moment and Little Goody Two-Shoes the next? I don't know, but it sure wasn't sane.

For weeks before we went, the word was whispered from ear to ear among us: *Jamaica.*

Jamaica High School was the first "away" game we went to in my senior year. The word was full of terror. Jamaica had black kids. Forest Hills High School had been redistricted every year and there were *no* blacks in the school. Aside from the rocks and hitter chicks, nearly everyone was white, middle class, and Jewish. We held mirrors up to each other and told each other we were very heavenly and the whole world was like us, except we never really believed it. We called Manhattan "New York" or "The City." It was as far away and glamorous to us as it was to Clarence in Peoria or Pat in Kansas. Our mothers wouldn't let us go there.

I confess: when I left the Forest Hills ghetto for the first "away" game, I, Princess of the Pom-Poms, Our Lady of the Saddle Shoes, Culture Queen, carried with me, hidden in my purse, a menacing kitchen knife. For protection.

Every time I say "sure" when I mean "no," every time I smile brightly when I'm exploding with rage, every time I imagine my man's achievement is my own, I know the cheerleader never really died. I feel her shaking her ass inside me and I hear her breathless, girlish voice mutter "T-E-A-M, Yea, Team."

God knows, I tried hard to kill her. Forest Hills had a history of sending its red-skirted stars bouncing off for the big league at Cornell, and it looked for a few months just before I turned 17 as though I might follow their saddle-shoed footsteps, but something happened. I went to Barnard College instead.

Barnard was another kind of game, requiring a different kind of coin to play. No points there for having been a cheerleader. It was no longer a high-priced commodity, but now a social deficit. I, alert to the winds of change and being a good mimic, buried my cheerleader past. Fast.

"What did you do in high school?"

"I wrote poetry."

"I was in the theater."

"I listened to jazz."

And the cheerleader stayed buried until recently, when I had a series of strange revelations:

Beautiful, exotic Janet, painter-poet, was a cheerleader in Connecticut.

Acid-freak Nina, unwed hippie mother, was a cheerleader in Ohio.

Elegant Susan, theatrical and literary, was a cheerleader in Philadelphia.

Shaggy Bob, radical lawyer, was a basketball player at Midwood.

Junk dealer Joe was on the Bayside team.

I am not alone.

It *was* the only game in town for middle-class kids in the American fifties.

The world is full of us.

T-E-A-M.

Yea, Team!

FROM *HOW CHILREN FAIL*, by John Holt

February 27, 1958

A few days ago Nell came up to the desk, and looking at me steadily and without speaking, as usual, put on the desk her ink copy of the latest composition. Our rule is that on the ink copy there must be no more than three mistakes per page, or the page must be copied again. I checked her paper, and on the first page found five mistakes. I showed them to her, and told her, as gently as I could, that she had to copy it again, and urged her to be more careful — typical teacher's advice. She looked at me, heaved a sigh, and went back to her desk. She is left-handed, and doesn't manage a pen very well. I could see her frowning with concentration as she worked and struggled. Back she came after a while with the second copy. This time the first page had seven mistakes, and the handwriting was noticeably worse. I told her to copy it again. Another bigger sigh, and she went back to her desk. In time the third copy arrived, looking much worse than the second, and with even more mistakes.

At that point Bill Hull asked me a question, one I should have asked myself, one we ought all to keep asking ourselves: "Where are you trying to get, and are you getting there?"

The question sticks like a burr. In schools — but where isn't it so? — we so easily fall into the same trap: the means to an end becomes an end in itself. I had on my hands this three-mistake rule meant to serve the ends of careful work and neat compositions. By applying it rigidly was I getting more careful work and neater compositions? No; I was getting a child who was so worried about having to recopy her paper that she could not concentrate on doing it, and hence did it worse and worse, and would probably do the next papers badly as well.

We need to ask more often of everything we do in school. "Where are we trying to get, and is this thing we are doing helping us to get there?" Do we do something because we want to help the children and can see that what we are doing is helping them? Or do we do it because it is inexpensive or convenient for school, teachers, administrators? Or because everyone else does it? We must beware of making a virtue of necessity, and cooking up high-sounding educational reasons for doing what is done really for reasons of administrative economy or convenience. The still greater danger is that, having started to do something for good enough reasons, we may go on doing it stubbornly and blindly, as I did that day, unable or unwilling to see that we are doing more harm than good.

March 20, 1959

Today Jane did one of those things that, for all her rebellious and annoying behavior in class, make her one of the best and most appealing people, young or old, that I have ever known. I was at the board, trying to explain to her a point on long division, when she said, in self-defense, "But Miss W. (her fourth-grade teacher) told us that we should take the first number . . ." Here she saw the smallest shadow of doubt on my face. She knew instantly that I did not approve of this rule, and without so much as a pause she continued, ". . . it wasn't Miss W., it was someone else . . ." and then went on talking about long division.

I was touched and very moved. How many adults would have seen what she saw, that what she was saying about Miss W.'s teaching was, in some slight degree, lowering my estimate of Miss W.? Even more to the point, how many adults, given this opportunity to shift the blame for their difficulties onto the absent Miss W., would instead have instantly changed their story to protect her from blame? For all our yammering about loyalty, not one adult in a thousand would have shown the loyalty that this little girl gave to her friend and former teacher. And she scarcely had to think to do it; for her, to defend one's friends from harm, blame, or even criticism was an instinct as natural as breathing.

Teachers and schools tend to mistake good behavior for good character. What they prize above all else is docility, suggestibility; the child who will do what he is told; or even better, the child who will do what is wanted without even having to be told. They value most in children what children least value in themselves. Small wonder that their effort to build character is such a failure; they don't know it when they see it. Jane is a good example. She has been a trial to everyone who has taught her. Even this fairly lenient school finds her barely tolerable; most schools long since would have kicked her out in disgrace. Of the many adults who have known her, probably very few have recognized her extraordinary qualities or appreciated their worth. Asked for an estimate of her character, most of them would probably say that it was bad. Yet, troublesome as she is, I wish that there were more children like her.

WHEN YOUR PROFESSION TAKES YOU TO HOLLYWOOD, by Liv Ullmann

I came to Hollywood with a suitcase packed for ten days. I had been invited to the premiere of *The Emigrants*. I remained for many months.

An astounded actress from Trondhjem was showered with offers. People smiled and said welcome, opened their homes, picked fruit from their trees and placed it in my child's hands.

I began working, and Linn and I moved into an enormous house with five bathrooms and a swimming pool and a guest cottage; wrote letters to friends saying that people here must be crazy, but it was fun. My bathroom was the size of an ordinary Oslo apartment. It was so grand that the toilet was built like a throne so that one should never feel confused being a film star when nature called.

"You must cut your hair," said one producer.

"No!"

"I'll make you the biggest star if you'll just dress a little differently."

"I'm used to dressing this way."

"Perhaps you should wear some more make-up. Send the beauty-parlor bill to me."

"Certainly not."

And then they left me alone. After all, I enjoyed the status of a serious actress. I had soul and depth, and was European. I didn't use make-up, and I came from Norway.

I met with generosity, found friends and acquaintances, bathed in heated swimming pools, sat in soft chairs watching films in private screening rooms, walked on long sandy beaches by the sea.

I stood on my lawn in the morning squinting up at the sun, was driven to the studio before most people were awake—at half-past five, when the best of day and night meet.

As I sat in his chair, the make-up artist and I gossiped. He gave me good advice for my new life and was always around, as if he wanted to make sure that I didn't get into difficulties. For many years, even before I was born, he had been bending over world-famous faces, covering them with creams and rouges and powders. The bodies of women who had been the cause of sweet dreams for men all over the world had relaxed here in loose dressing gowns, enjoying a moment of freedom before being taken to the wardrobe and laced in and padded out in the appropriate places.

"Life is so short," said the make-up artist, "and no one can persuade me to give something up today for the possibilities of tomorrow, promises of the future." His neck and hands were covered with chains and amulets, and he jingled gaily as he moved. He wore a little cap to hide his baldness.

"Sparkle," he whispered to me as I went in to the lights and the heat and the cameras. "That's what Shirley Temple's mother always said to her little daughter."

I spent some months in Hollywood and tried to sparkle. When something inside me protested, I reminded myself I would soon be home again. I was looking forward to making a film on the island in Sweden, living with old friends in primitive summer cottages where there was no hot water or electricity. Walk a hundred yards to an outhouse, whatever the weather.

Sit there and see the sea through the cracks in the wall, and feel that it is good to be alive.

When your profession takes you one day to Hollywood and the next to a barren island in the Baltic.

HEATHER LAMB [A TELEPHONE OPERATOR AND HER WORK], by Studs Terkel

For almost two years she has been working as a long distance telephone operator at Illinois Bell. A naval base is nearby. She works three nights a week, split shift, during the high-school season and a full forty hours in the summertime. She is turning eighteen.

It's a strange atmosphere. You're in a room about the size of a gymnasium, talking to people thousands of miles away. You come in contact with at least thirty-five an hour. You can't exchange any ideas with them. They don't know you, they never will. You feel like you might be missing people. You feel like they put a coin in the machine and they've got you. You're there to perform your service and go. You're kind of detached.

A lot of the girls are painfully shy in real life. You get some girls who are outgoing in their work, but when they have to talk to someone and look them in the face, they can't think of what to say. They feel self-conscious when they know someone can see them. At the switchboard, it's a feeling of anonymousness.

There are about seven or eight phrases that you use and that's it: "Good morning, may I help you?" "Operator, may I help you?" "Good afternoon." "Good evening." "What number did you want?" "Would you repeat that again?" "I have a collect call for you from so-and-so, will you accept the charge?" "It'll be a dollar twenty cents." That's all you can say.

A big thing is not to talk with a customer. If he's upset, you can't say more than "I'm sorry you've been having trouble." If you get caught talking with a customer, that's one mark against you. You can't help but want to talk to them if they're in trouble or if they're just feeling bad or something. For me it's a great temptation to say, "Gee, what's the matter?" You don't feel like you're really that much helping people.

Say you've got a guy on the line calling from Vietnam, his line is busy and you can't interrupt. God knows when he'll be able to get on his line again. You know he's lonesome and he wants to talk to somebody, and there you are and you can't talk to him. There's one person who feels badly and you can't do anything. When I first started, I asked the operator and she says, "No, he can always call another time."

One man said, "I'm lonesome, will you talk to me?" I said, "Gee I'm sorry, I just can't." But you *can't*. (Laughs.) I'm a communications person but I can't communicate.

I've worked here almost two years and how many girls' first names do I know? Just their last name is on their headset. You might see them every day and you won't know their names. At Ma Bell they speak of teamwork, but you don't even know the names of the people who are on your team.

It's kind of awkward if you meet someone from the company and say, "Hi there, Jones," or whatever. (Laughs.) It's very embarrassing. You sit in the cafeteria and you talk to people and you don't even know their names. (Laughs.) I've gone to a lot of people I've been talking to for a week and I've said, "Tell me your name." (Laughs.)

You have a number—mine's 407. They put your number on your tickets, so if you made a mistake they'll know who did it. You're just an instrument. You're there to dial a number. It would be just as good for them to punch out the number.

The girls sit very close. She would be not even five or six inches away from me. The big thing is elbows, especially if she's left-handed. That's why we have so many colds in the winter, you're so close. If one person has a cold, the whole office has a cold. It's very catchy.

You try to keep your fingernails short because they break. If you go to plug in, your fingernail goes. You try to wear your hair simple. It's not good to have your hair on top of your head. The women don't really come to work if they've just had their hair done. The headset flattens it.

Your arms don't really get tired, your mouth gets tired. It's strange, but you get tired of talking, 'cause you talk constantly for six hours without a break.

Half the phones have a new system where the quarter is three beeps, a dime is two beeps, and a nickel is one beep. If the guy's in a hurry and he keeps throwing in money, all the beeps get all mixed up together (laughs), and you don't know how much money is in the phone. So it's kinda hard.

When you have a call, you fill it out on this IBM card. Those go with a special machine. You use a special pencil so it'll go through this computer and pick up the numbers. It's real soft lead, it just goes all over the desk and you're all dirty by the time you get off. (Laughs.) And sometimes your back hurts if your chair isn't up at the right height and you have to bend over and write. And keeping track. You don't get just one call at a time.

There is also the clock. You've got a clock next to you that times every second. When the light goes off, you see the party has answered, you have to write down the hour, the minute, and the second. Okay, you put that in a special slot right next to the cord light. You're ready for another one. Still you've got to watch the first one. When the light goes on, they disconnect and you've got to take that card out again and time down the hour, the minute, and the second—plus keeping on taking other calls. It's hectic.

GOODBYE TO ALL THAT, by Joan Didion

How many miles to Babylon?
Three score miles and ten —
Can I get there by candlelight?

Yes, and back again —
If your feet are nimble and light
You can get there by candlelight.

It is easy to see the beginnings of things, and harder to see the ends. I can remember now, with a clarity that makes the nerves in the back of my neck constrict, when New York began for me, but I cannot lay my finger upon the moment it ended, can never cut through the ambiguities and second starts and broken resolves to the exact place on the page where the heroine is no longer as optimistic as she once was. When I first saw New York I was twenty, and it was summertime, and I got off a DC-7 at the old Idlewild temporary terminal in a new dress which had seemed very smart in Sacramento but seemed less smart already, even in the old Idlewild temporary terminal, and the warm air smelled of mildew and some instinct, programmed by all the movies I had ever seen and all the songs I had ever heard sung and all the stories I had ever read about New York, informed me that it would never be quite the same again. In fact it never was. Some time later there was a song on all the jukeboxes on the upper East Side that went "but where is the school-girl who used to be me," and if it was late enough at night I used to wonder that. I know now that almost everyone wonders something like that, sooner or later and no matter what he or she is doing, but one of the mixed blessings of being twenty and twenty-one and even twenty-three is the conviction that nothing like this, all evidence to the contrary notwithstanding, has ever happened to anyone before.

Of course it might have been some other city, had circumstances been different and the time been different and had I been different, might have been Paris or Chicago or even San Francisco, but because I am talking about myself I am talking here about New York. That first night I opened my window on the bus into town and watched for the skyline, but all I could see were the wastes of Queens and the big signs that said MIDTOWN TUNNEL THIS LANE and then a flood of summer rain (even that seemed remarkable and exotic, for I had come out of the West where there was no summer rain), and for the next three days I sat wrapped in blankets in a hotel room air-conditioned to 35° and tried to get over a bad cold and a high fever. It did not occur to me to call a doctor, because I knew none, and although it did occur to me to call the desk and ask that the air conditioner be turned off, I never called, because I did not know how much to tip whoever might come — was anyone ever so young? I am here to tell you that someone was. All I could do during those three days was talk long-distance to the boy I already knew I would never marry in the spring. I would stay in New York, I told him, just six months, and I could see the Brooklyn Bridge from my window. As it turned out the bridge was the Triborough, and I stayed eight years.

In retrospect it seems to me that those days before I knew the names of all the bridges were happier than the ones that came later, but perhaps you will see that as we go along. Part of what I want to tell you is what it is like to be young in New York, how six months can become eight years with the deceptive case of a film dissolve, for that is how those years appear to me now, in a long sequence of sentimental dissolves and old-fashioned trick shots—the Seagram Building fountains dissolve into snowflakes, I enter a revolving door at twenty and come out a good deal older, and on a different street. But most particularly I want to explain to you, and in the process perhaps to myself, why I no longer live in New York. It is often said that New York is a city for only the very rich and the very poor. It is less often said that New York is also, at least for those of us who came there from somewhere else, a city for only the very young.

I remember once, one cold bright December evening in New York, suggesting to a friend who complained of having been around too long that he come with me to a party where there would be, I assured him with the bright resourcefulness of twenty-three, "new faces." He laughed literally until he choked, and I had to roll down the taxi window and hit him on the back. "New faces," he said finally, "don't tell me about *new faces*." It seemed that the last time he had gone to a party where he had been promised "new faces," there had been fifteen people in the room, and he had already slept with five of the women and owed money to all but two of the men. I laughed with him, but the first snow had just begun to fall and the big Christmas trees glittered yellow and white as far as I could see up Park Avenue and I had a new dress and it would be a long while before I would come to understand the particular moral of the story.

It would be a long while because, quite simply, I was in love with New York. I do not mean "love" in any colloquial way, I mean that I was in love with the city, the way you love the first person who ever touches you and never love anyone quite that way again. I remember walking across Sixty-second Street one twilight that first spring, or the second spring, they were all alike for a while. I was late to meet someone but I stopped at Lexington Avenue and bought a peach and stood on the corner eating it and knew that I had come out of the West and reached the mirage. I could taste the peach and feel the soft air blowing from a subway grating on my legs and I could smell lilac and garbage and expensive perfume and I knew that it would cost something sooner or later—because I did not belong there, did not come from there—but when you are twenty-two or twenty-three, you figure that later you will have a high emotional balance, and be able to pay whatever it costs. I still believed in possibilities then, still had the sense, so peculiar to New York, that something extraordinary would happen any minute, any day, any month. I was making only $65 or $70 a week then ("Put yourself in Hattie Carnegie's hands," I was advised without the slightest trace of irony by an editor of the magazine for which I worked), so little money that some weeks I had to charge food at Bloomingdale's gourmet shop in order to eat, a fact which went unmentioned in the letters I wrote to California. I never told my father that I needed money because then he would have sent it, and I would never know if I could do it by myself. At that time making a living seemed a game to me, with arbitrary but quite inflexible rules. And except on a certain kind of winter evening—six-thirty in the Seventies, say, already dark and bitter with a wind off the river, when I would be walking very fast toward a bus and would look in the bright windows of brownstones and see cooks working in clean kitchens and imagine women lighting candles on the floor above and beautiful children being bathed on the floor above that—except on nights like those, I never felt poor; I had the feeling that if I needed money I could always get it. I could write a syndicated column for teenagers under the name "Debbi Lynn" or I could smuggle gold into India or I could become a $100 call girl, and none of it would matter.

Nothing was irrevocable; everything was within reach. Just around every corner lay something curious and interesting, something I had never before seen or done or known about. I could go to a party and meet someone who called himself Mr. Emotional Appeal and ran The Emotional Appeal Institute or Tina Onassis Blandford or a Florida cracker who was then a regular on what he called "the Big C," the Southampton-El Morocco circuit ("I'm well-connected on the Big C, honey," he would tell me over collard greens on his vast borrowed terrace), or the widow of the celery king of the Harlem market or a piano salesman from Bonne Terre, Missouri, or someone who had already made and lost two fortunes in Midland, Texas. I could make promises to myself and to other people and there would be all the time in the world to keep them. I could stay up all night and make mistakes, and none of it would count.

You see I was in a curious position in New York: it never occurred to me that I was living a real life there. In my imagination I was always there for just another few months, just until Christmas or Easter or the first warm day in May. For that reason I was most comfortable in the company of Southerners. They seemed to be in New York as I was, on some indefinitely extended leave from wherever they belonged, disinclined to consider the future, temporary exiles who always knew when the flights left for New Orleans or Memphis or Richmond or, in my case, California. Someone who lives always with a plane schedule in the drawer lives on a slightly different calendar. Christmas, for example, was a difficult season. Other people could take it in stride, going to Stowe or going abroad or going for the day to their mothers' places in Connecticut; those of us who believed that we lived somewhere else would spend it making and canceling airline reservations, waiting for weatherbound flights as if for the last plane out of Lisbon in 1940, and finally comforting one another, those of us who were left, with the oranges and mementos and smoked-oyster stuffings of childhood, gathering close, colonials in a far country.

Which is precisely what we were. I am not sure that it is possible for anyone brought up in the East to appreciate entirely what New York, the idea of New York, means to those of us who came out of the West and the South. To an Eastern child, particularly a child who has always had an uncle on Wall Street and who has spent several hundred Saturdays first at F. A. O. Schwartz and being fitted for shoes at Best's and then waiting under the Biltmore clock and dancing to Lester Lanin, New York is just a city, albeit *the* city, a plausible place for people to live. But to those of us who came from places where no one had heard of Lester Lanin and Grand Central Station was a Saturday radio program, where Wall Street and Fifth Avenue and Madison Avenue were not places at all but abstractions ("Money," and "High Fashion," and "The Hucksters"), New York was no mere city. It was instead an infinitely romantic notion, the mysterious nexus of all love and money and power, the shining and perishable dream itself. To think of "living" there was to reduce the miraculous to the mundane; one does not "live" at Xanadu.

In fact it was difficult in the extreme for me to understand those young women for whom New York was not simply an ephemeral Estoril but a real place, girls who bought toasters and installed new cabinets in their apartments and committed themselves to some reasonable future. I never bought any furniture in New York. For a year or so I lived in other people's apartments; after that I lived in the Nineties in an apartment furnished entirely with things taken from storage by a friend whose wife had moved away. And when I left the apartment in the Nineties (that was when I was leaving everything, when it was all breaking up) I left everything in it, even my winter clothes and the map of Sacramento County I had hung on the bedroom wall to remind me who I was, and I moved into a monastic four-room floor-through on Seventy-fifth Street. "Monastic" is perhaps misleading here, implying some chic severity; until after I was married and my husband moved some furniture in, there was nothing at all in those four rooms except a cheap double mattress and box springs, ordered by telephone the day I decided to move, and two French garden chairs lent me by a friend who imported them. (It strikes me now that the people I knew in New York all had curious and self-defeating sidelines. They imported garden chairs which did not sell very well at Hammacher Schlemmer or they tried to market hair straighteners in Harlem or they ghosted exposés of Murder Incorporated for Sunday supplements. I think that perhaps none of us was very serious, engagé only about our most private lives.)

All I ever did to that apartment was hang fifty yards of yellow theatrical silk across the bedroom windows, because I had some idea that the gold light would make me feel better, but I did not bother to weight the curtains correctly and all that summer the long panels of transparent golden silk would blow out the windows and get tangled and drenched in the afternoon thunderstorms. That was the year, my twenty-eighth, when I was discovering that not all of the promises would be kept, that some things are in fact irrevocable and that it had counted after all, every evasion and every procrastination, every mistake, every word, all of it.

That is what it was all about, wasn't it? Promises? Now when New York comes back to me it comes in hallucinatory flashes, so clinically detailed that I sometimes wish that memory would effect the distortion with which it is commonly credited. For a lot of the time I was in New York I used a perfume called *Fleurs de Rocaille,* and then *L'Air du Temps,* and now the slightest trace of either can short-circuit my connections for the rest of the day. Nor can I smell Henri Bendel jasmine soap without falling back into the past, or the particular mixture of spices used for boiling crabs. There were barrels of crab boil in a Czech place in the Eighties where I once shopped. Smells, of course, are notorious memory stimuli, but there are other things which affect me the same way. Blue-and-white striped sheets. Vermouth cassis. Some faded nightgowns which were new in 1959 or 1960, and some chiffon scarves I bought about the same time.

I suppose that a lot of us who have been young in New York have the same scenes on our home screens. I remember sitting in a lot of apartments with a slight headache about five o'clock in the morning. I had a friend who could not sleep, and he knew a few other people who had the same trouble, and we would watch the sky lighten and have a last drink with no ice and then go home in the early morning light, when the streets were clean and wet (had it rained in the night? we never knew) and the few cruising taxis still had their headlights on and the only color was the red and green of traffic signals. The White Rose bars opened very early in the morning; I recall waiting in one of them to watch an astronaut go into space, waiting so long that at the moment it actually happened I had my eyes not on the television screen but on a cockroach on the tile floor. I liked the bleak branches above Washington Square at dawn, and the monochromatic flatness of Second Avenue, the fire escapes and the grilled storefronts peculiar and empty in their perspective.

It is relatively hard to fight at six-thirty or seven in the morning without any sleep, which was perhaps one reason we stayed up all night, and it seemed to me a pleasant time of day. The windows were shuttered in that apartment in the Nineties and I could sleep a few hours and then go to work. I could work then on two or three hours' sleep and a container of coffee from Chock Full O'Nuts. I liked going to work, liked the soothing and satisfactory rhythm of getting out a magazine, liked the orderly progression of four-color closings and two-color closings and black-and-white closings and then The Product, no abstraction but something which looked effortlessly glossy and could be picked up on a newsstand and weighed in the hand. I liked all the minutiae of proofs and layouts, liked working late on the nights the magazine went to press, sitting and reading *Variety* and waiting for the copy desk to call. From my office I could look across town to the weather signal on the Mutual of New York Building and the lights that alternately spelled out TIME and LIFE above Rockefeller Plaza; that pleased me obscurely, and so did walking uptown in the mauve eight o'clocks of early summer evenings and looking at things, Lowestoft tureens in Fifty-seventh Street windows, people in evening clothes trying to get taxis, the trees just coming into full leaf, the lambent air, all the sweet promises of money and summer.

Some years passed, but I still did not lose that sense of wonder about New York. I began to cherish the loneliness of it, the sense that at any given time no one need know where I was or what I was doing. I liked walking, from the East River over to the Hudson and back on brisk days, down around the Village on warm days. A friend would leave me the key to her apartment in the West Village when she was out of town, and sometimes I would just move down there, because by that time the telephone was beginning to bother me (the canker, you see, was already in the rose) and not many people had that number. I remember one day when someone who did have the West Village number came to pick me up for lunch there, and we both had hangovers, and I cut my finger opening him a beer and burst into tears, and we walked to a Spanish restaurant and drank Bloody Marys and *gazpacho* until we felt better. I was not then guilt-ridden about spending afternoons that way, because I still had all the afternoons in the world.

And even that late in the game I still liked going to parties, all parties, bad parties, Saturday-afternoon parties given by recently married couples who lived in Stuyvesant Town, West Side parties given by unpublished or failed writers who served cheap red wine and talked about going to Guadalajara, Village parties where all the guests worked for advertising agencies and voted for Reform

Democrats, press parties at Sardi's, the worst kinds of parties. You will have perceived by now that I was not one to profit by the experience of others, that it was a very long time indeed before I stopped believing in new faces and began to understand the lesson in that story, which was that it is distinctly possible to stay too long at the Fair.

I could not tell you when I began to understand that. All I know is that it was very bad when I was twenty-eight. Everything that was said to me I seemed to have heard before, and I could no longer listen. I could no longer sit in little bars near Grand Central and listen to someone complaining of his wife's inability to cope with the help while he missed another train to Connecticut. I no longer had any interest in hearing about the advances other people had received from their publishers, about plays which were having second-act trouble in Philadelphia, or about people I would like very much if only I would come out and meet them. I had already met them, always. There were certain parts of the city which I had to avoid. I could not bear upper Madison Avenue on weekday mornings (this was a particularly inconvenient aversion, since I then lived just fifty or sixty feet east of Madison), because I would see women walking Yorkshire terriers and shopping at Gristede's, and some Veblenesque gorge would rise in my throat. I could not go to Times Square in the afternoon, or to the New York Public Library for any reason whatsoever. One day I could not go into a Schrafft's; the next day it would be Bonwit Teller.

I hurt the people I cared about, and insulted those I did not. I cut myself off from the one peson who was closer to me than any other. I cried until I was not even aware when I was crying and when I was not, cried in elevators and in taxis and in Chinese laundries, and when I went to the doctor he said only that I seemed to be depressed, and should see a "specialist." He wrote down a psychiatrist's name and address for me, but I did not go.

Instead I got married, which as it turned out was a very good thing to do but badly timed, since I still could not walk on upper Madison Avenue in the mornings and still could not talk to people and still cried in Chinese laundries. I had never before understood what "despair" meant, and I am not sure that I understand now, but I understood that year. Of course I could not work. I could not even get dinner with any degree of certainty, and I would sit in the apartment on Seventy-fifth Street paralyzed until my husband would call from his office and say gently that I did not have to get dinner, that I could meet him at Michael's Pub or at Toots Shor's or at Sardi's East. And then one morning in April (we had been married in January) he called and told me that he wanted to get out of New York for a while, that he would take a six-month leave of absence, that we would go somewhere.

It was three years ago that he told me that, and we have lived in Los Angeles since. Many of the people we knew in New York think this a curious aberration, and in fact tell us so. There is no possible, no adequate answer to that, and so we give certain stock answers, the answers everyone gives. I talk about how difficult it would be for us to "afford" to live in New York right now, about how much "space" we need. All I mean is that I was very young in New York, and that at some point the golden rhythm was broken, and I am not that young any more.

The last time I was in New York was in a cold January, and everyone was ill and tired. Many of the people I used to know there had moved to Dallas or had gone on Antabuse or had bought a farm in New Hampshire. We stayed ten days, and then we took an afternoon flight back to Los Angeles, and on the way home from the airport that night I could see the moon on the Pacific and smell jasmine all around and we both knew that there was no longer any point in keeping the apartment we still kept in New York. There were years when I called Los Angeles "the Coast," but they seem a long time ago.

BATTLE ROYAL, by Ralph Ellison

It goes a long way back, some twenty years. All my life I had been looking for something, and everywhere I turned someone tried to tell me what it was. I accepted their answers too, though they were often in contradiction and even self-contradictory. I was naïve. I was looking for myself and asking everyone except myself questions which I, and only I, could answer. It took me a long time and much painful boomeranging of my expectations to achieve a realization everyone else appears to have been born with: That I am nobody but myself. But first I had to discover that I am an invisible man!

And yet I am no freak of nature, nor of history. I was in the cards, other things having been equal (or unequal) eighty-five years ago. I am not ashamed of my grandparents for having been slaves. I am only ashamed of myself for having at one time been ashamed. About eighty-five years ago they were told that they were free, united with others of our country in everything pertaining to the common good, and, in everything social, separate like the fingers of the hand. And they believed it. They exulted in it. They stayed in their place, worked hard, and brought up my father to do the same. But my grandfather is the one. He was an odd old guy, my grandfather, and I am told I take after him. It was he who caused the trouble. On his deathbed he called my father to him and said, "Son, after I'm gone I want you to keep up the good fight. I never told you, but our life is a war and I have been a traitor all my born days, a spy in the enemy's country ever since I give up my gun back in the Reconstruction. Live with your head in the lion's mouth. I want you to overcome 'em with yeses, undermine 'em with grins, agree 'em to death and destruction, let 'em swoller you till they vomit or bust wide open." They thought the old man had gone out of his mind. He had been the meekest of men. The younger children were rushed from the room, the shades drawn and the flame of the lamp turned so low that it sputtered on the wick like the old man's breathing. "Learn it to the younguns," he whispered fiercely; then he died.

But my folks were more alarmed over his last words than over his dying. It was as though he had not died at all, his words caused so much anxiety. I was warned emphatically to forget what he had said and, indeed, this is the first time it has been mentioned outside the family circle. It had a tremendous effect upon me, however. I could never be sure of what he meant. Grandfather had been a quiet old man who never made any trouble, yet on his deathbed he had called himself a traitor and a spy, and he had spoken of his meekness as a dangerous activity. It became a constant puzzle which lay unanswered in the back of my mind. And whenever things went well for me I remembered my grandfather and felt guilty and uncomfortable. It was as though I was carrying out his advice in spite of myself. And to make it worse, everyone loved me for it. I was praised by the most lily-white men of the town. I was considered an example of desirable conduct—just as my grandfather had been. And what puzzled me was that the old man had defined it as *treachery*. When I was praised for my conduct I felt a guilt that in some way I was doing something that was really against the wishes of the white folks, that if they had understood they would have desired me to act just the opposite, that I should have been sulky and mean, and that that really would have been what they wanted, even though they were fooled and thought they wanted me to act as I did. It made me afraid that some day they would look upon me as a traitor and I would be lost. Still I was more afraid to act any other way because they didn't like that at all. The old man's words were like a curse. On my graduation day I delivered an oration in which I showed that humility was the secret, indeed, the very essence of progress. (Not that I believed this—how could I, remembering my grandfather?—I only believed that it worked.) It was a great success. Everyone praised me and I was invited to give the speech at a gathering of the town's leading white citizens. It was a triumph for our whole community.

It was in the main ballroom of the leading hotel. When I got there I discovered that it was on the occasion of a smoker, and I was told that since I was to be there anyway I might as well take part in the battle royal to be fought by some of my school-mates as part of the entertainment. The battle royal came first.

All of the town's big shots were there in their tuxedoes, wolfing down the buffet food, drinking beer and whiskey and smoking black cigars. It was a large room with a high ceiling. Chairs were arranged in neat rows around three sides of a portable boxing ring. The fourth side was clear, revealing a gleaming space of polished floor. I had some misgivings over the battle royal, by the way. Not from a distaste for fighting, but because I didn't care too much for the other fellows who were to take part. They were tough guys who seemed to have no grandfather's curse worrying their minds. No one could mistake their toughness. And besides, I suspected that fighting a battle royal might detract from the dignity of my speech. In those pre-invisible days I visualized myself as a potential Booker T. Washington. But the other fellows didn't care too much for me either, and there were nine of them. I felt superior to them in my way, and I didn't like the manner in which we were all crowded together into the servants' elevator. Nor did they like my being there. In fact, as the warmly lighted floors flashed past the elevator we had words over the fact that I, by taking part in the fight, had knocked one of their friends out of a night's work.

We were led out of the elevator through a rococo hall into an anteroom and told to get into our fighting togs. Each of us was issued a pair of boxing gloves and ushered out into the big mirrored hall, which we entered looking cautiously about us and whispering, lest we might accidentally be heard above the noise of the room. It was foggy with cigar smoke. And already the whiskey was taking effect. I was shocked to see some of the most important men of the town quite tipsy. They were all there — bankers, lawyers, judges, doctors, fire chiefs, teachers, merchants. Even one of the more fashionable pastors. Something we could not see was going on up front. A clarinet was vibrating sensuously and the men were standing up and moving eagerly forward. We were a small tight group, clustered together, our bare upper bodies touching and shining with anticipatory sweat; while up front the big shots were becoming increasingly excited over something we still could not see. Suddenly I heard the school superintendent, who had told me to come, yell, "Bring up the shines, gentlemen! Bring up the little shines!"

We were rushed up to the front of the ballroom, where it smelled even more strongly of tobacco and whiskey. Then we were pushed into place. I almost wet my pants. A sea of faces, some hostile, some amused, ringed around us, and in the center, facing us, stood a magnificent blonde — stark naked. There was dead silence. I felt a blast of cold air chill me. I tried to back away, but they were behind me and around me. Some of the boys stood with lowered heads, trembling. I felt a wave of irrational guilt and fear. My teeth chattered, my skin turned to goose flesh, my knees knocked. Yet I was strongly attracted and looked in spite of myself. Had the price of looking been blindness, I would have looked. The hair was yellow like that of a circus kewpie doll, the face heavily powdered and rouged, as though to form an abstract mask, the eyes hollow and smeared a cool blue, the color of a baboon's butt. I felt a desire to spit upon her as my eyes brushed slowly over her body. Her breasts were firm and round as the domes of East Indian temples, and I stood so close as to see the fine skin texture and beads of pearly perspiration glistening like dew around the pink and erected buds of her nipples. I wanted at one and the same time to run from the room, to sink through the floor, or go to her and cover her from my eyes and the eyes of the others with my body; to feel the soft thighs, to caress her and destroy her, to love her and murder her, to hide from her, and yet to stroke where below the small American flag tattooed upon her belly her thighs formed a capital V. I had a notion that of all in the room she saw only me with her impersonal eyes.

And then she began to dance, a slow sensuous movement; the smoke of a hundred cigars clinging to her like the thinnest of veils. She seemed like a fair bird-girl girdled in veils calling to me from the angry surface of some gray and threatening sea. I was transported. Then I became aware of the clarinet playing and the big shots yelling at us. Some threatened us if we looked and others if we did not. On my right I saw one boy faint. And now a man grabbed a silver pitcher from a table and stepped close as he dashed ice water upon him and stood him up and forced two of us to support him as his head hung and moans issued from his thick bluish lips. Another boy began to plead to go home. He was the largest of the group, wearing dark red fighting trunks much too small to conceal the erection which projected from him as though in answer to the insinuating low-registered moaning of the clarinet. He tried to hide himself with his boxing gloves.

And all the while the blonde continued dancing, smiling faintly at the big shots who watched her with fascination, and faintly smiling at our fear. I noticed a certain merchant who followed her hungrily, his lips loose and drooling. He was a large man who wore diamond studs in a shirtfront which swelled with the ample paunch underneath, and each time the blonde swayed her undulating hips he ran his hand through the thin hair of his bald head and, with his arms upheld, his posture clumsy like that of an intoxicated panda, wound his belly in a slow and obscene grind. This creature was completely hypnotized. The music had quickened. As the dancer flung herself about with a detached expression on her face, the men began reaching out to touch her. I could see their beefy fingers sink into the soft flesh. Some of the others tried to stop them and she began to move around the floor in graceful circles, as they gave chase, slipping and sliding over the polished floor. It was mad. Chairs went crashing, drinks were spilt, as they ran laughing and howling after her. They caught her just as she reached a door, raised her from the floor, and tossed her as college boys are tossed at a hazing, and above her red, fixed-smiling lips I saw the terror and disgust in her eyes, almost like my own terror and that which I saw in some of the other boys. As I watched, they tossed her twice and her soft breasts seemed to flatten against the air and her legs flung wildly as she spun. Some of the more sober ones helped her to escape. And I started off the floor, heading for the anteroom with the rest of the boys.

Some were still crying and in hysteria. But as we tried to leave we were stopped and ordered to get into the ring. There was nothing to do but what we were told. All ten of us climbed under the ropes and allowed ourselves to be blindfolded with broad bands of white cloth. One of the men seemed to feel a bit sympathetic and tried to cheer us up as we stood with our backs against the ropes. Some of us tried to grin. "See that boy over there?" one of the men said. "I want you to run across at the bell and give it to him right in the belly. If you don't get him, I'm going to get you. I don't like his looks." Each of us was told the same. The blindfolds were put on. Yet even then I had been going over my speech. In my mind each word was as bright as flame. I felt the cloth pressed into place, and frowned so that it would be loosened when I relaxed.

But now I felt a sudden fit of blind terror. I was unused to darkness. It was as though I had suddenly found myself in a dark room filled with poisonous cottonmouths. I could hear the bleary voices yelling insistently for the battle royal to begin.

"Get going in there!"

"Let me at that big nigger!"

I strained to pick up the school superintendent's voice, as though to squeeze some security out of that slightly more familiar sound.

"Let me at those black sonsabitches!" someone yelled.

"No, Jackson, no!" another voice yelled. "Here, somebody, help me hold Jack."

"I want to get at that ginger-colored nigger. Tear him limb from limb," the first voice yelled.

I stood against the ropes trembling. For in those days I was what they called ginger-colored, and he sounded as though he might crunch me between his teeth like a crisp ginger cookie.

Quite a struggle was going on. Chairs were being kicked about and I could hear voices grunting as with a terrific effort. I wanted to see, to see more desperately than ever before. But the blindfold was as tight as a thick skin-puckering scab and when I raised my gloved hands to push the layers of white aside a voice yelled, "Oh, no you don't, black bastard! Leave that alone!"

"Ring the bell before Jackson kills him a coon!" someone boomed in the sudden silence. And I heard the bell clang and the sound of the feet scuffling foward.

A glove smacked against my head. I pivoted, striking out stiffly as someone went past, and felt the jar ripple along the length of my arm to my shoulder. Then it seemed as though all nine of the boys had turned upon me at once. Blows pounded me from all sides while I struck out as best I could. So many blows landed upon me that I wondered if I were not the only blindfolded fighter in the ring, or if the man called Jackson hadn't succeeded in getting me after all.

Blindfolded, I could no longer control my motions. I had no dignity. I stumbled about like a baby or a drunken man. The smoke had become thicker and with each new blow it seemed to scar and further restrict my lungs. My saliva became like hot bitter glue. A glove connected with my head, filling my mouth with warm blood. It was everywhere. I could not tell if the moisture I felt upon my body was sweat or blood. A blow landed hard against the nape of my neck. I felt myself going over, my head hitting the floor. Streaks of blue light filled the black world behind the blindfold. I lay prone, pretending that I was knocked out, but felt myself seized by hands and yanked to my feet. "Get going, black boy! Mix it up!" My arms were like lead, my head smarting from blows. I managed to feel my way to the ropes and held on, trying to catch my breath. A glove landed in my mid-section and I went over again, feeling as though the smoke had become a knife jabbed into my guts. Pushed this way and that by the legs milling around me, I finally pulled erect and discovered that I could see the black, sweat-washed forms weaving in the smoky-blue atmosphere like drunken dancers weaving to the rapid drum-like thuds of blows.

Everyone fought hysterically. It was complete anarchy. Everybody fought every body else. No group fought together for long. Two, three, four, fought one, then turned to fight each other, were themselves attacked. Blows landed below the belt and in the kidney, with the gloves open as well as closed, and with my eyes partly opened now there was not so much terror. I moved carefully, avoiding blows, although not too many to attract attention, fighting from group to group. The boys groped about like blind, cautious crabs crouching to protect their mid-sections, their heads pulled in short against their shoulders, their arms stretched nervously before them, with their fists testing the smoke-filled air like the knobbed feelers of hypersensitive snails. In one corner I glimpsed a boy violently punching the air and heard him scream in pain as he smashed his hand against a ring post. For a second I saw him bent over holding his hand, then going down as a blow caught his unprotected head. I played one group against the other, slipping in and throwing a punch then stepping out of range while pushing the others into the melee to take the blows blindly aimed at me. The smoke was agonizing and there were no rounds, no bells at three minute intervals to relieve our exhaustion. The room spun round me, a swirl of lights, smoke, sweating bodies surrounded by tense white faces. I bled from both nose and mouth, the blood spattering upon my chest.

The men kept yelling, "Slug him, black boy! Knock his guts out!"

"Uppercut him! Kill him! Kill that big boy!"

Taking a fake fall, I saw a boy going down heavily beside me as though we were felled by a single blow, saw a sneaker-clad foot shoot into his groin as the two who had knocked him down stumbled upon him. I rolled out of range, feeling a twinge of nausea.

The harder we fought the more threatening the men became. And yet, I had began to worry about my speech again. How would it go? Would they recognize my ability? What would they give me?

I was fighting automatically when suddenly I noticed that one after another of the boys was leaving the ring. I was surprised, filled with panic, as though I had been left alone with an unknown danger. Then I understood. The boys had arranged it among themselves. It was the custom for the two men left in the ring to slug it out for the winner's prize. I discovered this too late. When the bell sounded two men in tuxedoes leaped into the ring and removed the blindfold. I found myself facing Tatlock, the biggest of the gang. I felt sick at my stomach. Hardly had the bell stopped ringing in my ears than it changed again and I saw him moving swiftly toward me. Thinking of nothing else to do I hit him smash on the nose. He kept coming, bringing the rank sharp violence of stale sweat. His face was a black blank of a face, only his eyes alive—with hate of me and aglow with a feverish terror from what had happened to us all. I became anxious. I wanted to deliver my speech and he came at me as though he meant to beat it out of me. I smashed him again and again, taking his blows as they came. Then on a sudden impulse I struck him lightly and as we clinched, I whispered, "Fake like I knocked you out, you can have the prize."

"I'll break your behind," he whispered hoarsely.

"For *them?*"

"For *me*, sonofabitch!"

They were yelling for us to break it up and Tatlock spun me half around with a blow, and as a joggled camera sweeps in a reeling scene, I saw the howling red faces crouching tense beneath the cloud of blue-gray smoke. For a moment the world wavered, unraveled, flowed, then my head cleared and Tatlock bounced before me. That fluttering shadow before my eyes was his jabbing left hand. Then falling forward, my head against his damp shoulder, I whispered.

"I'll make it five dollars more."

"Go to hell!"

But his muscles relaxed a trifle beneath my pressure and I breathed, "Seven?"

"Give it to your ma," he said, ripping me beneath the heart.

And while I still held him I butted him and moved away. I felt myself bombarded with punches. I fought back with hopeless desperation. I wanted to deliver my speech more than anything else in the world, because I felt that only these men could judge truly my ability, and now this stupid clown was ruining my chances. I began fighting carefully now, moving in to punch him and out again with my greater speed. A lucky blow to his chin and I had him going too— until I heard a loud voice yell, "I got my money on the big boy."

Hearing this, I almost dropped my guard. I was confused: Should I try to win against the voice out there? Would not this go against my speech, and was not this a moment for humility, for nonresistance? A blow to my head as I danced about sent my right eye popping like a jack-in-the-box and settled my dilemma. The room went red as I fell. It was a dream fall, my body languid and fastidious as to where to land, until the floor became impatient and smashed up to meet me. A moment later I came to. An hypnotic voice said FIVE emphatically. And I lay there, hazily watching a dark red spot of my own blood shaping itself into a butterfly, glistening and soaking into the soiled gray world of the canvas.

When the voice drawled TEN I was lifted up and dragged to a chair. I sat dazed. My eye pained and swelled with each throb of my pounding heart and I wondered if now I would be allowed to speak. I was wringing wet, my mouth still bleeding. We were grouped along the wall now. The other boys ignored me as they congratulated Tatlock and speculated as to how much they would be paid. One boy whimpered over his smashed hand. Looking up front, I saw attendants in white jackets rolling the portable ring away and placing a small square rug in the vacant space surrounded by chairs. Perhaps, I thought, I will stand on the rug to deliver my speech.

Then the M.C. called to us, "Come on up here boys and get your money."

We ran forward to where the men laughed and talked in their chairs, waiting. Everyone seemed friendly now.

"There it is on the rug," the man said. I saw the rug covered with coins of all dimensions and a few crumpled bills. But what excited me, scattered here and there, were the gold pieces.

"Boys, it's all yours," the man said. "You get all you grab."

"That's right, Sambo," a blond man said, winking at me confidentially.

I trembled with excitement, forgetting my pain. I would get the gold and the bills, I thought. I would use both hands. I would throw my body against the boys nearest me to block them from the gold.

"Get down around the rug now," the man commanded, "and don't anyone touch it until I give the signal."

"This ought to be good," I heard.

As told, we got around the square rug on our knees. Slowly the man raised his freckled hand as we followed it upward with our eyes.

I heard, "These niggers look like they're about to pray."

Then, "Ready," the man said, "Go!"

I lunged for a yellow coin lying on the blue design of the carpet, touching it and sending a surprised shriek to join those rising around me. I tried frantically to remove my hand but could not let go. A hot, violent force tore through my body, shaking me like a wet rat. The rug was electrified. The hair bristled up on my head as I shook myself free. My muscles jumped, my nerves jangled, writhed. But I saw that this was not stopping the other boys. Laughing in fear and embarrassment, some were holding back and scooping up the coins knocked off by the painful contortions of the others. The men roared above us as we struggled.

"Pick it up, goddammit, pick it up!" someone called like a bass-voiced parrot. "Go on, get it!"

I crawled rapidly around the floor, picking up the coins, trying to avoid the coppers and to get greenbacks and the gold. Ignoring the shock by laughing, as I brushed the coins off quickly, I discovered that I could contain the electricity — a contradiction, but it works. Then the men began to push us onto the rug. Laughing embarrassedly, we struggled out of their hands and kept after the coins. We were all wet and slippery and hard to hold. Suddenly I saw a boy lifted into the air, glistening with sweat like a circus seal, and dropped, his wet back landing flush upon the charged rug, heard him yell and saw him literally dance upon his back, his elbows beating a frenzied tattoo upon the floor, his muscles twitching like the flesh of a horse stung by many flies. When he finally rolled off, his face was gray and no one stopped him when he ran from the floor amid booming laughter.

"Get the money," the M.C. called. "That's good hard American cash!"

And we snatched and grabbed, snatched and grabbed. I was careful not to come too close to the rug now, and when I felt the hot whiskey breath descend upon me like a cloud of foul air I reached out and grabbed the leg of a chair. It was occupied and I held on desperately.

"Leggo, nigger! Leggo!"

The huge face wavered down to mine as he tried to push me free. But my body was slippery and he was too drunk. It was Mr. Colcord, who owned a chain of movie houses and "entertainment palaces." Each time he grabbed me I slipped out of his hands. It became a real struggle. I feared the rug more than I did the drunk, so I held on, surprising myself for a moment by trying to topple *him* upon the rug. It was such an enormous idea that I found myself actually carrying it out. I tried not to be obvious, yet when I grabbed his leg, trying to tumble him out of the chair, he raised up roaring with laughter, and looking at me with soberness dead in the eye, kicked me viciously in the chest. The chair leg flew out of my hand and I felt myself going and rolled. It was as though I had rolled through a bed of hot coals. It seemed a whole century would pass before I would roll free, a century in which I was seared through the deepest level of my body to the fearful breath within me and the breath seared and heated to the point of explosion. It'll all be over in a flash, I thought as I rolled clear. It'll all be over in a flash.

But not yet, the men on the other side were waiting, red faces swollen as though from apoplexy as they bent forward in their chairs. Seeing their fingers coming toward me I rolled away as a fumbled football rolls off the receiver's fingertips, back into the coals. That time I jerkily sent the rug sliding out of place and heard the coins ringing against the floor and the boys scuffling to pick them up and the M.C. calling, "All right, boys, that's all. Go get dressed and get your money."

I was limp as a dish rag. My back felt as though it had been beaten with wires.

When we had dressed the M.C. came in and gave us each five dollars, except Tatlock, who got ten for being last in the ring. Then he told us to leave. I was not to get a chance to deliver my speech, I thought. I was going out into the dim alley in despair when I was stopped and told to go back. I returned to the ball-room, where the men were pushing back their chairs and gathering in groups to talk.

The M.C. knocked on a table for quiet. "Gentlemen," he said, "we almost forgot an important part of the program. A most serious part, gentlemen. This boy was brought here to deliver a speech which he made at his graduation yesterday . . ."

"Bravo!"

"I'm told that he is the smartest boy we've got out there in Greenwood. I'm told that he knows more big words than a pocket-sized dictionary."

Much applause and laughter.

"So now, gentlemen, I want you to give him your attention."

There was still laughter as I faced them, my mouth dry, my eye throbbing. I began slowly, but evidently my throat was tense, because they began shouting, "Louder! Louder!"

"We of the younger generation extol the wisdom of that great leader and educator," I shouted, "who first spoke these flaming words of wisdom: 'A ship lost at sea for many days suddenly sighted a friendly vessel. From the mast of the unfortunate vessel was seen a signal: "Water, water, we die of thirst!" The answer from the friendly vessel came back: "Cast down your bucket where you are." The captain of the distressed vessel, at last heeding the injunction, cast down his bucket, and it came up full of fresh sparkling water from the mouth of the Amazon River.' And like him I say, and in his words, 'To those of my race who depend upon bettering their condition in a foreign land, or who underestimate the importance of cultivating friendly relations with the Southern white man, who is his next-door neightbor, I would say: "Cast down your bucket where you are"—cast it down in making friends in every manly way of the people of all races by whom we are surrounded . . .' "

I spoke automatically and with such fervor that I did not realize that the men were still talking and laughing until my dry mouth, filling up with blood from the cut, almost strangled me. I coughed, wanting to stop and go to one of the tall brass, sand-filled spittoons to relieve myself, but a few of the men, especially the superintendent, were listening and I was afraid. So I gulped it down, blood, saliva and all, and continued. (What powers of endurance I had during those days! What enthusiasm! What a belief in the rightness of things!) I spoke even louder in spite of the pain. But still they talked and still they laughed, as though deaf with cotton in dirty ears. So I spoke with greater emotional emphasis. I closed my ears and swallowed blood until I was nauseated. The speech seemed a hundred times as long as before, but I could not leave out a single word. All had to be said, each memorized nuance considered, rendered. Nor was that all. Whenever I uttered a word of three or more syllables a group of voices would yell for me to repeat it. I used the phrase "social responsibility" and they yelled:

"What's that word you say, boy?"

"Social responsibility," I said.

"What?"

"Social . . ."

"Louder."

". . . responsibility."

"More!"

"Respon—"

"Repeat!"

"—sibility."

The room filled with the uproar of laughter until, no doubt, distracted by having to gulp down my blood, I made a mistake and yelled a phrase I had often seen denounced in newspaper editorials, heard debated in private.

"Social . . ."

"What?" they yelled.

". . . equality—"

The laughter hung smokelike in the sudden stillness. I opened my eyes, puzzled. Sounds of displeasure filled the room. The M.C. rushed forward. They shouted hostile phrases at me. But I did not understand.

A small dry mustached man in the front row blared out, "Say that slowly, son!"

"What sir?"

"What you just said!"

"Social responsibility, sir," I said.

"You weren't being smart, were you, boy?" he said, not unkindly.

"No, sir!"

"You sure that about 'equality' was a mistake?"

"Oh, yes, sir," I said, "I was swallowing blood."

"Well, you had better speak more slowly so we can understand. We mean to do right by you, but you've got to know your place at all times. All right, now, go on with your speech."

I was afraid. I wanted to leave but I wanted also to speak and I was afraid they'd snatch me down.

"Thank you, sir," I said, beginning where I had left off, and having them ignore me as before.

Yet when I finished there was a thunderous applause. I was surprised to see the superintendent come forth with a package wrapped in white tissue paper, and gesturing for quiet, address the men.

"Gentlemen, you see that I did not overpraise this boy. He makes a good speech and some day he'll lead his people in the proper paths. And I don't have to tell you that that is important in these days and times. This is a good, smart boy, and so to encourage him in the right direction, in the name of the Board of Education I wish to present him a prize in the form of this . . ."

He paused, removing the tissue paper and revealing a gleaming calfskin brief case.

". . . in the form of this first-class article from Shad Whitmore's shop."

"Boy," he said, addressing me, "take this prize and keep it well. Consider it a badge of office. Prize it. Keep developing as you are and some day it will be filled with important papers that will help shape the destiny of your people."

I was so moved that I could hardly express my thanks. A rope of bloody saliva forming a shape like an undiscovered continent drooled upon the leather and I wiped it quickly away. I felt an importance that I had never dreamed.

"Open it and see what's inside," I was told.

My fingers a-tremble, I complied, smelling the fresh leather and finding an official-looking document inside. It was a scholarship to the state college for Negroes. My eyes filled with tears and I ran awkwardly off the floor.

I was overjoyed; I did not even mind when I discovered that the gold pieces

I had scrambled for were brass pocket tokens advertising a certain make of automobile.

When I reached home everyone was excited. Next day the neighbors came to congratulate me. I even felt safe from grandfather, whose deathbed curse usually spoiled my triumphs. I stood beneath his photograph with my brief case in hand and smiled triumphantly into his stolid black peasant's face. It was a face that fascinated me. The eyes seemed to follow everywhere I went.

That night I dreamed I was at a circus with him and that he refused to laugh at the clowns no matter what they did. Then later he told me to open my brief case and read what was inside and I did, finding an official envelope stamped with the state seal; and inside the envelope I found another, endlessly, and I thought I would fall of weariness. "Them's years," he said, "Now open that one." And I did and in it I found an engraved document containing a short message in letters of gold. "Read it," my grandfather said. "Out loud."

"To Whom It May Concern," I intoned. "Keep This Nigger-boy Running."

I awoke with the old man's laughter in my ears.

(It was a dream I was to remember and dream again for many years after. But at that time I had no insight into its meaning. First I had to attend college.)

BURDEN OF PARENTAL LOVE CAN BE TOO HEAVY TO BEAR,
by Sydney Harris

The boy returned home from college for the Christmas holidays, and he seemed drawn and depressed. Somebody asked me why, and I said, "Too much pressure."

"Too much pressure of school work?" I shook my head. "No, too much pressure at home. A boy can't carry so big a burden."

The burden I referred to was the expectations of his parents. They are pinning too many hopes on his career; his success is too important to them. And he feels this keenly, and resents it without knowing why.

Even the burden of parental love is sometimes too heavy for a growing child to bear. He feels this warm, moist, concentrated affection pressing down upon him, almost suffocating in its intensity. But most young people eventually learn how to cope with that.

What is much harder to handle is the sense that you have to live up to the mark someone else has set for you. The grades become too important, the competition too frantic, the fear of disappointing those who believe in you turns into an overwhelming nightmare.

And it's desperately unfair to the boy. He cannot live his parents' lives over again for them. He cannot make up for their own lacks, their own unfulfillments. He cannot carry their torch — only his own.

I know boys who do not try — either in high school or in college — simply

Strictly Personal by Sidney J. Harris. © 1980 Field Enterprises, Inc. Courtesy of Field Newspaper Syndicate.

because their parents' standards are too high for them, and they are afraid of letting down the team.

If they do not try, the parents can always say, "He's very bright, he's very capable; if only he would try, he would do marvelously well." But the boy knows that no matter how hard he tries he will not do as well as his parents' expectations; and so by refusing to try, he is keeping his psychological cake and eating it, too.

All this, sadly enough, is truer of the more educated, higher-income, professional families. It is here that the competition is the greatest, the expectations most elevated. If the boy would be happier as a telephone linesman or a forest ranger, he is in a hopeless bind. His goals have been set for him by his milieu, and he cannot be his own man; so he simply refuses to play the game. He "does not try."

A poor boy has difficult odds to struggle against; but at least he sets the terms of his life-work. A child from a more affluent home is given the terms—doctor, lawyer, business chief—and the Lord help him if he wants to be an auto mechanic or a painter or some other occupation outside the prescribed limits of genteel activity.

As Warden Lawes once said of convicts, no man can be called a failure until he has tried something he really likes, and fails at it.

CHANNELLED WHELK, by Anne Morrow Lindbergh

The shell in my hand is deserted. It once housed a whelk, a snail-like creature, and then temporarily, after the death of the first occupant, a little hermit crab, who has run away, leaving his tracks behind him like a delicate vine on the sand. He ran away, and left me his shell. It was once a protection to him. I turn the shell in my hand, gazing into the wide open door from which he made his exit. Had it become an encumbrance? Why did he run away? Did he hope to find a better home, a better mode of living? I too have run away, I realize. I have shed the shell of my life, for these few weeks of vacation.

But his shell—it is simple; it is bare, it is beautiful. Small, only the size of my thumb, its architecture is perfect, down to the finest detail. Its shape, swelling like a pear in the center, winds in a gentle spiral to the pointed apex. Its color, dull gold, is whitened by a wash of salt from the sea. Each whorl, each faint knob, each criss-cross vein in its egg-shell texture, is as clearly defined as on the day of creation. My eye follows with delight the outer circumference of that diminutive winding staircase up which this tenant used to travel.

My shell is not like this, I think. How untidy it has become! Blurred with moss, knobby with barnacles, its shape is hardly recognizable any more. Surely, it had a shape once. It has a shape still in my mind. What is the shape of my life?

The shape of my life today starts with a family. I have a husband, five children and a home just beyond the suburbs of New York. I have also a craft, writing, and therefore work I want to pursue. The shape of my life, is of course, determined by many other things; my background and childhood, my mind and its education, my conscience and its pressures, my heart and its desires. I want to give and take from my children and husband, to share with friends and community, to carry out my obligations to man and to the world, as a woman, as an artist, as a citizen.

But I want first of all—in fact, as an end to these other desires—to be at peace with myself. I want a singleness of eye, a purity of intention, a central core to my life that will enable me to carry out these obligations and activities as well as I can. I want, infact—to borrow from the language of the saints—to live "in grace" as much of the time as possible. I am not using this term in a strictly theological sense. By grace I mean an inner harmony, essentially spiritual, which can be translated into outward harmony. I am seeking perhaps what Socrates asked for in the prayer from the *Phaedrus* when he said, "May the outward and inward man be at one." I would like to achieve a state of inner spiritual grace from which I could function and give as I was meant to in the eye of God.

Vague as this definition may be, I believe most people are aware of periods in their lives when they seem to be "in grace" and other periods when they feel "out of grace," even though they may use different words to describe these states. In the first happy condition, one seems to carry all one's tasks before one lightly, as if borne along on a great tide; and in the opposite state one can hardly tie a shoestring. It is true that a large part of life consists in learning a technique of tying the shoestring, whether one is in grace or not. But there are techniques of living too; there are even techniques in the search for grace. And techniques can be cultivated. I have learned by some experience, by many examples, and by the writings of countless others before me, also occupied in the search, that certain environments, certain modes of life, certain rules of conduct are more conducive to inner and outer harmony than others. There are, in fact, certain roads that one may follow. Simplification of life is one of them.

I mean to lead a simple life, to choose a simple shell I can carry easily—like a hermit crab. But I do not. I find that my frame of life does not foster simplicity. My husband and five children must make their way in the world. The life I have chosen as wife and mother entrains a whole caravan of complications. It involves a house in the suburbs and either household drudgery or household help which wavers between scarcity and non-existence for most of us. It involves food and shelter; meals, planning, marketing, bills, and making the ends meet in a thousand ways. It involves not only the butcher, the baker, the candlestickmaker but countless other experts to keep my modern house with its modern "simplifications" (electricity, plumbing, refrigerator, gas-stove, oil-burner, dish-washer, radios, car, and numerous other labor-saving devices) functioning properly. It involves health; doctors, dentists, appointments, medicine, codliver oil, vitamins, trips to the drugstore. It involves education, spiritual, intellectual, physical; schools, school conferences, car-pools, extra trips for basketball or orchestra practice; tutoring; camps, camp equipment and transportation. It involves clothes, shopping, laundry, cleaning, mending, letting skirts down and sewing buttons on, or finding someone else to do it. It involves friends, my husband's, my children's, my own, and endless arrangements to get together; letters, invitations, telephone calls and transportation hither and yon.

For life today in America is based on the premise of ever-widening circles of contact and communication. It involves not only family demands, but community demands, national demands, international demands on the good citizen, through social and cultural pressures, through newspapers, magazines, radio programs, political drives, charitable appeals, and so on. My mind reels with it. What a circus act we women perform every day of our lives. It puts the trapeze artist to shame. Look at us. We run a tight rope daily, balancing a pile of books on the head. Baby-carriage, parasol, kitchen chair, still under control. Steady now!

This is not the life of simplicity but the life of multiplicity that the wise men warn us of. It leads not to unification but to fragmentation. It does not bring grace; it destroys the soul. And this is not only true of my life, I am forced to conclude; it is the life of millions of women in America. I stress America, because today, the American woman more than any other has the privilege of choosing such a life. Woman in large parts of the civilized world has been forced back by war, by poverty, by collapse, by the sheer struggle to survive, into a smaller circle of immediate time and space, immediate family life, immediate problems of existence. The American woman is still relatively free to choose the wider life. How long she will hold this enviable and precarious position no one knows. But her particular situation has a signficance far above its apparent economic, national or even sex limitations.

For the problem of the multiplicity of life not only confronts the American woman, but also the American man. And it is not merely the concern of the American as such, but of our whole modern civilization, since life in America today is held up as the ideal of a large part of the rest of the world. And finally, it is not limited to our present civilization, though we are faced with it now in an exaggerated form. It has always been one of the pitfalls of mankind. Plotinus was preaching the dangers of multiplicity of the world back in the third century. Yet, the problem is particularly and essentially woman's. Distraction is, always has been, and probably always will be, inherent in woman's life.

For to be a woman is to have interests and duties, raying out in all directions from the central mother-core, like spokes from the hub of a wheel. The pattern of our lives is essentially circular. We must be open to all points of the compass; husband, children, friends, home, community; stretched out, exposed, sensitive like a spider's web to each breeze that blows, to each call that comes. How difficult for us, then, to achieve a balance in the midst of these contradictory tensions, and yet how necessary for the proper functioning of our lives. How much we need, and how arduous of attainment is that steadiness preached in all rules for holy living. How desirable and how distant is the ideal of the contemplative, artist, or saint — the inner inviolable core, the single eye.

With a new awareness, both painful and humorous, I begin to understand why the saints were rarely married women. I am convinced it has nothing to do, as I once supposed, with chastity or children. It has to do primarily with distractions. The bearing, rearing, feeding and educating of children; the running of a house with its thousand details; human relationships with their myriad pulls — woman's normal occupations in general run counter to creative life, or contemplative life, or saintly life. The problem is not merely one of *Woman and Career, Woman and the Home, Woman and Independence.* It is more basically: how to remain whole in the midst of the distractions of life; how to remain balanced, no matter what centrifugal forces tend to pull one off center; how to remain strong, no matter what shocks come in at the periphery and tend to crack the hub of the wheel.

What is the answer? There is no easy answer, no complete answer. I have only clues, shells from the sea. The bare beauty of the channelled whelk tells me that one answer, and perhaps a first step, is in simplification of life, in cutting out some of the distractions. But how? Total retirement is not possible. I cannot shed my responsibilities. I cannot permanently inhabit a desert island. I cannot be a nun in the midst of family life. I would not want to be. The solution for me, surely, is neither in total renunciation of the world, nor in total acceptance of it. I must find a balance somewhere, or an alternating rhythm between these two extremes; a swinging of the pendulum between solitude and communion, between retreat and return. In my periods of retreat, perhaps I can learn something to carry back into my worldly life. I can at least practice for these two weeks the simplification of outward life, as a beginning. I can follow this superficial clue, and see where it leads. Here, in beach living, I can try.

One learns first of all in beach living the art of shedding; how little one can get along with, not how much. Physical shedding to begin with, which then mysteriously spreads into other fields. Clothes, first. Of course, one needs less in the sun. But one needs less anyway, one finds suddenly. One does not need a closet-full, only a small suitcase-full. And what a relief it is! Less taking up and down of hems, less mending, and — best of all — less worry about what to wear. One finds one is shedding not only clothes — but vanity.

Next, shelter. One does not need the airtight shelter one has in winter in the North. Here I live in a bare sea-shell of a cottage. No heat, no telephone, no plumbing to speak of, no hot water, a two-burner oil stove, no gadgets to go wrong. No rugs. There were some, but I rolled them up the first day; it is easier to sweep the sand off a bare floor. But I find I don't bustle about with unnecessary sweeping and cleaning here. I am no longer aware of the dust. I have shed my Puritan conscience about absolute tidiness and cleanliness. Is it possible that, too, is a material burden? No curtains. I do not need them for privacy; the pines around my house are enough protection. I want the windows open all the time, and I don't want to worry about rain. I begin to shed my Martha-like anxiety about many things. Washable slipcovers, faded and old — I hardly see them; I don't worry about the impression they make on other people. I am shedding pride. As little furniture as possible; I shall not need much. I shall ask into my shell only those friends with whom I can be completely honest. I find I am shedding hypocrisy in human relationships. What a rest that will be! The most exhausting thing in life, I have discovered, is being insincere. That is why so much of social life is exhausting; one is wearing a mask. I have shed my mask.

I find I live quite happily without those things I think necessary in winter in the North. And as I write these words, I remember, with some shock at the disparity in our lives, a similar statement made by a friend of mine in France who spent three years in a German prison camp. Of course, he said, qualifying his remark, they did not get enough to eat, they were sometimes atrociously treated, they had little physical freedom. And yet, prison life taught him how little one can get along with, and what extraordinary, spiritual freedom and peace such simplification can bring. I remember again, ironically, that today more of us in America than anywhere else in the world have the luxury of choice between simplicity and complication of life. And for the most part we, who could use simplicity, choose complication. War, prison, survival periods, enforce a form of simplicity on man. The monk and the nun choose it of their own free will. But if one accidentally finds it, as I have for a few days, one finds also the serenity it brings.

Is it not rather ugly, one may ask? One collects material possessions not only for security, comfort or vanity, but for beauty as well. Is your sea-shell house not ugly and bare? No, it is beautiful, my house. It is bare, of course, but the wind, the sun, the smell of the pines blow through its bareness. The unfinished beams in the roof are veiled by cobwebs. They are lovely, I think, gazing up at them with new eyes; they soften the hard lines of the rafters as grey hairs soften the lines on a middle-aged face. I no longer pull out grey hairs or sweep down cobwebs. As for the walls, it is true they looked forbidding at first. I felt cramped and enclosed by their blank faces. I wanted to knock holes in them, to give them another dimension with pictures or windows. So I dragged home from the beach grey arms of driftwood, worn satin-smooth by wind and sand. I gathered trailing green vines with floppy red-tipped leaves. I picked up the whitened skeletons of conchshells, their curious hollowed-out shapes faintly reminiscent of abstract sculpture. With these tacked to walls and propped up in corners, I am satisfied. I have a periscope out to the world. I have a window, a view, a point of flight from my sedentary base.

I am content. I sit down at my desk, a bare kitchen table with a blotter, a bottle of ink, a sand dollar to weight down one corner, a clam shell for a pen tray, the broken tip of a conch, pink-tinged, to finger, and a row of shells to set my thoughts spinning.

I love my sea-shell of a house. I wish I could live in it always. I wish I could transport it home. But I cannot. It will not hold a husband, five children and the necessities and trappings of daily life. I can only carry back my little channelled whelk. It will sit on my desk in Connecticut, to remind me of the ideal of a simplified life, to encourage me in the game I played on the beach. To ask how little, not how much, can I get along with. To say — is it necessary? — when I am tempted to add one more accumulation to my life, when I am pulled toward one more centrifugal activity.

Simplification of outward life is not enough. It is merely the outside. But I am starting with the outside. I am looking at the outside of the shell, the outside of my life — the shell. The complete answer is not to be found on the outside, in an outward mode of living. This is only a technique, a road to grace. The final answer, I know, is always inside. But the outside can give a clue, can help one to find the inside answer. One is free, like the hermit crab, to change one's shell.

Channelled whelk, I put you down again, but you have set my mind on a journey, up an inwardly winding spiral staircase of thought.

POLIO [HIKING IN THE MOUNTAINS], by William O. Douglas

I took my early hikes into the hills to try to strengthen my legs, but they were to strengthen me in subtler ways. As I came to be on intimate terms with the hills, I learned something of their geology and botany. I heard the Indian legends associated with them. I discovered many of their secrets. I learned that they were always clothed in garments of delicate hues, though they seemed to be barren; though they looked dead and monotonous, they teemed with life and had many moods.

It was a real ordeal for me to walk the hills in the dead of summer, for then they were parched and dry and offered no shade from the hot sun and no springs or creeks where thirst could be quenched. Then the rattlesnake seemed to thrive. But in the spring, fall, and winter, there were interesting places to explore; my walks then were more fun than ordeal.

When I tramped the foothills in dead of winter, the pulse of life on the ridges was slow. The wind swept down from Mount Adams and Mount Rainier, cold and piercing, and I would find some black rimrock where I could sit, my back to the rock, protected from the wind, hoping the warmth of my sagebrush fire would not awaken a den of rattlers with the false message that spring had arrived. And when I turned around and started home, the same strong wind at my back made me feel as if the strength of giants was in me. I strode along the barren ridge with ease, commanding the city that lay at my feet.

Sometimes the chinook, the soft and balmy breeze from the west side of the Cascade Mountains, would blow. With the chinook came a light and gentle rain; and as it swept across this desert area it always carried the refreshing smell of dampened dust and the pungent but delicate odor of sage. Often I walked at night, when the chinook blew hardest and the outdoors always seemed most alive.

When I stretched out on the ground and listened, I could hear the cheatgrass singing softly in the wind. The sage, too, would join the symphony. The legend is that as the wind goes softly through the sage, it sings in memory of the Idaho Indians whose plains it covered as far as the eye could see and whose mountains it decorated far above the deep-snow line. And the verse of its song is always the same, "Shoshone, Shoshone."

I discovered, too, that if I looked carefully I could find a variety of wild-flowers surprising in so arid an environment. I remember looking down one spring afternoon, fresh from the man-made gardens of the valley, and seeing at my feet among the sagebrush a scattering of delicate pink. It was the rock rose, or bitterroot, a gentle membrane that the Creator seemed to have fashioned from bare rock-dust simply to decorate desolate places. A low plant, with waxy pale-pink flowers ribbed in a darker hue, the bitterroot has a translucent quality that makes it look as fragile to the touch as the gossamer winds of a tropical butterfly. Its leaves, I later learned, dry and vanish when the flowers appear, and its blossoms open with the sun and close with the darkness.

But the bitterroot is sturdier than it looks, and useful as well as decorative. The plant was collected by Lewis at the mouth of the Lou Lou Fork of the Bitterroot River in Montana. Its roots are the spatlum known to Indians, explorers, and early settlers as valued food. They contain a rich supply of starch, slightly bitter, thence its name. I never see the bitterroot blooming among the sage without feeling that I should take off my hat and stand in adoration at the wondrous skill of the Creator. I'll always remember the words of the artist who said, "I have grown to feel that there is nothing more amazing about a personal God than there is about the blossoming of the gorgeous little bitterroot."

I do not envy those whose introduction to nature was lush meadows, lakes, and swamps where life abounds. The desert hills of Yakima had a poverty that sharpened perception. Even a minute violet quickens the heart when one has walked far or climbed high to find it. Where nature is more bountiful, even the the tender bitterroot might go unnoticed. Yet when a lone plant is seen in bloom on scabland between batches of bunch grass and sage, it can transform the spot as completely as only a whole bank of flowers could do in a more lush environment. It is the old relationship between scarcity and value, one of the lessons which the foothills of Yakima taught me.

There are two early trips that stand out especially in my memory. One was in the coolness of early spring. I left town before dusk and climbed the barren ridge west of Selah Gap. On the way up I had crossed a draw and caught the sweet odor of the mock orange. In the darkness I could vaguely see the lone shrub that filled this draw with the fragrance of its blossoms. It stood six feet high, and in this barren ravine the delicacy of its fragrance seemed strangely out of place.

The night was clear and the moon had just reached this horizon. Mount Adams loomed in the west, "high-humped," as Lewis and Clark aptly described it when they saw it on April 2, 1806. Along the ridge of the Cascades to the north was Mount Rainier, cold, aloof, and forbidding. Below at my feet the lights of the town had come on, blinking like stars of a minor firmament. A faint streak of light, sparkling in the moonlight, marked the course of the Yakima River as it wound its way across the valley, through dark splotches of sumac, cottonwood, and willow.

Above the dark rim of the foothills were the stars of the universe. They were the same stars that saw these valleys and hills and mountains rise from the murk of the ocean, reaching for the sun. They saw the Columbia lava, hot and steaming, pour in molten form across this land again and again, scorching to cinders everything it touched, burying great ponderosa pine four and five feet thick under its deep folds, and filling the sky with smoke that finally drew a curtain over the sun. They saw a subtropical land touched by the chill of the Arctic and rimmed with ice and snow. They saw the mighty Columbia and the Yakima grow from driblets to minor drainage canals to great rivers. They saw the glaciers recede and floods come. After the floods they saw the emergence of a desert that some unseen hand had sown with fragrant sage and populated with coyotes, rabbits, kangaroo rats, sage hens, sage sparrows, desert sparrows, blue-birds, and doves. They saw the Indians first appear on the horizon to the north, spreading out to all parts of the continent in their long trek from Asia. And thousands of years later they saw some newcomers arrive, the ones that fought, quarreled, and loved, the ones that built houses and roads and planted orchards, the ones that erected spires and lifted their eyes to the sky in prayer.

I think it was that night that I got my first sense of Time. I began to appreciate some of the lessons that geology taught. In the great parade of events that this region unfolded, man was indeed insignificant. He appeared under this firmament only briefly and then disappeared. His transit was too short for geological time to measure.

As I walked the ridge that evening, I could hear the chinook on distant ridges before it reached me. Then it touched the sage at my feet and made it sing. It brushed my cheek, warm and soft. It ran its fingers through my hair and rippled away in the darkness. It was a friendly wind, friendly to man throughout time. It was beneficent, carrying rain to the desert. It was soft, bringing warmth to the body. It had almost magical qualities, for it need touch the snow only lightly to melt it.

It became for me that night a measure of the kindliness of the universe to man, a token of the hospitality that awaits man when he puts foot on this earth. It became for me a promise of the fullness of life to him who, instead of shaking his fist at the sky, looks to it for health and strength and courage.

That night I felt at peace. I felt that I was a part of the universe, a companion to the friendly chinook that brought the promise of life and adventure. That night, I think, there first came to me the germ of a philosophy of life: that man's best measure of the universe is in his hopes and his dreams, not his fears, that man is part of a plan, only a fraction of which he, perhaps, can ever comprehend.

Another trip into those hills marked a turning point in my life. It was April and the valley below was in bloom, lush and content with fruit blossoms. Then came a sudden storm, splattering rain in the lower valley and shooting tongues of lightning along the ridges across from me. As the weather cleared, Adams and Rainier stood forth in power and beauty, monarchs to every peak in their range.

Away from town, in the opposite direction from its comforts, the back-bone of the Cascades was clear against the western sky, the slopes and ravines dark blue in the afternoon sun. The distant ridges and canyons seemed soft and friendly. They appeared to hold untold mysteries and to contain solitude many times more profound than that of the barren ridge on which I stood. They offered streams and valleys and peaks to explore, snow fields and glaciers to conquer, wild animals to know. That afternoon I felt that the high mountains in the distance were extending to me an invitation to get acquainted with them, to tramp their trails and sleep in their high basins.

My heart filled with joy, for I knew I could accept the invitation. I would have legs and lungs equal to it.

CIRCLES AND SQUARES, by John G. Neihardt

After the heyoka ceremony, I came to live here where I am now between Wounded Knee Creek and Grass Creek. Others came too, and we made these little gray houses of logs that you see, and they are square. It is a bad way to live, for there can be no power in a square.

You have noticed that everything an Indian does is in a circle and that is because the Power of the World always works in circles, and everything tries to be round. In the old days when we were a strong and happy people, all our power came to us from the sacred hoop of the nation, and so long as the hoop was unbroken, the people flourished. The flowering tree was the living center of the hoop, and the circle of the four quarters nourished it. The east gave peace and light, the south gave warmth, the west gave rain, and the north with its cold and mighty wind gave strength and endurance. This knowledge came to us from the outer world with our religion. Everything the Power of the World does is done in a circle. The sky is round, and I have heard that the earth is round like a ball, and so are all the stars. The wind, in its greatest power, whirls. Birds make their nests in circles, for theirs is the same religion as ours. The sun comes forth and goes down again in a circle. The moon does the same, and both are round. Even the seasons form a great circle in their changing and always come back again to where they were. The life of a man is a circle from childhood to childhood, and so it is in everything where power moves. Our tepees were round like the nests of birds, and these were always set in a circle, the nation's hoop, a nest of many nests, where the Great Spirit meant for us to hatch our children.

But the Wasichus have put us in these square boxes. Our power is gone and we are dying, for the power is not in us any more. You can look at our boys and see how it is with us. When we were living by the power of the circle in the way we should, boys were men at twelve or thirteen years of age. But now it takes them very much longer to mature.

AN 18-YEAR-OLD LOOKS BACK ON LIFE, by Joyce Maynard

Every generation thinks it's special — my grandparents because they remember horses and buggies, my parents because of the Depression. The over-30's are special because they knew the Red Scare of Korea, Chuck Berry and beatniks. My older sister is special because she belonged to the first generation of teen-agers (before that, people in their teens were *adolescents*), when being a teen-ager was still fun. And I — I am 18, caught in the middle. Mine is the generation of unfulfilled expectations. "When you're older," my mother promised, "you can wear lipstick." But when the time came, of course, lipstick wasn't being worn. "When we're big, we'll dance like that," my friends and I whispered, watching Chubby Checker twist on "American Bandstand." But we inherited no dance steps, ours was a limp, formless shrug to watered-down music that rarely made the feet tap. "Just wait till we can vote," I said, bursting with 10-year-old fervor, ready to fast, freeze, march and die for peace and freedom as Joan Baez, barefoot, sang "We Shall Overcome." Well, now we can vote, and we're old enough to attend rallies and knock on doors and wave placards, and suddenly it doesn't seem to matter any more.

My generation is special because of what we missed rather than what we got, because in a certain sense we are the first and the last. The first to take technology for granted. (What was a space shot to us, except an hour cut from Social Studies to gather before a TV in the gym as Cape Canaveral counted down?) The first to grow up with TV. My sister was 8 when we got our set, so to her it seemed magic and always somewhat foreign. She had known books already and would never really replace them. But for me, the TV set was, like the kitchen sink and the telephone, a fact of life.

We inherited a previous generation's hand-me-downs and took in the seams, turned up the hems, to make our new fashions. We took drugs from the college kids and made them a high-school commonplace. We got the Beatles, but not those lovable look-alikes in matching suits with barber cuts and songs that made you want to cry. They came to us like a bad joke — aged, bearded, discordant. And we inherited the Vietnam war just after the crest of the wave — too late to burn draft cards and too early not be drafted. The boys of 1953 — my year — will be the last to go.

So where are we now? Generalizing is dangerous. Call us the apathetic generation and we will become that. Say times are changing, nobody cares about prom queens and getting into the college of his choice any more — say that (because it sounds good, it indicates a trend, gives a symmetry to history) and you make a movement and a unit out of a generation unified only in its common fragmentation. If there is a reason why we are where we are, it comes from where we have been.

Like overanxious patients in analysis, we treasure the traumas of our childhood. Ours was more traumatic than most. The Kennedy assassination has become our myth: Talk to us for an evening or two—about movies or summer jobs or Nixon's trip to China or the weather—and the subject will come up ("Where were *you* when you heard?"), as if having lived through Jackie and the red roses, John-John's salute and Oswald's on-camera murder justifies our disenchantment.

We haven't all emerged the same, of course, because our lives were lived in high-school corridors and drive-in hamburger joints as well as in the pages of Time and Life, and the images on the TV screen. National events and personal memory blur so that, for me, Nov. 22, 1963, was a birthday party that had to be called off and Armstrong's moon-walk was my first full can of beer. If you want to know who we are now; if you wonder how we'll vote, or whether we will, or whether, 10 years from now, we'll end up just like all those other generations that thought they were special—with 2.2 kids and a house in Connecticut—if that's what you're wondering, look to the past because, whether we should blame it or not, we do.

I didn't know till years later that they called it the Cuban Missile Crisis. But I remember Castro. (We called him Castor Oil and were awed by his beard—beards were rare in those days.) We might not have worried so much (what would the Communists want with our small New Hampshire town?) except that we lived 10 miles from an air base. Planes buzzed around us like mosquitoes that summer. People talked about fallout shelters in their basements and one family on our street packed their car to go to the mountains. I couldn't understand that. If everybody was going to die, I certainly didn't want to stick around, with my hair falling out and—later—a plague of thalidomide-type babies. I wanted to go quickly, with my family.

Dying didn't bother me so much—I'd never known anyone who died, and death was unreal, fascinating. (I wanted Doctor Kildare to have more terminal cancer patients and fewer love affairs.) What bothered me was the business of immortality. Sometimes, the growing-up sort of concepts germinate slowly, but the full impact of death hit me like a bomb, in the night. Not only would my body be gone—that I could take—but I would cease to think. That I would no longer be a participant I had realized before; now I saw that I wouldn't even be an observer. What especially alarmed me about The Bomb (always singular like, a few years later, The Pill) was the possibility of total obliteration. All traces of me would be destroyed. There would be no grave and, if there were, no one left to visit it.

Newly philosophical, I pondered the universe. If the earth was in the solar system and the solar system was in the galaxy and the galaxy was in the universe, what was the universe in? And if the sun was just a dot—the head of a pin—what was I? We visited a planetarium that year, in third grade, and saw a dramatization of the sun exploding. Somehow the image of that orange ball zooming toward us merged with my image of The Bomb. The effect was devastating, and for the first time in my life—except for Easter Sundays, when I wished I went to church so I could have a fancy new dress like my Catholic and Protestant friends—I longed for religion.

I was 8 when Joan Baez entered our lives, with long, black, beatnik hair and a dress made out of a burlap bag. When we got her first record (we called her Joan *Baze* then — soon she was simply Joan) we listened all day, to "All My Trials" and "Silver Dagger" and "Wildwood Flower." My sister grew her hair and started wearing sandals, making pilgrimages to Harvard Square. I took up the guitar. We loved her voice and her songs but, even more, we loved the idea of Joan, like the 15th-century Girl of Orleans, burning at society's stake, marching along or singing, solitary, in a prison cell to protest segregation. She was the champion of nonconformity and so — like thousands of others — we joined the masses of her fans.

I knew she must but somehow I could never imagine Jackie Kennedy going to the bathroom. She was too cool and poised and perfect. We had a book about her, filled with color pictures of Jackie painting, in a spotless yellow linen dress, Jackie on the beach with Caroline and John-John, Jackie riding elephants in India and Jackie, in a long white gown, greeting Khrushchev like Snow White welcoming one of the seven dwarfs. (No, I wasn't betraying Joan in my adoration. Joan was beautiful but human, like us; Jackie was magic.) When, years later, she married Rumpelstiltskin, I felt like a child discovering, in his father's drawer, the Santa Claus suit. And, later still, reading some Ladies' Home Journal exposé ("Jacqueline Onassis's secretary tells all . . .") I felt almost sick. After the first few pages I put the magazine down. I wasn't interested in the fragments, only in the fact that the glass had broken.

If I had spent at the piano the hours I gave to television, on all those afternoons when I came home from school, I would be an accomplished pianist now. Or if I'd danced, or read, or painted. . . . But I turned on the set instead, every day, almost, every year, and sank into an old green easy chair, smothered in quilts, with a bag of Fritos beside me and a glass of milk to wash them down, facing life and death with Dr. Kildare, laughing at Danny Thomas, whispering the answers — out loud sometimes — with "Password" and "To Tell the Truth." Looking back over all those afternoons, I try to convince myself they weren't wasted. I must have learned something; I must, at least, have changed.

What I learned was certainly not what TV tried to teach me. From the reams of trivia collected over years of quiz shows, I remember only the questions, never the answers. I loved "Leave It to Beaver" for the messes Beaver got into, not for the inevitable lecture from Dad at the end of each show. I saw every episode two or three times, witnessed Beaver's aging, his legs getting longer and his voice lower, only to start all over again with young Beaver every fall. (Someone told me recently that the boy who played Beaver Cleaver died in Vietnam. The news was a shock — I kept coming back to it for days until another distressed Beaver fan wrote to tell me that it wasn't true after all.)

I got so I could predict punch lines and endings, not really knowing whether I'd seen the episode before or only watched one like it. There was the bowling-ball routine, for instance: Lucy, Dobie Gillis, Pete and Gladys — they all used it. Somebody would get his finger stuck in a bowling ball (Lucy later updated the gimmick using Liz Taylor's ring) and then they'd have to go to a wedding or give a speech at the P.T.A. or have the boss to dinner, concealing one hand all the while. We weren't supposed to ask questions like "Why don't they just tell the truth?" These shows were built on deviousness, on the longest distance between two points, and on a kind of symmetry which decrees that no loose ends shall be left untied, no lingering doubts allowed. (The Surgeon General is off the track in worrying about TV violence, I think. I grew up in the days before law-men became peacemakers. What carries over is not the gunfights but the memory that everything always turned out all right.) Optimism shone through all those half hours I spent in the dark shadows of the TV room – out of evil shall come good.

Most of all, the situation comedies steeped me in American culture. I emerged from years of TV viewing indifferent to the museums of France, the architecture of Italy, the literature of England. A perversely homebound Ameri-can, I pick up paperbacks in bookstores, checking before I buy to see if the characters have foreign names, whether the action takes place in London or New York. Vulgarity and banality fascinate me. More intellectual friends (who watch no TV) can't understand what I see in "My Three Sons." "Nothing happens," they say. "The characters are dull, plastic, faceless. Every show is the same." I guess that's why I watch them – boring repetition is, itself, a rhythm – a steady pulse of flashing Coca-Cola signs, McDonald's Golden Arches and Howard Johnson roofs.

I don't watch TV as an anthropologist, rising loftily above my subject to analyze. Neither do I watch, as some kids now tune in to reruns of "The Lone Ranger" and "Superman" (in the same spirit they enjoy comic books and pop art) for their camp. I watch in earnest. How can I do anything else? Five thou-sand hours of my life have gone into this box.

There were almost no blacks in our school. They were Negroes then; the word black was hard to say at first. Negro got hard to say for a while too, so I said nothing at all and was embarrassed. If you had asked me, at 9, to describe Cassius Clay, I would have taken great, liberal pains to be color-blind, men-tioning height, build, eye color and shoe size, disregarding skin. I knew black people only from newspapers and the TV screen – picket lines. National Guards-men at the doors of schools. (There were few black actors on TV then, except for Jack Benny's Rochester.) It was easy, in 1963, to embrace the Negro cause. Later, faced with cold stares from an all-black table in the cafeteria or heckled by a Panther selling newspapers, I first became aware of the fact that maybe the little old lady didn't want to be helped across the street. My visions of black-and-white-together look at me now like shots from "To Sir With Love." If a black is friendly to me, I wonder as other blacks might, if he's a sellout.

I had no desire to scream or cry or throw jelly beans when I first saw the Beatles on the Ed Sullivan Show. An eighth-grader would have been old enough to revert to childhood, but I was too young to act anything but old. So mostly we laughed at them. We were in fifth grade, the year of rationality, the calm before the storm. We still screamed when the boys came near us (which they rarely did) and said they had cooties. Barbie dolls tempted us. That was the year when I got my first Barbie. Perhaps they were produced earlier, but they didn't reach New Hampshire till late that fall, and the stores were always sold out. So at the close of our doll-playing careers there was a sudden dramatic switch from lumpy, round-bellied Betsy Wetsys and stiff-legged little-girl dolls to slim, curvy Barbie, just 11 inches tall, with a huge, expensive wardrobe that included a filmy black negligee and a mouth that made her look as if she'd just swallowed a lemon.

Barbie wasn't just a toy, but a way of living that moved us suddenly from tea parties to dates with Ken at the Soda Shoppe. Our short careers with Barbie, before junior high sent her to the attic, built up our expectations for teen-age life before we had developed the sophistication to go along with them. Children today are accustomed to having a tantalizing youth culture all around them. (They play with Barbie in the nursery school.) For us, it broke like a cloudburst, without preparation. Caught in the deluge, we were torn—wanted to run for shelter but tempted, also, to sing in the rain.

Marijuana and the class of '71 moved through high school together. When we came in, as freshmen, drugs were still strange and new; marijuana was smoked only by a few marginal figures while those in the mainstream guzzled beer. It was called pot then—the words grass and dope came later; hash and acid and pills were almost unheard of. By my sophomore year, lots of the seniors and even a few younger kids were trying it. By the time I was a junior—in 1969— grass was no longer reserved for the hippies; basketball players and cheerleaders and boys with crew-cuts and boys in black-leather jackets all smoked. And with senior year—maybe because of the nostalgia craze—there was an odd liquor revival. In my last month of school, a major bust led to the suspension of half a dozen boys. They were high on beer.

Now people are saying that the drug era is winding down. (It's those statisticians with their graphs again, charting social phenomena like the rise and fall of hemlines.) I doubt if it's real, this abandonment of marijuana. But the frenzy is gone, certainly, the excitement and the fear of getting caught and the worry of where to get good stuff. What's happened to dope is what happens to a new record: you play it constantly, full volume, at first. Then, as you get to know the songs, you play them less often, not because you're tired of them exactly, but just because you know them. They're with you always, but quietly, in your head.

My position was a difficult one, all through those four years when grass took root in Oyster River High. I was on the side of all those things that went along with smoking dope—the clothes, the music, the books, the candidates. More and more of my friends smoked, and many people weren't completely my friends, I think, because I didn't. Drugs took on a disproportionate importance. Why was it I could spend half a dozen evenings with someone without his ever asking me what I thought of Beethoven or Picasso but always, in the first half hour, he'd ask whether I smoked?

It became—like hair length and record collection—a symbol of who you were, and you couldn't be all the other things—progressive and creative and free-thinking—without taking that crumpled roll of dry, brown vegetation and holding it to your lips. You are what you eat—or what you smoke, or what you don't smoke. And when you say "like—you know," you're speaking the code, and suddenly the music of the Grateful Dead and the poetry of Bob Dylan and the general brilliance of Ken Kesey all belong to you as if, in those three fuzzy, mumbled words, you'd created art yourself and uttered the wisdom of the universe.

The freshman women's dorm at Yale has no house mother. We have no check-in hours or drinking rules or punishments for having boys in our rooms past midnight. A guard sits by the door to offer, as they assured us at the beginning of the year, physical – not moral – protection. All of which makes it easy for many girls who feel, after high-school curfews and dating regulations, suddenly liberated. (The first week of school last fall, many girls stayed out all night, every night, displaying next morning the circles under their eyes the way some girls show off engagement rings.)

We all received the "Sex at Yale" book, a thick, black pamphlet filled with charts and diagrams and a lengthy discussion of contraceptive methods. And at the first women's assembly, the discussion moved quickly from course-signing-up procedures to gynecology, where it stayed for much of the evening. Somebody raised her hand to ask where she could fill her pill prescription, someone else wanted to know about abortions. There was no standing in the middle any more – you had to either take out a pen and paper and write down the phone numbers they gave out or stare stonily ahead, implying that those were numbers *you* certainly wouldn't be needing. From then on it seemed the line had been drawn.

But of course the problem is that no lines, no barriers, exist. Where, five years ago a girl's decisions were made for her (she had to be in at 12 and, if she was found – in – with her boyfriend . . .); today the decision rests with her alone. She is surrounded by knowledgeable, sexually experienced girls and if *she* isn't willing to sleep with her boyfriend, somebody else will. It's peer-group pressure, 1972 style – the embarrassment of virginity.

Everyone is raised on nursery rhymes and nonsense stories. But it used to be that when you grew up, the nonsense disappeared. Not for us – it is at the core of our music and literature and art and, in fact, of our lives. Like characters in an Ionesco play, we take absurdity unblinking. In a world where military officials tell us "We had to destroy the village in order to save it," Dylan lyrics make an odd kind of sense. They aren't meant to be understood; they don't jar our sensibilities because we're used to *non sequiturs*. We don't take anything too seriously these days. (Was it a thousand earthquake victims or a million? Does it matter?) The casual butcher's-operation in the film "M*A*S*H" and the comedy in Vonnegut and the album cover showing John and Yoko, bareback, are all part of the new absurdity. The days of the Little Moron joke and the elephant joke and the knock-knock joke are gone. It sounds melodramatic, but the joke these days is life.

You're not supposed to care too much any more. Reactions have been scaled down from screaming and jelly-bean-throwing to nodding your head and maybe – if the music really gets to you (and music's the only thing that does any more) – tapping a finger. We need a passion transfusion, a shot of energy in the veins. It's what I'm most impatient with, in my generation – this languid, I-don't-give-a-s – ism that stems in part, at least, from a culture of put-ons in which any serious expression of emotion is branded sentimental and old-fashioned. The fact that we set such a premium on being cool reveals a lot about my generation; the idea is not to care. You can hear it in the speech of college students today: cultivated monotones, low volume, punctuated with four-letter words that come off sounding only bland. I feel it most of all on Saturday morning, when the sun is shining and the crocuses are about to bloom and, walking through the corridors of my dorm, I see there isn't anyone awake.

I'm basically an optimist. Somehow, no matter what the latest population figures say, I feel everything will work out — just like on TV. I may doubt man's fundamental goodness, but I believe in his power to survive. I say, sometimes, that I wonder if we'll be around in 30 years, but then I forget myself and speak of "when I'm 50. . . ." Death has touched me now — from Vietnam and Biafra and a car accident that makes me buckle my seat belt — but like negative numbers and the sound of a dog whistle (too high-pitched for human ears), it's not a concept I can comprehend. I feel immortal while all the signs around me proclaim that I'm not.

We feel cheated, many of us — the crop of 1953 — which is why we complain about inheriting problems we didn't cause. (Childhood notions of justice, reinforced by Perry Mason, linger on. Why should I clean up someone else's mess? Who can I blame?) We're excited also, of course: I can't wait to see how things turn out. But I wish I weren't quite so involved, I wish it weren't my life that's being turned into a suspense thriller.

When my friends and I were little, we had big plans. I would be a famous actress and singer, dancing on the side. I would paint my own sets and compose my own music, writing the script and the lyrics and reviewing the performance for the New York Times. I would marry and have three children (they don't allow us dreams like that any more) and we would live, rich and famous (donating lots to charity, of course, and periodically adopting orphans), in a house we designed ourselves. When I was older I had visions of good works. I saw myself in South American rain forests and African deserts, feeding the hungry and healing the sick with an obsessive selflessness, I see now, as selfish, in the end, as my original plans for stardom.

Now my goal is simpler. I want to be happy. And I want comfort — nice clothes, a nice house, good music and good food, and the feeling that I'm doing some little thing that matters. I'll vote and I'll give to charity, but I won't give myself. I feel a sudden desire to buy land — not a lot, not a business investment, but just a small plot of earth so that whatever they do to the country I'll have a place where I can go — a kind of fallout shelter, I guess. As some people prepare for their old age, so I prepare for my 20's. A little house, a comfortable chair, peace and quiet — retirement sounds tempting.

AFTER ALL, MOSS IS KIND OF NICE STUFF, by Nickie McWhirter

We tend to live according to cliches, and for every useful one there are a couple of others that are downright dangerous to the human psyche.

If honesty is the best policy, why do we lie to our children about Santa Claus and the Easter Bunny? You wrestle with that one for a while. Mouthing cliches releases us from the serious work of thinking, not to mention feeling, evaluating and acting on our own decisions.

Cliches can scare us and make us feel guilty, without cause. Don't get too big for your britches! They can cajole us and make us feel content, without cause. Virtue is its own reward!

Cliches can do a lot of things but, in general, what they do is immobilize people, obviating personal expression, discovery, growth and the accumulation of valid, useful knowledge.

We learn them from our parents and pass them on to our children. We consider them useful intellectual trinkets, or worse—Words to Live By. Cliches are potent and dangerous. Ben Franklin neglected to tell us that. It's time we find out.

We all get into miserable situations from time to time. The bills pile up, the dog dies, the job goes ppffffttttt and the spouse and kids run off with the Moonies. They each leave a rude note.

Never mind. Society has a collection of cliche confections available to distract you from your misery and, at the same time, lock you into it. That's one trouble with cliches designed for use in time of misery. They are never meant to get you out, just to make you feel at home in the morass. These are a few:

It's always darkest before the dawn. Every cloud has a silver lining. Things always work out for the best. Don't cry over spilt milk. They've made their bed, now let them lie in it. (Or, you've made your bed, now you lie in it.) The grass always looks greener on the other side of the fence. Look at the doughnut, not at the hole.

I won't get into the religious cliches, for which we can all . . . count our blessings.

Some of these cliches are more gentle and sympathetic than others, but all of them say essentially the same thing, which is "Too bad about your troubles. Live with them; don't try to change anything; rely on magic."

Well, phooey. What kind of cockamamie counsel is that? What kind of phony comfort can be derived from it? All these verbal geegaws do is help a troubled person put off addressing the trouble and deciding how to get out. Sometimes the grass really is greener on the other side, and every cloud does not have a silver lining. Magic rarely saves persons from drowning. Why should it be relied upon to save you or me from the bill collector?

When a sensible person finally comes up with some plan to solve his or her problems, there are lots of cliches to spur the action. Strike while the iron's hot; he who hesitates is lost; when the going gets tough, the tough . . . You know. There are matching cliches to slow everything down. Make haste slowly; look before you leap, and try not to get in over your head, let alone too involved.

Bless us!—doesn't it all sound wonderful and wise. That's the secret of cliches. They each have this tiny throwaway chip of wisdom all done up inside a glittering word wrap. It's like a carton of strawberry yogurt with the wonderful picture of dew-kissed ripe strawberries on the package, but inside it's plain old yogurt, slightly pink with one shred of tired strawberry hiding in the bottom, somewhere.

It greatly distresses me that so many otherwise sane people are dazzled by the wrappings and settle for the pathetic little shreds of wisdom inside cliches. At the very least, I think persons raised on a constant diet of this razzle-dazzle junk probably suffer some sort of spiritual and intellectual malnutrition. At worst, some folks are addicted. In times of discomfort a cliche fix is the only thing that keeps them going. On their feet, as we say.

I remember one parent who regularly strapped the bejesus out of his three sons—who were somewhat unruly—and explained it all by saying, "Spare the rod and spoil the child!" It was convenient. I don't know if this man was a sadist or a dolt. If he had normal intelligence, he didn't use it. The cliche saved him from having to think about what he was doing and whether his actions were likely to accomplish what he hoped to accomplish. It also served to thwart criticism from his wife, family and the school authorities. Who can argue with a cliche-spouting father? No sane person.

Then there was a woman of my acquaintance who stayed married much too long to a man who knocked her around and brought girl friends home, just for fun. The wife used to weep and say, "Andy will come to his senses." He had as much sense as he would ever have and he knew what he was doing. This woman decided to stay married "for the sake of the children," until she finally decided that none of the cliches were making her life any more bearable. Logically and pragmatically she decided what to do. So long, Andy.

Cliches are of absolutely no help. You can find one to explain or justify any action or inaction. Money doesn't buy happiness; money isn't everything. That is the standard excuse to stay in a second-rate job. Every pinch-penny in the world uses "A fool and his money are soon parted" as a crutch. Spendthrifts, conversely, rely on "It's only money; you can't take it with you."

Cliches are code for larger, much more complicated ideas. Unless you explore the larger ideas and their implications, you really don't know what you're thinking, or talking about.

When I was a kid, we studied some about Ben Franklin and Poor Richard. "A rolling stone gathers no moss" nearly drove me crazy.

I wondered if it was good for a stone NOT to gather mosss, and why. Moss is kind of nice—soft, green, pretty. I could see that if you rode your bike really fast through the creekbed, you wouldn't get stuck in the mud. OK. But did the cliche also mean if you were a traveling salesman, like my granddad was for a while, you wouldn't gather possessions? Was that good? Did it mean if you moved around real fast from friend to friend, none of them would glom onto you? That wasn't good, I was sure.

Cliches and I never got along very well after the fifth grade.

MENDING WALL, by Robert Frost

Something there is that doesn't love a wall,
That sends the frozen-ground-swell under it

And spills the upper boulders in the sun,
And makes gaps even two can pass abreast.
The work of hunters is another thing:
I have come after them and made repair
When they have left not one stone on a stone,
But they would have the rabbit out of hiding,
To please the yelping dogs. The gaps I mean,
No one has seen them made or heard them made,
But at spring mending-time we find them there.
I let my neighbor know beyond the hill;
And on a day we meet to walk the line
And set the wall between us once again.
We keep the wall between us as we go.
To each the boulders that have fallen to each.
And some are loaves and some so nearly balls
We have to use a spell to make them balance:
"Stay where you are until our backs are turned!"
We wear our fingers rough with handling them.
Oh, just another kind of outdoor game,
One on a side. It comes to little more:
There where it is we do not need the wall:
He is all pine and I am apple orchard.
My apple trees will never get across
And eat the cones under his pines, I tell him.
He only says, "Good fences make good neighbors."
Spring is the mischief in me, and I wonder
If I could put a notion in his head:
"Why do they make good neighbors? Isn't it
Where there are cows? But here there are no cows.
Before I built a wall I'd ask to know
What I was walling in or walling out,
And to whom I was like to give offense.
Something there is that doesn't love a wall,
That wants it down." I could say "Elves" to him,
But it's not elves exactly, and I'd rather
He said it for himself. I see him there,
Bringing a stone grasped firmly by the top
In each hand, like an old stone-age savage armed.
He moves in darkness as it seems to me,
Not of woods only and the shade of trees.
He will not go behind his father's saying,
And he likes having thought of it so well
He says again, "Good fences made good neighbors."

THE RABBITS WHO CAUSED ALL THE TROUBLE, by James Thurber

Within the memory of the youngest child there was a family of rabbits who lived near a pack of wolves. The wolves announced that they did not like the way the rabbits were living. (The wolves were crazy about the way they themselves were living, because it was the only way to live.) One night several wolves were killed in an earthquake and this was blamed on the rabbits, for it is well known that rabbits pound on the ground with their hind legs and cause earthquakes. On another night one of the wolves was killed by a bolt of lightning and this was also blamed on the rabbits, for it is well known that lettuce-eaters cause lightning. The wolves threatened to civilize the rabbits if they didn't behave, and the rabbits decided to run away to a desert island. But the other animals, who lived at a great distance, shamed them, saying, "You must stay where you are and be brave. This is no world for escapists. If the wolves attack you, we will come to your aid, in all probability." So the rabbits continued to live near the wolves and one day there was a terrible flood which drowned a great many wolves. This was blamed on the rabbits, for it is well known that carrot-nibblers with long ears cause floods. The wolves descended on the rabbits, for their own good, and imprisoned them in a dark cave, for their own protection.

When nothing was heard about the rabbits for some weeks, the other animals demanded to know what had happened to them. The wolves replied that the rabbits had been eaten and since they had been eaten the affair was a purely internal matter. But the other animals warned that they might possibly unite against the wolves unless some reason was given for the destruction of the rabbits. So the wolves gave them one. "They were trying to escape," said the wolves, "and, as you know, this is no world for escapists."

Moral: Run, don't walk, to the nearest desert island.

Copyright © 1940 by James Thurber. Copyright 1968 Helen Thurber. From *Fables for Our Time*, published by Harper & Row.

LETTER FROM CHIEF SEATHL TO FRANKLIN PIERCE, by Allmonde Kinder

London – The United Kingdom World Wildlife Fund is bringing to the attention of its members the following, which is presented as a letter written to the President of the United States, Democrat Franklin Pierce, in 1855. Chief Seathl

Reprinted by permission of the *Chicago Sun-Times*; courtesy of Allmonde Kinder.

(Seattle), of the Suwamish tribe of the State of Washington, is said to have written it, regarding the proposed purchase of the tribe's land.

The Great Chief in Washington sends word that he wishes to buy our land. The Great Chief also sends us words of friendship and goodwill. This is kind of him, since we know that he has little need of our friendship in return. But we will consider your offer, for we know that if we do not do so, the white man may come with guns and take our land. What Chief Seathl says, the Great Chief in Washington can count on us truly as our white brothers can count on the return of the seasons. My words are like the stars – they do not set.

How can you buy or sell the sky – the warmth of the land? The idea is strange to us. Yet we do not own the freshness of the air or the sparkle of the water. How can you buy them from us? We will decide in our time. Every part of this earth is sacred to my people. Every shining pine needle, every sandy shore, every mist in the dark woods, every clearing and humming insect is holy in the memory of the experience of my people.

We know that the white man does not understand our ways. One portion of the land is the same to him as the next, for he is a stranger who comes in the night and takes from the land whatever he needs. The earth is not his brother, but his enemy, and when he has conquered it, he moves on. He leaves his fathers' graves behind and he does not care. He kidnaps the earth from his children. He does not care. His fathers' graves and his children's birthright are forgotten. His appetite will devour the earth and leave behind only a desert.

The sight of your cities pains the eyes of the redman. But perhaps it is because the redman is a savage and does not understand.

There is no quiet place in the white man's cities. No place to hear the leaves of spring or the rustle of insect wings. But perhaps I am a savage and do not understand – the clatter only seems to insult the ears. And what is there to life if a man cannot hear the lovely cry of the whippoorwill or the arguments of the frogs around a pond at night.

The Indian prefers the soft sound of the wind darting over the face of the pond, and the smell of the wind itself cleansed by a mid-day rain, or scented with a pine. The air is precious to the redman. For all things share the same breath – the beasts, the trees, the man. The white man does not seem to notice the air he breathes. Like a man dying for many days, he is numb to the smell.

If I decide to accept, I will make one condition. The white man must treat the beasts of this land as his brothers. I am a savage and I do not understand any other way.

I have seen a thousand rotting buffaloes on the prairie, left by the white man who shot them from a passing train. I am a savage and I do not understand how the smoking iron horse can be more important than the buffalo that will kill only to stay alive.

What is man without the beasts? If all the beasts were gone, men would die from great loneliness of spirit, for whatever happens to the beasts also happens to the man. All things are connected. Whatever befalls the earth befalls the sons of the earth.

DECLARATION OF INDEPENDENCE, by
Thomas Jefferson and Others

IN CONGRESS, JULY 4, 1776
THE UNANIMOUS DECLARATION OF THE
THIRTEEN UNITED STATES OF AMERICA

When in the Course of human events it becomes necessary for one people to dissolve the political bands which have connected them with another, and to assume among the powers of the earth, the separate and equal station to which the Laws of Nature and of Nature's God entitle them, a decent respect to the opinions of mankind requires that they should declare the causes which impel them to the separation.

We hold these truths to be self-evident, that all men are created equal, that they are endowed by their Creator with certain unalienable Rights, that among these are Life, Liberty and the pursuit of Happiness. That to secure these rights, Governments are instituted among Men, deriving their just powers from the consent of the governed, That whenever any Form of Government becomes destructive of these ends, it is the Right of the People to alter or to abolish it, and to institute new Government, laying its foundation on such principles and organizing its powers in such form, as to them shall seem most likely to affect their Safety and Happiness. Prudence, indeed, will dictate that Governments long established should not be changed for light and transient causes; and accordingly all experience hath shewn that mankind are more disposed to suffer, while evils are sufferable, than to right themselves by abolishing the forms to which they are accustomed. But when a long train of abuses and usurpations, pursuing invariably the same Object evinces a design to reduce them under absolute Despotism, it is their right, it is their duty, to throw off such Government, and to provide new Guards for their future security. Such has been the patient sufferance of these Colonies; and such is now the necessity which constrains them to alter their former Systems of Government. The history of the present King of Great Britain is a history of repeated injuries and usurpations, all having in direct object the establishment of an absolute Tyranny over these States. To prove this, let Facts be submitted to a candid world.

He has refused his Assent to Laws, the most wholesome and necessary for the public good.

He has forbidden his Governors to pass laws of immediate and pressing importance, unless suspended in their operation till his Assent should be obtained; and when so suspended, he has utterly neglected to attend to them.

He has refused to pass other Laws for the accommodation of large districts of people, unless those people would relinquish the right of Representation in the Legislature, a right inestimable to them and formidable to tyrants only.

He has called together legislative bodies at places unusual, uncomfortable, and distant from the depository of their Public Records, for the sole purpose of fatiguing them into compliance with his measures.

He has dissolved Representative Houses repeatedly, for opposing with manly firmness his invasions of the rights of the people.

He has refused for a long time, after such dissolutions, to cause others to be elected; whereby the Legislative Powers, incapable of Annihilation, have returned to the People at large for their exercise; the State remaining in the mean time exposed to all the dangers of invasion from without, and convulsions within.

He has endeavored to prevent the population of these States; for that purpose obstructing the Laws for Naturalization of Foreigners; refusing to pass others to encourage their migration hither, and raising the conditions of new Appropriations of Lands.

He has obstructed the Administration of Justice, by refusing his Assent to Laws for establishing Judiciary Powers.

He has made Judges dependent on his Will alone, for the tenure of their offices, and the amount and payment of their salaries.

He has erected a multitude of New Offices, and sent hither swarms of Officers to harass our people, and eat out their substance.

He has kept among us, in times of peace, Standing Armies without the Consent of our legislatures.

He has affected to render the Military independent of and superior to the Civil Power.

He has combined with others to subject us to a jurisdiction foreign to our constitution, and unacknowledged by our laws; giving his Assent to their Acts of pretented Legislation: For quartering large bodies of armed troops among us: For protecting them, by a mock Trial, from punishment for any Murders which they should commit on the Inhabitants of these States: For cutting off our Trade with all parts of the world: For imposing Taxes on us without our Consent: For depriving us in many cases, of the benefits of Trial by Jury: For transporting us beyond Seas to be tried for pretended offenses: For abolishing the free System of English Laws in a neighboring Province, establishing therein an Arbitrary government, and enlarging its Boundaries so as to render it at once an example and fit instrument for introducing the same absolute rule into these Colonies: For taking away our Charters, abolsihing our most valuable Laws and altering fundamentally the Forms of our Governments: For suspending our own Legislatures, and declaring themselves invested with power to legislate for us in all cases whatsoever.

He has abdicated Government here, by declaring us out of his Protection and waging War against us.

He has plundered our seas, ravaged our Coasts, burnt our towns, and destroyed the lives of our people.

He is at this time transporting large Armies of foreign Mercenaries to complete the works of death, desolation and tyranny, already begun with circumstances of Cruelty & Perfidy scarcely paralleled in the most barbarous ages, and totally unworthy the Head of a civilized nation.

He has constrained our fellow Citizens taken Captive on the high Seas to bear Arms against their Country, to become the executioners of their friends and Brethren, or to fall themselves by their Hands.

He has excited domestic insurrections amongst us, and has endeavored to bring on the inhabitants of our frontiers, the merciless Indian Savages, whose known rule of warfare, is an undistinguished destruction of all ages, sexes, and conditions.

In every stage of these Oppressions We have Petitioned for Redress in the most humble terms: Our repeated Petitions have been answered only by repeated injury. A Prince, whose character is thus marked by every act which may define a Tyrant, is unfit to be the ruler of a free people.

Nor have We been wanting in attention to our British brethren. We have warned them from time to time of attempts by their legislature to extend an unwarrantable jurisdiction over us. We have reminded them of the circumstances of our emigration and settlement here. We have appealed to their native justice and magnanimity, and we have conjured them by the ties of our common kindred to disavow these usurpations, which would inevitably interrrupt our connections and correspondence. They too have been deaf to the voice of justice and of consanguinity. We must, therefore, acquiesce in the necessity, which denounces our Separation, and hold them, as we hold the rest of mankind, Enemies in War, in Peace Friends.

We, THEREFORE, the Representatives of the UNITED STATES OF AMERICA, in General Congress, Assembled, appealing to the Supreme Judge of the world for the rectitude of our intentions, do, in the Name, and by Authority of the good People of these Colonies, solemnly publish and declare, That these United Colonies are, and of Right ought to be FREE AND INDEPENDENT STATES; that they are Absolved from all Allegiance to the British Crown, and that all political connection between them and the State of Great Britain, is and ought to be totally dissolved; and that as Free and Independent States, they have full Power to levy War, conclude Peace, contract Alliances, establish Commerce, and to do all other Acts and Things which Independent States may of right do. And for the support of this Declaration, with a firm reliance on the protection of Divine Providence, we mutually pledge to each other our Lives, our Fortunes, and our sacred Honor.

CIVIL DISOBEDIENCE, by Henry David Thoreau

I heartily accept the motto, — "That government is best which governs least;" and I should like to see it acted up to more rapidly and systematically. Carried out, it finally amounts to this, which also I believe, — "That government is best which governs not at all;" and when men are prepared for it, that will be the kind of government which they will have. Government is at best but an expedient; but most governments are usually, and all governments are sometimes, inexpedient. The objections which have been brought against a standing army, and they are many and weighty, and deserve to prevail, may also at last be brought against a standing government. The standing army is only an arm of the standing government. The government itself, which is only the mode which the people have chosen to execute their will, is equally liable to be abused and perverted before the people can act through it. Witness the present Mexican war, the work of comparatively a few individuals using the standing government as their tool; for, in the outset, the people would not have consented to this measure.

This American government,—what is it but a tradition, though a recent one, endeavoring to transmit itself unimpaired to posterity, but each instant losing some of its integrity? It has not the vitality and force of a single living man; for a single man can bend it to his will. It is a sort of wooden gun to the people themselves. But it is not the less necessary for this; for the people must have some complicated machinery or other, and hear its din, to satisfy that idea of government which they have. Governments show thus how successfully men can be imposed on, even impose on themselves, for their own advantage. It is excellent, we must all allow. Yet this government never of itself furthered any enterprise, but by the alacrity with which it got out of its way. *It* does not keep the country free. *It* does not settle the West. *It* does not educate. The character inherent in the American people has done all that has been accomplished; and it would have done somewhat more, if the government had not sometimes got in its way. For government is an expedient by which men would fain succeed in letting one another alone; and, as has been said, when it is most expedient, the governed are most let alone by it. Trade and commerce, if they were not made of india-rubber, would never manage to bounce over the obstacles which legislators are continually putting in their way; and, if one were to judge these men wholly by the effects of their actions and not partly by their intentions, they would deserve to be classed and punished with those mischievous persons who put obstructions on the railroads.

But, to speak practically and as a citizen, unlike those who call themselves no-government men, I ask for, not at once no government, but *at once* a better government. Let every man make known what kind of government would command his respect, and that will be one step toward obtaining it.

After all, the practical reason why, when the power is once in the hands of the people, a majority are permitted, and for a long period continue, to rule is not because they are most likely to be in the right, nor because this seems fairest to the minority, but because they are physically the strongest. But a government in which the majority rule in all cases cannot be based on justice, even as far as men understand it. Can there not be a government in which majorities do not virtually decide right and wrong, but conscience?—in which majorities decide only those questions to which the rule of expediency is applicable? Must the citizen ever for a moment, or in the least degree, resign his conscience to the legislator? Why has every man a conscience, then? I think that we should be men first, and subjects afterward. It is not desirable to cultivate a respect for the law, so much as for the right. The only obligation which I have a right to assume is to do at any time what I think right. It is truly enough said that a corporation has no conscience; but a corporation of conscientious men is a corporation *with* a conscience. Law never made men a whit more just; and, by means of their respect for it, even the well-disposed are daily made the agents of injustice. A common and natural result of an undue respect for law is, that you may see a file of soldiers, colonel, captain, corporal, privates, powder-monkeys and all, marching in admirable order over hill and dale to the wars, against their wills, ay, against their common sense and consciences, which makes it very steep marching indeed, and produces a palpitation of the heart. They have no doubt that it is damnable business in which they are concerned; they are all peaceably inclined. Now, what are they? Men at all? or small movable forts and magazines, at the service of some unscrupulous man in power? Visit the Navy-Yard, and behold a marine, such a man as an American government can make, or such as it can make a man with its black arts,—a mere shadow and reminiscence of humanity, a man laid out alive and standing, and already, as one may say, buried under arms with funeral accompaniments, though it may be,—

"Not a drum was heard, not a funeral
note,
As his corse to the rampart we
hurried;
Not a soldier discharged his farewell
shot
O'er the grave where our hero we
buried."

The mass of men serve the state thus, not as men mainly, but as machines, with their bodies. They are the standing army, and the militia, jailers, constables, *posse comitatus,* etc. In most cases there is no free exercise whatever of the judgment or of the moral sense; but they put themselves on a level with wood and earth and stones; and wooden men can perhaps be manufactured that will serve the purpose as well. Such command no more respect than men of straw or a lump of dirt. They have the same sort of worth only as horses and dogs. Yet such as these even are commonly esteemed good citizens. Others—as most legislators, politicians, lawyers, ministers, and office-holders—serve the state chiefly with their heads, and, as they rarely make any moral distinctions, they are as likely to serve the devil, without *intending* it, as God. A very few,—as heroes, patriots, martyrs, reformers in the great sense and *men*—serve the state with their consciences also, and so necessarily resist it for the most part; and they are commonly treated as enemies by it. A wise man will only be useful as a man, and will not submit to be "clay," and "stop a hole to keep the wind away," but leave that office to his dust at least:—

"I am too high-born to be propertied,
To be a secondary at control,
Or useful serving-man and instrument
To any sovereign state throughout the
world."

He who gives himself entirely to his fellow-men appears to them useless and selfish; but he who gives himself partially to them is pronounced a benefactor and philanthropist.

How does it become a man to behave toward this American government to-day? I answer, that he cannot without disgrace be associated with it. I cannot for an instant recognize that political organization as *my* government which is the *slave's* government also.

All men recognize the right of revolution; that is, the right to refuse allegiance to, and to resist, the government, when its tyranny or its inefficiency are great and unendurable. But almost all say that such is not the case now. But such was the case, they think, in the Revolution of '75. If one were to tell me that this was a bad government because it taxed certain foreign commodities brought to its ports, it is most probable that I should not make an ado about it, for I can do without them. All machines have their friction; and possibly this does enough good to counterbalance the evil. At any rate, it is a great evil to make a stir about it. But when the friction comes to have its machine, and oppression and robbery are organized, I say, let us not have such a machine any longer. In other words, when a sixth of the population of a nation which has undertaken to be the refuge of liberty are slaves, and a whole country is unjustly overrun and conquered by a foreign army, and subject to military law, I think that is is not too soon for honest men to rebel and revolutionize. What makes this duty the more urgent is the fact that the country so overrun is not our own, but ours is the invading army.

Paley, a common authority with many on moral questions, in his chapter on the "Duty of Submission to Civil Government," resolves all civil obligation into expediency; and he proceeds to say "that so long as the interest of the whole society requires it, that is, so long as the established government cannot be resisted or changed without public inconveniency, it is the will of God . . . that the established government be obeyed, — and no longer. This principle being admitted, the justice of every particular case of resistance is reduced to a computation of the quantity of the danger and grievance on the one side, and of the probability and expense of redressing it on the other." Of this, he says, every man shall judge for himself. But Paley appears never to have contemplated those cases to which the rule of expediency does not apply, in which a people, as well as an individual, must do justice, cost what it may. If I have unjustly wrested a plank from a drowning man, I must restore it to him though I drown myself. This, according to Paley, would be inconvenient. But he that would save his life, in such a case, shall lose it. This people must cease to hold slaves, and to make war on Mexico, though it cost them their existence as a people.

In their practice, nations agree with Paley; but does any one think that Massachusetts does exactly what is right at the present crisis?

> "A drab of state, a cloth-o'-silver slut,
>   To have her train borne up, and her soul
>   trail in the dirt."

Practically speaking, the opponents to a reform in Massachusetts are not a hundred thousand politicians at the South, but a hundred thousand merchants and farmers here, who are more interested in commerce and agriculture than they are in humanity, and are not prepared to do justice to the slave and to Mexico, *cost what it may.* I quarrel not with far-off foes, but with those who, near at home, coöperate with, and do the bidding of, those far away, and without whom the latter would be harmless. We are accustomed to say, that the mass of men are unprepared; but improvement is slow, because the few are not materially wiser or better than the many. It is not so important that many should be as good as you, as that there be some absolute goodness somewhere; for that will leaven the whole lump. There are thousands who are *in opinion* opposed to slavery and to the war, who yet in effect do nothing to put an end to them; who, esteeming themselves children of Washington and Franklin, sit down with their hands in their pockets, and say that they know not what to do, and do nothing; who even postpone the question of freedom to the question of free trade, and quietly read the prices-current along with the latest advices from Mexico, after dinner, and, it may be, fall asleep over them both. What is the price-current of an honest man and patriot to-day? They hesitate, and they regret, and sometimes they petition; but they do nothing in earnest and with effect. They will wait, well disposed, for others to remedy the evil, that they may no longer have it to regret. At most, they give only a cheap vote, and a feeble countenance and God-speed, to the right, as it goes by them. There are nine hundred and ninety-nine patrons of virtue to one virtuous man. But it is easier to deal with the real possessor of a thing than with the temporary guardian of it. . . .

It is not a man's duty, as a matter of course, to devote himself to the eradication of any, even the most enormous, wrong; he may still properly have other concerns to engage him; but it is his duty, at least, to wash his hands of it, and, if he gives it no thought longer, not to give it practically his support. If I devote myself to other pursuits and contemplations, I must first see, at least, that I do not pursue them sitting upon another man's shoulders. I must get off him first, that he may pursue his contemplations too. See what gross inconsistency is tolerated. I have heard some of my townsmen say, "I should like to have them order me out to help put down an insurrection of the slaves, or to march to Mexico;—see if I would go;" and yet these very men have each, directly by their allegiance, and so indirectly, at least, by their money, furnished a substitute. The soldier is applauded who refuses to serve in an unjust war by those who do not refuse to sustain the unjust government which makes the war; is applauded by those whose own act and authority he disregards and sets at naught; as if the state were penitent to that degree that it hired one to scourge it while it sinned, but not to that degree that it left off sinning for a moment. Thus, under the name of Order and Civil Government, we are all made at last to pay homage to and support our own meanness. After the first blush of sin comes its indifference; and from immoral it becomes as it were, *un*moral and not quite unnecessary to that life which we have made. . . .

Unjust laws exist: shall we be content to obey them or shall we endeavor to amend them, and obey them until we have succeeded, or shall we transgress them at once? Men generally, under such a government as this, think that they ought to wait until they have persuaded the majority to alter them. They think that, if they should resist, the remedy would be worse than the evil. But it is the fault of the government itself that the remedy *is* worse than the evil. *It* makes it worse. Why is it not more apt to anticipate and provide for reform? Why does it not cherish its wise minority? Why does it cry and resist before it is hurt? Why does it not encourage its citizens to be on the alert to point out its faults, and do better than it would have them? Why does it always crucify Christ, and excommunicate Copernicus and Luther, and pronounce Washington and Franklin rebels?

One would think, that a deliberate and practical denial of its authority was the only offense never contemplated by government; else, why has it not assigned its definite, its suitable and proportionate penalty? If a man who has no property refuses but once to earn nine shillings for the State, he is put in prison for a period unlimited by any law that I know, and determined only by the discretion of those who placed him there; but if he should steal ninety times nine shillings from the State, he is soon permitted to go at large again.

If the injustice is part of the necessary friction of the machine of government, let it go, let it go: perchance it will wear smooth, — certainly the machine will wear out. If the injustice has a spring, or a pulley, or a rope, or a crank, exclusively for itself, then perhaps you may consider whether the remedy will not be worse than the evil; but if it is of such a nature that it requires you to be the agent of injustice to another, then, I say, break the law. Let your life be a counter friction to stop the machine. What I have to do is to see, at any rate, that I do not lend myself to the wrong which I condemn.

As for adopting the ways which the State has provided for remedying the evil, I know not of such ways. They take too much time, and a man's life will be gone. I have other affairs to attend to. I came into this world, not chiefly to make this a good place to live in, but to live in it, be it good or bad. A man has not everything to do, but something; and because he cannot do *everything*, it is not necessary that he should do *something* wrong. . . .

I do not hesitate to say, that those who call themselves Abolitionists should at once effectually withdraw their support, both in person and property, from the government of Massachusetts, and not wait till they constitute a majority of one, before they suffer the right to prevail through them. I think that it is enough if they have God on their side, without waiting for that other one. Moreover any man more right than his neighbors constitutes a majority of one already.

I meet this American government, or its representative, the State government, directly, and face to face, once a year — no more — in the person of its taxgatherer; this is the only mode in which a man situated as I am necessarily meets it; and it then says distinctly, Recognize me; and the simplest, the most effectual, and, in the present posture of affairs, the indispensablest mode of treating with it on this head, of expressing your little satisfaction with and love for it, is to deny it then. My civil neighbor, the tax-gatherer, is the very man I have to deal with, — for it is, after all, with men and not with parchment that I quarrel, — and he has voluntarily chosen to be an agent of the government. How shall he ever know well what he is and does as an officer of the government, or as a man, until he is obliged to consider whether he shall treat me, his neighbor, for whom he has respect, as a neighbor and well-disposed man, or as a maniac and disturber of the peace, and see if he can get over this obstruction to his neighborliness without a ruder and more impetuous thought or speech corresponding with his action. I know this well, that if one thousand, if one hundred, if ten men whom I could name, — if ten *honest* men only, — ay, if *one* HONEST man, in this State of Massachusetts, CEASING TO HOLD SLAVES, were actually to withdraw from this copartnership, and be locked up in the county jail therefor, it would be the abolition of slavery in America. For it matters not how small the beginning may seem to be: what is once well done is done forever. But we love better to talk about it: that we say is our mission. Reform keeps many scores of newspapers in its service, but not one man. If my esteemed neighbor, the State's ambassador,[1] who will devote his days to the settlement of the question of human rights in the Council Chamber, instead of being threatened with the prisons of Carolina, were to sit down the prisoner of Massachusetts, that State which is so anxious to foist the sin of slavery upon her sister, — though at present she can discover only an act of inhospitality to be the ground of a quarrel with her, — the Legislature would not wholly waive the subject the following winter.

Under a government which imprisons any unjustly, the true place for a just man is also a prison. The proper place to-day, the only place which Massachusetts has provided for her freer and less desponding spirits, is in her prisons, to be put out and locked out of the State by her own act, as they have already put themselves out by their principles. It is there that the fugitive slave, and the Mexican prisoner on parole, and the Indian come to plead the wrongs of his race should find them; on that separate, but more free and honorable ground, where the State places those who are not *with* her, but *against* her, — the only house in a slave State in which a free man can abide with honor. If any think that their influence would be lost there, and their voices no longer afflict the ear of the State, that they would not be as an enemy within its walls, they do not know by how much truth is stronger than error, nor how much more eloquently and effectively he can combat injustice who has experienced a little in his own person. Cast your whole vote, not a strip of paper merely, but your whole influence. A minority is powerless while it conforms to the majority; it is not even a minority then; but it is irresistible when it clogs by its whole weight. If the alternative is to keep all just men in prison, or give up war and slavery, the State will not hesitate which to choose. If a thousand men were not to pay their tax-bills this year, that would not be a violent and bloody measure, as it would be to pay them, and enable the State to commit violence and shed innocent blood. This is, in fact, the definition of a peaceable revolution, if any such is possible. If the tax-gatherer, or any other public officer, asks me, as one has done, "But what shall I do?" my answer is, "If you really wish to do anything, resign your office." When the subject has refused allegiance, and the officer has resigned his office, then the revolution is accomplished. But even suppose blood should flow. Is there not a sort of blood shed when the conscience is wounded? Through this wound a man's real manhood and immortality flow out, and he bleeds to an everlasting death. I see this blood flowing now. . . .

---

[1] Thoreau is referring to a Concord congressman, Samuel Hoar, who journeyed to South Carolina to test that state's laws prohibiting black Massachusetts seamen from entering their ports. Hoar was expelled from the state by the South Carolina legislature.

The authority of government, even such as I am willing to submit to, — for I will cheerfully obey those who know and can do better than I, and in many things even those who neither know nor can do so well, — is still an impure one; to be strictly just, it must have the sanction and consent of the governed. It can have no pure right over my person and property but what I concede to it. The progress from an absolute to a limited monarchy, from a limited monarchy to a democracy, is a progress toward a true respect for the individual. Even the Chinese philosopher was wise enough to regard the individual as the basis of the empire. It a democracy, such as we know it, the last improvement possible in government? Is it not possible to take a step further towards recognizing and organizing the rights of man? There will never be a really free and enlightened State until the State comes to recognize the individual as a higher and independent power, from which all its own power and authority are derived, and treats him accordingly. I please myself with imagining a State at last which can afford to be just to all men, and to treat the individual with respect as a neighbor; which even would not think it inconsistent with its own repose if a few were to live aloof from it, not meddling with it, nor embraced by it, who fulfilled all the duties of neighbors and fellow-men. A State which bore this kind of fruit, and suffered it to drop off as fast as it ripened, would prepare the way for a still more perfect and glorious State, which also I have imagined, but not yet anywhere seen.

GAYLORD FREEMAN, by Studs Terkel

It is a morning in 1975.

He is chairman of the board of the First National Bank of Chicago. It is his last year; he has chosen his successor. His tie bears the bank's insignia: the name and the coin. "I got one of our boys to design it. I have never worn any other tie on a business day. I wear this as an indication to the troops that I'm thinkin' about the bank."

It is an expansive office, with objets d'art here and in the anteroom. Adjacent is his private dining room. On the fifty-seventh floor is a huge dining room where, this noon, his successor will host a luncheon for the ambassador of Japan; among the several hundred guests will be the city's leading industrialists and Mayor Richard Daley.

I came in in '34 and go out in '75. That's more than forty-one years. Do I feel withdrawal symptoms? A friend was telling me of her father, Edward Ryerson (chairman of the board of directors of Inland Steel Company, during the forties, and a leading civic figure). After his retirement, nobody invited him to lunch. He had to find somebody who didn't have a damn thing to do. I've already sensed it. As soon as we designated Bob as our successor, it was inevitable that people would say: "Gale Freeman, he's a nice guy, but Bob's the fella we should be talking to."

I find now that every couple of weeks, I have a free luncheon engagement. It tickles me. It doesn't upset me. I kind of laugh at myself because when I retire, where will I have lunch? I've had a magnificent dining room. I'll go to a club. I've belonged to the Mid-Day Club for over thirty years, and I've never had lunch there. Now I'll have places to go to.

I won't be in demand. I'll be seeking company rather than being sought. If you're happy, that's all right. I'm very lucky. I've achieved everything I hoped to achieve. I'm not rich, but I'll be comfortable. I don't aspire to anything more. I don't feel short-circuited or let down. I'm graduating from business with a good report card. Already I feel less competitive. Let somebody else have the credit. I don't have to fight for that anymore.

It can be very pleasing if it doesn't come too late. I remember a friend of mine who was a very tough man in business. When he was retiring, he said: "There's nobody in town that really likes me. From now on, I'm going to lead my life to be liked." It was too late. Attitudes were set, his habits were so ingrained, he couldn't make the change. He died an unhappy man, with great tension between himself and the children. The trick is to put all that competitiveness into your life when it's necessary but to moderate it with a degree of love and modesty.

My good friend Professor Milton Friedman says the worst thing is for businessmen to feel responsible to society. He says that's a lot of baloney and it's contrary to the businessman's assignment. It's an arrogance he should not have. I don't accept that, though I greatly admire Milton.

Is this a Christian thought? No, we hope we'll be in business for years. There's nothing sacred about a profit-oriented society. There's no guarantee in the Bible or the Constitution that you can have private property. If we're going to continue to have these opportunities, it's only because this is acceptable to a high enough proportion of our people that they don't change the laws to prevent it.

I work hard. I try to be here about a quarter of seven. I work until five-thirty or six. I haven't played bridge in thirty years. I haven't played golf in twenty years. I like work better than golf. I don't like the artificial camaraderie of the locker room, havin' four, five drinks and goin' home a little plastered and havin' to take a long nap so it ruins the whole goddamn day.

Which would you rather be doing: traveling through Europe and calling on the ministers of finance and heads of state, or playing bridge with people who haven't had a new thought in twenty years? This is going to be the problem of retirement. No intellectual stimulation.

Three years later. It is a morning in 1978. We are seated in a smaller office on another floor. There are no objets d'art around.

I don't feel I've sacrificed anything. As a younger man, I sacrificed closeness with my children. But in our mature life, it isn't a sacrifice. We have two grandsons, eighteen and sixteen, who've been with us the past few days. Very idealistic.

I run into the businessman in the board room or the locker room, and by God, he's for the American Way one hundred percent. Anybody that deviates from that is a goddamn Communist, I say to him: "What do you mean by 'the American Way'?" "Well, everybody knows that." I say: "What were the concepts that led to the creation of our country?" He's ill at ease, he doesn't want to talk about it because (a) he's never given it much thought; and (b) he's not sure he can defend a system that permits as wide a variety of income as we have.

My feeling's always been that no system is perfect. But ours has done more, not only for the rich, but for the poor, than any other system. Let's not be embarrassed about it; let's understand it more. I wouldn't have pursued this as much if I didn't have doubts.

I think our nation has grown old, and very rapidly. We've lost a lot of the dream. We're like people my age, whose world narrows. A young man comes out of school and he's interested in everything. Then he gets a job, and his world narrows a bit. He marries. Job, home, family. And it narrows a bit more. Finally, he gets older. Through with his job, his family gone away, his ultimate concern is his bowel movement every morning. Our country is going through a great deal of that now.

This January, I sat down in the afternoon and read a novel. That's the first one I read since I got out of school in 1934. I never felt I could waste a minute. It was cheating. I felt I had a terrible duty to the bank and a duty to society. It took a hell of a lot of my time. People are silly. I'm not as good as I was. I'm not as physically strong. I'm not as mentally sharp. I have a hell of a time with names. So I don't feel the same duty I had when I was a more efficient machine.

Machine?

(Laughs softly.) I know. I shouldn't have said that.

It's worse if you've been top dog. It's harder to retire than if you never were the boss. (Suddenly sharp.) Business is so goddamn competitive! The head of a business is really competing with everybody all the time, not only with his competitors. You're competing with your friends in other businesses, your dearest friends. It influences your life tremendously. And not necessarily in a good way. (Laughs.) It tends to make business friendships not quite friendships.

The guy who's been intensely competitive all his life and then —click! —he's retired, it's hard for him to joyously admire the success of his associates, his friends. He can't help feeling it's a little at his expense. Of course, it isn't. He's not in that league anymore. This is a hard thing for many men to take.

I've been retired a year and a half now. I wrote some poems about it.

Our names are as they were. We look the same. Our wives are just as kind. In fact, more thoughtful. But we don't feel the same, not quite. The young men do not stand, we never felt they should. Our old friends smile, but turn a moment sooner to the younger man. And that is fair. We're just as good friends as we were, but not quite so important anymore. Not so important. No. But wiser?

WALDEN, by E. B. White

Miss Nims, take a letter to Henry David Thoreau. Dear Henry: I thought of you the other afternoon as I was approaching Concord doing fifty on Route 62. That is a high speed at which to hold a philosopher in one's mind, but in this century we are a nimble bunch.

On one of the lawns in the outskirts of the village a woman was cutting the grass with a motorized lawn mower. What made me think of you was that the machine had rather got away from her, although she was game enough, and in the brief glimpse I had of the scene it appeared to me that the lawn was mowing the lady. She kept a tight grip on the handles, which throbbed violently with every explosion of the one-cylinder motor, and as she sheered around bushes and lurched along at a reluctant trot behind her impetuous servant, she looked like a puppy who had grabbed something that was too much for him. Concord hasn't changed much, Henry; the farm implements and the animals still have the upper hand.

I may as well admit that I was journeying to Concord with the deliberate intention of visiting your woods; for although I have never knelt at the grave of a philosopher nor placed wreaths on moldy poets, and have often gone a mile out of my way to avoid some place of historical interest, I have always wanted to see Walden Pond. The account which you left of your sojourn there is, you will be amused to learn, a document of increasing pertinence; each year it seems to gain a little headway, as the world loses ground. We may all be transcendental yet, whether we like it or not. As our common complexities increase, any tale of individual simplicity (and yours is the best written and the cockiest) acquires a new fascination; as our goods accumulate, but not our well-being, your report of an existence without material adornment takes on a certain awkward credibility.

My purpose in going to Walden Pond, like yours, was not to live cheaply or to live dearly there, but to transact some private business with the fewest obstacles. Approaching Concord, doing forty, doing forty-five, doing fifty, the steering wheel held snug in my palms, the highway held grimly in my vision, the crown of the road now serving me (on the right-hand curves), now defeating me (on the lefthand curves), I began to rouse myself from the stupefaction which a day's motor journey induces. It was a delicious evening, Henry, when the whole body is one sense, and imbibes delight through every pore, if I may coin a phrase. Fields were richly brown where the harrow, drawn by the stripped Ford, had lately sunk its teeth; pastures were green; and overhead the sky had that same everlasting great look which you will find on Page 144 of the Oxford pocket edition. I could feel the road entering me, through tire, wheel, spring, and cushion; shall I not have intelligence with earth too? Am I not partly leaves and vegetable mold myself? — a man of infinite horsepower, yet partly leaves.

Stay with me on 62 and it will take you into Concord. As I say, it was a delicious evening. The snake had come forth to die in a bloody S on the highway, the wheel upon its head, its bowels flat now and exposed. The turtle had come up too to cross the road and die in the attempt, its hard shell smashed under the rubber blow, its intestinal yearning (for the other side of the road) forever squashed. There was a sign by the wayside which announced that the road had a "cotton surface." You wouldn't know what that is, but neither, for that matter, did I. There is a cryptic ingredient in many of our modern improvements—we are awed and pleased without knowing quite what we are enjoying. It is something to be traveling on a road with a cotton surface.

The civilization round Concord to-day is an odd distillation of city, village, farm, and manor. The houses, yards, fields look not quite suburban, not quite rural. Under the bronze beech and the blue spruce of the departed baron grazes the milch goat of the heirs. Under the porte-cochère stands the reconditioned station wagon; under the grape arbor sit the puppies for sale. (But why do men degenerate ever? What makes families run out?)

It was June and everywhere June was publishing her immemorial stanza; in the lilacs, in the syringa, in the freshly edged paths and the sweetness of moist beloved gardens, and the little wire wickets that preserve the tulips' front. Farmers were already moving the fruits of their toil into their yards, arranging the rhubarb, the asparagus, the strictly fresh eggs on the painted stands under the little shed roofs with the patent shingles. And though it was almost a hundred years since you had taken your ax and started cutting out your home on Walden Pond, I was interested to observe that the philosophical spirit was still alive in Massachusetts: in the center of a vacant lot some boys were assembling the framework of a rude shelter, their whole mind and skill concentrated in the rather inauspicious helter-skeleton of studs and rafters. They too were escaping from town, to live naturally, in a rich blend of savagery and philosophy.

That evening, after supper at the inn, I strolled out into the twilight to dream my shapeless transcendental dreams and see that the car was locked up for the night (first open the right front door, then reach over, straining, and pull up the handles of the left rear and the left front till you hear the click, then the handle of the right rear, then shut the right front but open it again, remembering that the key is still in the ignition switch, remove the key, shut the right front again with a bang, push the tiny keyhold cover to one side, insert key, turn, and withdraw). It is what we all do, Henry. It is called locking the car. It is said to confuse thieves and keep them from making off with the laprobe. Four doors to lock behind one robe. The driver himself never uses a laprobe, the free movement of his legs being vital to the operation of the vehicle; so that when he locks the car it is a pure and unselfish act. I have in my life gained very little essential heat from laprobes, yet I have ever been at pains to lock them up.

The evening was full of sounds, some of which would have stirred your memory. The robins still love the elms of New England villages at sundown. There is enough of the thrush in them to make song inevitable at the end of day, and enough of the tramp to make them hang round the dwellings of men. A robin, like many another American, dearly loves a white house with green blinds. Concord is still full of them.

Your fellow-townsmen were stirring abroad—not many afoot, most of them in their cars; and the sound which they made in Concord at evening was a rustling and a whispering. The sound lacks steadfastness and is wholly unlike that of a train. A train, as you know who lived so near the Fitchburg line, whistles once or twice sadly and is gone, trailing a memory in smoke, soothing to ear and mind. Automobiles, skirting a village green, are like flies that have gained the inner ear — they buzz, cease, pause, start, shift, stop, halt, brake, and the whole effect is a nervous polytone curiously disturbing.

As I wandered along, the toc toc of ping pong balls drifted from an attic window. In front of the Reuben Brown house a Buick was drawn up. At the wheel, motionless, his hat upon his head, a man sat, listening to Amos and Andy on the radio (it is a drama of many scenes and without an end). The deep voice of Andrew Brown, emerging from the car, although it originated more than two hundred miles away, was unstrained by distance. When you used to sit on the shore of your pond on Sunday morning, listening to the church bells of Acton and Concord, you were aware of the excellent filter of the intervening atmosphere. Science has attended to that, and sound now maintains its intensity without regard for distance. Properly sponsored, it goes on forever.

A fire engine, out for a trial spin, roared past Emerson's house, hot with readiness for public duty. Over the barn roofs the martins dipped and chittered. A swarthy daughter of an asparagus grower, in culottes, shirt, and bandanna, pedalled past on her bicycle. It was indeed a delicious evening, and I returned to the inn (I believe it was your house once) to rock with the old ladies on the concrete veranda.

Next morning early I started afoot for Walden, out of Main Street and down Thoreau, past the depot and the Minuteman Chevrolet Company. The morning was fresh, and in a bean field along the way I flushed an agriculturalist, quietly studying his beans. Thoreau Street soon joined Number 126, an artery of the State. We number our highways nowadays, our speed being so great we can remember little of their quality or character and are lucky to remember their number. (Men have an indistinct notion that if they keep up this activity long enough all will at length ride somewhere, in next to no time.) Your pond is on 126.

I knew I must be nearing your woodland retreat when the Golden Pheasant lunchroom came into view — Sealtest ice cream, toasted sandwiches, hot frankfurters, waffles, tonics, and lunches. Were I the proprietor, I should add rice, Indian meal, and molasses — just for old time's sake. The Pheasant, incidentally, is for sale: a chance for some nature lover who wishes to set himself up beside a pond in the Concord atmosphere and live deliberately, fronting only the essential facts of life on Number 126. Beyond the Pheasant was a place called Walden Breezes, an oasis whose porch pillars were made of old green shutters sawed into lengths. On the porch was a distorting mirror, to give the traveler a comical image of himself, who had miraculously learned to gaze in an ordinary glass without smiling. Behind the Breezes, in a sun-parched clearing, dwelt your philosophical descendants in their trailers, each trailer the size of your hut, but all grouped together for the sake of congeniality. Trailer people leave the city, as you did, to discover solitude and in any weather, at any hour of the day or night, to improve the nick of time; but they soon collect in villages and get bogged deeper in the mud than ever. The camp behind Walden Breezes was just rousing itself to the morning. The ground was packed hard under the heel, and the sun came through the clearing to bake the soil and enlarge the wry smell of cramped housekeeping. Cushman's bakery truck had stopped to deliver an early basket of rolls. A camp dog, seeing me in the road, barked petulantly. A man emerged from one of the trailers and set forth with a bucket to draw water from some forest tap.

Leaving the highway I turned off into the woods toward the pond, which was apparent through the foliage. The floor of the forest was strewn with dried old oak leaves and *Transcripts.* From beneath the flattened popcorn wrapper (*granum explosum*) peeped the frail violet. I followed a footpath and descended to the water's edge. The pond lay clear and blue in the morning light, as you have seen it so many times. In the shallows a man's waterlogged shirt undulated gently. A few flies came out to greet me and convoy me to your cove, past the No Bathing signs on which the fellows and the girls had scrawled their names. I felt strangely excited suddenly to be snooping around your premises, tiptoeing along watchfully, as though not to tread by mistake upon the intervening century. Before I got to the cove I heard something which seemed to me quite wonderful: I heard your frog, a full, clear *troonk*, guiding me, still hoarse and solemn, bridging the years as the robins had bridged them in the sweetness of the village evening. But he soon quit, and I came on a couple of young boys throwing stones at him.

Your front yard is marked by a bronze tablet set in a stone. Four small granite posts, a few feet away, show where the house was. On top of the tablet was a pair of faded blue bathing trunks with a white stripe. Back of it is a pile of stones, a sort of cairn, left by your visitors as a tribute I suppose. It is a rather ugly little heap of stones, Henry. In fact the hillside itself seems faded, brow-beaten; a few tall skinny pines, bare of lower limbs, a smattering of young maples in suitable green, some birches and oaks, and a number of trees felled by the last big wind. It was from the bole of one of these fallen pines, torn up by the roots, that I extracted the stone which I added to the cairn—a sentimental act in which I was interrupted by a small terrier from a nearby picnic group, who confronted me and wanted to know about the stone.

I sat down for a while on one of the posts of your house to listen to the bluebottles and the dragon flies. The invaded glade sprawled shabby and mean at my feet, but the flies were tuned to the old vibration. There were the remains of a fire in your ruins, but I doubt that it was yours; also two beer bottles trodden into the soil and become part of earth. A young oak had taken root in your house, and two or three ferns, unrolling like the ticklers at a banquet. The only other furnishings were a DuBarry pattern sheet, a page torn from a picture magazine, and some crusts in wax paper.

Before I quit I walked clear round the pond and found the place where you used to sit on the northeast side to get the sun in the fall, and the beach where you got sand for scrubbing your floor. On the eastern side of the pond, where the highway borders it, the State has built dressing rooms for swimmers, a float with diving towers, drinking fountains of porcelain, and rowboats for hire. The pond is in fact a State Preserve, and carries a twenty-dollar fine for picking wild flowers, a decree signed in all solemnity by your fellow-citizens Walter C. Wardwell, Erson B. Barlow, and Nathaniel I. Bowditch. There was a smell of creosote where they had been building a wide wooden stairway to the road and the parking area. Swimmers and boaters were arriving; bodies plunged vigorously into the water and emerged wet and beautiful in the bright air. As I left, a boatload of town boys were splashing about in mid-pond, kidding and fooling, the young fellows singing at the tops of their lungs in a wild chorus:

> Amer-ica, Amer-i-ca, God shed his grace on thee,
> And crown thy good with brotherhood
> From sea to shi-ning sea!

I walked back to town along the railroad, following your custom. The rails were expanding noisily in the hot sun, and on the slope of the roadbed the wild grape and the blackberry sent up their creepers to the track.

The expense of my brief sojourn in Concord was:

Canvas shoes	$1.95	
Baseball bat	.25	gifts to take back
Left-handed fielder's glove	1.25	to a boy
Hotel and meals	4.25	
In all	$7.70	

As you see, this amount was almost what you spent for food for eight months. I cannot defend the shoes or the expenditure for shelter and food: they reveal a meanness and grossness in my nature which you would find contemptible. The baseball equipment, however, is the kind of impediment with which you were never on even terms. You must remember that the house where you practiced the sort of economy which I respect was haunted only by mice and squirrels. You never had to cope with a shortstop.

TRYING TO RESTORE A SEA OF GRASS, by Dennis Farney

Wildflowers and grass, rippling in the wind; a landscape in motion beneath the wide Midwestern sky.

That is late spring on the prairie. It is a placid time of meadowlarks singing from sun-splashed hillsides and cattle lowing in a gathering dusk. The prairie then is a gentle landscape, a world of low green hills and little wooded valleys that rolls away toward a far-off horizon.

It seems an unlikely place for anything of significance to be happening. Yet a quiet development hereabouts may tell something about the changing mood of the nation:

People are finally coming to value what Walt Whitman once called "North America's characteristic landscape," the American prairie.

Some think this is a reflection of a deep-felt national anxiety about the dizzying pace of social change in the last decade and a half, a yearning for simple, enduring things. Others think it's just an indication that the environmental movement has matured enough to appreciate unspectacular landscapes as well as spectacular ones. Whatever the reason, there is a growing appreciation for the landscape regarded through most of U.S. history as good only for plowing up or mowing down.

Here in the Kansas Flint Hills, a 50-mile-wide band that runs north-south across the state, environmentalists are struggling to establish a Tallgrass Prairie National Park. It would preserve the kind of prairie the homesteaders crossed and conquered, a sea of grass up to nine feet tall, with a root system so matted that it broke the pioneer plows.

Other types of prairie, which have shorter grasses, still survive in large tracts in the drier parts of the Great Plains. But the tallgrass prairie, which once occupied more humid country from western Ohio to eastern Kansas, has long since vanished beneath the plow. It has become the Corn Belt—except for here where it's protected by a topsoil too thin to plow.

It is a widespread misconception that prairies are always flat; most of them have a pitch and roll. Another misconception is that they are monotonous landscapes of grass and only grass. A virgin prairie sparkles with the color of from 200 to 300 kinds of wildflowers from April to October. But above all else, a prairie is an utterly open landscape, a place of lonely windmills turning in a ceaseless wind, of redtailed hawks circling in an empty sky, of endless distances receding toward infinity.

This openness tends either to invigorate people or to terrify them. "Between that earth and that sky, I felt erased, blotted out," Willa Cather wrote in *My Antonia*, her classic novel on the settlement of the prairie. All through such prairie novels, and the letters and diaries of the early sodbusters, there is an eerie ambivalence: the prairie will enchant you with its solitude and its serenity—if it doesn't devour you with its loneliness, its enervating winds, its blizzards and its broiling sun.

Perhaps it is only now, after the prairie has been conquered by the plow, the air conditioner and the interstate highway, that men can safely appreciate its harsh and sharp-edged beauty. Perhaps that is the reason a new movement of sorts has sprung up in recent years, waxing strongest in those states like Illinois and Iowa where the prairie has all but disappeared. It is the prairie restoration movement, composed of a diverse assemblage of people who are trying, with seeds and infinite patience, to re-create—from plowed ground—a semblance of the virgin prairie.

It is no hobby for those who like their payoffs quick and their results guaranteed. The native prairie grasses are difficult to reestablish and many of the wildflowers are next to impossible. Some scientists estimate it may be possible to create a pretty good facsimile of the original prairie in 300 years. Others think 500 years. It's an inexact science.

And yet the prairie movement continues to grow. Practically every college and university in the Midwest seems to have its own little plot of restored prairie now. More surprisingly, a growing collection of individuals are toiling in prairie plantations—everybody from academic types to retired farmers, from little old ladies to Madison Avenue admen.

Maybe all this is part of a broader phenomenon, being one of many ways that Americans are trying to ward off future shock. This, at least, is the suspicion of one man who is as much an authority on the subject as anybody.

"People long for something that will give them a sense of security and continuity and permanence," ventures Jim Wilson, a sort of philosopher-activist in the prairie restoration movement. He is an ex-saxophone player, ex-explorer (by motorcycle) of the sub-Sahara region, ex-English professor, ex-farmer and now, late in a life well-spent, a writer and seller of grass and wildflower seeds in Polk, Nebraska.

For years Jim Wilson and his wife Alice have been selling prairie grass seed to ranchers and farmers, who have been planting it for the usual utilitarian reasons. In recent years, though, they've been flooded with orders from a new kind of customer—people who seem to be planting prairie grass and wildflowers just for the innate rightness of it. "They think in poetry," explains Jim Wilson, "whereas the agricultural people think in prose."

All those prairie restorations may or may not endure for the 300 years, or 500 years, necessary before nature slowly shapes them into something approaching the prairie that Willa Cather knew. And the proposed Tallgrass Prairie National Park for the Flint Hills of Kansas may or may not make it through the congressional labyrinth. It's snagged right now, as usually happens with national park proposals before they ultimately pass.

But something subtle does seem to be happening in lots of unheralded ways and places, all across the country. It may be no coincidence that, at the same time the prairie restoration movement is booming, manufacturers of old-fashioned Mason jars report they can't keep up with demand. In recent years, it seems, many people have begun home canning again. It may be no coincidence that in city after city, the rush is on to restore old houses and warehouses instead of tearing them down; that handicrafts are more than ever in vogue; that for the first time in decades, there is a modest movement from the cities to the small towns and countryside.

People seem to be searching for authentic, enduring things. They seem to want to do things for themselves. They seem to believe that if the world has fragmented into countless problems, people, acting individually and together in countless small ways, may yet be able to knit it back together again.

No doubt it would be a mistake to read too much into these quiet and ephemeral developments having to do with Mason jars and prairie cone-flowers. Yet they are hardly insignificant, or pessimistic, developments either. And, at a time when our political leaders seem increasingly befuddled and disheartened by events, they just may be a truer gauge of the national temper.

LITTLE BOXES, by Malvina Reynolds

Little boxes on the hillside
Little boxes made of ticky tacky.
Little boxes on the hillside,
Little boxes all the same.

There's a green one and a pink one
And a blue one and a yellow one,
And they're all made out of ticky-tacky,
And they all look just the same.

And all the people in the houses
All go to the university,
Where they were put in boxes
And they came out all the same,

And there's doctors and lawyers,
And business executives,
And they're all made out of ticky-tacky
And they all look just the same.

And they all play on the golf course
And drink their martinis dry,
And they all have pretty children
And the children go to school,
And the children go to summer camp
And then to the university.
Where they are put in boxes
And they all come out the same.

And the boys go into business
And marry and raise a family.
In boxes made of ticky-tacky
And they all look just the same.

There's a green one and a pink one,
And a blue one and a yellow one.
And they're all made out of ticky-tacky
And they all look just the same.

BILL VEECK, by Studs Terkel

He's nursing a beer at a table in the Bards Room, a casual restaurant-saloon under the stands of Comiskey Park.

He is president of the Chicago White Sox. He is sixty-four.

For the most part, we're losers. We're losers in a country where winning means you're great, you're beautiful, you're moral. If you don't make a lot of money, you're a loser. The bigness, the machines, the establishment, imbue us with the idea that unless you make a lot of money, you're nothing. Happiness has nothing to do with it. I'm challenging that, and I'm having fun doing it.

We have a lousy team out in the field right now, but they're singing in the stands. We have just about the worst ball club and the oldest park in the country. We have an exploding scoreboard in Comiskey Park. At first, they declared it illegal, immoral, fattening, terrible, too bush. (Laughs.) Funny how you pick things up. It came from reading Saroyan's play *The Time of Your Life.* All took place in a saloon. There's a pinball machine and the fella, he goes up to the bartender and he wants more nickels. He plays and plays, no luck; and just before the final curtain, he hits a winner. The bells rang and the flag went up and it played "Dixie" and all sorts of extravagant things. That's what happens on our exploding scoreboard. Saroyan was sayin' something: You keep tryin' and tryin', and finally you do hit a winner. You hope, you dream, the guy's gonna hit a homer. Suddenly he hits it. The rockets go off, the bombs burst in air. (Laughs.) The loser has his day.

There is in all of us a competitive spirit, but winning has become life and death. We lose sight that it's only a game. It's a delightful game that is occasionally played by skillful men. Phil Wrigley once said that all you need is a winning club. It's a damning comment. We all like winners, but winning without joy isn't worth the candle. I hate to lose, but it's not the end of the world. Tomorrow may be better. (Laughs.) I'm the guy at that pinball machine waiting for all those rockets to explode.

I guess that's one of the reasons I was thrown out of organized baseball. I'd like to say I withdrew gracefully. They agreed to let the St. Louis Browns move to Baltimore if I withdrew. It was '53 when they terminated me. When I came back to the Sox thirteen years later, I was not welcomed with open arms. I didn't show proper respect.

I've reached the conclusion that I'm an anachronism. My wife and I have created a couple of other anachronisms: our sons. I'll settle for that.

Postscript: In 1954, I ran into Eddie Gaedel. He was a midget, three feet seven, who worked as a messenger. In 1951, Veeck had hired him as a ball player, as a member of the St. Louis Browns, for one turn at bat. "He got on base," Veeck recalls. "*He had a foot and a half strike zone. If I had any courage, I might have signed eight midgets, and we might have won a game in '51.*"

Gaedel, wistful, rueful, remembered: "*I batted a thousand that year. One time at bat, I get on base. I'm disappointed in Mr. Veeck. I sure thought he'd use me again. But,*" *he smiled beatifically,* "*I'll never forget that day as long as I live. The fans went wild. I still think I can do it.*" *It was his one glory moment.*

THE STEREOTYPE, by Germaine Greer

In that mysterious dimension where the body meets the soul the stereotype is born and has her being. She is more body than soul, more soul than mind. To her belongs all that is beautiful, even the very word beauty itself. All that exists, exists to beautify her. The sun shines only to burnish her skin and gild her hair; the wind blows only to whip up the color in her cheeks; the sea strives to bathe her; flowers die gladly so that her skin may luxuriate in their essence. She is the crown of creation, the masterpiece. The depths of the sea are ransacked for pearl and coral to deck her; the bowels of the earth are laid open that she might wear gold, sapphires, diamonds and rubies. Baby seals are battered with staves, unborn lambs ripped from their mothers' wombs, millions of moles, muskrats, squirrels, minks, ermines, foxes, beavers, chinchillas, ocelots, lynxes, and other small and lovely creatures die untimely deaths that she might have furs. Egrets, ostriches and peacocks, butterflies and beetles yield her their plumage. Men risk their lives hunting leopards for her coats, and crocodiles for her handbags and shoes. Millions of silkworms offer her their yellow labors; even the seamstresses roll seams and whip lace by hand, so that she might be clad in the best that money can buy.

The men of our civilization have stripped themselves of the fineries of the earth so that they might work more freely to plunder the universe for treasures to deck my lady in. New raw materials, new processes, new machines are all brought into her service. My lady must therefore be the chief spender as well as the chief symbol of spending ability and monetary success. While her mate toils in his factory, she totters about the smartest streets and plushiest hotels with his fortune upon her back and bosom, fingers and wrists, continuing that essential expenditure in his house which is her frame and her setting, enjoying the silken idleness which is the necessary condition of maintaining her mate's prestige and her qualification to demonstrate it. Once upon a time only the aristocratic lady could lay claim to the title of crown of creation: only her hands were white enough, her feet tiny enough, her waist narrow enough, her hair long and golden enough; but every well-to-do burgher's wife set herself up to ape my lady and to follow fashion, until my lady was forced to set herself out like a gilded doll overlaid with monstrous rubies and pearls like pigeons' eggs. Nowadays the Queen of England still considers it part of her royal female role to sport as much of the family jewelry as she can manage at any one time on all public occasions, although the male monarchs have escaped such showcase duty, which develops exclusively upon their wives.

At the same time as woman was becoming the showcase for wealth and caste, while men were slipping into relative anonymity and "handsome is as handsome does," she was emerging as the central emblem of western art. For the Greeks the male and female body had beauty of a human, not necessarily a sexual, kind; indeed they may have marginally favored the young male form as the most powerful and perfectly proportioned. Likewise the Romans showed no bias towards the depiction of femininity in their predominantly monumental art. In the Renaissance the female form began to predominate, not only as the mother in the predominate emblem of *madonna con bambino,* but as an aesthetic study in herself. At first naked female forms took their chances in crowd scenes or diptychs of Adam and Eve, but gradually Venus claims ascendancy, Mary Magdalene ceases to be wizened and emaciated, and becomes nubile and ecstatic, portraits of anonymous young women, chosen only for their prettiness, begin to appear, are gradually disrobed, and renamed Flora or Primavera. Painters begin to paint their own wives and mistresses and royal consorts as voluptuous beauties, divesting them of their clothes if desirable, but not of their jewelry. Susanna keeps her bracelets on in the bath, and Hélène Fourment keeps ahold of of her fur as well!

What happened to women in painting happened to her in poetry as well. Her beauty was celebrated in terms of the riches which clustered around her: her hair was gold wires, her brow ivory, her lips ruby, her teeth gates of pearl, her breasts alabaster veined with lapis lazuli, her eyes as black as jet. The fragility of her loveliness was emphasized by the inevitable comparisons with the rose, and she was urged to employ her beauty in love-making before it withered on the stem. She was for consumption; other sorts of imagery spoke of her in terms of cherries and cream, lips as sweet as honey and skin white as milk, breasts like cream uncrudded, hard as apples. Some celebrations yearned over her finery as well, her lawn more transparent than morning mist, her lace as delicate as gossamer, the baubles that she toyed with and the favors that she gave. Even now we find the thriller hero describing his classy dames' elegant suits, cheeky hats, well-chosen accessories and footwear; the imagery no longer dwells on jewels and flowers but the consumer emphasis is the same. The mousy secretary blossoms into the feminine stereotype when she reddens her lips, lets down her hair, and puts on something frilly.

Nowadays women are not expected, unless they are Paola di Liegi or Jackie Onassis, and then only on gala occasions, to appear with a king's ransom deployed upon their bodies, but they are required to look expensive, fashionable, well-groomed, and not to be seen in the same dress twice. If the duty of the few may have become less onerous, it has also become the duty of the many. The stereotype marshals an army of servants. She is supplied with cosmetics, underwear, foundation garments, stockings, wigs, postiches and hairdressing as well as her outer garments, her jewels and furs. The effect is to be built up layer by layer, and it is expensive. Splendor has given way to fit, line and cut. The spirit of competition must be kept up, as more and more women struggle towards the top drawer, so that the fashion industry can rely upon an expanding market. Poorer women fake it, ape it, pick up on the fashions a season too late, use crude effects, mistaking the line, the sheen, the gloss of the high-class article for a garish simulacrum. The business is so complex that it must be handled by an expert. The paragons of the stereotype must be dressed, coifed and painted by the experts and the style-setters, although they may be encouraged to give heart to the housewives studying their lives in pulp magazines by claiming a lifelong fidelity to their own hair and soap and water. The boast is more usually discouraging than otherwise, unfortunately.

As long as she is young and personable, every woman may cherish the dream that she may leap up the social ladder and dim the sheen of luxury by sheer natural loveliness; the few examples of such a feat are kept before the eye of the public. Fired with hope, optimism and ambition, young women study the latest forms of the stereotype, set out in *Vogue, Nova, Queen* and other glossies, where the mannequins stare from among the advertisements for fabulous real estate, furs and jewels. Nowadays the uniformity of the year's fashions is severely affected by the emergence of the pert female designers who direct their appeal to the working girl, emphasizing variety, comfort, and simple, striking effects. There is no longer a single face of the year: even Twiggy has had to withdraw into marketing and rationed personal appearances, while the Shrimp works mostly in New York. Nevertheless the stereotype is still supreme. She has simply allowed herself a little more variation.

The stereotype is the Eternal Feminine. She is the Sexual Object sought by all men, and by all women. She is of neither sex, for she has herself no sex at all. Her value is solely attested by the demand she excites in others. All she must contribute is her existence. She need achieve nothing, for she is the reward of achievement. She need never give positive evidence of her moral character because virtue is assumed from her loveliness, and her passivity. If any man who has no right to her be found with her she will not be punished, for she is morally neuter. The matter is solely one of male rivalry. Innocently she may drive men to madness and war. The more trouble she can cause, the more her stocks go up, for possession of her means more the more demand she excites. Nobody wants a girl whose beauty is imperceptible to all but him; and so men welcome the stereotype because it directs their taste into the most commonly recognized areas of value, although they may protest because some aspects of it do not tally with their fetishes. There is scope in the stereotype's variety for most fetishes. The leg man may follow miniskirts, the tit man can encourage see-through blouses and plunging necklines, although the man who likes fat women may feel constrained to enjoy them in secret. There are stringent limits to the variations on the stereotype, for nothing must interfere with her function as a sex object. She may wear leather, as long as she cannot actually handle a motorbike; she may wear rubber, but it ought not to indicate that she is an expert diver or waterskier. If she wears athletic clothes the purpose is to underline her unathleticism. She may sit astride a horse, looking soft and curvy, but she must not crouch over its neck with her rump in the air.

Because she is the emblem of spending ability and the chief spender, she is
also the most effective seller of this world's goods. Every survey ever held
has shown that the image of an attractive woman is the most effective advertising gimmick. She may sit astride the mudguard of a new car, or step into it
ablaze with jewels; she may lie at a man's feet stroking his new socks; she may
hold the petrol pump in a challenging pose, or dance through woodland glades
in slow motion in all the glory of a new shampoo; whatever she does her image
sells. The gynolatry of our civilization is written large upon its face, upon
hoardings, cinema screens, television, newspapers, magazines, tins, packets,
cartons, bottles, all consecrated to the reigning deity, the female fetish. Her
dominion must not be thought to entail the rule of women, for she is not a
woman. Her glossy lips and mat complexion, her unfocused eyes and flawless
fingers, her extraordinary hair all floating and shining, curling and gleaming,
reveal the inhuman triumph of cosmetics, lighting, focusing and printing, crop-
ping and composition. She sleeps unruffled, her lips red and juicy and closed, her
eyes as crisp and black as if new painted, and her false lashes immaculately
curled. Even when she washes her face with a new and creamier toilet soap her
expression is as tranquil and vacant and her paint as flawless as ever. If ever she
should appear tousled and troubled, her features are miraculously smoothed to
their proper veneer by a new washing powder or a bouillon cube. For she is a
doll: weeping, pouting or smiling, running or reclining, she is a doll. She is an
idol, formed of the concatenation of lines and masses, signifying the lineaments
of satisfied impotence.

Her essential quality is castratedness. She absolutely must be young, her
body hairless, her flesh buoyant, and *she must not have a sexual organ.* No
musculature must distort the smoothness of the lines of her body, although she
may be painfully slender or warmly cuddly. Her expression must betray no hint
of humor, curiosity or intelligence, although it may signify hauteur to an extent
that is actually absurd, or smoldering lust, very feebly signified by drooping
eyes and a sullen mouth (for the stereotype's lust equals irrational submission),
or, most commonly, vivacity and idiot happiness. Seeing that the world despoils
itself for this creature's benefit, she must be happy; the entire structure would
topple if she were not. So the image of woman appears plastered on every surface imaginable, smiling interminably. An apple pie evokes a glance of tender
beatitude, a washing machine causes hilarity, a cheap box of chocolates brings
forth meltingly joyous gratitude, a Coke is the cause of a rictus of unutterable
brilliance, even a new stick-on bandage is saluted by a smirk of satisfaction. A
real woman licks her lips and opens her mouth and flashes her teeth when photographers appear: *she* must arrive at the premiere of her husband's film in a
paroxysm of delight, or his success might be murmured about. The occupational
hazard of being a Playboy Bunny is the aching facial muscles brought on by the
obligatory smiles.

So what is the beef? Maybe I couldn't make it. Maybe I don't have a pretty
smile, good teeth, nice tits, long legs, a cheeky arse, a sexy voice. Maybe I don't
know how to handle men and increase my market value, so that the rewards due
to the feminine will accrue to me. Then again, maybe I'm sick of the masquer-
ade. I'm sick of pretending eternal youth. I'm sick of belying my own intelligence, my own will, my own sex. I'm sick of peering at the world through

false eyelashes, so everything I see is mixed with a shadow of bought hairs; I'm sick of weighting my head with a dead mane, unable to move my neck freely, terrifed of rain, of wind, of dancing too vigorously in case I sweat into my lacquered curls. I'm sick of the Powder Room. I'm sick of pretending that some fatuous male's self-important pronouncements are the objects of my undivided attention. I'm sick of going to films and plays when someone else wants to, and sick of having no opinions of my own about either. I'm sick of being a transvestite. I refuse to be a female impersonator. I am a woman, not a castrate.

April Ashley was born male. All the information supplied by genes, chromosomes, internal and external sexual organs added up to the same thing. April was a man. But he longed to be a woman. He longed for the stereotype, not to embrace, but to be. He wanted soft fabrics, jewels, furs, makeup, the love and protection of men. So he was impotent. He couldn't fancy women at all, although he did not particularly welcome homosexual addresses. He did not think of himself as a pervert, or even as a transvestite, but as a woman cruelly transmogrified into manhood. He tried to die, became a female impersonator, but eventually found a doctor in Casablanca who came up with a more acceptable alternative. He was to be castrated, and his penis used as the lining of a surgically constructed cleft, which would be a vagina. He would be infertile, but that has never affected the attribution of femininity. April returned to England, resplendent. Massive hormone treatment had eradicated his beard, and formed tiny breasts: he had grown his hair and bought feminine clothes during the time he had worked as an impersonator. He became a model, and began to illustrate the feminine stereotype as he was perfectly qualified to do, for he was elegant, voluptuous, beautifully groomed, and in love with his own image. On an ill-fated day he married the heir to a peerage, the Hon. Arthur Corbett, acting out the highest achievement of the feminine dream, and went to live with him in a villa in Marbella. The marriage was never consummated. April's incompetence as a woman is what we must expect from a castrate, but it is not so very different after all from the impotence of feminine women, who submit to sex without desire, with only the infantile pleasure of cuddling and affection, which is their favorite reward. As long as the feminine stereotype remains the definition of the female sex, April Ashley is a woman, regardless of the legal decision ensuing from her divorce. She is as much a casualty of the polarity of the sexes as we all are. Disgraced, unsexed April Ashley is our sister and our symbol.

THE INCOMPARABLE BUZZ-SAW, by H. L. Mencken

The allurement that women hold out to men is precisely the allurement that Cape Hatteras holds out to sailors: they are enormously dangerous and hence enormously fascinating. To the average man, doomed to some banal drudgery all his life long, they offer the only grand hazard that he ever encounters. Take them away and his existence would be flat and secure as that of a moo-cow. Even to the unusual man, the adventurous man, the imaginative and romantic man, they offer the adventure of adventures. Civilization tends to dilute and cheapen all other hazards. Even war has been largely reduced to caution and calculation; already, indeed, it employs almost as many press-agents, letter-openers and generals as soldiers. But the duel of sex continues to be fought in the Berserker manner. Whoso approaches women still faces the immemorial dangers. Civilization has not made them a bit more safe than they were in Solomon's time; they are still inordinately menacing, and hence inordinately provocative, and hence inordinately charming.

The most disgusting cad in the world is the man who, on grounds of decorum and morality, avoids the game of love. He is one who puts his own ease and security above the most laudable of philanthropies. Women have a hard time of it in this world. They are oppressed by man-made laws, man-made social customs, masculine egoism, the delusion of masculine superiority. Their one comfort is the assurance that, even though it may be impossible to prevail against man it is always possible to enslave and torture a man. This feeling is fostered when one makes love to them. One need not be a great beau, a seductive catch, to do it effectively. Any man is better than none. To shrink from giving so much happiness at such small expense, to evade the business on the ground that it has hazards — this is the act of a puling and tacky fellow.

THE IMPULSE TO WRITE, by Ray Bradbury

If you are writing without zest, without gusto, without love, without fun, you are only half a writer. . . . For the first thing a writer should be is — excited. He should be a thing of fevers and enthusiasms. Without such vigor, he might as well be out picking peaches or digging ditches. God knows it'd be better for his health.

How long has it been since you wrote a story where your real love or your real hatred somehow got onto the paper? When was the last time you dared release a cherished prejudice so it slammed the page like a lightning bolt? What are the best things and the worst things in your life, and when are you going to get around to whispering or shouting them?

Wouldn't it be wonderful, for instance, to throw down a copy of *Harper's Bazaar* you happened to be leafing through at the dentist's, and leap to your typewriter and ride off with hilarious anger, attacking their silly and sometimes shocking snobbishness? I did just that a few years back. I came across an issue where the *Bazaar* photographers, with their perverted sense of equality once again utilized natives in a Puerto Rican back-street as props in front of which their starved-looking manikins postured for the benefit of yet more emaciated half-women in the best salons in the country. The photographs so enraged me I ran, did not walk, to my machine and wrote "Sun and Shadow," the story of an old Puerto Rican who ruins the *Bazaar* photographer's afternoon by sneaking into each picture and dropping his pants.

I dare say there are a few of you who would like to have done this job. I had the fun of doing it; the cleansing after-effects of the hoot, the holler, and the great horselaugh. Probably the editors at the *Bazaar* never heard. But a lot of readers did and cried, "Go it, *Bazaar*; go it, Bradbury!" I claim no victory. But there was blood on my gloves when I hung them up.

When was the last time you did a story like that, out of pure indignation?

When was the last time you were stopped by the police in your neighborhood because you like to walk, and perhaps think, at night? It happened to me just often enough that, irritated, I wrote "The Pedestrian," a story of a time, fifty years from now, when a man is arrested and taken off for clinical study because he insists on looking at un-televised reality, and breathing unair-conditioned air.

Irritations and angers aside, what about loves? What do you love most in the world? The big and little things, I mean. A trolley car, a pair of tennis shoes? These, at one time when we were children, were invested with magic for us. During the past year I've published one story about a boy's last ride in a trolley that smells of all the thunderstorms in time, full of cool green moss-velvet seats and blue electricity, but doomed to be replaced by the more prosaic, more practical-smelling bus. Another story concerned a boy who wanted to own a pair of new tennis shoes for the power they gave him to leap rivers and houses and streets, and even bushes, sidewalks, and dogs. The shoes were to him, the surge of antelope and gazelle on African summer veldt. The energy of unleashed rivers and summer storms lay in the shoes; he had to have them more than anything else in the world.

So, simply then, here is my formula.

What do you want more than anything else in the world? What do you love, or what do you hate?

Find a character, like yourself, who will want something or not want something, with all his heart. Give him running orders. Shoot him off. Then follow as fast as you can go. The character, in his great love, or hate, will rush you through to the end of the story. The zest and gusto of his need, and there *is* zest in hate as well as in love, will fire the landscape and raise the temperature of your typewriter thirty degrees.

All of this is primarily directed to the writer who has already learned his trade; that is, has put into himself enough grammatical tools and literary knowledge so he won't trip himself up when he wants to run. The advice holds good for the beginner, too, however, even though his steps may falter for purely technical reasons. Even here, passion often saves the day.

The history of each story, then, should read almost like a weather report: Hot today, cool tomorrow. This afternoon, burn down the house. Tomorrow, pour cold critical water upon the simmering coals. Time enough to think and cut and rewrite tomorrow. But today — explode — fly apart — disintegrate! The other six or seven drafts are going to be pure torture. So why not enjoy the first draft, in the hope that your joy will seek and find others in the world who, reading your story, will catch fire, too?

It doesn't have to be a big fire. A small blaze, candlelight perhaps; a longing for a mechanical wonder like a trolley or an animal wonder like a pair of sneakers rabbiting the lawns of early morning. Look for the little loves, find and shape the little bitternesses. Savor them in your mouth, try them on your typewriter. . . . Ideas lie everywhere, like apples fallen and melting in the grass for lack of wayfaring strangers with an eye and a tongue for beauty whether absurd, horrific, or genteel.

HOW TO WRITE A BUSINESS LETTER, by Malcolm Forbes

A good business letter can get you a job interview.

Get you off the hook.

Or get you money.

It's totally asinine to blow your chances of getting *whatever* you want—with a business letter that turns people off instead of turning them on.

The best place to learn to write is in school. If you're still there, pick your teachers' brains.

If not, big deal. I learned to ride a motorcycle at 50 and fly balloons at 52. It's never too late to learn.

Over 10,000 business letters come across my desk every year. They seem to fall into three categories: stultifying if not stupid, mundane (most of them), and first rate (rare). Here's the approach I've found that separates the winners from the losers (most of it's just good common sense)—it starts *before* you write your letter:

KNOW WHAT YOU WANT

If you don't, write it down—in one sentence. "I want to get an interview within the next two weeks." That simple. List the major points you want to get across—it'll keep you on course.

If you're *answering* a letter, check the points that need answering and keep the letter in front of you while you write. This way you won't forget anything—*that* would cause another round of letters.

And for goodness' sake, answer promptly if you're going to answer at all. Don't sit on a letter—*that* invites the person on the other end to sit on whatever you want from *him*.

PLUNGE RIGHT IN

Call him by name—not "Dear Sir, Madam, or Ms." "Dear Mr. Chrisanthopoulos"—and be sure to spell it right. That'll get him (thus, you) off to a good start.

(Usually, you can get his name just by phoning his company—or from a business directory in your nearest library.)

Tell what your letter is about in the first paragraph. One or two sentences. Don't keep you reader guessing or he might file your letter away—even before he finishes it.

In the round file.

Reprinted by permission of the International Paper Company.

If you're answering a letter, refer to the date it was written. So the reader won't waste time hunting for it.

People who read business letters are as human as thee and me. Reading a letter shouldn't be a chore — *reward* the reader for the time he gives you.

WRITE SO HE'LL ENJOY IT

Write the entire letter from his point of view — what's in it for *him?* Beat him to the draw — surprise him by answering the questions and objections he might have.

Be positive — he'll be more receptive to what you have to say.

Be nice. Contrary to the cliché, genuinely nice guys most often finish first or very near it. I admit it's not easy when you've got a gripe. To be agreeable while disagreeing — that's an art.

Be natural — write the way you talk. Imagine him sitting in front of you — what would you *say* to him?

Business jargon too often is cold, stiff, unnatural.

Suppose I came up to you and said, "I acknowledge receipt of your letter and I beg to thank you." You'd think, "Huh? You're putting me on."

The acid test — read your letter *out loud* when you're done. You might get a shock — but you'll know for sure if it sounds natural.

Don't be cute or flippant. The reader won't take you seriously. This doesn't mean you've got to be dull. You prefer your letter to knock 'em dead rather than bore 'em to death.

Three points to remember:

Have a sense of humor. That's refreshing *anywhere* — a nice surprise in a business letter.

Be specific. If I tell you there's a new fuel that could save gasoline, you might not believe me. But suppose I tell you this:

"Gasohol" — 10% alcohol, 90% gasoline — works as well as straight gasoline. Since you can make alcohol from grain or corn stalks, wood or wood waste, coal — even garbage, it's worth some real follow through.

Now you've got something to sink your teeth into.

Lean heavier on nouns and verbs, lighter on adjectives. Use the active voice instead of the passive. Your writing will have more guts.

Which of these is stonger? Active voice: "I kicked out my money manager." Or, passive voice: "My money manager was kicked out by me." (By the way, neither is true. My son, Malcolm Jr., manages most Forbes money — he's a brilliant moneyman.)

GIVE IT THE BEST YOU'VE GOT

When you don't want something enough to make *the* effort, making *an* effort is a waste.

Make your letter look appetizing — or you'll strike out before you even get to bat. Type it — on good-quality 8½" × 11" stationery. Keep it neat. And use paragraphing that makes it easier to read.

Keep your letter short — to one page, if possible. Keep your paragraphs short. After all, who's going to benefit if your letter is quick and easy to read?

You.

For emphasis, *underline* important words. And sometimes indent sentences as well as paragraphs.

Like this. See how well it works? (But save it for something special.)

Make it perfect. No typos, no misspellings, no factual errors. If you're sloppy and let mistakes slip by, the person reading your letter will think you don't know better or don't care. Do you?

Be crystal clear. You won't get what you're after if your reader doesn't get the message.

Use good English. If you're still in school, take all the English and writing courses you can. The way you write and speak can really help — or *hurt*.

If you're not in school (even if you are), get the little 71-page gem by Strunk & White, *Elements of Style*. It's in paperback. It's fun to read and loaded with tips on good English and good writing.

Don't put on airs. Pretense invariably impresses only the pretender.

Don't exaggerate. Even once. Your reader will suspect everything else you write.

Distinguish opinions from facts. Your opinions may be the best in the world. But they're not gospel. You owe it to your reader to let him know which is which. He'll appreciate it and he'll admire you. The dumbest people I know are those who Know It All.

Be honest. It'll get you further in the long run. If you're not, you won't rest easy until you're found out. (The latter, not speaking from experience.)

Edit ruthlessly. Somebody ~~has~~ said that words are ~~a lot~~ like inflated money — the more ~~of them that~~ you use, the less, each one ~~of them~~ is worth. ~~Right on.~~ Go through your entire letter ~~just~~ as many times as it takes. ~~Search out and~~ Annihilate all unnecessary words, and sentences — even ~~entire~~ paragraphs.

SUM IT UP AND GET OUT

The last paragraph should tell the reader exactly what you want *him* to or what *you're* going to do. Short and sweet. "May I have an appointment? Next Monday, the 16th, I'll call your secretary to see when it'll be most convenient for you."

Close with something simple like, "Sincerely." And for heaven's sake sign legibly. The biggest ego trip I know is a completely illegible signature.

Good luck.

I hope you get what you're after.

Sincerely,

Malcolm S. Forbes

HOW TO WRITE CLEARLY, by Edward T. Thompson

If you are afraid to write, don't be.

If you think you've got to string together big fancy words and high-flying phrases, forget it.

To write well, unless you aspire to be a professional poet or novelist, you only need to get your ideas across simply and clearly.

It's not easy. But it *is* easier than you might imagine.

There are only three basic requirements:

First, you must *want* to write clearly. And I believe your really do, if you've stayed this far with me.

Second, you must be willing to *work hard*. Thinking means work — and that's what it takes to do anything well.

Third, you must know and follow some *basic guidelines.*

If, while you're writing for clarity, some lovely, dramatic or inspired phrases or sentences come to you, fine. Put them in.

But then with cold, objective eyes and mind ask yourself: "Do they detract from clarity?" If they do, grit your teeth and cut the frills.

FOLLOW SOME BASIC GUIDELINES

I can't give you a complete list of "dos and don'ts" for every writing problem you'll ever face.

But I can give you some fundamental guidelines that cover the most common problems.

1. OUTLINE WHAT YOU WANT TO SAY.

I know that sounds grade-schoolish. But you can't write clearly until, *before you start,* you know where you will stop.

Ironically, that's even a problem in writing an outline (i.e., knowing the ending before you begin).

So try this method:

• On 3" X 5" cards, write — one point to a card — all the points you need to make.

• Divide the cards into piles — one pile for each group of points *closely related* to each other. (If you were describing an automobile, you'd put all the points about safety in another, and so on.)

• Arrange your piles of points in a sequence. Which are most important and should be given first or saved for last? Which must you present before others in order to make the others understandable?

• Now, *within* each pile, do the same thing — arrange the *points* in logical, understandable order.

There you have your outline, needing only an introduction and conclusion.

This is a practical way to outline. It's also flexible. You can add, delete or change the location of points easily.

2. START WHERE YOUR READERS ARE.

How much do they know about the subject? Don't write to a level higher than your readers' knowledge of it.

Reprinted by permission of the International Paper Company.

CAUTION: Forget that old – and wrong – advice about writing to a 12-year-old mentality. That's insulting. But do remember that your prime purpose is to *explain* something, not prove that you're smarter than you readers.

3. AVOID JARGON.

Don't use words, expressions, phrases known only to people with specific knowledge or interests.

Example: A scientist, using scientific jargon, wrote, "The biota exhibited a one hundred percent mortality response." He could have written: "All the fish died."

4. USE FAMILIAR COMBINATIONS OF WORDS.

A speech writer for President Franklin D. Roosevelt wrote, "We are endeavoring to construct a more inclusive society." F.D.R. changed it to, "We're going to make a country in which no one is left out."

CAUTION: By familiar combinations of words, I do *not* mean incorrect grammar. *That* can be *unclear*. Example: John's father says he can't go out Friday. (Who can't go out? John or his father?)

5. USE "FIRST-DEGREE" WORDS.

These words immediately bring an image to your mind. Other words must be "translated" through the first-degree word before you see the image. Those are second/third-degree words.

First-degree words	Second/third-degree words
face	visage, countenance
stay	abide, remain, reside
book	volume, tome, publication

First degree words are usually the most precise words, too.

6. STICK TO THE POINT.

Your outline – which was more work in the beginning – now saves you work. Because now you can ask about any sentence you write: "Does it relate to a point in the outline? If it doesn't, should I add it to the outline? If not, I'm getting off the track." Then, full steam ahead – on the main line.

7. BE AS BRIEF AS POSSIBLE.

Whatever you write, shortening – *condensing* – almost always makes it tighter, straighter, easier to read and understand.

Condensing, as *Reader's Digest* does it, is in large part artistry. But it involves techniques that anyone can learn and use.

• *Present your points in logical ABC order:* Here again, your outline should save you work because, if you did it right, your points already stand in logical ABC order – A makes B understandable, B makes C understandable and so on.

To write in a straight line is to say something clearly in the fewest possible words.

• *Don't waste words telling people what they already know:* Notice how we edited this: "Have you ever wondered how banks rate you as a credit risk? ~~You know, of course, that it's some combination of facts about your income, your job, and so on. But actually,~~ Many banks have a scoring system. . . ."

• *Cut out excess evidence and unnecessary anecdotes:* Usually, one fact or example (at most, two) will support a point. More just belabor it. And while writing about something may remind you of a good story, ask yourself: "Does it *really help* to tell the story, or does it slow me down?"

(Many people think *Reader's Digest* articles are filled with anecdotes. Actually, we use them sparingly and usually for one of two reasons: either the subject is so dry it needs some "humanity" to give it life; or the subject is so hard to grasp, it needs anecdotes to help readers understand. If the subject is both lively and easy to grasp, we move right along.)

• *Look for the most common word wasters:* windy phrases.

Windy phrases	Cut to...
at the present time	now
in the event of	if
in the majority of instances	usually

• *Look for passive verbs you can make active:* Invariably, this produces a shorter sentence. "The cherry tree *was* chopped down by George Washington." (Passive verb and nine words.) "George Washington *chopped* down the cherry tree." (Active verb and seven words.)

• *Look for positive/negative sections from which you can cut the negative:* See how we did it here: "The answer ~~does not rest with carelessness or incompetence. It lies largely in~~ is having enough people to do the job."

• Finally, to write more clearly by saying it in fewer words: when you've finished, stop.

HOW TO WRITE WITH STYLE, by Kurt Vonnegut

Newspaper reporters and technical writers are trained to reveal almost nothing about themselves in their writings. This makes them freaks in the world of writers, since almost all of the other ink-stained wretches in that world reveal a lot about themselves to readers. We call these revelations, accidental and intentional, elements of style.

These revelations tell us as readers what sort of person it is with whom we are spending time. Does the writer sound ignorant or informed, stupid or bright, crooked or honest, humorless or playful—? And on and on.

Why should you examine your writing style with the idea of improving it? Do so as a mark of respect for your readers, whatever you're writing. If you scribble your thoughts any which way, your readers will surely feel that you care nothing about them. They will mark you down as an egomaniac or a chowderhead — or, worse, they will stop reading you.

The most damning revelation you can make about yourself is that you do not know what is interesting and what is not. Don't you yourself like or dislike writers mainly for what they choose to show you or make you think about? Did you ever admire an empty-headed writer for his or her mastery of the language? No.

So your own winning style must begin with ideas in your head.

1. FIND A SUBJECT YOU CARE ABOUT

Find a subject you care about and which you in your heart feel others should care about. It is this genuine caring, and not your games with language, which will be the most compelling and seductive element in your style.

I am not urging you to write a novel, by the way — although I would not be sorry if you wrote one, provided you genuinely cared about something. A petition to the mayor about a pothole in front of your house or a love letter to the girl next door will do.

2. DO NOT RAMBLE, THOUGH

I won't ramble on about that.

3. KEEP IT SIMPLE

As for your use of language: Remember that two great masters of language, William Shakespeare and James Joyce, wrote sentences which were almost childlike when their subjects were most profound. "To be or not to be?" asks Shakespeare's Hamlet. The longest word is three letters long. Joyce, when he was frisky, could put together a sentence as intricate and as glittering as a necklace for Cleopatra, but my favorite sentence in his short story "Eveline" is this one: "She was tired." At that point in the story, no other words could break the heart of a reader as those three words do.

Simplicity of language is not only reputable, but perhaps even sacred. The *Bible* opens with a sentence well within the writing skills of a lively fourteen-year-old: "In the beginning God created the heaven and the earth."

4. HAVE THE GUTS TO CUT

It may be that you, too, are capable of making necklaces for Cleopatra, so to speak. But your eloquence should be the servant of the ideas in your head. Your rule might be this: If a sentence, no matter how excellent, does not illuminate your subject in some new and useful way, scratch it out.

5. SOUND LIKE YOURSELF

The writing style which is most natural for you is bound to echo the speech you heard when a child. English was the novelist Joseph Conrad's third language, and much that seems piquant in his use of English was no doubt colored by his first language, which was Polish. And lucky indeed is the writer who has grown up in Ireland, for the English spoken there is so amusing and musical. I myself grew up in Indianapolis, where common speech sounds like a band saw cutting galvanized tin, and employs a vocabulary as unornamental as a monkey wrench.

In some of the more remote hollows of Appalachia, children still grow up hearing songs and locutions of Elizabethan times. Yes, and many Americans grow up hearing a language other than English, or an English dialect a majority of Americans cannot understand.

All these varieties of speech are beautiful, just as the varieties of butterflies are beautiful. No matter what your first language, you should treasure it all your life. If it happens not be standard English, and if it shows itself when you write standard English, the result is usually delightful, like a very pretty girl with one eye that is green and one that is blue.

I myself find that I trust my own writing most, and others seem to trust it most, too, when I sound most like a person from Indianapolis, which I am. What alternatives to I have? The one most vehemently recommended by teachers has no doubt been pressed on you, as well: to write like cultivated Englishmen of a century or more ago.

6. SAY WHAT YOU MEAN TO SAY

I used to be exasperated by such teachers, but am no more. I understand now that all those antique essays and stories with which I was to compare my own work were not magnificent for their datedness or foreignness, but for saying precisely what their authors meant them to say. My teachers wished me to write accurately, always selecting the most effective words, and relating the words to one another unambiguously, rigidly, like parts of a machine. The teachers did not want to turn me into an Englishman after all. They hoped that I would become understandable—and therefore understood. And there went my dream of doing with words what Pablo Picasso did with paint or what any number of jazz idols did with music. If I broke all the rules of punctuation, had words mean whatever I wanted them to mean, and strung them together higgledy-piggledy, I would simply not be understood. So you, too, had better avoid Picasso-style or jazz-style writing, if you have something worth saying and wish to be understood.

Readers want our pages to look very much like pages they have seen before. Why? This is because they themselves have a tough job to do, and they need all the help they can get from us.

7. PITY THE READERS

They have to identify thousands of little marks on paper, and make sense of them immediately. They have to *read*, an art so difficult that most people don't really master it even after having studied it all through grade school and high school—twelve long years.

So this discussion must finally acknowledge that our stylistic options as writers are neither numerous nor glamorous, since our readers are bound to be such imperfect artists. Our audience requires us to be sympathetic and patient teachers, ever willing to simplify and clarify—whereas we would rather soar high above the crowd, singing like nightingales.

That is the bad news. The good news is that we Americans are governed under a unique Constitution, which allows us to write whatever we please without fear of punishsment. So the most meaningful aspect of our styles, which is what we choose to write about, is utterly unlimited.

8. FOR REALLY DETAILED ADVICE

For a discussion of literary style in a narrower sense, in a more technical sense, I commend to your attention *The Elements of Style,* by William Strunk, Jr., and E. B. White (Macmillan, 1979). E. B. White is, of course, one of the most admirable literary stylists this country has so far produced.

You should realize, too, that no one would care how well or badly Mr. White expressed himself, if he did not have perfectly enchanting things to say.

INDEX